WORLD POETS

WORLD POETS

Ron Padgett

Editor in Chief

VOLUME 1

CHARLES SCRIBNER'S SONS
An imprint of The Gale Group
New York

Text and photo credits begin on page 407 of volume 3.

Charles Scribner's Sons
1633 Broadway
New York, NY 10019

Library of Congress Cataloging-in-Publication Data

World poets / Ron Padgett, editor in chief.
    p. cm.
  "Mainly for use by students aged 14 to 18 . . . and for anyone interested in learning more about poetry"—Introd., vol. 1.
  Includes bibliographical references and index.
  Contents: v. 1. Apollinaire-Homer — v. 2. Hopkins-Shakespeare — v. 3. Shelley-Yeats.
  Summary: Alphabetically arranged articles on 107 poets from around the world, accompanied by fifteen essays on various genres and schools of poetry.
  ISBN 0-684-80591-X (set) — ISBN 0-684-80610-X (v. 1) — ISBN 0-684-80609-6 (v. 2) — ISBN 0-684-80592-8 (v. 3)
  1. Poetry—Bio-bibliography—Dictionaries—Juvenile literature. 2. Poets—Biography—Dictionaries—Juvenile literature. [1. Poets—Encyclopedias. 2. Poetry.] I. Padgett, Ron.

PN1021.W67 2000
809.1'003—dc21
[B]
                                   00-024801

1 3 5 7 9 11 13 15 17 19 20 18 16 14 12 10 8 6 4 2

Printed in the United States of America.

The paper used in this publication meets the minimum requirements of the American National Standard for Information Sciences—Permanence of Paper for Printed Library Materials, ANSI Z39.48-1992.

EDITORIAL STAFF

CONTENTS

INTRODUCTION

by Ron Padgett

Few people even glance at the introduction in a reference book, so if you are reading these words, you are either a librarian or a person with a lot of curiosity or both. In any case, welcome. The purpose of this introduction is to tell you what this book is and what it isn't, and to suggest some ways for you to use it.

How This Book Came About

In 1998 Charles Scribner's Sons invited me to assemble a book on poetry and poets, mainly for use by students aged 14 to 18, but also for teachers looking for assignment information and for anyone interested in learning more about poetry. In recent years, poetry had become increasingly popular, partly through television programs about poetry and films such as *Dead Poets Society* and *Il Postino* (*The Postman*), through rap poetry and rock lyrics, and through public readings and poetry slams, but also through a widespread hunger for emotional and spiritual nourishment. At the same time, a lot more poetry was being studied and written in school. Although Scribners Writers Series sets, such as *American Writers* and *British Writers*, include poets, the articles in them were not written for young people. And so Scribners began to plan a book that would have articles describing the lives and works of around 110 poets, supplemented by general articles about different kinds of poetry, about certain periods and groups of poets, and about writing poetry, along with some handy lists. The idea sounded great to me, but which poets would be included? Scribners told me that I would make that decision, but to keep in mind that the book would be used often by students who had gone to the school library to look up a certain poet who had been assigned in English class. Therefore I should be sure to include poets who are often studied in school. Around this core group I could add other poets who might catch the fancy of a student thumbing through the book. This, then, was my assignment.

I began compiling a list of the poets frequently assigned and of the additional poets that I thought high school students might like, consulting with a number of teachers and poets who teach. Instead of the 110 required by the publisher, my first list had 340 poets on it. I took a deep breath and started crossing off names, which became harder and harder the more I cut. I hated leaving certain poets out, but I felt better when I saw how much I liked the final selection.

I was happy with it because it had poets from all over the world and from all times, from prehistory to the present day, poets who used traditional poetic forms and poets who were wildly experimental, poets of differrent cultures writing in different languages, poets deeply religious and poets irreverent. I took this approach because, first of all, it represents what I think is a healthy attitude toward world poetry, and second because the people who would be using the book—American students—mirror that variety of taste, race, native language, religion, and culture more than ever before.

A Wider World of Poetry

Before the 1970s, high school textbooks included mainly English-language poets such as Robert Frost, Emily Dickinson, and William Shakespeare, and fine poets they are, well worthy of attention. But more and more teachers began to notice that these poets appealed to some students, but not to others, who might like a different kind of poet if given the chance. These teachers brought in poems by poets not included in the textbooks, poets whose work they themselves admired. This trend has snowballed, so that now the members of the core group (Frost, Dickinson, and so on) have been joined by a wide variety of poets previously excluded from the curriculum—women poets and minority poets, but also poets such as André Breton and Allen Ginsberg whose style or subject matter represented a radical departure from the usual high school curriculum.

Robert Frost is quoted as saying that poetry is that which is lost in translation, which means that translations of poems aren't as good as their original versions: the real poetry disappears. This is true—when the translation is a bad one. But it is not true when the translation equals or surpasses the original. In any case, we are lucky to have had so many good translators of poetry in recent years, translators who are often poets themselves, because they have helped open up our view of poetry from around the world, a world with a lot of interesting poems in it! There is no reason why we should be limited to reading poems written only in English. In compiling this book, whenever possible I assigned the articles on foreign-language poets to people who had done good translations of those poets, people who know the poetry from the inside out. In general, my guiding principle was to invite poets to write the articles, particularly poets who had worked with students, either as regular classroom teachers or as visiting writers.

Is This Book Perfect?

In putting this book together, have I made all the right choices? No, because there are too many possible right choices, and no one can make them all in any one anthology. Some readers will be upset by my including certain poets, and some will be upset by my omitting others. That always happens when an anthology is assembled. The French poet Paul Eluard realized this when he compiled one that he wittily called *The Best Anthology Is the One You Make for Yourself*. Although I have kept the reader (you) in mind throughout, the project reflects my taste and my sense of the possibilities in poetry. In other words, this book has a point of view, for which I happily accept responsibility.

The Aim of This Book

But for you even more important than my taste is the question of this book's usefulness. The editors at Scribners and I have tried our best to make this book as helpful as possible. First, we invited experts to write articles that deliver solid information in a clear and interesting way. Then we added photographs of the poets, sample poems, bibliographies, and notes that explain ideas and words that an average high school reader may not understand. In some cases, we listed websites and historic sights for further information. Too often, poetry is thought of as something difficult, remote, boring, or just plain weird, which is true—of bad or mediocre poetry. But good poetry is exciting, nourishing, encouraging, and sometimes even funny, once you get past a few obstacles. Our aim in this book is to remove those obstacles as quickly as possible.

Doing a Classroom Assignment

If you are working on an assigned poet, then you will want to go directly to the article about that person. Different people read in different ways, but in general I would suggest that you read the sample poem (the one in the box) first, without worrying about what it means: just let the words flow through your mind. Read it silently and then aloud. As you do, you will probably start to like or dislike the poem, but what really matters at this point is your willingess simply to *experience* the poem, to let your mind go as you read. Then read the article, which will tell you about both the life and the work of the poet. Look at the poet's picture and allow yourself to daydream a little. Go back and read the sample poem again and any poems quoted in the article. Then, to do a thorough job, find more poems by that person, in a textbook, an anthology, or a whole volume devoted to the poet's work, and read other commentaries on the poet's work. Feel free to ask your teacher, a librarian, or a book dealer how to find these books. If resources are not readily available, try the Internet, through which you can find an amazing variety of new and used books, even rare ones.

The Dream House

Think of poetry as an enormous house with hundreds and hundreds of rooms, from magically exciting ones to very quiet and beautifully simple ones, each with its own objects, colors, people, and activities in progress. Now think of the articles in this book as doorways into that house. Pick any door. Walk right in and wander down the hallways. Be our guest. If you stay long enough, you will start to feel at home in the entire mansion. You may even end up adding a room of your own.

ACKNOWLEDGMENTS

I am grateful to the many people who helped me bring this book into the world. First of all, to Sylvia Miller at Charles Scribner's Sons, who invited me to take on the project and who cheerfully oversaw it much of the way, and to her colleagues at Scribners, publisher Karen Day, editor Stephen Wagley, editor Jeff Chen, and editor Laura Smid. Laura deserves many extra kudos for the daily energy and attention she brought to our detailed work together over a long period.

I benefited from the advice of those writers and teachers that Scribners consulted before I joined the project: Mike Angelotti, John C. Anzul, Molly Bendall, David Black, Andrea Davis, Stephen Dunning, Ann Folsom, Carol Jago, Edward Lueders, and Debra Wetzel Nycum.

I wish to thank the many students and classroom teachers—from kindergarten through college level—I have worked with, as a poetry teacher, since 1969. I also learned from the experiences of the high school teachers who took part in a series of seminars conducted at Teachers & Writers Collaborative by C. K. Williams.

Many other people advised me along the way, among them Roy Alin, Janet Allen, L. S. Asekoff, Neil Baldwin, Kathleen Bell, Mary Burchenal, Judith Ortiz Cofer, William Corbett, Dante della Terza, Ed Farrell, Michael Greer, Geof Hewitt, Ted Hipple, Carolyn Lott, Christopher Merrill, Angela Nielsen, Geoffrey O'Brien, David Rosenberg, Jack Sasson, Brian Swann, Edward Tayler, Lorenzo Thomas, David Unger, George Viglirolo, and Marlo Welshons, but two people, George Stade and Seymour Yessner, merit an extra special thanks.

My appreciation also goes to Allen Foresta and Anca Oana Meret at the Milbank Memorial Library (Teachers College, New York City), and to the librarians at the Research Division and the Mid-Manhattan Branch of the New York Public Library, Butler Library (Columbia University), and the Kellogg-Hubbard Library in Montpelier, Vermont.

One book in particular was of great value in helping me shape this work: Arthur N. Applebee's *Literature in the Secondary School: Studies of Curriculum and Instruction in the United States*, issued as NCTE Research Report No. 25 by the National Council of Teachers of English. Applebee's book, an

xvii

extensive and fairly recent survey, went a long way toward answering several difficult questions, including the most germane one: Which poets are studied in contemporary American high schools?

Thanks to colleagues past and present at Teachers & Writers Collaborative: Dierdra Colzie, Jordan Davis, Christopher Edgar, Darlene Gold, Alba Delia Hernández, Jill Jackson, Elizabeth Fox, Daniel Kane, Simon Kilmurry, Lynn Michau, Bruce Morrow, Patricia Padgett, Barbara Pucci, Nancy Larson Shapiro, and Susan Straub, and to the writers who have taught in the Teachers & Writers Collaborative program and written about their experiences, writers such as Jack Collom, Kenneth Koch, Herbert Kohl, Larry Fagin, Phillip Lopate, Bernadette Mayer, Sheryl Noethe, Stephen O'Connor, Daniel Sklar, Meredith Sue Willis, Dale Worsley, Alan Ziegler, and Bill Zavatsky.

A huge and hearty thanks to the authors of the articles in this book, who showed generosity and grace in handling what turned out to be challenging assignments. Many of them told me that they took on the work as a labor of love and as a chance to contribute something positive to the way young people feel about poetry.

On a personal level, I would like to acknowledge three of my teachers. Lilly Roberts, my junior high school English teacher for three years, performed a miracle by awakening in me a sense of the beauty of literature. Two of my professors in college, F. W. Dupee and Kenneth Koch, showed me, among many other things, that reading and writing poetry is a sensible and healthy thing to do.

Finally, I give thanks to my friend and agent Robert Cornfield and to my wife Patricia, the ultimate sounding board.

GUILLAUME APOLLINAIRE

(1880–1918)

by Michael Leddy

On 26 August 1880 in Rome, Italy, a boy was born to Angelica de Kostrowitzki, the young, unmarried daughter of Michal Apollinaris Kostrowitzki, a Polish military man who had settled in that city with his Italian wife. In September the boy was baptized in a Catholic church as Guillaume Apollinaire Albert. In November, Angelica registered her son's birth with city authorities, giving him the name Guillaume Albert Vladimir Alexandre Apollinaire Kostrowitzki.

This extraordinary name was only an early stage in Guillaume's adventures in identity. Among his family, he was always known as Wilhelm (the German equivalent of Guillaume). To an early girlfriend, he was "Kostro"; to other lovers and friends he was "Gui." In late adolescence he toyed with the pseudonym "Guillaume Macabre," and he later created the persona of "Louise Lalanne," under whose name he published poems and reviews. As the occasional author of erotic fiction, he wrote under no name at all. To his fellow soldiers in the French infantry in World War I he was "Cointreauwhiskey."* To readers of poetry he was and is known as Guillaume Apollinaire, the

Except where otherwise noted, quotations from Apollinaire's poetry throughout are translated by Ron Padgett. See bibliography for published sources of specific poems.

*****Cointreau** a French liqueur

name that he settled on for publication in 1902 and a name well suited for a poet, suggesting the god Apollo, patron of poets in Greek mythology.

How much of a person's identity is tied to a name? Apollinaire's story suggests that names and the identities that go with them can be shifting, flexible, and multiple. One person can, in a way, be two or three people—say, Wilhelm the son, Gui the lover, and Apollinaire the poet—all at once. That sense of shifting, flexible, multiple possibilities, in oneself and in the world, is very important to Apollinaire's poetry and helps explain how the son of a young Polish-Italian woman living in Rome grew up to be a French poet.

Early Years

In Apollinaire's poem "Le larron" ("The Thief"), a chorus of voices tells the title character: "A sphinx* was your father and your mother a night" (*Alcools*). That line gives a strong sense of the poet's feelings toward his own parents: a wholly absent father whose identity was a riddle (and has never been established with complete certainty) and a mother preoccupied with nightlife and her own shadowy love life. Young Wilhelm and his brother, Alberto (also born to an unknown father), grew up with little sense of a stable family or stable home.

In 1887, Angelica moved with her sons from Rome to the gambling center and resort country of Monaco, on the Mediterranean Sea, where she worked as an *entraîneuse*.* She enrolled her sons at a Catholic school, where Wilhelm roomed and studied until 1895. His youthful piety,* which he recalls in "Zone" and other poems, was to fade, but his years at the Collège Saint-Charles and other schools in the French cities of Cannes and Nice had other, lasting effects. Wilhelm was developing into an extraordinary talker and reader, and by his late teens he was writing what a schoolmate remembered as "strange" poetry (Steegmuller, p. 35). Wilhelm had found his way to the innovative poetry of French symbolists such as Stéphane Mallarmé and Arthur Rimbaud, and was becoming, in spirit if not yet in nationality, a French poet himself. The symbolists believed in a poetry of mystery and suggestion, evoking feelings and moods in all their indefinable complexity through the description of objects and scenes. Apollinaire's mature po-

*sphinx in Greek mythology, a monster who killed anyone unable to answer her riddle. The word also means a person whose character is mysterious.

*entraîneuse a woman paid by nightclubs and casinos to encourage men to spend money drinking and gambling

*piety religious devotion

etry retained something of the mystery and strangeness of symbolist poetry. His early interest in symbolist innovation* foreshadowed* his own role as an innovator.

Paris—Germany—Paris

In 1897, Wilhelm's formal education ended, and, in 1899, Angelica and her sons moved to Paris. Paris in the late nineteenth century was the center of European culture and a highly modern city. Its international expositions of 1889 and 1900 celebrated industrial and scientific progress; its Eiffel Tower, built in 1889, was then the world's tallest structure. Paris was also the scene of considerable activity in music, theater, art, and literature, with its cafés providing a setting for artistic and intellectual dialogue. And in just a few years the city was to be the center of fresh and exciting developments in painting and poetry in which Wilhelm, by then Guillaume Apollinaire, was to play a central role.

Apollinaire's efforts to make a living, though, took him away from his new home for a time. In August 1901 he became the tutor of an aristocratic family's daughter and traveled with the family to the German Rhineland* and, later, throughout Europe. The scenery of the Rhineland region made a strong impression on the poet, but a colleague made an even stronger impression: Apollinaire was falling in love with his pupil's governess,* a young Englishwoman named Annie Playden, who in the end rejected "Kostro" and emigrated to the United States.

Apollinaire's difficulties and frustrations in this relationship found voice in many poems, including a long lover's complaint in rhymed stanzas, "La chanson du mal-aimé" ("The Song of the Poorly Loved"). The short poem "Annie" suggests some of the abiding characteristics of Apollinaire's poetry:

> On the coast of Texas
> Between Mobile and Galveston there's a
> Large garden filled with roses
> It also contains a villa
> Which is a large rose
>
> Often a woman strolls along
> In the garden all alone

*innovation new development

*foreshadow to give clues that suggest events yet to come

*Rhineland the area of Germany west of the Rhine river

*governess a woman who takes care of a child or children in a private household

A Mennonite is a member of a Protestant religious sect founded in the sixteenth century. Apollinaire may be confusing the Mennonites with a related sect, the Amish, who use hooks and eyes instead of buttons to fasten clothing.

*free verse poetry that does not follow traditional forms, meters, or rhyme schemes

And when I walk along the line of lime trees by the road
My eyes meet hers and hers meet mine

Since that woman is a Mennonite
There are no rosebuds and no buttons on her clothes
Two of them are missing from my coat
The lady and I follow nearly the same rite

One might first be struck by the poem's appearance: like all of Apollinaire's mature poems, "Annie" is without punctuation, giving it a flat, modern appearance. Like many of Apollinaire's poems, "Annie" is written in free verse,* though its unexpected rhymes are a reminder of Apollinaire's interest in traditional stanza forms. And, like many of Apollinaire's poems, "Annie" shows us the poet's genius for re-imagining and transforming the familiar: a villa becomes a rose; Texas grows to contain Mobile, Alabama; and Annie is changed into a Mennonite woman. To object that Apollinaire has things wrong (for neither lime trees nor Mennonites are particularly associated with Texas) is to miss the point: the poem is not a picture of the real Texas but a fantasy of a strange, surprising, remarkable place. "Annie" also helps us understand Apollinaire's complexities of tone. If the ragged poet and the respectable Mennonite "lady" both wear clothes that lack buttons, they do so for very different reasons—the poet because of his poverty and the lady because of her religion. They seem to have much in common but they are really very different. Rather than daydream of Annie in a purely hopeful or hopeless way, Apollinaire offers a more complicated emotional response in a poem that is at once charming, funny, and sad.

In August 1902, Apollinaire gave up tutoring and returned to Paris. He worked as a bank clerk, but his real work was his writing—poems, art criticism, literary criticism, stories, and the occasional erotic novel to bring in some money. He also edited two literary magazines of his own. In 1909 he published his first literary book, *L'Enchanteur pourrissant (The Rotting Magician),* a dialogue between the legendary magician Merlin and his mistress, Viviane. In 1910, *L'Hérésiarque et Cie (The Heresiarch and Co.)* appeared, a collection of stories whose settings and events drew upon his year of European travels. In 1911 *La Bestiaire (The Bestiary)*, Apollinaire's first collection of poetry, was published, with woodcuts by the French artist Raoul Dufy. The year 1911 also saw one of the

The Pretty Redhead (excerpt)

Here I am before all an utterly sensible man
Knowing as much of life and death as a living person can
    know
Having been through the sorrows and joys of love
Having occasionally known how to impose his ideas on
    others
Knowing several languages
Having traveled quite a bit
Having seen the war in the Artillery* and the Infantry*
Wounded in the head trepanned* under chloroform*
Having lost his best friends in the horrible fight
I know as much of the old and the new as any one man
    can know of them both
And without getting upset today over that war
Just between us and for us my friends
I am giving my opinion on the long quarrel between
    tradition and invention

          Order and Adventure
You whose mouth is made in the image of the mouth
    of God
Mouth which is order itself
Be indulgent when you compare us
With those who were the perfection of order
We who look everywhere for adventure

We're not your enemies
We want to give you vast and strange territories
Where flowering mystery offers itself to anyone who
    wishes to gather it
There there are new fires and colors never seen before
A thousand unfathomable phantoms
To which reality must be given

*artillery the part of the army equipped with cannons or other large guns

*infantry the part of the army consisting of foot-soldiers

*trepanned had surgery to relieve pressure on the brain

*chloroform a chemical that used to be inhaled and used as anesthesia during surgery

strangest and most troubling events of Apollinaire's life: he was arrested for the theft of the *Mona Lisa,* a painting by the Italian artist Leonardo da Vinci, from the Louvre art museum in Paris and was held in prison for several days before being released as innocent.

All the while Apollinaire was becoming a central figure in a Parisian community of artists and writers, a man whose enthusiasm for life and poetry and art was unbounded. Among his associates were the painters Georges Braque, Pablo Picasso, and Robert Delaunay and the poets Max Jacob and André Salmon. Apollinaire's circle also included the painter Marie Laurencin, with whom he had a turbulent relationship from 1907 to 1912. During this time the new and exciting developments in painting that became known as cubism were profoundly influencing Apollinaire's poetry.

Cubism and *Alcools*

Life and art were changing rapidly and dramatically in the early twentieth century. The airplane and automobile offered remarkable mobility and speed. Photography, cinema, the telephone, radio, and the phonograph made possible a new multiplicity* in human experience. Watching a movie or speaking on a telephone, a person could almost be in two places at once. Some painters and poets began to feel that familiar ways of painting and writing were no longer adequate to capture the pace and variety of their modern world. Picasso, for instance, began to paint so as to suggest objects and scenes seen from several directions at once, as if a painting had been cut into pieces. The resulting style of painting, with its many-sided objects and shifting, multiple planes on a single canvas, became known as cubism.

Apollinaire was a great lover of modern life; his poems celebrate airplanes, automobiles, elevators, and even the weaponry of World War I. He was also an advocate of cubist painting and in 1913 brought together his writings on art as *Les Peintres Cubistes—Méditations esthétiques* (*The Cubist Painters: Aesthetic Meditations*), offering a passionate defense of art that did not obviously resemble what it depicted: "Real resemblance," he wrote, "no longer has any importance, since everything is sacrificed by the artist to truth" (p. 12). This observation helps us in approaching "Zone," a major poem that introduces Apollinaire's best-known volume of poetry, *Alcools* (1913).

As Apollinaire once remarked, each poem in *Alcools* commemorates an event in his life—his travels, his love affairs, and his imprisonment among those events. It is "Zone," however, that marks a radically new development in Apollinaire's poetry. Apollinaire called "Zone" a *poème-promenade,* a walking poem; it is the record of a sunrise to sunrise walk through

*multiplicity variation

Paris to the city's outskirts (known to Parisians as *La Zone*). Like a cubist painting, which does not in any simple way resemble the objects it depicts, "Zone" does not resemble that walk; it is not a straightforward account. Instead, the poem presents the many shifting exterior and interior realities of a walk through a city. Sometimes we see Paris from the poet's perspective, as he transforms the Eiffel Tower into a shepherdess of the city's bridges (her sheep). Sometimes we are elsewhere, as Apollinaire refers to past events in other places as though they, too, are now happening: "Here you are in Marseilles* among the watermelons / Here you are in Coblenz* at the Hotel Gnome." Even the poet himself takes on several dimensions; he is sometimes "I" sometimes "you."

As a picture of the complex sweep of everyday urban experience, "Zone" is a remarkable poem; one critic has suggested that it may be the most influential poem of the twentieth century. Its premise—a poet walking on city streets, looking, thinking, dreaming, and remembering—deeply influenced the work of many poets, including William Carlos Williams and Frank O'Hara.

War and *Calligrammes*

The outbreak of war—the Great War, later known as World War I—brought Apollinaire's life in Paris to a halt. In August 1914, Germany invaded France; Apollinaire, though not yet a French citizen, soon volunteered to fight for his adopted country. Military service, however, did not stop his literary activity. To the contrary, it gave him new possibilities for his poetry, reflected in the poems of *Calligrammes*, the final volume of poetry published during his lifetime.

Like *Alcools*, *Calligrammes* contains many love poems, written for Countess Louise de Coligny Châtillon and Madeleine Pagès, with whom Apollinaire was involved from 1914 to 1916, and for Jacqueline Kolb, the "pretty redhead" of the volume's last poem. *Calligrammes*, like *Alcools*, contains many poems in traditional forms, but *Calligrammes* also features much greater literary experimentation. The most obvious signs of experimentation are the calligrams* themselves, poems such as "Ocean-Letter" and "It's Raining," whose shapes and unusual typography* give a visual dimension to their language. Apollinaire originally planned to publish his

*Marseilles a port city in France

*Coblenz a city in Germany

*calligram like calligraphy, this term suggests beauty (from the Greek *kallos,* meaning, beauty) and writing (from the Greek *gramma,* letter writing). See also separate essay "Calligrammatic and Concrete Poetry" in these volumes.

*typography the font, style, or arrangement of typeset words or letters

calligrams under the title "Moi aussi je suis peintre" ("And I Too Am a Painter"), and these poems indeed suggest a painter's freedom to arrange elements on a canvas.

Perhaps even more innovative is the extreme cubist fragmentation of such poems as "Lundi rue Christine" ("Monday Rue Christine") and "Les fenêtres" ("The Windows"). "The Windows," said to be inspired by the planes of color in Robert Delaunay's paintings, is a dazzling blur of color, light, and movement;

> From red to green all the yellow dies
> Paris Vancouver Thenburg Nowsville New York and the
>   Antilles
> The window is opening like an orange
> The beautiful fruit of light

How might a window resemble an orange? Perhaps in that each opens to reveal a multifaceted, brilliant reality.

Calligrammes also focuses on the reality of war. Apollinaire wrote many poems in the trenches, and his war poems have prompted much debate. He was not blind to the human cost of war; as he says in "La jolie rousse" "The Pretty Redhead") he "lost his best friends in the horrible fight." Yet Apollinaire did enter into the war with the enthusiasm that he brought to all his activities. Some readers see in the resulting poems a glorification of battle, while others see a poet's determination to transform even war itself into poetry. In our own time, with the danger posed by nuclear weapons, Apollinaire's images of bombshells as beautiful birds and dancing women offer unfamiliar and unsettling ways of seeing the activity of war.

Return to Paris

In March 1916, Apollinaire was naturalized as a French citizen, only days before he was wounded in the head by shell fragments. The injury, which damaged his skull and affected his health generally, required trepanation. With his combat service ended, Apollinaire worked in the Press Relations Office of the French Ministry of War and published a novel, *Le Poète assassiné* (*The Poet Assassinated*) and a play, *Les Mamelles de Tirésias*

(*The Breasts of Tiresias*). Back in Paris, Apollinaire gave an important public lecture in November 1917, "The New Spirit and the Poets." In it he emphasized both the continuity of the old and new in art and literature and the importance of surprise in innovative work: "It is by surprise . . . that the new spirit distinguishes itself from all the literary and artistic movements which have preceded it" (*Selected Writings*, p. 233). The poem "The Pretty Redhead" also speaks on behalf of the new spirit in art and literature, which opens up "vast and strange territories" and discovers "new fires and colors never seen before."

Apollinaire by now had become an inspiration to a younger generation of writers associated with surrealism. In May 1918 he married Jacqueline Kolb. The poet of "The Song of the Poorly Loved" was now well loved, but he was not to survive the war. On 9 November 1918, two days before the armistice* that brought the war to an end, Apollinaire died in Paris of influenza. His wife later reported what he said to his doctor: "I want to live! I still have so many things to say!" (Steegmuller, p. 328). In January 1919, Angelica de Kostrowitzky visited the office of the literary review *Mercure de France*, curious to see copies of her son's books. "Madame," she was told, "you certainly seem to have no idea of the great reputation Apollinaire had made for himself by the time he died" (Steegmuller, p. 30). Today Apollinaire's reputation is greater still; he stands as a major figure in twentieth-century poetry.

Apollinaire's grave is located in the Père Lachaise cemetery in Paris. Many of the sights of Apollinaire's Paris can still be seen in the city today.

*armistice a truce or peace agreement between opposing sides.

Selected Bibliography

WORKS BY GUILLAUME APOLLINAIRE
In French

L'Enchanteur pourrissant (*The Rotting Magician*) (1909). Fiction.

L'Hérésiarque et Cie (*The Heresiarch and Co.*) (1910). Stories.

La Bestiaire (*The Bestiary*) (1911). Poetry.

IF YOU LIKE the poetry of Apollinaire, you might also like the poetry of Blaise Cendrars or Frank O'Hara.

Les Peintres Cubistes—Méditations esthétiques (The Cubist Painters: Aesthetic Meditations) (1913). Writings on art.

Alcools (1913). Poetry.

Le Poète assassiné (The Poet Assassinated) (1916). Fiction.

Les Mamelles de Tirésias (The Breasts of Tiresias) (1918). Play.

Calligrammes (1918). Poetry.

Poems Discussed in the Essay
(Translated by Ron Padgett)

"Annie." *Sulfur* 42:145 (spring 1998).

"The Pretty Redhead." Unpublished manuscript. 1998.

"The Windows." In Padgett, *Blood Work: Selected Prose.* Flint, Mich.: Bamberger, 1993.

"Zone." In *Sleeping on the Wing: An Anthology of Modern Poetry, with Essays on Reading and Writing.* Edited by Kenneth Koch and Kate Farrell. New York: Random House, 1981.

Available Collections

Alcools. Edited and translated by Anne Hyde Greet. Berkeley: University of California Press, 1965. A bilingual edition with extensive notes.

Apollinaire on Art: Essays and Reviews, 1902–1918. Edited by LeRoy C. Breunig. Translated by Susan Suleiman. New York: Da Capo, 1972; repr. 1988.

Calligrammes: Poems of Peace and War (1913–1916). Translated by Anne Hyde Greet. Berkeley: University of California Press, 1980. A bilingual edition with extensive notes.

The Cubist Painters: Aesthetic Meditations, 1913, 2d ed. Translated by Lionel Abel. New York: Wittenborn, Schultz, 1949.

The Heresiarch and Co. Translated by Rémy Inglis Hall. Garden City, N.Y.: Doubleday, 1965; Cambridge, Mass.: Exact Change, 1991.

The Poet Assassinated and Other Stories. Translated by Ron Padgett. San Francisco: North Point Press, 1984.

Selected Writings of Guillaume Apollinaire. Edited and translated by Roger Shattuck. New York: New Directions, 1971. A bilingual collection of poems, fiction, and critical prose.

WORKS ABOUT GUILLAUME APOLLINAIRE

Adéma, Marcel. *Apollinaire.* Translated by Denise Folliot. New York: Grove, 1955.

Bates, Scott. *Guillaume Apollinaire.* New York: Twayne, 1967.

Bohn, Willard. *Apollinaire and the International Avant-Garde.* Albany: State University of New York Press, 1997.

Cailler, Pierre. *Guillaume Apollinaire.* 2 vols. Visages d'hommes célèbres (Faces of famous men). Geneva: Pierre Cailler, 1965. A photographic record of Apollinaire's life, useful even to a reader with little or no French.

Padgett, Ron. "Four French Poets and the Cubist Painters." In his *Blood Work Selected Prose.* Flint, Mich.: Bamberger, 1993.

Shattuck, Roger. *The Banquet Years: The Origins of the Avant Garde in France, 1885 to World War I,* rev. ed. New York: Vintage, 1968.

Steegmuller, Francis. *Apollinaire: Poet Among the Painters.* New York: Farrar, Straus, 1963.

MUSICAL SETTINGS OF POEMS BY GUILLAUME APOLLINAIRE

Poulenc, Francis. *Mélodies.* EMI compact disc CMS 764087. Contains settings for voice and piano of thirty-three Apollinaire poems, including one by "Louise Lalanne."

✍

More About Apollinaire

You can find information about Apollinaire on the Internet in French at: http://www.wiu.edu/Apollinaire

Or in English at: http://www.kirjasto.sci.fi/apollina.htm

MATTHEW ARNOLD

(1822–1888)

by Karen Odden

It is somewhat imprecise to refer to Matthew Arnold simply as a "poet" because during his lifetime, he also wrote essays, letters, journal articles, prefaces, theater reviews, and lectures. His published work reflects his ability to juggle multiple projects; for example, his 1853 volume, *Poems,* includes an important essay as well as new and previously published poetry. Significantly, Arnold composed the volume while pursuing a second career, beginning in 1851, as an inspector of schools, working to administer and improve the British school system. This balance that Arnold sustained between poetry and prose, between old and new, and between two different careers is characteristic of the way he attempted to understand the world around him. Arnold believed in the value of looking at two—or more—sides of a question. He appreciated balanced points of view and he despised people who were narrow-minded and rigid or who refused to engage in debate. In fact, instead of simply ignoring his critics, he often exchanged a series of letters with them, arguing points back and forth. His humor, energy, and liveliness charmed many of his friends—

Quotations from Arnold's work throughout are taken from AMS Press, *The Works of Matthew Arnold in Fifteen Volumes.*

13

although sometimes his clever remarks got him into hot water with his superiors. But he was a successful poet, essayist, teacher, social critic, and civil servant in great part because he was broad-minded and thoughtful, always conscious of the drastic changes that England was undergoing in the 1800s and persistently trying to find ways that human beings could be happy amid these changes.

Early Years and Influences

The Thames (pronounced "temms") is the river that runs through London.

*Celtic related to the Celts—an ethnic group native to the British Isles

Matthew Arnold was born on Christmas Eve 1822 to Thomas and Mary Penrose Arnold. The second child of a large family, he spent the first five years of his life in Laleham-on-Thames, England, which he later recalled as an idyllic spot, situated on the bend of the river. Mary was of Celtic* descent; she had a literary bent and was interested in political reform. When Arnold was young, she was concerned for his health. Later, she was proud of her son, offering advice and support when critics ignored his work or treated it harshly. Arnold had a good relationship with his mother, frequently writing to her and confiding in her, until she died in 1873.

Arnold's father was another matter altogether. Famous as the stern headmaster of Rugby School, a secondary boarding school, from 1828 to 1842, he was credited with transforming an institution full of hellions—boys who were notorious for getting drunk, boxing, and brawling—into a boarding school that instilled discipline and upheld rigorous standards of behavior and education. Nicknamed "Crabby" by his father because of his clumsiness and sometimes glum disposition, Matthew attended Rugby School from age fifteen, but in order to distance himself from his father, he sometimes pretended not to care about school, refusing to hand in his homework or coming late to class; and he fussed over his clothes like a dandy. Nevertheless, he was considered clever. From the time he was young, Arnold had shown the promise of genius: he was studying Latin and the Bible by the time he was six, and at age twelve he wrote his first poems.

When he was fifteen, Arnold met one of his father's star pupils, Arthur Hugh Clough, a boy a few years older than himself. Early on, Clough was his friend and mentor, and Arnold followed him to Oxford University in 1841. Then, like Clough, he became a fellow of Oriel College at Oxford in 1845. But

Arnold had mixed feelings about his friend: he admired Clough immensely but also felt somewhat jealous that Clough was such a favorite of his father's; later, Arnold was angry with Clough for sharply criticizing his ideas about poetry; yet he felt affectionate enough toward his friend to commemorate the memory of their time at school together in the moving pastoral elegy* "Thyrsis" after Clough died in 1861.

Poems of Legends, Loss, and Love

Throughout his career, Arnold was fascinated by the ways that old material—such as pastoral conventions and myths—could be refashioned in ways that would be meaningful for his time. When he was eighteen, he won a prize for a poem about Alaric, who led the Goths against Rome in the fifth century A.D., which shows the influence of Byron's *Childe Harold's Pilgrimage.* At twenty-one, Arnold won the Newdigate Prize for his poem "Cromwell,"* in which he imagines the seventeenth-century Puritan Lord Protector's thoughts as he stands on the banks of the Thames, looking at ships about to set sail.

Perhaps he envisioned Cromwell near the Thames because Arnold always looked back on the first five years of his life at Laleham-on-Thames with fondness. He wrote to a friend that he loved great rivers, and he often uses water imagery in his poetry. But it is interesting that in his prose, the river becomes a metaphor for the poetry itself. In 1880 he was asked to write a preface for an anthology called *The English Poets;* in his essay (later published as *The Study of Poetry*), he wrote

> [In this anthology] it is the course of one great contributory stream to the world-river of poetry that we are invited to follow. . . . We should conceive of poetry worthily, and more highly . . . as capable of higher uses, and called to higher destinies, than those which in general men have assigned to it hitherto. More and more mankind will discover that we have to turn to poetry to interpret life for us, to console us, to sustain us (Vol. 4, p. 2).

In this passage, Arnold makes some big claims for poetry. Throughout his life he believed that poetry was not just art to be enjoyed and then set aside, but that it had the power to shape our lives, our feelings, and our thoughts. However, it is

*pastoral elegy a poem of sorrow or reflection, usually about one who has died, located in a natural setting

*Cromwell, Oliver (1599–1658) Commander of the Puritan army during the English Civil War of the 1640s. After leading his army to victory, he ruled England as "Lord Protector" from 1653 until his death in 1658.

din a loud, sustained noise

benumb to make numb

The Buried Life (excerpt)

But often, in the world's most crowded streets,
But often, in the din* of strife,
There rises an unspeakable desire
After the knowledge of our buried life;
A thirst to spend our fire and restless force
In tracking out our true, original course;
A longing to inquire
Into the mystery of this heart which beats
So wild, so deep in us—to know
Whence our lives come and where they go.
And many a man in his own breast then delves,
But deep enough, alas! none ever mines.
And we have been on many thousand lines.
And we have shown, on each, spirit and power;
But hardly have we, for one little hour,
Been on our own line, have we been ourselves—
Hardly had skill to utter one of all
The nameless feelings that course through our breast,
But they course on forever unexpressed.
And long we try in vain to speak and act
Our hidden self, and what we say and do
Is eloquent, is well—but 'tis not true!
And then we will no more be racked
With inward striving, and demand
Of all the thousand nothings of the hour
Their stupefying power;
Ah yes, and they benumb* us at our call!

(*Poetical Works of Matthew Arnold*)

---

curious that while the water image here is a metaphor for poetry that will "sustain us," the water images in Arnold's poems often point to themes of grief and loss.

In 1849 Arnold published his first volume of poetry, *The Strayed Reveller, and Other Poems,* anonymously (under the name "A"). One of the most important poems in this collection is "The Forsaken Merman," which is based on a Danish legend. In it, the merman is abandoned by his wife, Margaret, who leaves him and her children to become human and live in a town. The poem ends with the sad lament:

> There dwells a loved one,
> But cruel is she!
> She left lonely for ever
> The kings of the sea.

A woman named Margaret who abandons a man appears again in the pair of poems "Isolation. To Marguerite" and "To Marguerite, Continued" that Arnold published (also anonymously) in his second collection of poems, *Empedocles on Etna, and Other Poems.* While in "The Forsaken Merman" water represents the home that Margaret leaves, in the two later poems water suggests the distance that separates people: people are like islands in the sea, isolated from one another. In the first poem, the speaker has been deserted by his lover, Marguerite, and he is in the process of giving up the "dream" that

> two human hearts might blend
> In one, and [could be] through faith released
> From isolation without end.

But the second poem suggests that he has now accepted the loss of the dream: from the beginning, he understands that "Yes! . . .We mortal millions live *alone.*" He pictures all of us as islands "in the sea of life" and his only consolation is that he knows that at one point, long ago, "we were / Parts of a single continent." When the "nightingales divinely sing; / And lovely notes" pass from island to island, we are all reminded of our common past, our enjoyment of beauty, and our longing to communicate with other people. Perhaps Arnold was thinking of the famous passage from a sermon in John Donne's *Devotions upon Emergent Occasions,* which states, "No man is an island, entire of itself; every man is a piece of the continent, a part of the main. . . . Any man's death diminishes me, because I am involved in mankind, and therefore never send to know for whom the bell tolls; it tolls for thee."

Arnold's poems of loss were not only about the loss of faith, but also about the loss of individuals, and he wrote many elegies over the course of his career. This may have been his way of coping with his personal losses. Although his marriage to Frances Lucy Wightman was happy, three of his six children died quite young. Besides "Thyrsis," he wrote "Memorial Verses" on the occasion of William Wordsworth's death in

1850; "Haworth Churchyard" on writers Charlotte Brontë and Harriet Martineau (published 1855); "Rugby Chapel" for his father (1867); "Westminster Abbey" for writer A. P. Stanley (1882); not to mention an elegy each for his canary (1882) and his beloved dachshund (1887).

In 1853, having decided that his poem "Empedocles on Etna" was an artistic failure because it was full of "suffering [that] finds no vent in action," he published his third volume, *Poems: A New Edition*—but this time he put his name on the title page and he prefaced the volume with an essay explaining why he had taken out his former title poem. This book contains the poignant "Stanzas from the Grande Chartreuse," which is one of the two famous poems that date from Arnold's honeymoon in 1851. Wordsworth had visited the Carthusian monastery in the Grande Chartreuse (a region in the French Alps) back in 1790. He saw the two rivers—the Guiers Mort, which flows from the monastery, and the Guiers Vif, which lies in the valley below it. In his long poem *The Prelude,* Wordsworth spoke of the two rivers as "the sister streams of Life and Death." In Arnold's poem, the speaker sees the two rivers as representing a modern dilemma: he has lost faith in the old forms of Christianity and hasn't yet found anything to take their place. He represents himself as

> Wandering between two worlds, one dead
> The other powerless to be born
> With nowhere yet to rest my head

Dover Beach is a famous beach in England. The cliffs nearby are white because they are made of limestone.

Arnold's most famous poem, "Dover Beach," also has to do with the loss of faith, and it too dates from his honeymoon, though it wasn't published until 1867, in *New Poems.* "Dover Beach" is a monologue in which the speaker addresses his silent lover. The poem begins by positioning France and England on opposite sides of the channel, the former as unstable ("the light / Gleams and is gone) and the latter as firm ("the cliffs of England stand"). Of course, the view from France would be different—the speaker sees only the view from his own "window":

> The sea is calm to-night.
> The tide is full, the moon lies fair
> Upon the straits;—on the French coast the light

Gleams and is gone; the cliffs of England stand,
Glimmering and vast, out in the tranquil bay.
Come to the window, sweet is the night-air!
Only, from the long line of spray
Where the sea meets the moon-blanch'd land,
Listen! you hear the grating roar
Of pebbles which the waves draw back, and fling,
At their return, up the high strand,*
Begin, and cease, and then again begin,
With tremulous cadence slow, and bring
The eternal note of sadness in.

> ***strand** beach or shoreline*

Note the sound imagery here—the poem itself is united by sound (the lines end in a rough rhyme scheme* *abacdbdce-fcgfg*) rather than by meter (the lines don't have a regular rhythm or even the same number of syllables). This sound imagery is balanced by images of warfare—you can almost picture the "long line of spray" like a long line of soldiers in an army, rushing the beach, "draw[ing] back and fling[ing]" pebbles as their weapons.

> ***rhyme scheme** in poetry, the pattern of rhymes formed by the last word (or two) of each line*

Next, the speaker compares the sea on the beach in front of him to the sea that the philosopher Sophocles saw in ancient Greece, and then to "The Sea of Faith," that he imagines has receded, leaving the world naked and unprotected. In the end, he recognizes that the world is full of chaos and pain but that even if there is little "faith," love might provide some solace:

Ah, love, let us be true
To one another! For the world, which seems
To lie before us like a land of dreams,
So various, so beautiful, so new,
Hath really neither joy, nor love, nor light,
Nor certitude, nor peace, nor help for pain;
And we are here as on a darkling plain
Swept with confused alarms of struggle and flight,
Where ignorant armies clash by night.

The insistent repetition of "nor" in two consecutive lines creates a tone of deep lament: the speaker suggests what the world *could* have (joy, love, light, peace) but simultaneously takes it away, creating a vacuum that nothing can fill—except maybe love.

Prose Works and Later Years

Although he published *New Poems* in 1867, after 1855 Arnold concentrated on writing essays, which varied from literary criticism to social commentary to reflections on religion. He was busy with his job as inspector of schools, making trips to Europe to learn about foreign educational systems in 1859, 1865, and 1885–1886. Sometimes he regretted that he had to work for a living and couldn't simply devote his time to writing poetry, like his contemporaries Robert Browning and Alfred Lord Tennyson. But his travels gave him the chance to observe different cultures, and many of his most famous essays came out of this experience. As a result of his travels and his conviction that all children—no matter how poor—deserve a good education, he wrote essays such as *Schools and Universities on the Continent* and "The Twice-Revised Code." In the latter essay, Arnold criticizes the unfair practice of giving funds to British elementary schools based on performance and attendance; this policy took money away from poorer schools and gave it to wealthier ones.

In 1857 he was elected professor of poetry at Oxford; his inaugural address, titled "On the Modern Element in Literature," was the first address to be given there in English instead of Latin. Throughout the 1860s, he was primarily interested in literary criticism, and he wrote a series of lectures and articles, collected as *On Translating Homer; Essays in Criticism;* and *On the Study of Celtic Literature.*

If the essays of the 1860s concerned literature, the 1870s found Arnold preoccupied with social questions. In *Culture and Anarchy,* he explains that there are two forces at work in society: Hellenism (based on Greek ideas of art and beauty) and Hebraism (based on Christian values such as hard work). He criticizes Victorian* society for being too industrious—for preferring what Wordsworth once called "getting and spending" to beauty. He also wrote essays on the Bible, arguing that it needed to be reinterpreted for the modern age, and he addressed the plight of the Irish.

To pay his son's gambling debts, Arnold traveled to the United States in the 1880s and gave a series of lectures to raise money. In some cities, he was received enthusiastically; in others, people didn't quite know what to think of his ideas. He returned to England and after a few more years of work, he finally retired from his job as inspector of schools in 1886. A few

* **Victorian** characteristic of the era of Queen Victoria (1837–1901)

"The plight of the Irish" refers to Ireland's poor education system, religious conflict, heavy taxation, unemployment, and poverty—problems due, in great part, to the economic and political domination by Britain and the potato famines of the 1840s.

days after he retired, he again traveled to the United States to visit his daughter Lucy and stayed with her for a few months before returning to England. On 15 April 1888, Arnold and his wife were in Liverpool, where Lucy's ship was to dock. Running for a streetcar, he had a fatal heart attack. His body was brought back to Laleham-on-Thames and buried at his beloved birthplace.

Selected Bibliography

WORKS BY MATTHEW ARNOLD

Collected Poems

Matthew Arnold: The Poetry. Edited by Carol Dawson. London: Routledge and Kegan Paul, 1973.

The Poems of Matthew Arnold. Edited by Kenneth Allott. 2d ed. Revised by Miriam Allott. London: Longman, 1979.

Poetical Works. Edited by C. B. Tinker and H. F. Lowry. London: Oxford University Press, 1950.

The Works of Matthew Arnold in Fifteen Volumes. New York: AMS Press, 1970.

Collected Prose

The Complete Prose Works of Matthew Arnold. 11 vols. Edited by R. H. Super. Ann Arbor: University of Michigan Press (1960–1977).

Collected Letters

The Letters of Matthew Arnold, 1848–1888. 2 vols. Edited by George W. E. Russell. New York and London: Macmillan, 1895.

Selected Letters of Matthew Arnold. Edited by Clinton Machann and Forrest D. Burt. Ann Arbor: University of Michigan Press, 1993.

WORKS ABOUT MATTHEW ARNOLD

ApRoberts, Ruth. *Arnold and God.* Berkeley: University of California Press, 1983.

Baum, Paull F. *Ten Studies in the Poetry of Matthew Arnold.* Durham, N.C.: Duke University Press, 1958.

IF YOU LIKE the poetry of Arnold, you might also like the poetry of William Wordsworth or Robert Browning.

🐦

Coulling, Sidney. *Matthew Arnold and His Critics: A Study of Arnold's Controversies.* Athens: Ohio University Press, 1974.

Honan, Park. *Matthew Arnold: A Life.* Repr. Cambridge, Mass.: Harvard University Press, 1983.

Machann, Clinton. *Matthew Arnold: A Literary Life.* New York: St. Martin's Press, 1998.

Madden, William A. *Matthew Arnold: A Study of the Aesthetic Temperament in Victorian England.* Bloomington: Indiana University Press, 1967.

Murray, Nicholas. *A Life of Matthew Arnold.* London: Hodder and Stoughton, 1996.

Stange, G. Robert. *Matthew Arnold: The Poet as Humanist.* Princeton, N.J.: Princeton University Press, 1967.

Trilling, Lionel. *Matthew Arnold.* New York: Columbia University Press, 1958.

More About Arnold:

You can find the University of Toronto's Matthew Arnold website at:
http://www.library.utoronto.ca/utel/authors/arnoldm.html

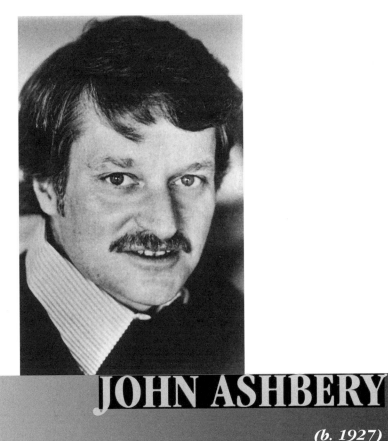

JOHN ASHBERY

(b. 1927)

by Ann Lauterbach

John Ashbery was born on 28 July 1927 in Rochester, New York, and grew up on a farm about thirty miles from there, in Sodus. He had a younger brother, Richard, who died at the age of nine. Ashbery loved his grandfather's house, where he often spent weekends after taking art lessons at the Rochester Art Museum. While attending Deerfield Academy, a college preparatory school in Massachusetts, he published his first poem in a student magazine at about age fifteen. At Harvard College he became friends with fellow student and poet Kenneth Koch and wrote his senior honors thesis on the poet W. H. Auden. After receiving his bachelor's degree in 1949, Ashbery went on to graduate school at Columbia and New York University, where he studied French literature. He worked in publishing from 1951 until 1955, when he received a Fulbright Fellowship to France, where he subsequently lived and worked as an art critic until he returned to New York City in 1965. His job as executive editor of *Art News* lasted until 1972, when he began teaching at Brooklyn College. In 1990 he became the Charles P. Stevenson Jr. Professor of Languages and Literature

If you have definite expectations of what is going to happen once you are inside the poem, you could be disappointed. . . .

at Bard College, dividing his time between New York City and Hudson, New York.

Ashbery has received many awards and prizes for his poetry, beginning with his very first book from a major publisher, *Some Trees,* which was chosen by Auden for the Yale Younger Poets Series in 1956. His book *Self-Portrait in a Convex Mirror* won the Pulitzer Prize, the National Book Award, and the National Book Critics Circle Award for poetry. Among his many other honors are the Bollingen Prize, the Shelley Memorial Award, a Guggenheim Fellowship, and a fellowship from the MacArthur Foundation.

How to Read His Poems

Many people, when they read a poem, ask, What is this poem *about?* Is it about a place? Is it about something that happened to someone? Is it about an important event in history? Is it about the poet? Is it about love or happiness or sorrow? When you read a poem by John Ashbery, these questions are often not easy to answer. Even though there are lots of things, places, persons, and events in his poems, the poems do not seem to be *about* them. One of the first things to do when you begin to read an Ashbery poem is not to worry too much about the subject of the poem but to go into it as you would any new experience, with curiosity, slowly, and with attention. If you have definite expectations of what is going to happen once you are inside the poem, you could be disappointed, and it might be better to begin with as blank a screen as you can manage. In fact, it might be useful to imagine that you are about to embark on a journey into a strange new landscape, where there are many familiar things in unfamiliar places.

One way to think about the "familiar things" in Ashbery's poems is to notice that they are *words,* like "tree" or "sky" or "mother" or "blue." Along with these familiar words, you are likely to find some you may never have heard or seen before, such words as "oxymoron," "convex," "sepulcher," and "Guadalajara." (It is always useful to have a dictionary nearby when you read an Ashbery poem.) Do not be surprised if you find phrases that seem to be from another time and are awkward enough to sound like someone struggling to speak English. You might encounter phrases that seem to be song lyrics or quotations from other books. You might even find a cartoon character, such as Daffy Duck! All of these elements could be found in any Ashbery poem, just the way, if you happen to be visiting New York City, you might see many people and things and signs and lights that do not belong to each other as much as they do to the city in which you find them.

A poem that can help us understand how to read Ashbery is from his second book, *Some Trees.* In this poem, "The Instruction Manual," the narrator is sitting in his office in a skyscraper and wishing he did not have to write "the instruction manual on the uses of a new metal." He looks out the window and sees all the people on the street below, "walking with an inner peace." Watching these far-off persons, he lets his mind wander:

> And, as my way is, I begin to dream, resting my elbows
>   on the desk
>   and leaning out of the window a little,
> Of dim Guadalajara! City of rose-colored flowers!
> City I wanted most to see, and most did not see, in
>   Mexico!

But no sooner does he begin to imagine this city in Mexico than he begins to describe it as if he were actually in it, just the way it might be in a dream or in a film in which the camera begins to move through the streets of a foreign city to show us all the sights. The narrator becomes a kind of tourist guide, pointing out the brightly colored world of Guadalajara, so different from his drab office. Here is how the poem concludes:

> Let us take this opportunity to tiptoe into one of the
>   side streets.
> Here you may see one of those white houses with green
>   trim
> That are so popular here. Look—I told you!
> It is cool and dim inside, but the patio is sunny.
> An old woman in gray sits there, fanning herself with a
>   plain leaf fan.
> She welcomes us to her patio, and offers us a cooling
>   drink.
> "My son is in Mexico City," she says. "He would welcome
>   you too
> If he were here. But his job is with a bank there.
> Look, here is a photograph of him."
> And a dark-skinned lad with pearly teeth grins out at us
>   from the worn leather frame.

We thank her for her hospitality, for it is getting late
And we must catch a view of the city, before we leave,
    from a good high place.
That church tower will do—the faded pink one, there
    against the fierce blue of the sky. Slowly we enter.
The caretaker, an old man dressed in brown and gray,
    asks us how long we have been in the city, and how
    we like it here.
His daughter is scrubbing the steps—she nods to us as
    we pass into the tower.
Soon we have reached the top, and the whole network
    of the city extends before us.
There is the rich quarter, with its houses of pink and
    white, and its crumbling, leafy terraces.
There is the poorer quarter, its homes a deep blue.
There is the market, where men are selling hats and
    swatting flies
And there is the public library, painted several shades of
    pale green and beige.
Look! There is the square we just came from, with the

promenader some-
one who is strolling

promenaders.*
There are fewer of them, now that the heat of the day
    has increased,
But the young boy and girl still lurk in the shadows of
    the bandstand.
And there is the home of the little old lady—
She is still sitting in the patio, fanning herself.

withal nevertheless

How limited, but how complete withal,* has been our
    experience of Guadalajara!
We have seen young love, married love, and the love of
    an aged mother for her son.
We have heard the music, tasted the drinks, and looked
    at colored houses.
What more is there to do, except stay? And that we
    cannot do.
And as a last breeze freshens the top of the weathered
    old tower, I turn my gaze
Back to the instruction manual which has made me
    dream of Guadalajara.

Ashbery tries not to call particular attention to himself in
his poetry. The "I" character who speaks in the poems is not always John Ashbery, but a partly invented person who is capable

of changing into a "you" or even into "we." In "The Instruction Manual," for example, even though there is a person who works in an office writing manuals about the uses of a new metal, this person is not Ashbery, but someone Ashbery imagined.

The fact that many of his poems move easily from "I" to "you" to "we" gives the impression of a sort of wind, and one of the ways you might think about Ashbery's poetry is to imagine the poet as a bird flying through the air and seeing all kinds of things or, perhaps, as a satellite dish. Ashbery also makes use of the ever-changing elements of air and water. Since the sounds of the voice and of music are carried on airwaves, and since so much of modern travel is through the air, it makes sense that a poet who wants to include as much as possible in his poems would often make reference to the air, to waves, to the sky, and to the sea. (One of John Ashbery's books is called *A Wave* and another, *Flow Chart.*) His poems often have the undulating* rhythms of the sea or of a gentle wind, and they seem to carry you along, showing you things as you go.

*undulating pulsating

Art and the New York School

John Ashbery has long been affiliated with a group of poets known as the New York school of poetry. A "school" in poetry is not a school in the ordinary sense, but suggests a common set of artistic concerns or a common place of origin. The New York school, which includes the poets Frank O'Hara, James Schuyler, Kenneth Koch, Barbara Guest, and Kenward Elmslie, grew out of a group of friends in New York. They liked to get together and read each other's poems, and sometimes they collaborated on projects. For example, Ashbery and Schuyler wrote a novel called *A Nest of Ninnies.*

One of the things these poets had in common was an interest in other arts. Frank O'Hara, for example, worked as a curator at the Museum of Modern Art and often wrote about paintings and painters. Ashbery wrote about art for many years. While he was living in Paris, he wrote art reviews for the *New York Herald Tribune* and for two art magazines, *Art International* and *Art News,* and in New York he was an editor at *Art News.* Many of his writings about art are now collected in a book called *Reported Sightings: Art Chronicles 1957–1987.*

You will find many references to paintings and painters in Ashbery's poems. One of his books, *The Double Dream of*

The Painter

Sitting between the sea and the buildings
He enjoyed painting the sea's portrait.
But just as children imagine a prayer
Is merely silence, he expected his subject
To rush up the sand, and, seizing a brush,
Plaster his own portrait on the canvas.

So there was never any paint on his canvas
Until the people who lived in the buildings
Put him to work: "Try using the brush
As a means to an end. Select, for a portrait,
Something less angry and large, and more subject
To a painter's moods, or, perhaps, to a prayer."

How could he explain to them his prayer
That nature, not art, might usurp* the canvas?
He chose his wife for a new subject,
Making her vast, like ruined buildings,
As if, forgetting itself, the portrait
Had expressed itself without a brush.

Slightly encouraged, he dipped his brush
In the sea, murmuring a heartfelt prayer:
"My soul, when I paint this next portrait
Let it be you who wrecks the canvas."
The news spread like wildfire through the buildings:
He had gone back to the sea for his subject.

*usurp** to seize or take over

Spring, has the same name as a painting by the early twentieth-century Italian painter Giorgio De Chirico. One of his most famous poems is called "Self-Portrait in a Convex Mirror," the title of another painting, by the sixteenth-century Italian painter Francesco Parmigianino. A very early poem, written in 1948, is called "The Painter." This poem is exciting because each line of the six six-line stanzas uses the same final words, in rotating order; then there is a last stanza, with only three lines, which has three of the same final words. A poem with this form is called a *sestina.*

Like many of Ashbery's poems, this one is both funny and serious. It is not really a story, but it is full of events. It has words like "prayer" and "crucified" and "soul," which seem to belong to the idea of religious feeling, but then there are

Imagine a painter crucified by his subject!
Too exhausted even to lift his brush,
He provoked some artists leaning from the buildings
To malicious mirth: "We haven't a prayer
Now, of putting ourselves on canvas,
Or getting the sea to sit for a portrait."

Others declared it a self-portrait.
Finally, all indications of a subject
Began to fade, leaving the canvas
Perfectly white. He put down the brush.
At once a howl, that was also a prayer,
Arose from the overcrowded buildings.

They tossed him, the portrait, from the tallest of buildings;
And the sea devoured the canvas and the brush
As though his subject had decided to remain a prayer.

(*Selected Poems*)

"buildings" and "plaster" and "work," which seem to belong to the day-to-day world. This kind of mixing of words from different areas of life gives Ashbery's work a playful feeling and allows readers to decide for themselves what is most interesting about the poem.

Different Forms

Ashbery has written many different kinds of poems, some of which use strict forms, like the sestina quoted earlier, in which you have to obey certain rules. One of his books, *Shadow Train,* is made up of fifty poems, all of which have the same shape: each poem has four stanzas containing four lines.

(These kinds of stanzas are called *quatrains.*) You could think of the book as a kind of train, in which each poem is a car that looks exactly like the next one but which contains different people with different experiences. Since Ashbery often takes a train from New York City to his country house, the idea for this book might have come from his many hours spent riding in a railroad car.

Other Ashbery poems are completely without formal limits. For example, his book called *Three Poems* is written in prose! The difference between poetry and prose is not always very clear. In the nineteenth century, in France, some poets began to write poems in prose, called *prose poems.* One of the best known of these French poets was Charles Baudelaire, who said that a prose poem allowed the poet to write a "poetic prose, musical without rhyme or rhythm, supple and rough enough to adapt to the lyrical movements of the soul, the undulations* of reverie,* the shocks of perception." You can see why a poet like Ashbery might want to write such a poem! Ashbery's three long prose poems are "The New Spirit," "The System," and "The Recital." They are almost like a kind of musical journey that carries the reader along in a sort of trance. Here is one paragraph from "The New Spirit":

> **This is shaped in the new merging, like ancestral smiles, common memories, remembering just how the light stood on the water that time. But it is also something new. Outside, can't you hear it, the traffic, the trees, everything getting nearer. To end up with, inside each other, moving upward like penance. For the continual pilgrimage has not stopped. It is only that you are both moving at the same rate of speed and cannot apprehend the motion. Which carries you beyond, alarmingly fast out into the confusion where the river pours into the sea. That place that seems even farther from shore. . . (*Three Poems*).**

This is another example of how Ashbery seems to be interested in the way things are always shifting and changing, first as we come closer to them and then as we move away. Many of his poems capture this feeling of motion, which is both exciting and a little scary, since you never know what is going to happen next. In this way, Ashbery's poems are very much like life, full of

*undulation a wave-like pulsation

*reverie daydream

unexpected surprises, some of which are sad, some funny, some confusing, and some mysterious and beautiful.

Selected Bibliography

WORKS BY JOHN ASHBERY

Poetry

Turandot and Other Poems (1953).

Some Trees (1956).

The Tennis Court Oath (1962).

Rivers and Mountains (1966).

Selected Poems (1967).

The Double Dream of Spring (1970).

Three Poems (1972).

Self-Portrait in a Convex Mirror (1975).

The Vermont Notebook (1975).

Houseboat Days (1977).

As We Know (1979).

Shadow Train (1981).

A Wave (1984).

Selected Poems (1985).

April Galleons (1987).

Flow Chart (1991).

Hotel Lautréamont (1992).

And the Stars Were Shining (1994).

Can You Hear, Bird (1995).

The Mooring of Starting Out: The First Five Books of Poetry (1997).

Wakefulness (1998).

Girls on the Run (1999).

IF YOU LIKE the poetry of Ashbery, you might also like the poetry of W. H. Auden, Frank O'Hara, or James Schuyler.

Other Works

A Nest of Ninnies (with James Schuyler) (1969). Novel.

Three Plays (1978).

Reported Sightings: Art Chronicles 1957–1987 (1989).

Syringa, composed by Elliott Carter. English poem by John Ashbery; text in Classical Greek by Aeschylus. New York: Associated Music Publishers, 1980.

WORKS ABOUT JOHN ASHBERY

Altieri, Charles. *Self and Sensibility in Contemporary American Poetry.* Cambridge, U.K., and New York: Cambridge University Press, 1984.

Blasing, Mutlu Kouuk. *Politics and Form in Post-Modern Poetry: O'Hara, Bishop, Ashbery and Merrill.* Cambridge, U.K., and New York: Cambridge University Press, 1995.

Eichbauer, Mary E. *Poetry's Self-Portrait: The Visual Arts as Mirror and Muse in René Char and John Ashbery.* New York: Peter Lang Publishers, 1992.

Hoeppner, Edward Haworth. *Echoes and Moving Fields: Structure and Subjectivity in the Poetry of W. S. Merwin and John Ashbery.* Cranbury, N.J.: Associated University Presses, 1994.

Kermani, David. *John Ashbery: A Comprehensive Bibliography, Including His Art Criticism, and with Selected Notes from Unpublished Materials.* New York: Garland Publishing, 1976.

Lehman, David, ed. *Beyond Amazement: New Essays on John Ashbery.* Ithaca, N.Y.: Cornell University Press, 1980.

Malinowska, Barbara. *Dynamics of Being, Space and Time in the Poetry of Czeslaw Milosz and John Ashbery.* New York: Peter Lang Publishers, 1997.

Murphy, Margueritte S. *A Tradition of Subversion: The Prose Poem in English from Wilde to Ashbery.* Amherst: University of Massachusetts Press, 1992.

Schultz, Susan M., ed. *The Tribe of John: Ashbery and Contemporary Poetry.* Tuscaloosa: University of Alabama Press, 1995.

Shapiro, David. *John Ashbery: An Introduction to the Poetry.* New York: Columbia University Press, 1979.

Shoptaw, John. *On the Outside Looking In: John Ashbery's Poetry.* Cambridge, Mass.: Harvard University Press, 1994.

Stitt, Peter. *Uncertainty and Plenitude: Five Contemporary Poets.* Iowa City: University of Iowa Press, 1997.

Ward, Geoff. *Statutes of Liberty: The New York School of Poets.* New York: St. Martin's Press, 1993.

✍

More About Ashbery

You can find information about John Ashbery on the Internet at:
http://www.poets.org/lit/poet/jashbfst.htm

W. H. AUDEN

(1907–1973)

by A. Michael Matin

One of the foremost poets of the twentieth century, W. H. Auden began his career with a meteoric rise to fame in his mid-twenties as the leader of a group of leftist* British writers. Although charismatic,* he was not really suited for such a role. After a flirtation with political writing during the 1930s, he rejected the notion of poetry as an effective vehicle for political ideas and emigrated to America, giving up his leadership of what had come to be known as the "Auden Group." Throughout his adult life Auden remained prolific, exploring a wide variety of themes and genres. Unlike the majority of his modernist elders, he preferred traditional verse forms, such as the sonnet. He insisted on the rigorous discipline of poetic creation, quipping that indulgence in free verse* leads to "squalor"—the artistic equivalent of "dirty sheets on the unmade bed and empty bottles on the unswept floor" (*The Dyer's Hand,* p. 22). An uncompromising perfectionist, he was never content with what he had written and continued to revise his work years after it had been published.

*leftist politically, very liberal

*charismatic having an exceptionally attractive personality and strong leadership skills

*free verse poetry that does not follow traditional forms, meters, or rhyme schemes

He said he agreed with the French poet Paul Valéry that "a poem is never finished; it is only abandoned" (*Collected Poems,* p. xxvi).

Early Life

*vicar a member of the clergy

Wystan Hugh Auden was born on 21 February 1907 in the northern English city of York to George and Constance Auden, both children of vicars.* Whereas Constance was a devout Christian, George, a doctor, was indifferent to religion. When Wystan was a baby, the Audens moved south to Birmingham when his father was appointed a professor of public health at the university there. His early years were characterized by middle class comfort and security. When World War I broke out, George Auden joined the Royal Army Medical Corps, and young Wystan saw very little of him during the four years of the conflict. (He later ascribed his homosexuality, in accordance with now outdated psychoanalytic theory, to his close relationship with his mother, a bond that, he observed, was intensified by the absence of his father during these formative years.) In 1915 he entered St. Edmunds, a Surrey school, where he met the future writer Christopher Isherwood, who became a lifelong friend. Five years later, he enrolled in Gresham's School in Norfolk. At the time, his ambition was to become a mining engineer. At the age of fifteen, however, he discovered his vocation as a poet.

In 1925 Auden entered Christ Church College, Oxford, where he met several other young writers with whom his name is usually linked—Cecil Day-Lewis, Louis MacNeice, and Stephen Spender. It was during his Oxford period that he wrote a poem aptly titled "The Watershed," which he later judged to be the first of his mature works. As a young artist, he was impressionable and learned his craft largely by imitating others. He referred to the poet and novelist Thomas Hardy as his "first Master," and he was briefly infatuated with the poetry of T. S. Eliot. After discovering the latter's work in 1926, he promptly announced, "I have torn up all my poems. . . . I've been reading Eliot. I now see the way I want to write" (Carpenter, p. 57). He soon discovered, however, that he did *not* want to write like the esoteric* Eliot. Auden viewed inaccessibility* in poetry as a fault, and he was particularly upset when some early critics identified an Eliot-like obscurity in his own youthful verse.

*esoteric exclusive, secretive

*inaccessibility inability to be grasped or understood

Early Work and Rise to Fame

Having completed his undergraduate studies, Auden traveled to Berlin in 1928, where he spent much of the next year learning German, writing poetry, and developing the radical political views that came to serve as the basis for much of his work over the next decade. A poem that he wrote in Berlin and later entitled "1929" conveys the spirit of the time and his own excitement at being a part of it:

> All this time was anxiety at night,
> Shooting and barricade in street.
> Walking home late I listened to a friend
> Talking excitedly of final war
> Of proletariat* against police—
> That one shot girl of nineteen through the knees,
> They threw that one down concrete stair—
> Till I was angry, said I was pleased.

*__proletariat__ the working class

After returning to England, he worked as a tutor until he got a job teaching at a boy's school in Scotland. His public breakthrough as a poet came in 1930, when the prestigious publishing house Faber and Faber—and specifically one of the firm's directors, his former idol, T. S. Eliot—published his first book, *Poems,* followed two years later by *The Orators.* These works gained extraordinary critical and popular acclaim and quickly made Auden the most renowned poet of his generation. He left Scotland in 1932 to teach at a school in Colwall, England. Although 1932 is often referred to as the beginning of his "Communist phase," his political convictions were by no means orthodox* and seem never to have been very strong at all. During the Great Depression of the 1930s, it was fashionable for young men in Britain to embrace socialism* and to declare solidarity with the working classes. Auden's own forays into political writing—as he himself would come to recognize in later years—consisted more of a rhetorical testing out of ideas than a committed endorsement of Marxist* principles.

Yet if his politics during this period were by no means clear, he was convinced of the authenticity of what he called a "vision of *agape*"* that he experienced in 1933: "I felt myself invaded by a power which . . . was irresistible and certainly not mine. For the first time in my life I knew exactly . . . what it means to love one's neighbor as oneself" (*Forewords and Afterwords*, p. 69).

*__orthodox__ conforming to established doctrine

*__socialism__ an economic system in which there is no private property

*__Marxist__ communist or socialist; relating to the ideas of Karl Marx

*__agape__ a Greek word meaning "love" in a nonromantic sense

Although he had thought that he had lost his belief in Christianity as a teenager, this episode suggests the persistence of the religious sensibility that, by 1940, returned him to the church.

Travels and Political Disillusionment

The most important of Auden's several dramatic collaborations with Christopher Isherwood, *The Ascent of F6,* was published in 1936 and performed the following year. Its theme—the hazards associated with the pursuit of glory—is symbolically expressed in the protagonist's* self-annihilating mountaineering endeavors. For Auden, who had come to feel that his role as a public figure in England was becoming intolerably burdensome, writing the play was an attempt to grapple with his mixed feelings about his own swift rise to fame. The outcome was decisive: "I knew I must leave [England] when I wrote it," he later remarked (Carpenter, p. 195). In fact, shortly after completing *The Ascent of F6,* he left home on the first of many long journeys.

He began with a voyage to Iceland with his friend and fellow poet Louis MacNeice, which resulted in their collaborative volume *Letters from Iceland.* While they were there, the Spanish Civil War broke out. This conflict was viewed by socialists as the opening salvo* in the great struggle against fascism.* Auden set off for Spain in early 1937 to support the anti-fascist Republican cause, hoping to serve as an ambulance driver. Once there, however, he discovered that the conflict was not at all the epic contest of good versus evil that he had hoped to see, and he soon left, deeply disillusioned. Yet he continued to believe in the evil of fascism, and on his return to England he wrote the call to arms "Spain 1937," a poem he would later disown for what he viewed to be its rhetorical excesses.

Even during the peak of his ostensibly "political" phase, Auden continued to write poetry that had nothing to do with politics, such as what is perhaps his most famous love poem, the tender confession of infidelity "Lullaby," which begins:

> Lay your sleeping head, my love,
> Human on my faithless arm;
> Time and fevers burn away
> Individual beauty from
> Thoughtful children, and the grave
> Proves the child ephemeral:*

*protagonist the major character in a literary work

*salvo discharge of weapons; a spirited verbal attack

*fascism a form of government that exalts a single ruler, greatly restricts personal freedom, and permits no opposition

*ephemeral short-lived

> But in my arms till break of day
> Let the living creature lie,
> Mortal, guilty, but to me
> The entirely beautiful.

As with most of the love lyrics he wrote throughout his career, he does not specify here the gender of the beloved, although he was not at all secretive about his homosexuality.

In 1938, during the Sino-Japanese War, Auden went to China, this time with Christopher Isherwood. Their experiences inspired their collaborative work *Journey to a War,* which includes the poems later called "Sonnets from China." Later that year they traveled to Belgium, where Auden wrote "Musée des Beaux Arts," a poem that takes as its subject a painting by the sixteenth-century Flemish painter Pieter Brueghel depicting the story of the mythical Icarus's doomed attempts to fly. In light of the impending Second World War, the poem describes how the world blithely ignores catastrophes:

> In Brueghel's *Icarus,* for instance: how everything turns
> away
> Quite leisurely from the disaster; the ploughman may
> Have heard the splash, the forsaken cry,
> But for him it was not an important failure; the sun shone
> As it had to on the white legs disappearing into the green
> Water; and the expensive delicate ship that must have
> seen
> Something amazing, a boy falling out of the sky,
> Had somewhere to get to and sailed calmly on.

Emigration to America

Early in 1939, Auden, along with Isherwood, arrived in New York City, where he made his home for a portion of nearly every year for the rest of his life. During his first several weeks in America he wrote the splendid elegy* "In Memory of W. B. Yeats." The last stanzas, which are addressed to the spirit of the great Irish poet, contain some of the finest and loftiest sentiments that he ever put to verse:

> Follow, poet, follow right
> To the bottom of the night,

*elegy a poem of sorrow or reflection, usually about someone who is dead

With your unconstraining voice
Still persuade us to rejoice;

With the farming of a verse
Make a vineyard of the curse,
Sing of human unsuccess
In a rapture of distress;

In the deserts of the heart
Let the healing fountain start,
In the prison of his days
Teach the free man how to praise.

Several months after his arrival in New York, Auden met a nineteen-year-old college student named Chester Kallman, who became his lifelong partner. When World War II began with the German invasion of Poland, Auden wrote "September 1, 1939," which contains the impassioned exhortation "We must love one another or die." As was the case with "Spain," however, he later disowned the poem because of what he termed its "dishonest" polemical rhetoric.* (Neither work appears in the *Collected Poems*, the volume that includes all of the verse by which he wanted to be remembered.) Soon after the outbreak of the war, Auden returned to the faith in which he had been raised. His "vision of *agape*" of 1933 demonstrates that even though he was not a practicing Christian, he had retained a deeply religious sensibility. Yet there was also a strong practical and intellectual aspect to his wartime return to faith: it provided him with an absolute moral foundation for his opposition to Nazism.*

Auden's poetry now became deeply philosophical and religious, beginning with the *New Year Letter,* in which he made a claim he would reaffirm for the rest of his life: "Art is not life and cannot be / A midwife to society." This does not mean that he endorsed the apolitical "art for art's sake" doctrine of such late-nineteenth-century British writers as Walter Pater and Oscar Wilde, but he did dissent* from those writers who believed that their work could have a meaningful impact on politics. The nineteenth-century Romantic poet Percy Bysshe Shelley had claimed in *A Defence of Poetry* that "poets are the unacknowledged legislators of the world." "'The unacknowledged legislators of the world' describes the secret police, not the poets," Auden retorted (*The Dyer's Hand,* p. 27).

Throughout the 1940s and the first half of the 1950s, Auden taught at various American universities and colleges,

*****polemical rhetoric** language that is used to instill ideas or beliefs

*****Nazism** a political doctrine put into effect in Germany in the 1930s that included a totalitarian form of government, a belief in the superiority of certain races, and the government control of industry
*****dissent** disagree

The Unknown Citizen
(To JS/07/M/378
This Marble Monument Is Erected by the State)

He was found by the Bureau of Statistics to be
One against whom there was no official complaint,
And all the reports on his conduct agree
That, in the modern sense of an old-fashioned word, he
    was a saint,
For in everything he did he served the Greater
    Community.
Except for the War till the day he retired
He worked in a factory and never got fired,
But satisfied his employers, Fudge Motors Inc.
Yet he wasn't a scab* or odd in his views,
For his Union reports that he paid his dues,
(Our report on his Union shows it was sound)
And our Social Psychology workers found
That he was popular with his mates and liked a drink.
The Press are convinced that he bought a paper every day
And that his reactions to advertisements were normal in
    every way.
Policies taken out in his name prove that he was fully
    insured,
And his Health-card shows he was once in hospital but left
    it cured.
Both Producers Research and High-Grade Living declare
He was fully sensible to the advantages of the Installment
    Plan
And had everything necessary to the Modern Man,
A phonograph, a radio, a car and a frigidaire.*
Our researchers into Public Opinion are content
That he held the proper opinions for the time of year;
When there was peace, he was for peace; when there was
    war, he went.
He was married and added five children to the population,
Which our Eugenist* says was the right number for a
    parent of his generation,
And our teachers report that he never interfered with their
    education.
Was he free? Was he happy? The question is absurd:
Had anything been wrong, we should certainly have heard.

***scab** a worker who refuses to join a labor union or who works during a strike

***frigidaire** a refrigerator

***Eugenist** a student or advocate of selective breeding

including the University of Michigan, Swarthmore, and Bryn Mawr. In 1946 he became a U.S. citizen, and in the following year the last of his long philosophical poems, *The Age of Anxiety,* appeared. In 1951 he published *Nones,* which includes "In Praise of Limestone" and other lovely poems recording his attachment to Ischia, the Italian island where he and Kallman regularly summered. It was also in Italy in 1951 that the first of his and Kallman's several opera librettos,* *The Rake's Progress,* commissioned by the renowned composer Igor Stravinsky, was performed.

*libretto the text for a musical work

The Shield of Achilles, judged by some to be Auden's finest volume of poems, appeared in 1955. The title work expands on some of the pessimistic* sentiments he had earlier registered about modern humanity in the poem "The Unknown Citizen," a mock-elegy delivered by the voice of the state in honor of a man whose exemplariness* is evidenced in his total lack of individuality. A similarly ironic devaluation of classical values is at work in "The Shield of Achilles," in which the war-glorifying world of Homeric* myth is seen through the lens of the antiheroic contemporary world, in which the chief outcome of war is not glory but suffering:

*pessimistic lacking hope for the future

*exemplariness praiseworthiness

*Homeric characteristic of Homer's long heroic epics, the *Iliad* and the *Odyssey* (ca. 750 B.C.)

> Out of the air a voice without a face
>   Proved by statistics that some cause was just
> In tones as dry and level as the place:
>   No one was cheered and nothing was discussed;
>   Column by column in a cloud of dust
> They marched away enduring a belief
> Whose logic brought them, somewhere else, to grief.

Late Work and Final Years

In 1956 Auden was elected Professor of Poetry at Oxford in England, where he spent several months of each of the next five years. He had by this time received numerous other honors, including the King's Gold Medal in 1937, the Pulitzer Prize in 1948, the Bollingen Prize in 1954, and the National Book Award in 1956. Yet he never obtained the award that he most coveted, the Nobel Prize, which he disingenuously* claimed he wanted not for the honor but for the money. Auden shifted his summer residence in 1958 from Ischia to the Austrian town of Kirchstetten, where he had purchased a house. His still substantial poetic output was complemented by prose works, such as *The Dyer's Hand,* which contains many of his finest essays.

*disingenuously deviously; faking simple honesty

His poetry during the 1960s increasingly tended toward the personal, as in *About the House,* a celebration of his home in Austria and of his life there with Kallman. Yet he still occasionally wrote about public events, as in "August 1968," a response to the crushing of democratic reforms in Czechoslovakia by Soviet tanks. Derisively likening the Soviet empire to an "ogre," he jeers:

> About a subjugated plain,
> Among its desperate and slain,
> The Ogre stalks with hands on hips,
> While drivel gushes from his lips.

Notably, however, the piece consists not of a call to action but rather a mere taunt, and hence does not contradict his assertion in the elegy on Yeats that "poetry makes nothing happen."

In his final years, Auden's verse increasingly registered his sense of the rapid aging that was visible on his deeply lined face. In addition to his awareness of his own declining health (a process accelerated by his heavy smoking and drinking), he wrote of his sense of being superseded by the American youth culture of the late 1960s and early 1970s. As he lamented in "Doggerel by a Senior Citizen," "Our earth in 1969 / Is not the planet I call mine." In 1972, a year before he died of a heart attack in Vienna, Austria, Auden attempted to relieve some of these feelings by taking up residence in the more traditional and hospitable environs of his old college, Christ Church, Oxford. While there, he wrote a verse encomium* to England entitled "Thank You, Fog," which charmingly conveys his sense of himself as a prodigal son who has returned home:

> Grown used to New York weather,
> all too familiar with Smog,
> You, Her unsullied Sister,
> I'd quite forgotten and what
> You bring to British winters:
> now native knowledge returns.

Selected Bibliography

WORKS BY W. H. AUDEN
Poetry
> *Poems* (1930).
>
> *The Orators* (1932).

*encomium an expression of praise

Prodigal son refers to the biblical story of a son who leaves home, wastes his inheritance, and then is welcomed back despite his mistake.

IF YOU LIKE the poetry of Auden, you might also like the poetry of William Butler Yeats.

On This Island (1936). Published in Britain as *Look, Stranger!*

Spain (1937).

Another Time (1940).

The Double Man (1941). Published in Britain as *New Year Letter.*

For the Time Being (1944).

The Age of Anxiety (1947).

Nones (1951).

The Shield of Achilles (1955).

Homage to Clio (1960).

About the House (1965).

City Without Walls (1969).

Epistle to a Godson (1972).

Thank You, Fog (1974).

Collected Poems (1976).

Plays

The Dance of Death (1933).

The Dog Beneath the Skin (with Christopher Isherwood) (1935).

The Ascent of F6 (with Christopher Isherwood) (1936).

On the Frontier (with Christopher Isherwood) (1938).

Opera Librettos

Paul Bunyan (1941).

The Rake's Progress (with Chester Kallman) (1951).

Elegy for Young Lovers (with Chester Kallman) (1961).

The Bassarids (with Chester Kallman) (1966).

Travel Books

Letters from Iceland (with Louis MacNeice) (1937).

Journey to a War (with Christopher Isherwood) (1939).

Prose

The Enchafèd Flood (1950).

The Dyer's Hand (1962).

Secondary Worlds (1969).

A Certain World (1970).

Forewords and Afterwords (1973).

Available Collections

The Complete Works of W. H. Auden, edited by Edward Mendelson and published by both Princeton University Press and Faber and Faber. Three of a projected eight volumes have thus far been published:

Plays and Other Dramatic Writings, 1927–1938 (1989).

Libretti and Other Dramatic Writings, 1939–1973 (1993).

Prose and Travel Books in Prose and Verse, 1926–1938 (1997).

The English Auden: Poems, Essays and Dramatic Writings, 1927–1939. Edited by Edward Mendelson. New York: Random House, 1977.

WORKS ABOUT W. H. AUDEN

Bloomfield, Barry C., and Edward Mendelson. *W. H. Auden: A Bibliography, 1924–1969,* 2nd ed. Charlottesville: University Press of Virginia, 1972.

Carpenter, Humphrey. *W. H. Auden: A Biography.* New York: Harcourt Brace Jovanovich, 1981.

Clark, Thekla. *Wystan and Chester: A Personal Memoir of W. H. Auden and Chester Kallman.* New York: Columbia University Press, 1996.

Davenport-Hines, Richard. *Auden.* New York: Pantheon Books, 1996.

Fuller, John. L. *W. H. Auden: A Commentary.* Princeton, N.J.: Princeton University Press, 1998.

Greenberg, Herbert M. *Quest for the Necessary: W. H. Auden and the Dilemma of Divided Consciousness.* Cambridge, Mass.: Harvard University Press, 1968.

Hynes, Samuel. *The Auden Generation.* New York: Viking, 1976.

Johnson, Richard A. *Man's Place: An Essay on Auden.* Ithaca, N.Y.: Cornell University Press, 1973.

More About Auden

You can find information about Auden on the Internet at:
http://www.lit.kobe-u.ac.jp/~hishika/auden.html
http://www.sat.dundee.ac.uk/~arb/speleo/auden.html
http://physserv1.physics.wisc.edu/~shalizi/Poetry/Auden/

Johnson, Wendell Stacy. *W. H. Auden.* New York: Continuum, 1990.

Mendelson, Edward. *Early Auden.* New York: Viking, 1981.

Mendelson, Edward. *Later Auden.* New York: Farrar, Straus and Giroux, 1999.

Page, Norman. *Auden and Isherwood: The Berlin Years.* New York: St. Martin's Press, 1998.

Spears, Monroe K. *The Poetry of W. H. Auden: The Disenchanted Island.* New York: Oxford University Press, 1963.

Spender, Stephen, ed. *W. H. Auden: A Tribute.* New York: Macmillan, 1975.

Wright, George T. *W. H. Auden,* rev. ed. New York: Twayne, 1981.

AMIRI BARAKA
(LeRoi Jones)
(b. 1934)

by Lorenzo Thomas

Amiri Baraka's popularity ranks him with such African American writers as Paul Laurence Dunbar, Langston Hughes, and Gwendolyn Brooks—poets whose works continue to be memorized and recited by readers from all walks of life. Baraka's role in the larger context of American literature is just as significant; as far as influence on the style of other writers is concerned, Baraka and John Ashbery have been the most influential American poets since 1960. Baraka was at first associated with the writers of the Beat Generation, and later became a leader of the important Black Arts Movement. Born Everett LeRoi Jones, he adopted Amiri Baraka as his Muslim name in 1967, though some of his works continued to be published under his original name. Baraka's writings earned him a vast popular audience and many honors, such as a Whitney Fellowship, a Rockefeller Foundation Fellowship, an Obie Award, a National Endowment for the Arts Fellowship, and the American Book Awards' Lifetime Achievement Award.

Quotations from Baraka's poetry throughout are taken from Vangelisti, ed. *Transbluesency: The Selected Poems of Amiri Baraka/LeRoi Jones (1961–1995)*.

The Beat Generation, known for their unconventional style, began publishing their work in the United States during the 1950s.

Early Life and Influences

Born in Newark, New Jersey, on 7 October 1934, Everett LeRoi Jones was the younger of two children of Coyette and Anna Lois Jones. He attended public schools, graduating with honors from Newark's Barringer High School in 1951. After attending Rutgers University and Howard University (where he studied with the poet and folklorist Sterling A. Brown), Baraka served in the U.S. Air Force. It was during his military service that he became serious about reading and writing poetry. After his discharge in 1957, Baraka settled in Greenwich Village—a New York City neighborhood with a long history of artistic activity—determined to pursue a literary career. From 1958 to 1963, he and his wife, Hettie Cohen, edited *Yugen,* a poetry magazine that presented work by such innovative writers as Gary Snyder, Michael McClure, and Charles Olson. He was also closely associated with Frank O'Hara and with the Beat writers Allen Ginsberg and Jack Kerouac.

Baraka's interest in music and the arts—and his skeptical attitude toward society's conventions—appeared early. As a teenager, he had ambitions that were more intellectual and visionary than concerned with material success. He recalled those adolescent dreams in the poem "Letter to E. Franklin Frazier":*

> By the projects* and small banks of my time. Counting
>   my steps
> on tar or new pavement, following the sun like a park. I
>   imagined
> a life, that was realer than speech, or the city's anonymous
> fish markets. Shuddering at dusk, with a mile or so up
>   the hill
>
> to get home. who did you love
> then, Mussolini?* What were you thinking,
> Lady Day?* A literal riddle of image
> was me, and my smell was a continent
> of familiar poetry. Walking the long way,
> always the long way, and up the steep hill.

The poem "Ostriches & Grandmothers!" expresses Baraka's understanding of poetry not simply as a pastime or a solace for loneliness, but rather as a sometimes daring (and perhaps dangerous) effort to confront one's own doubts.

Baraka and Cohen were married in 1958 at a Buddhist temple in New York. Divorced from Hettie in 1966, Baraka later married Amina Sylvia Robinson in a traditional Yoruba ceremony.

*__Frazier, E. Franklin__ (1894–1962) American sociologist

*__projects__ housing projects; government-subsidized low-income apartments

*__Mussolini, Benito__ (1883–1945). Fascist dictator of Italy from 1922 to 1943

*__Lady Day__ Billie Holiday (1915–1959). African American blues singer

Ostriches & Grandmothers! (excerpt)

It's these empty seconds
I fill with myself. Each
a recognition. A complete
utterance.

Here, it is color; motion;
the feeling of dazzling beauty
Flight.

As
the trapeeze rider
leans
with arms spread

wondering at the bar's
delay

Poetic Style

The poems in Baraka's first book, *Preface to a Twenty Volume Suicide Note,* reflect the irreverent* attitude of the Beat Generation. Reading his poems aloud in Greenwich Village coffeehouses, Baraka had developed an attractive and vividly colloquial* poetic style notable for urbane* wit and precise, evocative* diction. But this was also poetry that did not shy away from street slang or profanity. The subject matter of his poems was both personal and political, and a single work might often include social comment along with introspective* self-criticism. One theme that recurs throughout all of Baraka's work is his criticism of the hypocrisy,* conformity, and superficial values of middle-class lifestyles.

In "Hymn for Lanie Poo," for example, Baraka sarcastically ridicules the materialism of the affluent* but bland Eisenhower era.* He is particularly scornful of middle-class African Americans, especially his own peers—the grandchildren of those who fled the segregated South during the great migration at the beginning of the century:

*__irreverent__ lacking proper respect; not taking something seriously
*__colloquial__ characteristic of everyday conversation
*__urbane__ polished
*__evocative__ likely to cause an emotional response
*__introspective__ self-examining
*__hypocrisy__ self-contradiction; two-facedness
*__affluent__ abundantly wealthy
*__Eisenhower era__ Dwight Eisenhower was President of the United States from 1953 to 1961, a period now considered as marked by conventionality and conformity.

(O, generation revered
above all others,
O, generation of fictitious
Ofays*
I revere you . . .
You are all so beautiful)

my sister drives a green jaguar
my sister has her hair done twice a month
my sister is a school teacher
my sister took ballet lessons
my sister has a fine figure: never diets
my sister doesn't like to teach in Newark
    because there are too many colored
    in her classes

Other poems, of course, are just as disapproving of the self-centered shallowness of white Americans.

Social History and Drama

During this period Baraka also wrote *Blues People: Negro Music in White America,* a groundbreaking combination of social history and musicology that was soon recognized as a classic work of scholarship. His thesis was that such creative expression as music and literature accurately reflects social and economic conditions—and that changes in artistic styles are indicators of a society's ethical direction. This thesis influenced Baraka's own poetic development, and it has influenced many other writers. His 1964 play, *Dutchman,* later made into a movie, was also a major success and eloquently proclaimed the resentment felt by black Americans regarding a century of racial discrimination and exclusion from the mainstream. *Dutchman*'s searingly confrontational tone was new on the American stage and created much controversy with its portrayal of black people's internalized rage and white society's methodical brutality.

Black Arts Movement

Soon afterward, Baraka became a model for poets and playwrights of the Black Arts Movement (1965–1980) and an energetic organizer of the movement, which brought a new and militantly political focus to African American culture. In some ways the Black Arts Movement was a continuation of the Harlem Renaissance;* in other ways, though, it was a contrast. The writers of the 1920s had been much concerned with proving their equality to white Americans; the poets of the Black Arts Movement severely criticized the value system of American society and proposed a more Afrocentric or cultural nationalist* view for the black community. For some, Western culture itself was seen as a corrupt influence. From Baraka's point of view, a society's ethics, philosophy, and economic system are all inextricably* connected; a society that professes ideals of equality while deliberately harming some of its citizens was obviously hypocritical. Nevertheless, many of the poems he wrote during this period also directly chastise* the black community for self-destructive behavior and short-sighted choices. In *It's Nation Time,* Baraka points out that social progress is everyone's personal responsibility:

> The nation is like our selves, together
> seen in our various scenes, sets where ever we are
> what ever we are doing, is what the nation
> is
> doing
> or
> not doing
>
> "The Nation Is like Ourselves"

Later Work and Thought

Later, Baraka came to feel that racism and economic inequality are basic and unchangeable aspects of capitalist* society and that only a Marxist* reorganization could eliminate such problems. Much of his poetry from the late 1970s onward expresses this view.

In 1990, Baraka began work on a long series of poems entitled *Wise, Why's, Y's.* Meditative but concise, these poems recall lines from proverbs and spirituals, presenting direct philosophical comments inspired by musicians and other historical figures. Baraka has said that *Wise, Why's, Y's* is an attempt to write a postmodern* epic poem in the tradition of the West African *griots*—the poets and musicians who maintain the history and genealogies of their people through an oral tradition.

*__Harlem Renaissance__ a period (1920s) of enormous creativity in literature, music, and art in the African American community of Harlem in New York City

*__cultural nationalist__ subscribing to the belief, which first spread during the 1960s, that adoption of "African" culture in the United States should precede a revolution to end the oppression of African Americans.

*__inextricably__ inseparably

*__chastise__ to scold or punish

*__capitalist__ characterized by the private ownership and control of industry

*__Marxist__ based on the ideas of Karl Marx (1818–1883); communistic or socialistic

*__postmodern__ not bound by the categories or rules of "modern" art

*aphoristic characterized by aphorisms: brief, pithy statements of truth

*redemptive bringing about salvation

This work is also influenced by earlier American poets, such as Melvin B. Tolson, William Carlos Williams, and Charles Olson—who spent many years working on similar epic projects. In spite of its aphoristic* technique, *Wise, Why's, Y's* fully reflects Baraka's political and historical analysis.

Baraka's Marxist politics, however, never replaced his interest in African American culture and its traditions, especially as expressed in music. Indeed, his work never strays far from the theme of the life-affirming values of that tradition. His long poems "Reggae or Not" and "In the Tradition" both celebrate the communal creativity represented by jazz and by the talented artists—from anonymous folksingers to highly trained professionals—who have defined African American music and made their art popular throughout the world. Baraka sees this music as the prototype of a redemptive* African American value system, and this idea is reflected even in poems that contain the harshest social criticism. In "A Poem for Deep Thinkers," he carefully reiterates the positive hopefulness that underlies all of his work:

> Such intellectuals as we is baby, we need to deal in the
>   real
> world, and be be in the real world. We need to use, to
>   use, all
> the all the skills all the spills and thrills that we conjure,
>   that we
> construct, that we lay out and put together, to create
>   life as
> beautiful as we thought it could be, as we dreamed it
>   could be, . . .

The poem "In the Tradition" offers an even simpler statement of Baraka's basic philosophy:

>   the universal
> is the entire collection
> of particulars
>
> ours is one particular
> one tradition
> of love and suffering truth over lies

Throughout a prolific* career marked by both celebrity and much controversy, Amiri Baraka has demonstrated a total commitment to his art and to the belief that artistic activity has the power to change society for the better.

*prolific producing many works; fertile; productive

Selected Bibliography

WORKS BY AMIRI BARAKA

Poetry and Prose

Preface to a Twenty Volume Suicide Note (1961).

Blues People: Negro Music in White America (1963). Social history.

Dutchman and The Slave (1964). Two plays.

It's Nation Time (1970).

Wise, Why's, Y's (1990).

Video Recording

"Amiri Baraka." *Lannan Literary Series,* no. 26. Los Angeles: The Lannan Foundation, 1991.

Available Collections

The LeRoi Jones/Amiri Baraka Reader. Edited by William J. Harris. New York: Thunder's Mouth Press, 1991.

Transbluesency: The Selected Poems of Amiri Baraka/ LeRoi Jones (1961–1995). Edited by Paul Vangelisti. New York: Marsilio Publishers, 1995.

WORKS ABOUT AMIRI BARAKA

Brown, Lloyd W. *Amiri Baraka.* Boston: Twayne, 1980.

Melhem, D. H. *Heroism in the New Black Poetry: Introductions and Interviews.* Lexington: University Press of Kentucky, 1989.

Sollors, Werner. *Amiri Baraka/LeRoi Jones: The Quest for a "Populist Modernism."* New York: Columbia University Press, 1978.

MATSUO BASHŌ

(1644–1694)

by William J. Higginson

ashō has been called Japan's most important poet and is certainly its most famous. As a boy he showed an early interest in poetry; today virtually every Japanese over the age of twelve can quote his most famous poem from memory:

furuike ya   old pond . . .
kawazu tobikomu   a frog leaps in
mizu no oto   water's sound

Quotations from Bashō's poetry throughout are translated by William J. Higginson. See bibliography for published sources of specific poems.

Bashō is known worldwide through the popularity of his writings in translation. American poets from Ezra Pound and William Carlos Williams to Allen Ginsberg and Sonia Sanchez have been inspired by his poetry. And thousands of people all around the world now write haiku, which he helped establish as a major genre* of poetry.

*genre a type of literature with characteristic subject matter, style, tone, techniques, and so on, such as science fiction or epic poetry

The Poet's Life and Genres

Bashō, the son of Matsuo Yozaemon, was born in 1644 into the modest samurai (warrior class) family of Matsuo in the city of Ueno, Iga Province (now Mie Prefecture). Nothing is known of his mother. Bashō, the third of six children, became the personal servant and confidant of a young relative of the feudal lord of his province. Both boys were interested in *haikai,* the popular poetry of that time, and studied under various masters, including Kitamura Kigin (1624–1705), a leading poet and scholar. Bashō's first known poems were written before he was twenty years old.

Bashō's young master died in 1666, and not much is known about Bashō's life over the next few years. Evidently he associated with poets in Kyoto, then Japan's capital city. In 1672 he compiled a collection of short *haikai* verses by some thirty poets, called "The Seashell Game" (*Kai ōi*). This first major compilation was well received in manuscript form, and that same year Bashō moved to Edo (now known as Tokyo), where *Kai ōi* was published in 1674. *Haikai* poetry was becoming very popular there, and Bashō began to attract students.

In Bashō's day *haikai* was a recent development in the Japanese poetic tradition, but its roots go back to the earliest records of Japanese poetry and mythology, which include single poems written by two poets. In the thirteenth through the fifteenth centuries, Japanese poets developed long, collaborative poems called *renga* (linked poems) that involved many poets working together for days at a time.

The formal *renga* by court poets reached its artistic height in the fifteenth century under the leadership of Iio Sōgi (1421–1502), a poet to whom Bashō would look back as a major influence. But the old court poetry, including *renga,* was in serious decline by Bashō's time. Japan had suffered a prolonged period of sporadic civil wars that ended in 1601. Bashō came of age some decades into an era of peace and prosperity that gave members of the samurai and merchant classes the leisure and money to pursue the arts, especially literature.

As literature shifted from an aristocratic activity to the pastime of commoners, *haikai no renga* replaced courtly *renga* as the dominant poetry. "*Haikai*" means humorous, innovative in style, and commonplace in subject matter, as opposed to serious, stylistically tradition bound, and lofty in subject and tone, the hallmarks of court poetry. Before Bashō, *haikai* had become rather vulgar, but it had also expanded to include short solo stanzas called *hokku* and short humorous essays in prose called *haibun,* essays that often included one or more *hokku.*

During his lifetime Bashō was one of several acknowledged masters of linked poems in the *haikai* style. He and his disciples became known for a more serious approach to this playful type of writing; their work combined admiration for the great literature of the past with generous doses of images from the everyday experience of common people. Bashō also became a great writer of independent *hokku;* he is considered the father of what we now call *haiku,* those short, imagistic* verses that are a major part of the popular literature of Japan today.

The following haiku demonstrates Bashō's rejection of the joking, crude style that had dominated *haikai* for some years.

> *kare-eda ni*   on a leafless branch
> *karasu no tomarikeri*   a crow has come to perch—
> *aki no kure*   autumn dusk

This poem from 1680 takes a common subject in traditional Chinese painting, a crow on a leafless branch, and "translates" it into verse. The sense of desolation on an evening in late autumn penetrates both poem and reader. In the original, that desolate feeling is deepened by the use of the sharp "k" sounds, which also mimic the sounds the black bird might have made.

In 1686, Bashō wrote the "old pond" haiku quoted earlier, the single most famous poem in all of Japanese literature. Said to portray the dynamic intersection between the still surface of the pond and the action of the frog's leap, the poem is beautifully crafted, the onomatopoetic* *oto* ("sound") is precisely the grammatical as well as the imagistic point of the poem—and its last word. But one of the poem's most important aspects often gets lost in such discussions. The frog appears frequently in classical Japanese poetry, which celebrates its singing as an important sign of spring. After a thousand years of singing frogs, with the "old pond" poem Bashō restores the frog to its simple creaturehood and wryly comments on the tradition.

*****imagistic** using words that appeal to the senses by naming things that can be seen, heard, touched, and so on

*****onomatopoetic** using words that mimic or suggest the sounds or physical qualities of the thing spoken about, as in "out of the swamp in slimy, slippery shoes"

While he was a master of linked poetry and short verses in the *haikai* style, Bashō's greatness as a world author arises mainly from his *haikai* prose. He wrote a number of the brief poetic essays called *haibun,* many of which are masterpieces of their kind. Most important, Bashō adapted the travel diary, a major genre of Japanese literature for centuries, to the *haikai* style.

Throughout his adult life Bashō traveled from place to place in Japan, gathering new groups of disciples wherever he went. During his most productive period, from 1684 to his death ten years later, Bashō made seven major journeys resulting in five significant travel accounts, as well as a number of linked poems, short prose pieces, and independent verses; he also established many new groups of disciples. His last major work, the masterpiece *Narrow Road to the Interior* (*Oku no hosomichi,* 1694), was based on the first six months of a longer trip that he and a companion made on foot and horseback through twelve hundred miles of rural northern Japan in 1689.

As befits such a traveling poet, Bashō died while on yet another journey, in Osaka, far to the west of Edo. A number of his disciples gathered around him as he lay suffering from a stomach ailment, and they wrote down his last few haiku. The poem usually credited as his "death verse," a poem written when its author knows death is near, goes this way:

tabi ni yande	ill on a journey—
yume wa kareno o	my dreams wander over
kakemeguru	withered fields

On the following day Bashō revised an earlier poem, changing it so much that it seems like a new poem. Some scholars now suggest that this poem, rather than the verse on wandering dreams, should be considered Bashō's true death verse:

kiyotaki ya	Clear Cascade. . .
nami ni chirikomu	scattering down into the waves
aomatsuba	green pine needles

Clear Cascade is a place on the Ōi River near Kyoto, where pure waters plunge down a beautiful narrow gorge. The "green pine needles" are the tender tips of new growth in summer that easily snap off in the wind. While the first death verse captures the

A modest stone monument, with the poem carved on it, and a small pavilion on a cliffside path overlook the place celebrated in this poem. The stone is one of several hundred "poem stones" scattered around Japan containing haiku by Bashō and other poets.

uneasiness of a feverish sleep on a journey, the Clear Cascade verse suggests a calm acceptance of the temporary condition of human life and the beauty of the natural world.

Three days later, on the twelfth day of the tenth month of 1694, Bashō died. Japanese poets today celebrate his death anniversary on 12 October, but since Japan then used the lunar calendar, his actual death anniversary falls on 28 November in the Gregorian calendar.* (The Japanese celebrate the death anniversaries of important persons, rather than their birthdays.)

*Gregorian calendar the calendar generally used in Europe and the Americas. Until adopting it in 1873, Japan used the Chinese lunar calendar.

Bashō's Linked Poetry

The *haikai no renga* of Bashō and his disciples retains the best elements of earlier classical linked poetry but adds subtlety in linking and vivid images from the lives of common people. Today the Japanese call linked poems by Bashō and later poets "*renku,*" much as the earlier independent *hokku* are now called "*haiku.*"

Linked poetry was invented as a party game, with rules to keep the poets on track in the heat of composition. Someone agrees to host the party, and usually the chief guest writes the opening verse. This verse must reflect the time and place of composition by including something typical of the season and mentioning something for which that place is known. In the second verse, the host continues in the same season. The third verse must connect with the second but must also shift away from the things mentioned in the first two stanzas, opening up new territory in both subject and style.

Bashō and other poets of his day shortened the typical linked poem to thirty-six stanzas, rather than the usual one hundred of classical *renga*. This has continued to be the most popular length. In a thirty-six-stanza *renku,* the opening stanzas—the six on the first page—are like the introductions and polite conversations at the beginning of any party; they must avoid such subjects as illness and death, violence, love, and extreme images. Later, in the inner pages, the poets may take up any topic, and love is specifically required in certain places. Finally, the last six stanzas, on the last page, move quickly and straightforwardly from one image to the next, finishing in a light, optimistic tone.

In *renku* form the first verse is written in three phrases of 5, 7, and 5 "sounds" or short Japanese syllables. The second has two phrases of 7 sounds each. After this they alternate: 5-7-5, 7-7, 5-7-5, and so on. In English translations these are usually given in alternating stanzas of three and two lines.

Japanese linked poetry has another important feature that surprises those reading it for the first time: no single theme or plot unifies a completed poem. Like a traditional scroll painting, a linked poem moves through flowing seasonal landscapes, shifts perspectives and moods, and presents a variety of characters involved in many different and unrelated events. An action that seems part of a story will be given a setting in the following verse, and the verse after that may use the same setting to take up a different story altogether. Often the meaning of one stanza actually changes depending on whether it is read as connecting to the verse before or after it. In *renku,* the first and third of three successive stanzas usually do not seem connected, though both are connected to the one in the middle.

The boxed excerpt from an important *renku* demonstrates the features of the genre. "Summer Moon" was written in 1690 by Bashō and two of his best friends and leading disciples, Bonchō and Kyorai. It is one of four, thirty-six-stanza *renku* included in the most important book issued by Bashō and his disciples during his lifetime, *Monkey's Raincoat* (*Sarumino,* 1691). The three poets were at the height of their powers and were very comfortable working together—so comfortable that they relaxed the usual formality of the opening stanzas.

From left to right, the columns present the original Japanese in transliteration,* an English translation, and the author of each stanza plus brief notes to clarify the movement from stanza to stanza.

As "Summer Moon" shows, the world of *renku* is fluid. No one character dominates the poem for more than a verse or two. A young samurai in verse 6 becomes frightened in verse 7 and turns into a woman in verse 8; an old monk in verse 10 becomes toothless in verse 11 and then changes into a serving person in *The Tale of Genji,* Japan's greatest literary monument, in verse 12; a falling screen in verse 13 shifts locale from a private home to an inn in verse 14. And in the moving final stanzas the poet Komachi, remembering past loves, becomes an old beggar and then turns into a young wife, longing for her absent husband. Finally we are left with a different image of the same time period as a servant enjoys the freedom of the master's absence. Along with the action, the scenes and the seasons also shift from verse to verse and passage to passage.

*transliteration a script in one language or alphabet showing the sounds of another language

Summer Moon (excerpt)

Japanese	English Translation	Comments
1. *ichinaka wa*	Around the town	Bonchō. Summer (summer moon). The inelegant opening verse is unusual.
mono no nioi ya	the smells of things . . .	
natsu no tsuki	summer moon	
2. *atsushi atsushi to*	"It's hot! It's hot!"—	Bashō. Summer (hot). "Gate to gate" links with "town."
kado kado no koe	the voices from gate to gate	
3. *nibangusa*	the second weeding	Kyorai. Late summer (second weeding). The previous conversation shifts from town to the farm.
tori no hatasazu	not yet begun, and ears	
ho ni idete	out of the rice	
4. *hai uchitataku*	he knocks the ashes off	Bonchō. No season. Farmer's modest meal: sardine over an open fire.
urume ichimai	one piece of sardine	
5. *kono suji wa*	in these parts	Bashō. No season. Lunch shifts to a rural restaurant; a large denomination coin causes problems.
kane mo mishirazu	silver's an unknown sight—	
fujiyūsa yo	how inconvenient!	
6. *tada tohyōshi ni*	extravagantly long	Kyorai. No season. The customer, a young samurai, struts nervously.
nagaki wakizashi	that "short sword"	
7. *kusamura ni*	frightened by a thicket	Bonchō. Spring (frog). The nervous youth, now outside, shies at the croak of a frog.
kawazu kowagaru	with a froggy in it	
yūmagure	just at twilight	
8. *fuki no me tori ni*	picking butterbur* sprouts	Bashō. Early spring (butterbur sprouts). Now it is a woman surprised by the frog; she shakes, and her lamp goes out.
ando yurikesu	she shakes—the lantern out	

*__butterbur__ a wild plant similar to rhubarb

The Tale of Genji, a novel by Lady Murasaki (d. ca. A.D. 1015), details the lives and loves of a fictional Prince Genji and members of the next generation. It contains almost eight hundred poems and has been recognized since the thirteenth century as one of the greatest works of Japanese literature.

9. *dōshin no*

okori wa hana no

tsubomu toki

faith awakens

at the time when blossoms

come into bud

Kyorai. Mid spring (cherry blossom buds). The lamp going out brings enlightenment to mind.

10. *noto no nanao no*

fuyu wa sumiuki

in Nanao in Noto Province

life's hard in winter

Bonchō. Winter. A monk recalls his training in a desolate place.

11. *uo no hone*

shiwaburu made no

oi o mite

to the point of

sucking on fish bones

looking at old age

Bashō. No season. The cold poverty of a toothless old person.
(With the next verse, it echoes *The Tale of Genji.*)

12. *machibito ireshi*

komikado no kagi

the awaited one let in

with the key to the side gate

Kyorai. No season. Love. The old servant lets in the mistress's lover.

13. *tachi kakari*

byōbu o taosu

onagodomo

leaning on the screen

they knock it down—

the maidservants

Bonchō. No season. Love. The scene from an old courtly romance shifts to a merchant's house.

14. *yudono wa take no*
sunoko wabishiki

on the bathroom floor

a cheerless bamboo mat

Bashō. No season. The falling screen is now at an inn; a bather is surprised.

15. *uikyō no*

mi o fukiotosu

yūarashi

it blows and

scatters the fennel seeds

the night storm-wind

Kyorai. Mid-autumn (fennel seeds). The mood of cheerlessness shifts outdoors.

* * *

* * *

Verses 16–29 move through a great variety of new images, events, scenes, and characters.

30. *inochi ureshiki*

senjū no sata

a happy life—his poems

chosen for an anthology

Kyorai. No season. A wandering poet learns of his good luck.

31. *samazama ni*	how variously	Bonchō. No season. Love. The poet thinks back over a long life and many relationships.
shina kawaritaru	things change from one	
koi o shite	love to another	
32. *ukiyo no hate wa*	the end of our floating world	Bashō. No season. Love. Komachi, a famous poet and lover, became a Buddhist nun in old age.
mina komachi nari	we all become Komachis	
33. *nani yue zo*	why is it that	Kyorai. No season. An old beggar (Komachi?), receiving a bowl of porridge, sips and begins to cry.
kaya susuru ni mo	even while she sips porridge	
namidagumi	tears well up?	
34. *orusu to nareba*	while he's away	Bonchō. No season. Shifts to a lonely wife; the master absent, the main service room seems empty.
hiroki itajiki	the wooden floor is so wide	
35. *te no hira ni*	in the palm of the hand	Bashō. Mid-spring (cherry blossoms). Idle because the master's away, a servant enjoys the spring light.
shirami hawasuru	a louse crawls around	
hana no kage	in blossom-light	
36. *kasumi ugokanu*	spring haze motionless	Kyorai. Spring (haze/mist). The idle one is caught in spring fever.
hiru no nemutasa	the drowsiness of midday	

Bashō's Poetic Journals

When Bashō began writing, contemporary poets had already written short, humorous essays including *haikai* verses. But Bashō shifted the style to a higher level of seriousness and joined it with the long-standing tradition of literary diaries to create a new kind of journal with tremendous variety in tone and powerful use of allusions* to such earlier Chinese poets as Li Po and Tu Fu and to the high tradition of Japan. Starting with his "Records of a Weather-Exposed Skeleton" (*Nozarashi*

*__allusion__ a passing reference to fictional or historical characters, events, literature, or places the writer assumes the reader will recognize

kikō, journey of 1684–1685; in *The Narrow Road to the Deep North*), Bashō worked hard at creating a new prose style, which he later called *haibun* ("haikai" prose). This culminated in his last travel journal, *Narrow Road to the Interior (Oku no hosomichi)*. The journal includes some of the finest prose ever composed in Japanese as well as many of Bashō's most famous haiku. Although he traveled in 1689, he did not complete the journal until a few months before he died in 1694.

The following passage from *Narrow Road to the Interior* captures one of the high points of Bashō's journey, his visit to the famous Standing-Stone Temple (Ryūshakuji) far to the north of Edo. It ends with a powerful haiku, one of several that he worked on for years as he revised and refined this prose and verse masterpiece.

> **In the fief of Yamagata, there's a mountain temple called Ryūshakuji. Founded by Jikaku Daishi, it's an especially pure and tranquil place. "You must take a look," people advised, so, turning back from Obanazawa, we went about fifteen miles. Sun still not down, we reserved a lodging with priests at the bottom and climbed to the temple at the mountain-top. A mountain of massive rock heaped on stone, ancient pines and oaks; on old stones and velvet moss at the top of the crag were the temple buildings, doors closed, not a sound to be heard. Rounding the crest, crawling over rock, we worshipped at the Buddha hall. With beautiful views and deep silence our hearts steeped in clarity.**

shizukasa ya	the stillness . . .
iwa ni shimiiru	sinking into rock
semi no koe	cicada's* voice

*cicada a type of insect; a locust

Bashō's sensitive response to the tradition of Chinese and Japanese poets; to the landscape of Japan's sacred mountains, streams, and islands; to the seasonal cycle, and to his many diverse disciples, has deeply affected his people. Now, more than three hundred years after his death, Japanese poets and scholars study his works. And thanks to scholars, translators, and poets, we can find his influence in the literatures of many languages. Indeed, today haiku is probably the single most popular kind of poetry written worldwide.

Selected Bibliography

WORKS BY BASHŌ
Poems Discussed in This Essay (All Translated by William J. Higginson)

"Old Pond." In Higginson, William J., and Penny Harter. *The Haiku Handbook: How to Write, Share, and Teach Haiku*. Tokyo: Kodansha International, 1985.

"Summer Moon" (first 12 stanzas). In Higginson, William J. *The Haiku Seasons: Poetry of the Natural World*. Tokyo: Kodansha International, 1996.

Available Collections

Back Roads to Far Towns. Translated by Cid Corman and Kamaike Susumu. New York: Grossman Publishers, 1968; Hopewell, N.J.: Ecco Press, 1996. Still the best translation of *Oku no hosomichi*; includes full Japanese text on facing pages with aids for students of Japanese.

Bashō's Narrow Road: Spring and Autumn Passages. Translated by Hiroaki Sato. Berkeley, Calif.: Stone Bridge Press, 1996. Translations of *Oku no hosomichi* and a linked poem.

The Essential Bashō. Translated by Sam Hamill. Boston: Shambhala Publications, 1998. Includes Hamill's highly readable translations of *Narrow Road to the Interior* (cited below), three additional short travel journals, and a generous selection of haiku, but no *renku.*

Japanese Poetic Diaries. Compiled and translated by Earl Miner. Berkeley: University of California Press, 1969. Includes *Oku no hosomichi*.

Monkey's Raincoat. Translated by Cana Maeda. New York: Grossman Publishers, 1973. Translations of four *renku,* with an interesting theory of translation.

Monkey's Raincoat: Linked Poetry of the Bashō School with Haiku Selections. Translated by Lenore Mayhew. Rutland, Vt.: Charles E. Tuttle, 1985. Most readable translation of *renku* and haiku.

The Monkey's Straw Raincoat and Other Poetry of the Bashō School. Translated by Earl Miner and Hiroko Odagiri. Princeton, N.J.: Princeton University Press, 1981. The only complete English translation of the Bashō

IF YOU LIKE the poetry of Bashō, you might also like the poetry of Li Po, Tu Fu, Federico García Lorca, Sappho, Sonia Sanchez, or William Carlos Williams.

school anthology *Sarumino*; the layout makes the *renku* difficult to read.

The Narrow Road to the Deep North and Other Travel Sketches. Translated by Nobuyuki Yuasa. Baltimore: Penguin Books, 1966. Wordy, slack translations but the only readily available versions of Bashō's other diaries in English.

Narrow Road to the Interior. Translated by Sam Hamill. Boston: Shambhala Publications, 1991. Pocket edition.

The Narrow Road to Oku. Translated by Donald Keene. London: Kodansha International, 1996. Includes full Japanese text on facing pages with aids for students of Japanese; profusely illustrated.

On Love and Barley: Haiku of Basho. Translated by Lucien Stryk. New York: Penguin Books, 1985. Overly brief, sometimes abrupt translations.

The Way of Silence: Prose and Poetry of Basho. Edited by Richard Lewis. New York: Dial Press, 1970. Miscellaneous short selections by various translators; no linked poetry.

WORKS ABOUT BASHŌ AND *HAIKAI* LITERATURE

Aitken, Robert. *A Zen Wave: Bashō's Haiku and Zen*. New York: Weatherhill, 1978. Twenty-six chapters, each discussing a haiku by Bashō from a Zen Buddhist perspective.

Blyth, R. H. *Haiku*. vol. 1 of *Eastern Culture*. Tokyo: Hokuseido Press, 1949. One of the best books for an overview of *haikai* literature, though a little overbearing about the Zen influence.

Bowers, Faubion, ed. *The Classic Tradition of Haiku: An Anthology*. Mineola, N.Y.: Dover Publications, 1996. An excellent overview of haiku translations into English; includes poems by some fifty poets—Bashō is well represented—in versions by nearly as many translators.

Carter, Steven D., ed. and trans. *Traditional Japanese Poetry: An Anthology*. Stanford, Calif.: Stanford University Press, 1991. Excellent anthology; covers the range of Japanese traditional forms of poetry, with attention to Bashō and linked poetry.

Haas, Robert. *The Essential Haiku: Versions of Bashō, Buson, and Issa.* Hopewell, N.J.: Ecco Press, 1994. Largely revisions of Blyth's versions, but some work included here is not readily available elsewhere.

Henderson, Harold G. *An Introduction to Haiku: An Anthology of Poems from Bashō to Shiki.* Garden City, N.Y.: Doubleday, 1958. Compact, clear introductory treatment of haiku.

Higginson, William J. *The Haiku Handbook: How to Write, Share, and Teach Haiku.* New York: McGraw-Hill, 1985; Tokyo: Kodansha International, 1989. Includes section on Bashō and modern developments and the growth of haiku and related literature in English.

Higginson, William J. *The Haiku Seasons: Poetry of the Natural World.* Tokyo: Kodansha International, 1996. Stresses the nature content of *haikai* poetry, from pre-Bashō to contemporary examples.

Hoffman, Yoel, *Japanese Death Poems: Written by Zen Monks and Haiku Poets on the Verge of Death.* Rutland, Vt.: Charles E. Tuttle, 1986. Brief biographies and good translations of the last poems of more than three hundred haiku poets as well as a few dozen Zen monks; excellent introduction.

Miner, Earl. *Japanese Linked Poetry: An Account with Translations of Renga and Haikai Sequences.* Princeton, N.J.: Princeton University Press, 1979. The standard academic treatment of linked poetry, in a confusing layout.

Sato, Hiroaki. *One Hundred Frogs: From Renga to Haiku to English.* New York: Weatherhill, 1983. Excellent discussion and translations of linked poems, plus more than one hundred translations of Bashō's "old pond" haiku and haiku and linked poems by American poets.

Shirane, Haruo. *Traces of Dreams: Landscape, Cultural Memory, and the Poetry of Bashō.* Stanford, Calif.: Stanford University Press, 1998. Outstanding academic treatment of Bashō's poetics; many excellent translations.

Ueda, Makoto. *Bashō and His Interpreters: Selected Hokku with Commentary.* Stanford, Calif.: Stanford University Press, 1991. The best translations of Bashō's haiku available in English, set in a biographical narrative with notes on the circumstances of composition; very interesting

✍

More About Bashō

You can find information
about Matsuo Bashō on
the Internet at:
http://www.globaldialog.com/
~thefko/tom/gi_basho.
html

comments on Bashō's haiku by Japanese poets and
scholars from his day to ours.

Ueda, Makoto. *Literary and Art Theories in Japan*. Cleveland: Press of Western Reserve University, 1967. Valuable chapters on linked poetry and on Bashō's poetics.

Ueda, Makoto. *Matsuo Bashō*. New York: Twayne, 1970;
New York: Kodansha International, 1982. The standard
literary biography in English, with many translations.

Yasuda, Kenneth. *The Japanese Haiku: Its Essential Nature, History, and Possibilities in English, with Selected Examples*. Rutland, Vt.: Charles E. Tuttle, 1957. Somewhat dated, but good background on haiku; includes comments by early twentieth-century Japanese poets and scholars.

STEPHEN VINCENT BENÉT

(1898–1943)

by Joel Lewis

The American poet today is rarely identified as a flag-waving patriot. Although many American poets will be quick to tell you they love their country, they will also say they consider it important to identify the problems that they believe keep America from being as great as it could be.

Stephen Vincent Benét was the last significant patriotic poet to have emerged in America. His subject was America—its people, land, and democratic heritage. His famous poem *John Brown's Body* is still considered one of the greatest works written about the American Civil War. A committed political liberal in a period when many writers were socialists, he was a strong supporter of President Franklin D. Roosevelt. During World War II, he devoted his creative energies to writing radio plays and prose works that attempted to educate Americans about the dangers of both Nazism* and fascism.* One of his poetic dramas, "Listen to the People," aired on 4 July 1941 in a radio broadcast preceding a major speech by Roosevelt and was also published in *Life* magazine, one of the most widely read magazines of that era. Charles A. Fenton,

*Nazism a political doctrine put into effect in Germany in the 1930s that included a totalitarian form of government, a belief in the superiority of certain races, and government control of industry

*fascism a form of government that exalts a single ruler, greatly restricts personal freedom, and permits no opposition

*libretto the text of the words of an opera or other musical narrative

Benét's biographer, claimed that the poet was heard by more Americans than any other serious writer in the history of the United States. But Benét was not on the payroll of any government organization. He was asked to write his patriotic radio plays because so much of his poetry demonstrated his love of country.

Benét was, in that now rarely used term, a "man of letters"; that is, he wrote in many literary forms: novels, short stories, opera librettos,* dramas, movie scripts, reviews, and essays, in addition to poetry. He also earned money as a lecturer, a literary editor, and a judge of the Yale Series of Younger Poets literary competition. In fact, Benét lived entirely from his writing, and the enormous effort of trying to support a family this way ruined his fragile health and led to his premature death. Even after the great success of "Listen to the People," he complained about his lack of income. "No money," he wrote in a letter, "and owe more than in a long time." Although he did receive $500 for "Listen to the People," he gave the money to the United Service Organizations, a charity that serves U.S. military personnel. Benét would accept no payment from any of his writings connected to the war effort.

Even Benét's friends and admirers admitted that a good part of his literary output was "hack work"—stories and scripts written quickly in order to receive a badly needed check. After *John Brown's Body,* which made him famous, Benét wrote short stories matching the style of the magazine requesting the work, thereby producing some of his weakest writing. His poetry, however, remained uninfluenced by the demands of the market, and it is the poetry that we continue to read today.

A Precocious Poet

Stephen Vincent Benét was born on 22 July 1898 in Bethlehem, Pennsylvania, the third child and second son of James Walker Benét, captain of ordnance, U.S. Army, and Frances Neill Rose Benét. His siblings, Laura and William Rose, also grew up to become writers of note. In the 1930s and 1940s, the Benéts were among the best known literary families in America.

Benét grew up in a household of contradictions. His brother, twelve years his senior, was already publishing poetry and bringing poets and writers home from Yale. Their father, a career military officer, had hoped for military careers for his sons, but he was proud of his eldest son's achievements, and volumes of Dante and Shakespeare were in the family library.

Benét often said that he would have gone to the U.S. Military Academy at West Point had it not been for a bout of scarlet fever at age three that weakened his eyesight. "I was born and brought up in the Army—and in an intelligent branch of the Army, the ordnance," he wrote in the late 1930s. "My grandfather developed the rim-fire cartridge, my father was in charge of the first 16-inch gun ever made in this country, my uncle helped invent one of the earliest light machine guns, the Benét-Mercier."

It was the literary world, however, that would captivate young Benét. At the Summerville Academy in Augusta, Georgia, it became evident that he was something of a prodigy as a poet. At age thirteen, he won a three-dollar prize (a worker's day wage at the time) for a poem. By seventeen the *New Republic* had featured him in a two-page selection that included some of the major poets of the period. That year (1915), his brother arranged for the subsidized publication of Benét's first book, *Five Men and Pompey.* These early poems show influences of the socialist verse of the nineteenth-century English poet and artist William Morris and of Robert Browning's dramatic monologues. In the Browning mode, *Five Men* is a series of dramatic monologues* spoken by Roman leaders on the eve of Julius Caesar's becoming emperor. Early on, Benét was laying the groundwork for his magnum opus,* *John Brown's Body*—a poem that was concerned with history and politics told through dramatic monologues.

Benét entered Yale in 1915, the year his first book of poems was published. He excelled academically and was elected chairman of the editorial board of the *Yale Literary Magazine.* During World War I, he enlisted in the army but was honorably discharged quickly because of his bad eyesight. He reentered Yale and received a bachelor's degree in 1919 and a master's in 1920.

In 1921, Benét married Rosemary Carr, also a writer; they had two daughters and a son. She collaborated with her husband on a book of poems for children, *A Book of Americans* (1933), the only book by Benét that remains in print besides *John Brown's Body.* After a honeymoon in Europe, the Benéts settled in New York City.

*dramatic monologue** a poem written as a speech by one character

*magnum opus** masterpiece; greatest work

Tapping the American Past

Benét's reputation as a poet increased with the publication of "The Ballad of William Sycamore" in the *New Republic* in 1922. This poem exemplifies the style that made the poet such a popular figure in his day. In telling the story of this Daniel Boone pioneer figure, Benét employed an easy, songlike rhyme scheme, uncomplicated imagery, and simple language familiar to readers. Although his critics complained of his sentimentality, Benét borrowed freely from American folk mythology, including the modern myths found in the popular Wild West shows of that era, cheap Western novels, and silent films. Unlike his more radical contemporaries E. E. Cummings and T. S. Eliot, Benét wanted a wide readership and did not feel set apart from his fellow Americans. Benét's worldview was in accord with the mainstream American culture of his day, and his dramatic monologues were about characters and stories already familiar to his readers.

Benét was always struggling to support his family. In 1924 he coauthored two stage dramas; both flopped. He wrote romantic fiction for popular magazines. Despite his exhausting literary labors, he barely made ends meet. Often, a literary fee would go straight to pay a debt or back taxes, forcing the Benéts to borrow from friends and family.

John Brown's Body

In 1925, the Guggenheim Foundation awarded him a grant of $2,500 for a long historical poem on the Civil War. Benét set out for Paris with his family, where they could live more cheaply than in New York. Benét initially estimated that the poem might "take about 7 years to write & I'd have to read an entire library first." Actually, he finished his 15,000-line poem in less than two years, which left the poet physically exhausted for months.

Upon the publication of *John Brown's Body* in 1928, Benét was transformed from a highly regarded young poet to a national hero. In those years America was undergoing a redefinition of itself. With the passage of restrictive legislation in 1924, the great waves of immigration that began in the 1840s came to an end. America's substantial Jewish and Roman Catholic communities were beginning to enter the main-

---

Annotated Edition (excerpt)

And yet there are the words, in print,
And should an obdurate* old man
Remember half a dozen lines
Stuck in his mind like thistle-seed,
Or if, perhaps, some idle boy
Should sometimes read a page or so
In the deep summer, to his girl,
And drop the book half-finished there,
Since kissing was a better joy,
Why, I shall have been paid enough.
I'll have been paid enough indeed.

(John Brown's Body)

---

*obdurate stubborn; inflexible

stream. The Harlem Renaissance* spotlighted African American painters, writers, and musicians. And as the last of the Civil War veterans retired from public life, a reconciliation between the North and South seemed possible.

John Brown's Body is, simply, the history of the Civil War told in verse. The distinguished historian Bruce Catton considered it the best single book ever written on the subject. In the foreword to the 1941 edition of the book, Benét stated the aims of his book:

*Harlem Renaissance a period (1920s) of enormous creativity in literature, music, and art in the African American community of Harlem in New York City

> **What I was trying to do was to show certain realities, legends, ideas, landscapes, ways of living, faces of men that were ours, that did not belong to any other country. Our history is not just a list of names and dates, declarations and proclamations. It is made up of the lives of millions upon millions of ordinary men and women who lived through war and peace, strove, struggled, succeeded, failed, built something together.**

Although many book reviewers called the work an epic,* Benét described this poem as a "cyclodrama."* Each section of the poem is based on a different character's experience in the Civil War. The epic begins just before John Brown's raid on the Harper's Ferry arsenal, an event that many historians consider a prelude to the Civil War, and ends with the assassination of President Abraham Lincoln. Each of the poem's eight books features at least one major military conflict. The poem

*epic a long poem that tells the story of a hero's deeds

*cyclodrama a series of paintings placed around a room to tell a story

also includes numerous nonmilitary events, such as the hanging of Brown and the election of Lincoln.

What made the book so popular was Benét's ability to transform the complexities of the Civil War into a large cast of characters representing the many Americans involved in the war. Some characters are based on real individuals; others are entirely fictional creations who represent a particular community. Although Benét saw the Civil War as primarily a conflict between Puritan* New Englanders and Southern aristocrats, his view of the conflict was both tolerant and conciliatory. In his poem, there are no major villains, and all the main characters are treated with respect and sympathy.

Critics have accused Benét of ignoring the issue of slavery. His depiction of the Southern black is, in general, favorable to the South—there are no mistreated slaves, and the only slave who escapes to the North finds that he is treated worse there. Benét draws upon much of the stock imagery of the Civil War—the Southern aristocracy, the bravery of the Confederate generals Robert E. Lee and Stonewall Jackson, the savagery of William Tecumseh Sherman's march to the sea. Readers found nothing in the poem that was incompatible with their understanding of the conflict. Writing his epic only sixty years after the cessation of hostilities, Benét was well aware that there were still Civil War veterans alive and that millions of their children were now the generation leading the nation. In a small way, his book was an attempt to reunite two parts of the nation that still harbored resentment and suspicions of each other.

When *John Brown's Body* was published, it received an extraordinary reception. Allen Tate, a major poet and critic of the time, declared it to be "the most ambitious poem ever undertaken by an American on an American theme." In 1929, the book received the Pulitzer Prize for poetry. Benét's apartment in Paris was soon flooded with letters praising the book from Civil War veterans, children of veterans, and such prominent historians as Samuel Eliot Morison. Most noted his historical accuracy, and many praised his evenhanded treatment of the conflict. The novelist Sinclair Lewis cited the poem in his Nobel prize acceptance speech of 1930. Even Noel Coward, the sophisticated English songwriter and playwright, told Benét how much he enjoyed the book—much to the poet's astonishment.

John Brown's Body was more than a critical success—it was a best-seller. In the first year of publication it sold more

*__Puritan__ a Protestant Christian who opposed the traditions and forms of the Church of England. Most Puritans opposed elaborate ceremony and church hierarchy, believing that God's will was directly revealed to individuals through Bible reading. Puritans believed that only a few "elect" were chosen in advance by God for heaven.

than 150,000 copies—a huge number in the days before books were mass-marketed. The poem was a major money-maker for Doubleday, and it continued to sell steadily; the 1929 college edition went through forty-four printings over twenty-five years. It is estimated that five hundred schools, ranging from high schools to universities, made *John Brown's Body* required reading. Students who wrote to Benét requesting help with a term paper often received a personal reply.

Ordinary people discussed the poem and recited it to one another. The poem was often adapted for dramatic presentations on the new medium of radio. Soldiers in World War II wrote Benét to tell him how his poem gave them courage. As late as the 1950s, the actors Charles Laughton and Paul Osborn toured America three times in a staged version of the poem that played to capacity crowds.

Benét made more than $25,000 in the first year the book was published and was able to return with his family to America. However, he lost most of his profits in the great stock market crash of 1929. Soon he was again churning out short stories and reviews in order to help support his family. In 1930, he developed a serious case of arthritis that kept him in poor health the rest of his life.

Final Years

Benét devoted most of his creative energies after the publication of *John Brown's Body* to other literary forms. His short story "The Devil and Daniel Webster" is a modern classic, still found in high school anthologies. In 1939, Benét wrote a libretto for the American composer Douglas Moore's operetta of the same name, and this piece continues to be performed across the country. A 1942 movie version of the story, with a screenplay by Benét, was retitled *All That Money Can Buy.* It can still be seen on cable television.

The last few years of Benét's life were devoted to producing radio scripts warning of the dangers of fascism and promoting the idea of democracy. Although his health continued to deteriorate, he worked long hours in support of the war effort. He died in his wife's arms from a heart attack on 13 March 1943.

John Brown's Body was seen by its author as both a blessing and a curse. He was touched that this work had reached so many people and had made him such a respected national figure. He was also grateful that it was a steady source of income and made him a familiar figure on the lecture circuit, where he often recited from it. But he also grew exasperated by how closely associated he was with this single work. Nothing he wrote in the last fifteen years of his brief life came close to its critical and commercial success. And he was well aware that he could sell the slightest and most hastily written piece of writing because of the fame *John Brown's Body* had earned him.

In the end, he made his peace with the book that made him a literary star. When his publisher issued a new edition of *John Brown's Body,* complete with footnotes and scholarly material, he wrote a wry poem called "Annotated Edition" that reflected on the fame his poem had brought him.

Selected Bibliography

WORKS BY STEPHEN VINCENT BENÉT
Poetry

Five Men and Pompey (1915).

Heavens and Earth (1920).

Tiger Joy (1925).

John Brown's Body (1928).

A Book of Americans (with Rosemary Benét) (1933). Poems for children.

Prose

"The Devil and Daniel Webster" (1937).

Available Collections

John Brown's Body. Introduction and notes by Jack L. Capps and C. Robert Kemble. New York: Holt, Rinehart, and Winston, 1968.

The Last Circle. Introduction by Rosemary Benét. New York: Farrar, Straus, 1946. Stories and poems.

Selected Works. New York: Holt, Rinehart, and Winston, 1974.

WORKS ABOUT STEPHEN VINCENT BENÉT

Fenton, Charles A. *Stephen Vincent Benét: The Life and Times of an American Man of Letters 1898–1943.* Westport, Conn.: Greenwood Press, 1978.

Stroud, Parry Edmund. *Stephen Vincent Benét.* New York: Twayne, 1962.

TED BERRIGAN

(1934–1983)

by Alice Notley

*voraciously greedily; eagerly

As a teenager Ted Berrigan had no ambition to become a poet, though he read voraciously.* When he was a child, he had written a poem about the death of his grandfather, and he and a friend had often made up alternative lyrics for popular songs. Thus at an early age he showed a talent for using words in an expressive and musical way. But he was from a working-class family that had no connection to the arts, or to intellectual pursuits. He had an intuition of something mysterious in himself and in life that needed investigation. This mysterious something, which would turn out to be tied to poetry, seemed to have an irresistible power over him. Under its urging he would skip school in order simply to walk around and look at things. As he says in an interview with Tom Savage (*Talking in Tranquility,* 1991), he would visit "neighborhoods I didn't live in and walk out through the park and not think . . . thoughts, but I would feel neighborhoods and feel the lawns and the houses and the way that things looked, rather than see them" (p. 145).

Later on, Berrigan's poetry would often refer to walking around, being in an atmosphere with things and people and interacting with them rather than studying them, catching both an inner and outer process, as in "Tambourine Life":

What
　　excitement!
　　　　　　　crossing Saint Mark's Place
　　　　　face cold in air
　　　　　　　tonight
　　　　　　　　　when
　　　　　　　that girlish someone waving
　　　　　　　　　from a bicycle
　　　　　　　　　　turned me back on.
　　　　　　　(Saroyan, ed., *Selected Poems*)

"Tambourine Life" is a long poem written in a seemingly plain, but also witty, style, jokey but warm, and arranged in a way that makes use of the entire page. That style is one of several Berrigan would develop. He also wrote difficult and disjunctive* poetry; sometimes used "found" materials (words, phrases, or passages he did not write himself); experimented with different poem lengths from very long to as short as one word (for example, the word "bent" is an entire poem by Berrigan); worked with the series as a form;* and wrote in prose. He collaborated extensively with other poets and with visual artists. From a working-class kid in a kind of trance he developed into a prolific* poet, a poet who practiced his art full time, twenty-four hours a day.

The Road to New York City

Ted Berrigan was born in Providence, Rhode Island, on 15 November 1934, the oldest of four children in an Irish-American family. His father was in charge of maintenance of machines in a large baking company. His mother was a housewife who later, after she was widowed, worked in a school lunch service. Berrigan was educated in local Catholic schools. After he graduated from high school, he worked in Providence for a year or so, attended Providence College briefly, and then realized he had to leave the world in which he had grown up. Under another of his mysterious compulsions, as when he used to skip school,

*disjunctive broken up; not united

*form in poetry, a set of rules about the meter, rhyme, length, or tone of the poem.

*prolific producing many works; fertile; productive

he enlisted in the army in 1954 and did a tour of duty in Korea, after which he was stationed in Tulsa, Oklahoma. He entered the University of Tulsa on the GI Bill* and began his literary studies, writing his first poems in Tulsa and meeting people there who would be colleagues and friends for life and who would move to New York when he did: the poets Ron Padgett and Dick Gallup and the painter Joe Brainard. Berrigan earned a bachelor of arts degree and a master's degree in English. His first poems are simple and sentimental. After the 1959 publication of his first book, *A Lily for My Love,* in Tulsa, he tried to destroy all the copies because he realized the book was not very good. He kept one for himself though, to remember what he had changed from and perhaps still was deep down.

In 1960 Berrigan moved to New York City's Lower East Side, where he lived for eight years and again from 1976 for another seven years until his death in 1983. The Lower East Side, with its ethnic mix, its tolerance of poets and artists, and its lively, dirty streets, was always Berrigan's spiritual home. New York gave Berrigan his real education in the arts and his place in a community. Even when he was happily living elsewhere, as when he was in England in the early 1970s, he still wrote lines like "And New York City is the most beautiful city in the world / And it is horrible in that sense of hell. . . ." ("The Joke and the Stars," *Easter Monday,* unpublished). In the early 1960s New York was the base for such poets as John Ashbery, Frank O'Hara, James Schuyler, and Kenneth Koch—the so-called New York school. Berrigan became a second-generation member of the New York school, and its most humorous publicist. He liked to say that there really was a New York school and that anyone could join it no matter who—for a fee of five dollars. The point, aside from the fact that Berrigan rarely had any money, was that the New York school was both a state of mind and a joke. New York school poetry is witty and unpretentious. It is influenced by painting—seen in all those New York galleries—as well as by the fast talk experienced in every level of life in New York and by the internationalism of a city subject to waves of immigration. Berrigan was also influenced by poets other than those of the New York school, for example Philip Whalen and Robert Creeley, and by the musician and writer John Cage. He was a supremely "open" poet, able to appreciate and learn from others, although his own voice is unmistakable in all of his work and his words are weighted individually in a way that is unique to him.

*GI Bill legislation enabling members of armed forces to receive a college education paid for by the government

The Sonnets

Berrigan's first major work is his sequence of sonnets* called *The Sonnets,* first published in 1964. In *The Sonnets* Berrigan modernizes the sonnet form by breaking the reader's expectation of an easy connection between lines. He writes about his own friends and contemporary American artists, not only painters and poets but also movie stars and blues musicians, as in "Sonnet XV":

> In Joe Brainard's collage its white arrow
> He is not in it, the hungry dead doctor.
> Of Marilyn Monroe, her white teeth white-
> I am truly horribly upset because Marilyn
> and ate King Korn popcorn," he wrote in his
> of glass in Joe Brainard's collage
> Doctor, but they say "I LOVE YOU"
> and the sonnet is not dead.
> takes the eyes away from the gray words,
> Diary. The black heart beside the fifteen pieces
> Monroe died, so I went to a matinee B-movie
> washed by Joe's throbbing hands. "Today
> What is in it is sixteen ripped pictures
> does not point to William Carlos Williams.

The reader eventually realizes that he or she can make a more conventional poem out of this one by reading it according to a particular ordering of the lines: the first line, then the last line, then the second line, then the second-to-last line, and so on. The poem quotes a passage from his friend Joe Brainard's diary about the death of Marilyn Monroe, contradicts a famous statement by the poet William Carlos Williams that the sonnet as a form is dead, and describes a collage of Brainard's. The poem itself resembles a collage. Other sonnets in this sequence contain lines from old poems of Berrigan's, from other poems in the sequence, and from friends' poems that were given to him to change and use. Some incorporate material translated from foreign poets, some are simply earlier poems reprinted. Berrigan thought of the sequence as telling a story of relationships as Shakespeare's sonnets do; it is personal history seen as if it were a single moment of time.

The 1960s and 1970s

In 1962 Berrigan married Sandra Alper, and by the mid-1960s he was the father of two children, David and Kate. He earned a meager living in New York writing art reviews for the magazine *Art News,* working in a bookstore, giving readings, and selling signed editions of poetry books and manuscript materials. He taught the first poetry workshop at the St. Mark's Poetry Project, initiating a long association with that organization. Along with Padgett, Gallup, and Brainard, and others such as the poet Ed Sanders and the painter George Schneeman, he established the reputation of a generation of poets and artists born in the 1930s and early 1940s who lived a bohemian* existence in New York and who appreciated the qualities of both highbrow* and popular culture. Meanwhile his poetry evolved into the more open style of "Tambourine Life," a long poem containing seventy short sections that describe Berrigan's life, in process, in terms of words, ideas, and shapes that impinge on his consciousness. There is no real narration. Instead, the poem is meant to have an interesting "surface," just as a painting's surface is what its viewer is most aware of. In the course of his writing the poem, two people important to Berrigan died, the poet Frank O'Hara and a former lover, the flutist Anne Kepler. "Tambourine Life" acknowledges Kepler's death but ends with a very Berrigan-esque affirmation: "Joy is what I like, / That, and love." Those two lines create a little puzzle-shape: does the poet both like and love joy and/or like both joy and love? That shape is characteristic of the poem, which is replete with jokes, puns, and cross-references.

    In the late 1960s Berrigan became better known, as *The Sonnets* was republished and other works appeared. He was invited to teach at the Writers Workshop at the University of Iowa in 1968, embarking on a series of poet-in-residence jobs at universities that would continue off and on for the rest of his life. After their move to Iowa, Ted and Sandy Berrigan separated. In 1971 Berrigan married the poet Alice Notley with whom he had two sons, Anselm and Edmund, and with whom he lived until his death. Between 1969 and 1975 Berrigan lived in Ann Arbor, Michigan; New York City; Buffalo, New York; Southampton, Massachusetts; San Francisco; Bolinas, California; Chicago; London; and Essex, England, teaching creative writing at universities in most of these places. He was, as he

*bohemian unconventional

*highbrow intellectual

> ### Wind
>
> Every day when the sun comes up
> The angels emerge from the rivers
> Drily happy & all wet. Easy going
> But hard to keep my place. Easy
> On the avenue underneath my face.
> Difficult alone trying to get true.
> Difficult inside alone with you.
> The rivers' blackness flowing just sits
> Orange & reds blaze up inside the sky
> I sit here & I've been thinking this
> Red, blue, yellow, green, & white.
>
> (*So Going Around Cities*)

said, a migrant poet "so going around cities," to quote the title of the poem that became the title of his collected poems. In 1976 Berrigan moved back to New York, to 101 St. Mark's Place, where he lived until his death, maintaining, with Alice Notley, an informal salon* frequented by all sorts of people—poets, painters, and others—in a spirit of poetry and poverty. Berrigan was a leading poetic presence, ceaselessly talkative, the kind of person who changes other people's lives. He continued to read, write, talk, and respond to others' literary and emotional needs literally until the day of his death. Berrigan died in his own bed on 4 July 1983 of cirrhosis of the liver.

Later Poetry

Berrigan's poetry of the 1970s and early 1980s continued to develop along the several paths laid out by him in the 1960s. There are open-field poems,* there are deliberately sentimental poems toughly wrought, there are dense sonnetlike poems, there are poems incorporating found materials, and there are two book-length sequences, *Easter Monday*, and *A Certain Slant of Sunlight*. The poems of this later period are wiser and more sophisticated, more supple and various in surface as the years progress, his syntax* more inventive in accordance with a mental process that becomes quicker and more

*salon a place, usually a private home, where poets and artists meet and talk

*open-field poems poems that use the whole page as a field for the deployment of words, making space very important

*syntax the structure of a sentence; refers to word placement, as opposed to "diction," which refers to word choice

individual. "Personal Poem #9," an early poem included in *The Sonnets,* begins

> It's 8:54 a.m. in Brooklyn, it's the 26th of July
> and it's probably 8:54 in Manhattan but I'm
> in Brooklyn   I'm eating English muffins and drinking
> Pepsi and I'm thinking of how Brooklyn is New
> York City too how odd . . .

and ends with

> I think I was thinking
> when I was ahead I'd be somewhere like Perry Street
> erudite* dazzling slim and badly-loved
> contemplating my new book of poetry
> to be printed in simple type on old brown paper
> feminine marvelous and tough

erudite educated; well-read; scholarly

Written nearly twenty years later, "Red Shift" (in *So Going Around Cities: New and Selected Poems, 1958–1979*) begins

> Here I am at 8:08 p.m. indefinable ample rhythmic frame
> The air is biting, February, fierce arabesques*
>   on the way to tree in winter streetscape
> I drink some American poison liquid air which bubbles
>   and smoke to have character and to lean
> In. . . .

arabesque an ornamental curvy shape

and ends with

> I'm only pronouns, & I am all of them, & I didn't ask for
>   this
>   You did
> I came into your life to change it & it did so & now nothing
>   will ever change
> That, & that's that.
> Alone & crowded, unhappy fate, nevertheless
>   I slip softly into the air
> The world's furious song flows through my costume.

The first poem, deliberately imitative of Frank O'Hara's "personal poems," depends on clear meaning and clean conventional sentences. It ends in a mood of romantic self-pity,

*parody a humorous imitation intended to ridicule

*muse In Greek mythology, the nine Muses are goddesses who preside over the arts, sciences, song, and poetry. Today, the muse is considered a source of inspiration.

IF YOU LIKE the poetry of Berrigan, you might also like the poetry of Frank O'Hara or Ron Padgett.

accompanied by delicate self-parody.* In the later poem Berrigan assumes the form of the personal poem as his own, using it for a reflection on his previous twenty years. Berrigan is, still typically, in the process of taking a walk, but "Pepsi," Berrigan's trademark beverage, often mentioned in his poems, has become "American poison liquid air which bubbles." The sentences contain complex clauses and are less conversational. The mood is one of a fierce and true unhappiness, which is also a "costume." The poet nevertheless exults in the fact that he has changed and changed others.

Berrigan's poetry is for people. He tried to create himself on the page as an ordinary person, someone you might meet on a street corner and have a conversation with—light or deep. In life he was not an ordinary person, but nobody else is either. Meanwhile, Berrigan's work is of the highest skill and always executed with remarkable care; it is always operating on more than one level of meaning; it is often funny; and it is almost always amusing—has the muse* in it, as he explained the workings of that word.

Selected Bibliography

WORKS BY TED BERRIGAN
Poetry

The Sonnets (1967). Enlarged edition, New York: United Artists, 1982; further enlarged, New York: Penguin, 2000.

Bean Spasms (with Ron Padgett and Joe Brainard) (1967).

Many Happy Returns (1969).

In the Early Morning Rain (1970).

Red Wagon (1976).

Nothing for You (1977).

Train Ride (1978).

So Going Around Cities: New and Selected Poems 1958–1979 (1980).

A Certain Slant of Sunlight (1988).

Prose

Clear the Range (1977).

Interviews and Lectures

Ratcliffe, Stephen, and Leslie Scalapino, eds. *Talking in Tranquility: Interviews with Ted Berrigan.* Bolinas, Calif.: Avenue B, 1991.

Lewis, Joel, ed. *On the Level Everyday: Selected Talks on Poetry and the Art of Living.* Jersey City, N.J.: Talisman House, 1997.

Available Collections

Selected Poems. Edited by Aram Saroyan. New York: Penguin, 1994.

WORKS ABOUT TED BERRIGAN

Clark, Tom. *Late Returns.* Bolinas, Calif.: Tomboctou Books, 1985.

Fischer, Aaron. *Ted Berrigan: An Annotated Checklist.* New York: Granary Books, 1998.

Padgett, Ron. *Ted.* Great Barrington, Mass.: The Figures, 1993.

Waldman, Anne, ed. *Nice to See You: Homage to Ted Berrigan.* Minneapolis: Coffee House Press, 1991.

JOHN BERRYMAN

(1914–1972)

by Lea Baechler

To think of John Berryman as a person and a poet is to see him as a full-grown man with dark, heavy-framed glasses and a long, bushy beard, sequestered* in his study writing poems night after night into the late hours, whiskey glass and cigarettes at hand. This image of him persists partly because Berryman imposed that picture of himself on us and partly because in his poems he allows us to see only a glimpse or ghost of the child he was. Despite the numerous allusions* in his poems to the life-changing losses of his early years, Berryman refused to share the full experience of his childhood. While many of us recall the events and atmosphere of childhood fondly (sometimes reimagining the tough parts to suit ourselves), at the age of twelve John chose to erase his childhood after his father committed suicide. His refusal to revisit his childhood years in a comprehensive way strongly influenced the rest of his life and is the penetrating focus of his poetry.

*****sequestered** isolated; shut off from social interaction

*****allusion** a passing reference

Quotations from Berryman's poetry throughout are taken from the *Collected Poems* and *The Dream Songs.*

Troubled Beginnings

Born in McAlester, Oklahoma, on 25 October 1914 to John Allyn Smith and Martha (Little) Smith, John was christened John Allyn Smith, Jr. His brother, Robert Jefferson (Bob), was born in 1919. Their mother was a teacher and their father a banker. Life was relatively stable until 1924, when Smith abruptly quit his job. In the fall of 1925 he moved the family to Tampa, Florida, where he and Martha bought and ran a family restaurant, the Orange Blossom. Soon, however, the Florida real estate bust of 1926 put them out of business, and the family found itself living in difficult circumstances. It is not known whether marital problems, anxieties about money, a preexisting psychological condition, or the effect of such combined stress pushed him to his final tragic act, but early one June morning directly in front of the family's home, Smith shot himself. His son never recovered from his father's suicide: "Then came a departure / Thereafter nothing fell out as it might or ought" (Dream Song 1). Martha immediately moved the boys to Queens, New York, and soon afterward married a man she had been seeing in Tampa.

John accepted these changes and took his stepfather's name. As John Berryman, he put the past behind him and began his new life. He attended school in Queens until his mother realized that he and her husband were uneasy with each other, at which point she sent her son to boarding school in Connecticut. Bookish and physically awkward, Berryman never quite fit in at South Kent School, where chumming around with the other boys and playing sports was the norm. With effort he managed, and in 1932 he began studies on a partial scholarship at Columbia University. During his years at Columbia, Berryman's extraordinary brilliance became evident. His passion for literature and writing poetry developed, and he met a number of writers and intellectuals. The problems Berryman faced throughout his life also became apparent: an intellectual arrogance that consistently got him into trouble with peers and superiors, periods during which he worked furiously without sleeping for days, drunken binges that were followed by weeks of deep depression, and an obsession with love that led him into relationships that followed one of two paths—emotional devastation when the romance did not work out or an inability to commit to relatively stable and happy relationships.

A real estate bust occurs when property and businesses are sold at low prices but the predicted and necessary development to maintain them and make a profit does not take place.

His first year at Columbia was successful. A handsome, energetic young man with wit and intelligence, Berryman read, wrote, drank, and made himself popular with his fellow students and the women across the street at Barnard College. In the fall of 1933 he began studies with Mark Van Doren, an extraordinary teacher with an impressive reputation as a writer. For all his excitement about working with Van Doren, Berryman mistakenly assumed that Van Doren's recognition and his own brilliance would allow him to succeed without working. At the end of the year, he lost his scholarship and was suspended for the following term. Berryman returned in the spring of 1935 to immense pressures. He had to prove himself, complete two years of study within three semesters, and fulfill an extra demand he had placed on himself—to produce and publish his own work. Despite these pressures, combined with his anxiety about recognition through publication and the various problems that he had already exhibited, Berryman graduated on time and with honors.

Love and Work

In the fall of 1936, John left for England on a Kellett Fellowship from Columbia to study at Clare College, Cambridge, where he conducted his life much as he had at Columbia. During his two years in England, he studied mostly on his own, drank, and wrote obsessively. He met the Irish poet William Butler Yeats, as well as W. H. Auden and Dylan Thomas, and attended the lectures of T. S. Eliot. When he returned to the States in 1938, Berryman initially had difficulty finding a teaching position but began publishing his poems in literary journals. In 1940, at the age of twenty-five, he secured a lectureship at Harvard, followed by a Rockefeller Foundation Research Grant in 1944 and a creative writing position at Princeton in 1945. He also met the poets Delmore Schwartz, Theodore Roethke, Stanley Kunitz, and Robert Lowell, and the critic R. P. Blackmur.

Berryman traveled to Europe often and loved Ireland best. He married three times, had a son and two daughters, and engaged in a number of love affairs. Hospitalized periodically for exhaustion, breakdown, and alcoholism, Berryman occasionally turned to therapy. He also wrote and published prolifically.* Besides the individual poems, reviews, and critical essays he regularly published, mostly in literary journals,

prolifically productively; in great quantity

How is it that such an innovative, distinctive, and influential poet as John Berryman should have struggled so painfully to recognize his worth?

his first volume of poems, *The Dispossessed,* appeared in 1948, followed by *Stephen Crane* (1950), a psychologically probing biography of the American journalist who wrote *The Red Badge of Courage.* In 1956, he divorced his first wife, Eileen Simpson; immediately remarried; and published *Homage to Mistress Bradstreet,* a full-length poem that engages the work and life of the seventeenth-century American poet Anne Bradstreet. He remarried in 1961 and in 1964 published *77 Dream Songs,* the first three parts of his great Dream Song work. The concluding four parts, for which he won the National Book Award and the Bollingen Prize, were published in 1968 and were collectively entitled *His Toy, His Dream, His Rest.*

Over the years he taught and lectured at a number of universities, though from 1954 until his death he was based at the University of Minnesota. Along with Theodore Roethke, Berryman was known as the most penetrating and dynamic teacher of his time. Many of his students became well-known poets, and several wrote about Berryman's passionate and demanding teaching, among them, Philip Levine and Tess Gallagher. Yet despite his honored reputation as a distinguished teacher and mentor, his recognition as a poet and a scholar, and the numerous awards, fellowships, and grants (among them the Rockefeller, the Guggenheim, the Pulitzer, the National Book Award), Berryman remained insecure about his legitimacy as a "great" poet and about his ability to form lasting relationships with those he loved.

Poetic Work and Loss

How is it that such an innovative, distinctive, and influential poet as John Berryman should have struggled so painfully to recognize his worth? While there is no simple answer, we can consider what powers and thoughts compelled him to write the poems he did and what it is that makes Berryman's poetry innovative and distinctive. In the first Dream Song, the poet calls his father's suicide a "departure," after which nothing was as it should be. In an early 1940s piece, "The Ball Poem" (from *The Dispossessed*), Berryman asks, "What is the boy now, who has lost his ball, / What, what is he to do?" These opening lines ask what happens to a boy and who he becomes once he has lost something that matters. The poem also suggests that he is no longer a child. The boy "suffer[s]" as he watches the ball "go / Merrily bouncing, down the street" and experiences "an ultimate shaking grief." The poet concludes, "I am not a little boy," which suggests a loss of innocence and points, in the context of Berryman's other poems, to his desire to distance himself from childhood. Even though he occasionally gives us a glimpse of childhood happiness—"Once in a sycamore I was glad / all at the top, and I sang" (Dream Song 1)—he nearly always undercuts it with irony.* "Once" there was a boy at the top of a tree, and he "sang" and "was glad," but not anymore. For Berryman, that glad boy hardly existed, or if he did it was in a fairy tale, a made-up story of long ago, once upon a time.

The poet could not rub out of existence the problems rooted in his childhood, however. In his poems, Berryman repeatedly connects his current difficulties, his failed relationships, the losses of lovers and friends, his insecurities and anxieties, and his preoccupation with death in general and suicide in particular to that first "departure." For example, Dream Song 76 begins with an observation followed by a question, neither of which appears to have anything to do with his father: "Nothing very bad happen to me lately / How do you explain that?" For the poet, the answer to the question is obvious: nothing too bad can happen when one is in a state of "odd sobriety," one would not have to make the effort to be sober if one were not a drunk, and one would not be a drunk without a cause. He then declares, "in a modesty of death I join my father / who dared so long agone leave me." Notice the decision to join his father, as if to say, "If you can do this, so, too, can and will I." The use of the word "dared" reinforces this idea and also suggests that he regards his father's suicide as a presumptuous*—how *dare* you—and deliberate act of abandonment. He then turns to a specific detail: "A bullet on a concrete stoop." The bullet is not hurting anyone; it is simply lying there, neutrally situated on "a" step, not "the" step of Berryman's home. The beginning of the last stanza, "I offers you this handkerchief," further illustrates this emotional displacement. The poet offers consolation to some "you," but not to himself, and he will even share another's grief "shoulder to shoulder," though for him the whole thing—grief, consolation—is just "all that jazz." The concluding lines allude to the poet's loneliness, "I saw nobody coming," and his death wish, "so I went instead."

References to his father's death abound in *The Dream Songs*. The word "father" became for Berryman "the loneliest

*__irony__ saying the opposite of what you mean to make your point even more strongly

*__presumptuous__ overstepping bounds

word in the one language" (Dream Song 241). Even toward the end of Berryman's life the emotions are as intense as if his father's death had happened recently, not nearly fifty years earlier. In the penultimate* poem, Berryman stands over his father's grave "with rage" and asks, "When will indifference come, I moan & rave" (Dream Song 384). Unable to grow into indifference, he finds each new experience of separation, failure, and loss as devastating as the original—from his troubled marriages and relationships to the loss of close friends (including the writers Bhain Campbell, Dylan Thomas, Randall Jarrell, Theodore Roethke, and Delmore Schwartz) and the deaths of people with whom he was not particularly close but felt an intellectual or poetic affinity: the writers Hart Crane, W. B. Yeats, T. S. Eliot, and Sylvia Plath, to name only a few.

Dream Song: A Poet's Voice

Neither the impulse toward poetry nor a specific content or preoccupation is enough to make a writer distinctive and timely. A poet must also have an individual voice that speaks to and beyond his time and a style that characterizes him as unique and innovative. In his early work, Berryman was an accomplished poet, influenced by the poets he read and admired. The poems in *The Dispossessed* evoke intense emotion combined with admirable formal control, while the later *Homage to Mistress Bradstreet,* in which the poet enters the psyche* and voice of a woman poet who lived more than three centuries before him, is an achievement but not an effort easily repeated.

When Berryman began writing his Dream Songs in the late 1940s, he found that the form that allowed his lyric,* ironic voice to develop over time to tell the story of a life. Berryman's lyric form in the individual poems (three stanzas, six lines per stanza) is expansive enough to allow for irony, a high degree of emotion, and contradictions in emotion. In Dream Song 1, for example, we find both tender remembrance of a "glad boy" and despair ("then came a departure"). The poems work together to tell a story, and within the narrative structure, Berryman introduces characters who reappear: the "I" who speaks of his suffering and rage; Henry, the vulnerable, naive aspect of the "I"; and Mr. Bones, who is an extension of both the "I" and Henry but who is separate from them and has ironic distance from their pains, tribulations,*

*penultimate next to last

*psyche the psychological and sometimes spiritual character of a person

*lyric characterized by musical and personal expression

*tribulation a cause of suffering or distress

Henry's Confession (Dream Song 76)

Nothin very bad happen to me lately.
How you explain that? —I explain that, Mr Bones,
terms o' your bafflin odd sobriety.
Sober as man can get, no girls, no telephones,
what could happen bad to Mr Bones?
—If life is a handkerchief sandwich,

in a modesty of death I join my father
who dared so long agone leave me.
A bullet on a concrete stoop
close by a smothering southern sea
spreadeagled on an island, by my knee.
—You is from hunger, Mr Bones,

I offers you this handkerchief, now set
your left foot by my right foot,
shoulder to shoulder, all that jazz,
arm in arm, by the beautiful sea,
hum a little, Mr Bones.
—I saw nobody coming, so I went instead.

and sorrows. Where Henry might be "dazzled" and bewildered by the seriousness of something and the "I" cannot leave thought of it "alone," both turn to Mr. Bones for understanding of the suffering: "What for, Mr. Bones?" (Dream Song 38).

Berryman's addition of characters to his Dream Songs is supplemented by a rhythmic, bantering syntax* and wordplay. His playfulness with words, word arrangement, and grammar can be exuberant*—"all at the top" (in "once in a sycamore I was glad / all at the top") literally refers to a boy high up in a tree, yet also suggests the gladness rising up in him. The ironic, sometimes comedic surface it creates, however, reflects Berryman's painful subjects of disconnectedness and loss: in "my father / who so long agone dared leave me," we know that the "agone" literally means "ago," but Berryman's alteration of the word emphasizes the finality of a father *gone*.

When John Berryman leaped to his death from a bridge in Minneapolis over the Mississippi River, early on 7 January 1972, he had been sober for nearly a year, was about to begin a new term of teaching, and was working on the autobiographical novel *Recovery* and new poems. He left behind his family,

*__syntax__ the structure of a sentence; refers to word placement, as opposed to "diction," which refers to word choice

*__exuberant__ unrestrained; flamboyant

*cadence the rhythm of the flow of language or verse music

*premonition anticipation of something before it happens

his fears that he would inflict the trauma of his childhood on his own children, and the love and admiration of his students and many friends and fellow poets. He also left his work, in particular the Dream Songs. The cadences* and fragmented use of language in these poems mirror the lyric beauty of fleeting moments and capture our disconnected, conflicted sense of reality as we experience both the interior world of our fears and longings and the exterior world of their enactment. From reflections on loss and premonitions* of death emerges a haunting tenderness in the concluding poem of the Dream Songs. Referring to the heavy burden of parenthood, Berryman begins with physical observations—"My daughter's heavier," while all the while "light leaves are flying." He thinks about things he will never know—about death, about how "fall is grievy, brisk." Nearly at the point of despair, "tears behind the eyes," he wishes that life were better balanced so that he would not have to "scold" his "heavy daughter" (Dream Song 385). A similar tenderness appears in the concluding song (Dream Song 157) of his twelve-poem sequence for Delmore Schwartz. Here, he experiences "one solid block of agony" at the death of his friend before releasing himself from that grief by imagining Schwartz sitting happily in the afterlife among all the great writers and thinkers of the centuries. The closing lines convey what Berryman came to understand about his friend and what he desired, tenderly and longingly, for him. Perhaps they are words he took with him as well, or ones that we can wish for him: "I hope he's sitting with his peers: sit, sit, & recover & be whole."

IF YOU LIKE the poetry of Berryman, you might also like the poetry of Theodore Roethke.

Selected Bibliography

WORKS BY JOHN BERRYMAN
Poetry

The Dispossessed (1948).

Homage to Mistress Bradstreet, and Other Poems (1956).

77 Dream Songs (1964).

Berryman's Sonnets (1967). Written in 1947 and entitled "Sonnets to Chris" by Berryman, these poems record his first affair while married to Eileen Simpson.

Short Poems (1967).

His Toy, His Dream, His Pocket: 308 Dream Songs (1968).

Love & Fame (1970).

Delusions, etc. (1972).

Henry's Fate & Other Poems (1976).

Other Works

Berryman's Shakespeare. Edited by John Haffenden. New York: Farrar, Straus and Giroux, 1999. Essays based on work that Berryman began, but never finished, on a critical edition of *King Lear* and a study of Shakespeare.

The Freedom of the Poet. New York: Farrar, Straus and Giroux, 1976.

Recovery. New York: Farrar, Straus and Giroux, 1973.

Stephen Crane. Cleveland: World Publishing Co., 1950.

We Dream of Honour: John Berryman's Letters to His Mother. Edited by Richard Kelly. New York: Norton, 1988.

Available Collections

Collected Poems: 1937–1971. Edited by Charles Thornbury. New York: Farrar, Straus and Giroux, 1969; rev. ed., 1989.

The Dream Songs. New York: Farrar, Straus and Giroux, 1969.

WORKS ABOUT JOHN BERRYMAN

Bawer, Bruce. *The Middle Generation: The Lives and Poetry of Delmore Schwartz, Randall Jarrell, John Berryman, Robert Lowell.* Hamden, Conn.: Archon Books, 1986.

Conarroe, Joel. *Eight American Poets: Theodore Roethke, Elizabeth Bishop, Robert Lowell, John Berryman, Anne Sexton, Sylvia Plath, Allen Ginsberg, and James Merrill.* New York: Random House, 1994.

Conarroe, Joel. *John Berryman: An Introduction to the Poetry.* New York: Columbia University Press, 1977.

Haffenden, John. *The Life of John Berryman.* Boston: Routledge and Kegan Paul, 1982.

Halliday, E. M. *John Berryman and the Thirties: A Memoir.* Amherst: University of Massachusetts Press, 1987.

Hyde, Lewis. *Alcohol and Poetry: John Berryman and the Booze Talking.* Dallas: Dallas Institute Publications, 1986.

Kelly, Richard J., and Alan K. Lathrop, eds. *Recovering Berryman: Essays on a Poet.* Ann Arbor: University of Michigan Press, 1993.

Mariani, Paul L. *Dream Song: The Life of John Berryman.* New York: Morrow, 1990.

Simpson, Eileen. *Poets in Their Youth: A Memoir.* New York: Random House, 1982.

Vendler, Helen Hennessy. *The Given and the Made: Strategies of Poetic Redefinition.* Cambridge, Mass.: Harvard University Press, 1995.

ELIZABETH BISHOP

(1911–1979)

by Charles North

One of her schoolmates has provided this endearing picture of the sixteen-year-old Elizabeth Bishop:

> She looked remarkable, with tightly curly hair that stood straight up, while the rest of us all had straight hair that hung down. And she was remarkable in many ways besides. She had read more widely and deeply than we had. But she carried her learning lightly. She was very funny. She had a big repertory of stories she could *tell*, not read, and of wonderful songs she could sing, like ballads and sea chanteys. And if some school occasion called for a new song, or a skit, it would appear overnight like magic in her hands. . . . We called her "Bishop," spoke of her as "the Bishop," and we all knew with no doubt whatsoever that she was a genius (*The Collected Prose*, pp. xii–xiii).

Quotations from Bishop's poetry throughout are taken from *The Complete Poems, 1927–1979*.

*luminous glowing; shining

The imaginative teenager who had read so much and could tell stories and sing chanteys went on to win widespread acclaim for her luminous* poetry. The modesty, humor, intelligence, and inventiveness she displayed in school were characteristics of everything she wrote.

Traumatic Beginnings

And yet, if anyone had tried to predict Elizabeth Bishop's future on the basis of her childhood, there would have been little thought of success. She was born in Worcester, Massachusetts, on 8 February 1911, to William T. Bishop, who was vice president of a family building business and Gertrude May Boomer, who had descended from a British sailing family. But her life took a tragic turn when she was only eight months old. Her father died of kidney disease; soon after, her mother, already unstable, suffered a mental breakdown and was placed in a sanatorium. After the age of five, Elizabeth never saw her mother again.

"At night I lay blinking my flashlight off and on, and crying."

This traumatic loss and the dislocation that followed set the course for Elizabeth Bishop's life. She was moved from one relative to another, first to Canada to stay with her kindly maternal grandparents in tiny Grand Village, Nova Scotia, and then at the age of six, against her will, to the gloomy home of her paternal grandparents in Worcester. Extremely unhappy there, she developed chronic asthma, eczema, and bronchial infections and spent much of her time confined to bed. Feeling abandoned and isolated, she saw herself "aging, even dying. . . . At night I lay blinking my flashlight off and on, and crying" (*The Collected Prose*, p. 31).

The Fledgling Poet

Matters improved when she went to live with her aunt in Revere, Massachusetts, although illness plagued her. Often bedridden, she read a great deal and began to write poems and prose. In sixth grade she won an American Legion essay contest. At sixteen, enrolled at the Walnut Hill School for Girls, she emerged from her childhood depression—making friends; writing poems, stories, and plays; and editing the literary magazine. She continued to blossom at Vassar College, then a woman's college in Poughkeepsie, New York, which she entered in 1930. Stimulated by her bright, creative classmates—including the writer Mary McCarthy, who became a friend—she began to take herself seriously as a writer. She discovered the poetry of George Herbert and Gerard Manley Hopkins and began to publish her own poems in national magazines. The first, "Hymn to the Virgin," appeared in the *Magazine* in April 1934, her senior year at Vassar.

In her senior year, Bishop met the person who most influenced her as a poet, Marianne Moore, who lived quietly with her mother in Brooklyn, wore odd hats, wrote wonderfully precise poems, and became Bishop's mentor and close friend. (In her memoir "Efforts of Affection," Bishop colorfully describes their meeting on a bench in the New York Public Library, along with their subsequent trip to the circus.) Following college, under Moore's guidance, Bishop set out to become a poet. "I never left [Moore's house] without feeling happier: uplifted, even inspired, determined to be good, to work harder, not to worry about what other people thought, never to try to publish anything until I thought I'd done my best with it, no matter how many years it took—or never to publish at all" (*The Collected Prose,* p. 137). In these depression* years Bishop also looked for work and for a short time took a job as instructor at a correspondence school* for writers, the school whose sleazy operations she later exposed in "The U.S.A. School of Writing."

depression the period of economic hardship in America in the 1930s, following the stock market crash of 1929

correspondence school a school that offers courses conducted entirely by mail

The Sandpiper

Even after her emergence in the adult world, Elizabeth Bishop's childhood trauma remained with her. In addition to suffering from asthma attacks, she now drank heavily and was often in a state of depression that made it nearly impossible for her to write. Continuing the pattern of her childhood, she moved around restlessly, staying with friends, traveling in and out of the country, continually pondering new trips. She wrote, with reference to her poem "The Sandpiper," "Yes, all my life I have lived and behaved very much like that sandpiper—just running along the edges of different countries and continents, 'looking for something' " ("Laureate's Words of Acceptance," p. 12). What she was looking for, almost certainly, was a real home. She fell in love with one of the places she visited, Key West, Florida, and lived there on and off for nine years, beginning in 1938.

The fruit of her writing efforts in the 1930s and early 1940s was a long time in coming but well worth the wait. Her first book of poetry, *North & South,* short by poetry book standards, contains a number of remarkable poems, such as "The Map," "The Imaginary Iceberg," and "Florida." This book introduced Bishop's lifelong themes of travel, love, and loss. Also in the 1940s, Bishop formed one of her strongest literary friendships, with the poet Robert Lowell, and despite her insecurities, she was becoming recognized as an important poet. She was awarded the first of two Guggenheim Fellowships in 1947 and, with Lowell's help, was appointed to the prestigious position of poetry consultant to the Library of Congress (1949–1950).

A Home in Brazil

Of Bishop's travels, none proved as significant as a stopover in Brazil in 1951. Taken ill after eating fruit, she recuperated there for several months—and wound up staying for fifteen years as the companion of Lota de Macedo Soares, a highly accomplished Brazilian woman who had residences in Rio de Janeiro and in nearby Persepolis. The stability of a real home life together with the Brazilian landscape and culture inspired richly evocative poems, such as "Brazil, January 1, 1502," and "Questions of Travel." Bishop was also able to confront details of her childhood more directly than before, both in her poems and in such stories as "In the Village," which encapsulates* memories of her mother in the striking image: "A scream, the echo of a scream [that] hangs over that Nova Scotian Village" (*The Collected Prose,* p. 251).

*encapsulate to summarize or epitomize

Final Uprooting

Poems: North & South—A Cold Spring won the 1956 Pulitzer Prize, and *Questions of Travel* was nominated for the National Book Award. Also, Bishop translated the fascinating *Diary of Helena Morley,* written in Portuguese by a young Brazilian teenager who had lived in a diamond-mining village in the 1890s. But the 1960s were turbulent for Bishop. Although she still considered Brazil home, she hesitantly and with some fear took a position as poet-in-residence at the University of Washington in Seattle, her first serious attempt at teaching. Meanwhile, the political situation in Brazil had become increasingly unstable, and Lota's health was deteriorating. In America her dear friend Robert Lowell was having periodic mental breakdowns. Bishop drank in response to these stresses and at one point had the worst asthmatic attack of her life. She agonized about whether or not to leave Brazil for good. When Lota seemed well enough to visit her in New York, Bishop believed things were looking up. On her first night there, however, Lota took an overdose of tranquilizers and died without regaining consciousness.

After this violent turn, Bishop settled permanently in a waterfront apartment in downtown Boston. Needing income as well as stability, she took over Lowell's poetry-writing class at Harvard University. In Cambridge she met Alice Methfessel, who became her companion for the rest of her life. Bishop's remaining years saw her celebrated as one of America's major poets. Her *Complete Poems* won the National Book Award, and in 1976 she became the first woman, and the first American, to win the Books Abroad: Neustadt International Prize for literature. Her final collection, *Geography III,* won the National Book Critic's Circle Award and includes some of her finest poems. Often unwell, Bishop retired from Harvard, commuted from Boston to teach at New York University for a semester, and had just begun a poetry-writing class at the Massachusetts Institute of Technology when she died in her Boston apartment, on 6 October 1979, of a cerebral aneurysm.

The Perfectionist

Elizabeth Bishop was an exceptionally careful poet. She struggled with poems for years before deciding which ones should be published and which abandoned. As a result, her poetic output was small—only four short books in four decades of writing. Yet few American poets have become as widely admired or have written as many poems of lasting value. Readers and literary critics as well as fellow poets have marveled at her original viewpoints, her striking imagery, her ear for the music of the English language, and her perceptive and witty yet sympathetic depictions of people, landscapes, and animals.

One Art

The art of losing isn't hard to master;
so many things seem filled with the intent
to be lost that their loss is no disaster.

Lose something every day. Accept the fluster
of lost door keys, the hour badly spent.
The art of losing isn't hard to master.

Then practice losing farther, losing faster:
places, and names, and where it was you meant
to travel. None of these will bring disaster.

I lost my mother's watch. And look! my last, or
next-to-last, of three loved houses went.
The art of losing isn't hard to master.

I lost two cities, lovely ones. And, vaster,
some realms I owned, two rivers, a continent.
I miss them, but it wasn't a disaster.

—Even losing you (the joking voice, a gesture
I love) I shan't have lied. It's evident
the art of losing's not too hard to master
though it may look like (*Write* it!) like disaster.

Bishop was a talented watercolorist. Her paintings appear on the covers of her *Complete Poems, 1927–1979* and her *Collected Prose.*

*isinglass a semitransparent whitish substance like mica

In the early poem "The Fish," Bishop showed her remarkable eye for detail, as well as how evocative plain English can be:

I looked into his eyes
which were far larger than mine
but shallower, and yellowed,
the irises backed and packed
with tarnished tinfoil
seen through the lenses
of old scratched isinglass.*
They shifted a little, but not
to return my stare.

> —It was more like the tipping
> of an object toward the light.
> I admired his sullen face,
> The mechanism of his jaw,
> And then I saw that from his lower lip
> —if you could call it a lip—
> grim, wet, and weaponlike,
> hung five old pieces of fish-line . . .

The speaker eventually lets this battle-scarred warrior go, but not before she has transformed it through her precise use of language and imaginative associations. Similarly, in "Florida," she transforms an ordinary landscape:

> Cold white, not bright, the moonlight is coarse-meshed,
> and the careless, corrupt state is all black specks
> too far apart, and ugly whites; the poorest
> post-card of itself.

In both poems the language is clear and conversational and the perceptions vivid. Moreover, like her early favorite poets Hopkins and Herbert, she pays a great deal of attention to how words sound—individually, in phrases, and grouped into rhythmic poetic lines. The repetition of vowel and consonant sounds gives her language an almost physical presence.

Questions of Travel

Bishop's poems, like her life, are occupied with searching. Many begin with description and then proceed to wider considerations, often posing vital questions. They give the sense of a strongly independent mind at work. About her subject matter Bishop wrote, "Naturally I know, and it has been pointed out to me, that most of my poems are geographical, or about coasts, beaches and rivers running to the sea, and most of the titles of my books are geographical, too" ("Laureate's Words of Acceptance," p. 12). Yet the reader familiar with Bishop's life is aware that, underneath, her poems are as autobiographical as they are geographical. The places she writes about are those central to her life: Nova Scotia, Massachusetts,

Key West, Brazil. And the intense feelings associated with these places give her poetry a poignant undercurrent.

> *Continent, city, country, society:*
> *the choice is never wide and never free.*
> *And here, or there . . . No. Should we have stayed at*
>   *home,*
> *Wherever that may be?*

Given Bishop's lifelong quest for permanence, these lines from "Questions of Travel" are especially moving.

"You Are an Elizabeth"

Whereas in many of her poems, her regrets and longings surface only occasionally (more often they are hinted at in a suggestive image or concluding line), Bishop's late poems confront her personal difficulties openly. The difference can be seen by comparing her "Sestina"* with the equally wonderful "In the Waiting Room," from her final book. "Sestina" appears to depict an ordinary childhood scene:

> September rain falls on the house.
> In the failing light, the old grandmother
> sits in the kitchen with the child
> beside the Little Marvel Stove,
> reading the jokes from the almanac,
> laughing and talking to hide her tears.

The only surprising element in this first stanza is its final word. But by the time the sestina has concluded, the tears and other homely details have acquired a mysterious and haunting quality. By contrast, "In the Waiting Room," although it, too, begins with an ordinary scene—Elizabeth's accompanying her "foolish" aunt to the dentist—her aunt's cry of pain leads the poet to overt* and profound musings on her own identity:

> I said to myself: three days
> and you'll be seven years old.
> I was saying it to stop the sensation of falling off

*sestina an elaborate poetic form featuring the irregular repetition of six line-ending words through thirty-nine lines

*overt obvious; out in the open

the round, turning world
into cold, blue-black space.
But I felt: you are an *I,*
you are an *Elizabeth,*
you are one of *them.*
Why should you be one, too?
I scarcely dared to look
to see what it was I was.

One of Bishop's greatest strengths was her ability to write about such emotionally charged experiences in an objective, unsentimental way. Posing questions, qualifying initial impressions, "thinking on paper," she conveys vividly the sense that she discovers what to write in the process of writing.

Her poems about others—animals and people—and their various plights are equally vivid as well as clear-eyed. Life, she seems to be saying, is never a matter of certainties, and is always a matter for sympathetic understanding. The poems reveal her wit and lively sense of humor, and the underlying spirit is always generous and humane, whether she is depicting the eccentricities of Manuelzinho, the "Half squatter, half tenant . . . world's worst gardener since Cain" ("Manuelzinho") or, perhaps even more remarkably, the imaginative interior monologues* of a tropical toad, crab, and snail ("Rainy Season; Sub-Tropics").

The Art of Losing

Bishop's final book contains the superlative villanelle* "One Art." Written in one of the strictest poetic forms and simultaneously in the most natural English, "One Art" displays Bishop's poetic mastery as well as her probing mind—here focused directly on her lifelong "art of losing." From trivial losses like keys to more important ones like "places, and names, and where it was you meant / to travel" and finally to the most difficult loss of all, "losing you," the poet faces up to more personal central concerns. The final stanza, in which she interrupts herself, struggles to sum up, and exhorts* herself to write what is most painful to write, is Bishop at her best—which means American poetry at its best.

Always independent poetically, Bishop disapproved of the "confessional" style, which emphasized the difficult and often unpleasant feelings and experiences of the poet, and which was prominent in the 1950s and 1960s in the work of Sylvia Plath, Anne Sexton, and Robert Lowell.

*interior monologue a character's thoughts represented as words

*villanelle a rigorously formal poem in which whole lines and only two rhyming sounds are repeated

*exhort to urge or advise strongly

IF YOU LIKE the poetry of Bishop, you might also like the poetry of Marianne Moore or James Schuyler.

✍

Selected Bibliography

WORKS BY ELIZABETH BISHOP

Poetry

North & South (1946).

Poems: North & South—A Cold Spring (1955).

Questions of Travel (1965).

Geography III (1976).

Prose

The Collected Prose. New York: Farrar, Straus and Giroux, 1984. Includes "Efforts of Affection."

"Laureate's Words of Acceptance." *World Literature Today* 51:12 (winter 1977).

Letters

One Art. Edited by Robert Giroux. New York: Farrar, Straus and Giroux, 1994.

Editions and Translations

An Anthology of Twentieth Century Brazilian Poetry. Edited by Elizabeth Bishop and Emanuel Brasil. Middletown, Conn.: Wesleyan University Press, 1972.

The Diary of Helena Morley (by Alice Brant). Translated by Elizabeth Bishop. New York: Farrar, Straus and Cudahy, 1957.

Available Collection

The Complete Poems, 1927–1979. New York: Farrar, Straus and Giroux, 1983.

WORKS ABOUT ELIZABETH BISHOP

Costello, Bonnie. *Elizabeth Bishop: Questions of Mastery.* Cambridge, Mass.: Harvard University Press, 1991.

Fountain, Gary, and Peter Brazeau. *Remembering Elizabeth Bishop: An Oral Biography.* Amherst: University of Massachusetts Press, 1994.

Goldensohn, Lorrie. *Elizabeth Bishop: The Biography of a Poetry.* New York: Columbia University Press, 1992.

Kalstone, David. *Five Temperaments*. New York: Oxford University Press, 1977.

Kalstone, David. *Becoming a Poet*. New York: Farrar, Straus and Giroux, 1989.

Millier, Brett C. *Elizabeth Bishop: Life and the Memory of It.* Berkeley: California University Press, 1993.

Monteiro, George, ed. *Conversations with Elizabeth Bishop* (Interviews). Jackson: University Press of Mississippi, 1996.

Parker, Robert Dale. *The Unbeliever.* Urbana: Illinois University Press, 1988.

Schwartz, Lloyd, and Sybil Estess, eds. *Elizabeth Bishop and Her Art.* Ann Arbor: Michigan University Press, 1983.

Stevenson, Anne. *Elizabeth Bishop.* New York: Twayne, 1966.

Travisano, Thomas. *Elizabeth Bishop: Her Artistic Development.* Charlottesville: University Press of Virginia, 1988.

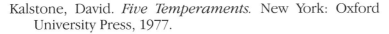

More About Bishop:

You can write to:
The Elizabeth Bishop Society
c/o Thomas Travisano
Department of English
Hartwick College
Oneota, NY 13820

WILLIAM BLAKE

(1757–1827)

by William Corbett

Between the ages of eight and ten William Blake had his first vision. A lonely boy, Blake took long walks through his native London to the farms on the city's outskirts. One day in the town of Peckham Rye, he saw a tree filled with angels. On a later walk he saw angels among the farmers who were gathering hay. Blake believed in the truth of these visions his entire life. If they came from his imagination, that made the angels no less real for him, since Blake believed that we know the truth not through reason but through imagination.

Life and Writing Style

Blake was born in London on 28 November 1757 and he lived in or around the city throughout his life. His father, James Blake, was a hosier who made and sold socks and stockings from a store on the first floor of their house. His mother was Catherine Hermitage Blake. Since Blake was all but unknown as a poet and artist in his lifetime, our knowledge of his life has great gaps. Of his early education, we know only that he read the Bible passionately and showed uncommon powers of imagination. His parents, recognizing his love for drawing, sent him to a drawing school at age ten. In 1772, now fifteen, Blake was apprenticed to a well-known engraver, James Basire. He completed his apprenticeship in 1779. From then on he earned his living as a printer and engraver, running a series of shops in which he sold the work he made.

Blake is commonly grouped with England's Romantic poets, but although he was their contemporary, he has little in common with Wordsworth, Coleridge, Byron, Shelley, and Keats. Unlike them, Blake worked at a trade; he is the only major British poet to have been a tradesman. Blake lived in the city while the other Romantics lived in the countryside or traveled in Europe. The others were all well known for their poetry, but Blake's poems were read by only a few during his lifetime. Indeed, Wordsworth and the rest probably never read a word of Blake's. Religion is at the center of Blake's visionary work; this is not true of other Romantic poetry. Blake stands today as the last great British religious poet.

Blake's is an unconventional religion drawn not from the church of his time but directly from the Bible. Much of his work satirizes* and condemns conventional religion for its corrupting influence on the imagination. He believed that he knew the true Christian religion, and he held so fiercely to his beliefs that many who knew him found him opinionated, ornery, and difficult. Even one of his great twentieth-century champions and editors, Geoffrey Keynes, called Blake "a strange individual." It is just this quality of strangeness that gives Blake's work a voice and vision as powerfully individual today as they were two centuries ago.

Songs of Innocence and of Experience

Blake's best-known work is *Songs of Innocence and of Experience.* He first printed *Songs of Innocence* in 1789; *Songs of Experience* followed in 1794. When he combined the two in 1815 he added the subtitle *Showing the Two Contrary States of the Human Soul.* Only twenty-five copies of this book now exist, and they are in the hands of private collectors, muse-

The Romantics were committed to individual expression of emotions and imagination and opposed to classical forms and social conventions. See article "Nineteenth-Century Romantic and Symbolist Poetry" in these volumes.

*satirize to criticize by mocking in a sarcastic, ironic way

ums, and libraries. Since Blake printed them over a period of years, they are all different in some way from one another.

The original *Songs of Innocence* contains twenty-seven pages, each bearing a design printed from a copper plate. Blake believed words and drawings said the same thing in different ways, but at first he did not know how to combine them. In 1787 his beloved younger brother Robert, the only member of his family Blake was close to, died. Robert remained as present and significant to Blake in death as he had been in life. In 1787, as Blake worked to unify word with image, Robert's spirit came and instructed him. Thus inspired, Blake invented the method that Geoffrey Keynes described in the introduction to *Songs of Innocence and Experience* as

> the laborious transfer of a written text to an etched copper-plate, from which an impression could be printed in ink of any color that he chose. The text would then be combined on the copper with illustrations or simple decorations harmonizing with the script, after which the whole print was colored with pen or paint-brush, varied as he pleased in each copy that he made (p. xiii).

To get the script to read left to right, Blake had to etch the words of his poems backward on the copper. This required many hours and great concentration. In the end Blake produced a hand-printed book similar to the illuminated* manuscripts that monks made during the Middle Ages. Over the years the books changed as his skill as an engraver grew and he employed fresh ideas about line and color.

The *Songs of Innocence,* Blake wrote in his introductory poem, are "happy songs / Every child may joy to hear." In this world, all is pure and joyous for children, shepherds, "Old John, with white hair," and the children's nurse whose "Nurse's Song" runs,

> When the voices of children are heard on the green
> And laughing is heard on the hill,
> My heart is at rest within my breast
> And every thing else is still.
>
> "Then come home, my children, the sun is gone down
> And the dews of night arise;

*illuminated decorated or illustrated

Come, come, leave off play, and let us away
Till the morning appears in the skies."

"No, no let us play, for it is yet day
And we cannot go to sleep;
Besides, in the sky the little birds fly
And the hills are all cover'd with sheep."

"Well, well, go & play till the light fades away
And then go home to bed."
The little ones leaped & shouted & laugh'd
And all the hills echoed.

The nurse hears the children's laughing voices and is content. But dusk is falling and night coming on. She calls the children to come in but they, seeing that there is still light in the sky, refuse. "It is yet day," they tell her, pointing to the birds and sheep, whose safety they see as extending to themselves. The nurse is persuaded and lets the children go on about their happy business. This is a world in perfect harmony, where the voices of children are not just heard but listened to. The children's innocent understanding of the world is a virtue and not something from which they need to be protected. Blake decorated the poem with an illustration of children playing ring-around-the-rosy at sunset. Seated under a tree, the nurse watches over them.

The parallel poem in *Songs of Experience* is in startling contrast to *Songs of Innocence.* The accompanying illustration is of a woman standing over a boy, whose hair she is grooming. Behind them sits a girl, her head down, seemingly forlorn. Here, "Nurse's Song" reads,

When the voices of children are heard on the green
And whisp'rings are in the dale,
The days of my youth rise fresh in my mind,
My face turns green and pale.

Then come home my children, the sun is gone down,
And the dews of night arise;
Your spring & your day are wasted in play,
And your winter and night in disguise.

No children laugh, but some whisper in the dale. They do not want to be overheard by the nurse, whom they may fear or dis-

The Tyger

Tyger Tyger, burning bright,
In the forests of the night;
What immortal* hand or eye,
Could frame thy fearful symmetry?

In what distant deeps or skies,
Burnt the fire of thine eyes?
On what wings dare he aspire?
What the hand, dare sieze the fire?

And what shoulder, & what art,
Could twist the sinews of thy heart?
And when thy heart began to beat,
What dread hand? & what dread feet?

What the hammer? what the chain,
In what furnace was thy brain?
What the anvil?* what dread grasp,
Dare its deadly terrors clasp?

When the stars threw down their spears
And water'd heaven with their tears:
Did he smile his work to see?
Did he who made the Lamb make thee?

Tyger Tyger burning bright,
In the forests of the night:
What immortal hand or eye,
Dare frame thy fearful symmetry?

(*The Complete Writings of William Blake*)

*immortal not vulnerable to death

*anvil a block on which metal is hammered into shape

trust. Hearing the children, the nurse thinks of her own youth, thoughts that turn her green with envy and then pale as if frightened. Fearful, she calls the children home, warning them that their play is a waste of time. Their winter and night, which she can see because of her "experience" but they cannot, will inevitably come. There are now two worlds, that of children, who are no longer innocent but whisper and hide in the dale, and that of the nurse, the voice of experience, who uses fear to keep the children in line.

The lamb, the very soul of innocence, which is depicted as so delighting children in *Songs of Innocence,* has its contrast in the *Songs of Experience* in "The Tyger," Blake's most famous poem. It is a poem that asks fourteen questions with the force of a hammer striking an anvil, but no answers come. "Did he who made the Lamb make thee?" the poem asks. Because the songs show two "contrary states," Blake may expect the reader to answer yes, God made the innocent lamb *and* the tiger of "fearful symmetry." But this leads to another, more profound question: If God made both the good of innocence and the evil of experience, how can we reconcile the two?

The Marriage of Heaven and Hell

For Blake these contrary states, as he wrote in *The Marriage of Heaven and Hell,* are fundamental: "Without Contraries is no progression. Attraction and Repulsion, Reason and Energy, Love and Hate, are necessary to Human existence." But, he continued, "From these contraries spring what the religious call Good & Evil. Good is the passive that obeys Reason. Evil is the active springing from Energy." But Blake believed this conception of the contraries to be wrong. In teaching children to passively accept her authority, the nurse of experience robs them of their innocence and capacity for joy. The "religious" who, in Blake's view, meant to enslave humankind, had it backward. Good is not passive but active. "Energy," he wrote, "is eternal delight." He believed, as "the Tyger" suggests, that we are caught between contraries, and that they are not to be resolved but maintained and learned from.

> *"You never know what is enough unless you know what is more than enough."*

To instruct us, *The Marriage of Heaven and Hell* gives seventy "Proverbs of Hell." They begin, "In seed time learn, in harvest teach, in winter enjoy." As seeds grow into plants, so do we as humans learn. We teach others how to harvest. In the winter we enjoy what has come of our labors. The process of learning is thus a natural cycle. That seems clear enough, but then Blake continues: "Drive your cart and your plow over the bones of the dead"; "The road of excess leads to the palace of wisdom"; "The cut worm forgives the plow." These lines that sound like folk wisdom are brainteasers. Does Blake mean that we should not honor the dead? Must we follow the road of excess to gain wisdom? Why should the worm forgive the plow? Another proverb states, "You never know what is enough unless you know what is more than enough." This may be key. If we learn what is more than enough then we will know what is enough. The road of excess will have led to the palace of wisdom. But does Blake expect us to live by these proverbs?

Peter Ackroyd, author of an excellent biography of Blake, holds that in the proverbs Blake is both "playful and serious." This is helpful because in thinking about Good and Evil it is easy to lose our sense of humor and easy to assume that the poet who writes about such big subjects has no sense of humor of his own. Blake liked to go too far, to mock, and to challenge, to follow his imagination wherever it led. "The cistern* contains," runs another proverb, "the fountain overflows." He did not hold on to his visions but poured them forth. "Exuberance* is beauty" is another line in *The Marriage of Heaven and Hell,* and the twenty-six-year-old Blake who wrote this work was certainly exuberant. "Enough! or Too Much" is the last proverb. Coming at the end of the list, this is both a joke and a reminder to the reader that to learn what is enough or too much we must satisfy our curiosity. Whatever Blake means here, he is against moderation in all things. The proverbs urge us to follow no authority other than that of our own senses and imagination.

Prophetic Books

Blake elaborated his visions in his so-called prophetic books, which he worked on from 1789, when he completed *The Book of Thel,* until 1818, when he completed *Jerusalem.* He created these books in the same illuminated form as the *Songs of Innocence and of Experience.* Although Blake came to master the method he had invented, it still demanded enormous effort and painstaking care. To support himself and his wife, Catherine Boucher, whom he married in 1782, Blake made and sold engravings illustrating popular books, such as Edward Young's *Night Thoughts,* or produced engravings for the poems of his patron, William Hayley.

While many of Blake's most beautiful and powerful designs illustrate the prophetic books, the poems themselves are hard going. In them Blake created his own mythological figures. Urizen, Rintrah, Enitharmon, and the rest must be understood before the poems can be grasped, but theirs is a private world as difficult to enter as the *Songs of Innocence and of Experience* is easy. In these books Blake is often so inspired

*cistern a well or other large container used to store water

*exuberance energetic, flamboyant, or unreserved expression of emotion

that he goes beyond sense. His powerful vision becomes so dense that while readers can be carried away, it is just as easy for us to get lost. This is not poetry of beautiful lines or passages nor is Blake's vision easy to paraphrase. It is pure poetry best approached with the help of a guide like the critic Harold Bloom.

The Man Behind the Writing

At Blake's death on 12 August 1827 he was remembered as an artist and engraver. Peter Ackroyd writes that the world Blake lived in "distrusted and despised" the revolutionary and uncompromising vision of his poetry. Thus Blake's genius went unrecognized until a biography by Alexander Gilchrist appeared in 1863. By that time it was already difficult to reconstruct the details of Blake's life. We still do not know the order in which he wrote his poems, and of the years between 1810 and 1816 we have scant knowledge. The record is not rich in anecdotes,* but there are two that reveal the social and political radical Blake was.

One summer day in the early 1790s their friend Thomas Butts came to call on the Blakes. He found them in a small house in a garden behind their apartment. "Come in!" cried Blake; "it's only Adam and Eve, you know." They were naked, free from what Blake called "those troublesome disguises," so as to better read aloud Milton's *Paradise Lost,* an epic poem about the expulsion of Adam and Eve from the Garden of Eden. Blake probably believed the practice of nudity to be liberating.

In 1803 Blake moved out of London to nearby Felpham. There he quarreled with a soldier named John Scofield and threw him off his property. Scofield claimed that Blake had spoken against England's king and for the emperor of France, Napoleon Bonaparte, then England's enemy who threatened to invade the country. Blake was charged with sedition,* a charge he denied. After several anxious months Blake, who had no great respect for the king and may have made that clear to the soldier, stood trial. He was acquitted, but the incident illustrates both Blake's fiery temper and his strong political convictions.

If William Blake ever put his unique vision in a nutshell, he may have done so in the first four lines of "Auguries of Innocence":

*anecdote a short, true human interest story

In the Bible the Garden of Eden is the first home of Adam, the first man, and his wife, Eve. God, their creator, tells them they may live forever in the Garden but warns them not to eat the fruit from the tree of the knowledge of good and evil. They disobey God, and God banishes them from the Garden.

*sedition advocating rebellion against the government

To see a World in a Grain of Sand
And a Heaven in a Wild Flower,
Hold Infinity in the palm of your hand
And Eternity in an hour.
(The Complete Writings of William Blake)

Selected Bibliography

WORKS BY WILLIAM BLAKE
Poetry

Songs of Innocence and of Experience. Edited by Sir Geoffrey Keynes. New York: Orion Press, 1967. Includes helpful comments about each poem and provides an informative introduction.

Blake. Everyman's Library Pocket Poets. New York: Knopf, 1994. Concentrates on the *Songs* and Blake's shorter poems.

Letters

The Letters of William Blake. Edited by Geoffrey Keynes. Cambridge, Mass.: Harvard University Press, 1968. Contains several illustrations and a helpful preface.

Available Collections

The Complete Writings of William Blake. Edited by Geoffrey Keynes. London: Oxford University Press, 1966.

The Poetry and Prose of William Blake. Edited by David V. Erdman; commentary by Harold Bloom. Garden City, N.Y.: Doubleday, 1970. Bloom provides eighty pages of insightful commentary.

WORKS ABOUT WILLIAM BLAKE

Ackroyd, Peter. *Blake.* New York: Knopf, 1996.

Keynes, Geoffrey, ed. *William Blake: Poet Printer Prophet.* New York: Orion Press, 1964. This coffee-table book is an excellent introduction to Blake's designs. This well written, lively biography is the work of an Englishman who knows a great deal about the London of Blake's time.

IF YOU LIKE the poetry of Blake, you might also like the poetry of Allen Ginsberg. In the late 1940s Ginsberg had a vision in which Blake read to him the poem "Ah! Sun-flower" from *Songs of Experience.*

More About Blake:

You can find information about Blake on the Internet at:
http://jefferson.village.virginia.edu/blake
http://www.betatesters.com/penn/blake.htm

ANNE BRADSTREET

(1612–1672)

by Ange Mlinko

Anne Bradstreet was America's first poet. When she was still a teenager, she embarked on a historic journey from England to America aboard the *Arabella,* the same ship as John Winthrop, the future first governor of Massachusetts. She was in many ways an ordinary woman of her time, devoted to her parents, her husband, her eight children, and her God. But her emigration to America, coupled with the support of her intellectual family, inspired Bradstreet to write poetry—even though it was at that time considered a male pursuit.

    "I am obnoxious to each carping* tongue / Who says my hand a needle better fits" she declares in the prologue to her most ambitious work, the *Quaternion.* Given the example of the Greek muses,* as well as England's own Queen Elizabeth I, Bradstreet was conscious of defending the female intellect. Yet she also says that she is not looking for laurel bays (given as the highest poetic honor); she would be happy with "thyme or parsley" (common, easily obtained herbs). Bradstreet's combination of modesty and pride gives her poetry a very human appeal.

Quotations from Bradstreet's work throughout are taken from Hensley, *The Works of Anne Bradstreet.*

*carping naggingly critical

*muse In Greek mythology, the nine Muses are goddesses who preside over the arts, sciences, song, and poetry.

Migration to America

Anne Bradstreet was born Anne Dudley in Lincolnshire, England, in 1612. For the first eighteen years of her life she led a comfortable existence in an intellectual, middle-class Puritan* family. Her father, Thomas Dudley, encouraged Anne's education—and her Christian devotion. At sixteen, she married Simon Bradstreet; at eighteen, she and her family set sail for the Massachusetts Bay Colony. Puritans were settling there to escape the religious persecution of King Charles I.

Not everyone survived the journey across the rough Atlantic. Those who did survive faced the prospect of starvation and disease in the colonies, where settlers led a very difficult existence, building roads and houses in the wilderness. Their most basic necessities, like tools, seeds, and cloth, had to come from England. Massachusetts had hotter summers, and colder winters, than the settlers were used to.

Bradstreet's first known poem dates from these early years of struggle. "Upon a Fit of Sickness, Anno 1632," written when she was nineteen, commemorates an illness that seems to have brought her to the brink of death. Written in fourteeners,* the popular ballad* meter, the poem moves from the acceptance of death (since life is only "care and strife") to the realization that she will "live" after all in eternity with God. Her rebuke* of death, "thou envious foe" is like that in the English poet John Donne's "Death Be Not Proud": both Bradstreet and Donne rejected the literal meanings of "life" and "death," since, as Christians, they believed in another life, an afterlife, in which one never dies.

In "To My Dear Children," Bradstreet's most autobiographical* writing, she emphasizes how adversity—her difficult migration, ill health, a period of infertility—is necessary to her faith. Adversity also inspired her to write much of her poetry. Surviving disaster became an occasion for thanking God in verse. Hence, her works tend to end on an inspirational note; they are vindications* of religious faith.

Poetic Fathers

Bradstreet's faith and her poetry were both based on her love of cosmic order. Of her rejection of atheism,* she wrote:

---

*Puritan** a Protestant Christian who opposed the traditions and forms of the Church of England. Most Puritans opposed elaborate ceremony and church hierarchy, believing that God's will was directly revealed to individuals through Bible reading. Puritans believed that only a few "elect" were chosen in advance by God for heaven.

*fourteener** a verse consisting of fourteen syllables (seven iambic feet)

*ballad** rhythmic poem that tells a story and is often meant to be sung

*rebuke** a reprimand or scolding

*autobiographical** related to the author's own life

*vindication** a justification or defense

*atheism** disbelief in the existence of God

That there is a God my reason would soon tell me by the wondrous works that I see, the vast frame of heaven and the earth, the order of all things, night and day, summer and winter, spring and autumn, the daily providing for this great household upon the earth, the preserving and directing of all to its proper end. ("To My Dear Children")

Her first poetic project, the *Quaternion,* testifies to this sheer wonder. Its five sections are "The Four Elements," "The Four Humours of Man," "Of the Four Ages," "The Four Seasons," and "The Four Monarchies"—long poems that attempt to give textbook histories of their subjects. She was inspired by the works of a French Calvinist,* Guillaume du Bartas, whose long poem—translated as *The Divine Weekes and Workes*— described the creation of the universe. Drawing from an ancient Greek view that held that God is at the center of the universe and all his works descend in rank to the tiniest organisms (a concept called the Great Chain of Being), Bradstreet took great pleasure in the task of fleshing out this orderly universe in orderly verse. As her biographer Elizabeth Wade White points out, she was the first English woman to write verse based on the scientific theories of her time.

*Calvinist a follower of the doctrines of John Calvin, who believed that God is present everywhere and that sinners could achieve salvation through the grace of God

Bradstreet's first muse was Thomas Dudley, her father, to whom she dedicated *Quaternion*: "From her that to yourself more duty owes / Than water in the boundless ocean flows." Dudley was a stern Puritan patriarch who supported his family during migration and hardship; he eventually rose to become the second governor of Massachusetts. The Dudleys and the Bradstreets were two of the most powerful families in New England. It was as an apprentice* and a daughter that Bradstreet wrote her early verse. She would later write her strongest work as a creator-mother.

*apprentice one who is learning the skills of a trade through hands-on experience

How Her First Book Was Published

It was common practice for a poet to write for a small audience, circulating manuscripts among friends. This is what Anne Bradstreet did until her poems were taken, without her knowledge, to a printer in England and published as *The Tenth Muse Lately Sprung Up in America*. It was the first book of poetry by an American. Imagine Bradstreet's shock when her brother-in-law, John Woodbridge, returned from England with copies of her poems in print! In the front of the book was a group of "testimonials," or what we call blurbs, celebrating the skill and wisdom to be found in its pages. Woodbridge, who was responsible for the publication (probably with the approval of Bradstreet's father and husband) wrote a personal introduction:

> **It is the work of a woman, honoured, and esteemed where she lives, for her gracious demeanor, her eminent parts, her pious conversation, her courteous disposition, her exact diligence in her place, and discreet managing of her family occasions, and more than so, these poems are the fruit but of some few hours, curtailed from her sleep, and other refreshments. ("Epistle to the Reader by John Woodbridge")**

An amazing woman emerges from Woodbridge's portrait. Considering that she was the mother of eight, manager of a household, and wife of a prominent man, it is striking that she had the energy to compose poetry in stolen moments. Considering that she was also "gracious," "pious," "courteous," and "discreet," it is perhaps even more striking that she had the drive to accomplish so much in what was considered a masculine realm. If there is any doubt that her ambition was unusual, look again at Woodbridge's preface, where he worries that the excellence of her poetry will make readers doubt that a woman could have written it. His response to this is to assure the audience that he is personally acquainted with the author and can vouch for her honor and respectability. She may be gifted, he implies, but she is not a threat to the social order.

The fragility of life in New England required that individuals put the community's needs above their own. But paradoxically, the New World held out the promise of a new life, new customs, new opportunities, and women were not immune from these yearnings. One woman, Anne Hutchinson, was branded a heretic* and exiled* for leading enthusiastic prayer meetings (Bradstreet's father was a judge at the trial). Another woman, Anne Bradstreet's own sister, Sarah, was divorced amid accusations of "preaching" and sexual looseness. Bradstreet would not have dreamed of putting these events into a poem, but she was probably troubled by these women's predicaments, since she herself came dangerously

*****heretic** someone whose opinions go against official church doctrine

*****exiled** forced to leave one's homeland

close to nonconformity just by putting pen to paper. Maybe Bradstreet's own boldness in writing was the product of that same sense of liberation, at the edge of the vast American wilderness.

In "The Author to Her Book," Bradstreet expresses dismay, acceptance, and finally affection for the book that launched her modest fame. She calls it "thou ill-formed offspring of my feeble brain" and "my rambling brat," establishing her relation to it as that of an exasperated mother. She is painfully aware of its flaws but must resign herself to letting it go out into the world, like a child who must find its own way. Bradstreet was thirty-eight when the book was published; never again did she plan such a grand project as the *Quaternion*. Maybe having officially published something made it possible for her to write more freely about matters closest to her heart—husband, children, God.

Prayers Against Disaster

Anne Bradstreet's later poems deal directly with loss and fear of loss: a fire that destroyed her home in 1666, the death of her parents and grandchildren, and the absences of her husband and sons on business. People of that time were much more intimate with the realities of death than we are now: illnesses came and went without explanation; infant mortality was high; women died during labor as a matter of course. If Anne's husband, Simon, were to perish on a transatlantic journey, the news would take months to reach his family. The many poems to Simon depict a happy marriage shadowed by the knowledge that death could come without warning. In "Before the Birth of One of Her Children," she begs him to remember her if she dies: "And when thou feel'st no grief, as I no harms, / Yet love thy dead, who long lay in thine arms." Her additional request that he protect their children from "stepdame's* injury" displays a touch of jealousy that moves the poem beyond formal grandeur to raw emotion.

*stepdame stepmother

In two poems about Simon's absence, she compares him to the sun that physically leaves her but never sets in her heart:

> O strange effect! now thou art southward gone,
> I weary grow the tedious day so long;

*Cancer in astrology, the sixth house of the zodiac, which represents domesticity and the home, and is where the summer solstice occurs

But when thou northward to me shalt return,
I wish my sun may never set, but burn
Within the Cancer* of my glowing breast,
The welcome house of him my dearest guest.
Where ever, ever stay, and go not thence,
Till nature's sad decree shall call thee hence;
Flesh of thy flesh, bone of thy bone,
I here, thou there, yet both but one.

"A Letter to Her Husband, Absent
Upon Public Employment"

In causing this metaphorical and unnatural winter, Simon's absence throws all of nature off balance. In another poem on the same theme, she compares herself to a deer, a dove, and a mullet* that have lost the will to live without their mates. These poems contrast sharply with another set of poems in which Bradstreet entrusts her husband's soul to God. The religious poems are a little less powerful, because she represses her fears for the sake of faith, but occasionally their reserved simplicity is very moving:

*mullet a kind of fish

Into Thy everlasting arms
Of mercy I commend
Thy servant, Lord. Keep and preserve
My husband, my dear friend.

"Upon My Dear and Loving Husband
His Going into England Jan. 16, 1661"

But when Bradstreet's poems allow grief to be fully expressed, their poetic beauty is stronger, as in "In Memory of My Dear Grandchild Elizabeth Bradstreet, who Deceased August, 1665, Being a Year and a Half Old." There, her mention of God is surprisingly ambivalent* as the "hand alone that guides nature and fate." In another poem on the death of a grandchild, there is greater comfort derived from a "Saviour," but less art.

*ambivalent uncertain or indecisive; being of two minds about something

Bradstreet expresses the complexity of her feelings in "Upon the Burning of Our House July 10, 1666." In the same breath as she praises the God who gives and takes away, she allows a glint of anger to emerge. For a moment, her humility almost seethes. She knows she should take comfort in her heavenly home with God—and she does—but not without distinctly swallowing her earthly pride. The family library—consisting of eight hundred precious books—was lost in that fire.

The Author to Her Book

Thou ill-formed offspring of my feeble brain,
Who after birth didst by my side remain,
Till snatched from thence by friends, less wise than true,
Who thee abroad, exposed to public view,
Made thee in rags, halting to th' press to trudge,
Where errors were not lessened (all may judge).
At thy return my blushing was not small,
My rambling brat (in print) should mother call,
I cast thee by as one unfit for light,
Thy visage* was so irksome in my sight;
Yet being mine own, at length affection would
Thy blemishes amend, if so I could:
I washed thy face, but more defects I saw,
And rubbing off a spot still made a flaw.
I stretched thy joints to make thee even feet,
Yet still thou run'st more hobbling than is meet;
In better dress to trim thee was my mind,
But nought save homespun cloth i' th' house I find.
In this array 'mongst vulgars may'st thou roam.
In critic's hands beware thou dost not come,
And take thy way where yet thou art not known;
If for thy father asked, say thou hadst none;
And for thy mother, she alas is poor,
Which caused her thus to send thee out of door.

*visage face

Since the single biggest event of her life had been her emigration to America, it was natural for her to use homelessness (or homesickness) as a metaphor, even before the fire. In a series of prose meditations,* written for her children, she emphasizes:

*meditation an essay or passage expressing the author's thinking or guiding the reader's thought

> We must, therefore, be here as strangers and pilgrims, that we may plainly declare that we seek a city above and wait all the days of our appointed time till our change shall come. (*Meditations Divine and Moral*, number 53)

In yet another poem, "Contemplations," Bradstreet considers the natural beauty of a New England autumn and is so carried away in the beginning that she can almost understand why trees were considered gods by pagans.* But by the end of the poem, she compares humans to sailors who long for a port

*pagan someone who does not accept the biblical God as the one and only god; a heathen

but cannot find security anywhere except in the thought of heaven.

Poetry and Motherhood

One of Bradstreet's most delightful poems, "In Reference to Her Children, 23 June 1659," is an allegory* of her life as a mother bird whose chicks are already leaving the nest. The tone of the poem is buoyant,* and we should not forget that it was rare for a mother to have eight pregnancies result in eight grown children. She is blunt about her fears for her children and her determination to protect them, but the poem's first striking note is tenderness: "I had eight birds hatched in one nest, / Four cocks there were, and hens the rest." As she goes on to describe the ones that grew up and flew away, she confesses that she continues to worry about their well-being. "O to your safety have an eye!" she begs them, now that she cannot look after them herself. The poem grows more and more beautiful as it goes on, ending with a vision of an aging Bradstreet as a bird singing on its branch ("my age I will not once lament") until finally the bird joins the angels in an everlasting springtime. Meanwhile, on earth, her little brood cares for their own little broods, remembering the example of their mother:

> In chirping language, oft them tell,
> You had a dam* that loved you well,
> That did what could be done for young,
> And nursed you up till you were strong,
> And 'fore she once would let you fly,
> She showed you joy and misery;
> Taught what was good, and what was ill,
> What would save life, and what would kill.
> Thus gone, amongst you I may live,
> And dead, yet speak, and counsel give:
> Farewell my birds, farewell adieu,
> I happy am, if well with you.
> "In Reference to Her Children, 23 June 1659"

The way that these lines mingle dignity and simplicity, tenderness and power, is what makes them so interesting 350 years

*allegory a story in which the fictional objects, characters, and actions are equated with meanings that lie outside the narrative itself

*buoyant cheerful; light

*dam a shortened version of the word "dame," which in this poem is used to mean mother

later. That they were written by a mother makes them rare in the history of English literature.

Bradstreet died at age sixty after a wasting illness. She was cared for to the end by her loving family. Her poems continue to be reprinted. In 1956 the American poet John Berryman wrote his *Homage to Mistress Bradstreet.* Berryman, who found his own life and times difficult, took inspiration from her fortitude* in continuing to write while enduring hardship. His poem creates a dialogue between the poets, the highest compliment that could be paid to Anne Bradstreet.

*__fortitude__ strength and determination

Selected Bibliography

WORKS BY ANNE BRADSTREET
Poetry and Prose

The Tenth Muse, Lately Sprung Up in America (1650).

Several Poems (1678).

Available Collections

The Tenth Muse and, from the Manuscripts, Meditations Divine and Morall Together with Letters and Occasional Pieces. Gainesville, Fla.: Scholars' Facsimiles and Reprints, 1965.

The Works of Anne Bradstreet. Edited by Jeannine Hensley. Cambridge, Mass.: The Belknap Press of Harvard University Press, 1967.

WORKS ABOUT ANNE BRADSTREET

Berryman, John. *Homage to Mistress Bradstreet.* New York: Farrar Straus and Giroux, 1956.

Caldwell, Patricia. "Why Our First Poet Was a Woman: Bradstreet and the Birth of an American Poetic Voice." *Prospects: An Annual Journal of American Cultural Studies*: 13 (1988): 1–35.

Cowell, Pattie, and Ann Stanford, eds. *Critical Essays on Anne Bradstreet.* Boston: G. K. Hall, 1983.

Hensley, Jeannine. "Anne Bradstreet's Wreath of Thyme." In *The Works of Anne Bradstreet.* Cambridge, Mass.: The Belknap Press of Harvard University Press, 1967.

Rich, Adrienne. "Anne Bradstreet and Her Poetry." In *The Works of Anne Bradstreet*. Cambridge, Mass.: The Belknap Press of Harvard University Press, 1967.

Rosenmeier, Rosamond. *Anne Bradstreet Revisited*. Boston: G. K. Hall, 1991.

White, Elizabeth Wade. *Anne Bradstreet: The Tenth Muse*. New York: Oxford University Press, 1971.

ANDRÉ BRETON
(1896–1966)

by Mark Polizzotti

Among the more curious aspects of André Breton's life is the fact that for nearly fifty years his existence and that of the surrealist movement he founded were virtually one and the same. "No one can deny that my life has formed one body [with surrealism]," he told an interviewer in 1952 (*Conversations,* p. 177). Not only did Breton try, with varying degrees of success, to act according to surrealism's principles, but the episodes of his personal life often merged into, even powered, the more public events of the surrealist group.

The surrealist movement, at its height during the 1920s and 1930s, aimed to express the workings of the unconscious or subconscious mind.

Early Influences

We can trace many of the recurring themes of Breton's life—his belief in the revolutionary power of poetry, his need for collective activity, his fierce opposition to religion and bourgeois* values, as well as his stubborn, often bossy personality—back to his childhood. André Breton was born in Tinchebray (Normandy), France, on 19 February 1896 and grew up in

*bourgeois relating to the middle class

hermetic very difficult to understand, as if sealed up

the working-class suburbs of Paris. His father, Louis, an ex-policeman, provided a relatively affectionate presence, but his mother, Marguerite, showed almost no love or warmth toward her only son. Still, it was from his mother that Breton got most of his attitudes, if only by opposition. Marguerite was rigidly Catholic and preoccupied with social standing and she considered the arts a waste of time. As a child, Breton was forbidden to play outside with other children—which no doubt fostered his lifelong need to be surrounded by a group as well as his sense that the street was his "true element," where he "could test like nowhere else the winds of possibility" (*Les pas perdus, Lost Steps,* p. 4). Instead, he turned to adventure stories, tales of the supernatural, and, in his adolescence, poetry, especially the hermetic* sonnets of the French poet Stéphane Mallarmé.

Some of Breton's earliest and most important friendships, in fact, were with poets, most notably Paul Valéry, Guillaume Apollinaire (who coined the term surrealism), and Pierre Reverdy. All three were older than Breton and were beginning to establish their reputations; they encouraged him in his literary interests (despite his mother's prohibition) and helped get his early poems published in magazines. Like Mallarmé's poems, these early verses were often obscure and complex, as in this example from 1913:

laureled crowned with leaves, an honor in Roman times

> Merry, and so imprudently laureled*
> With youth that a hastening fawn would enlace
> This Nymph on the rocks who the soul (If not depict
> Did I at least catch her on the blue of some forest edge)
> "Merry"

Breton's most important friendship from this period, however, was with a young rebel named Jacques Vaché, who laughed at poetry and everything else Breton loved. The two young men met during World War I, when Breton, forced by his parents to study medicine, was serving as an intern in the army hospital where Vaché was recovering from a leg wound. Vaché seemed to know as much about poetry as Breton, but he refused to share his friend's enthusiasm for it. The one literary creation he claimed to like was the French writer André Gide's antihero* Lafcadio (from *Lafcadio's Adventures*), "because he doesn't read and his only products are amusing experiments—such as Murder" (Vaché to Breton, 18 August 1917; in *Four Dada Suicides*).

antihero a main character who lacks heroic qualities

Vaché's personality was a mix of distant reserve and flamboyant outrageousness. He would go to a movie theater and nonchalantly begin spreading out a full picnic lunch or walk around town in a homemade uniform that was half-French and half-German. One time Breton found him at a theatrical premiere, threatening to shoot the audience with his pistol because he did not like the play. Once back at the front, Vaché sent Breton a series of letters in which he tried to define the concept he called "umor": "I believe it is a sensation—I almost said a SENSE—that too—of the theatrical (and joyless) pointlessness of everything" (Vaché to Breton, 29 April 1917). His death from a drug overdose in January 1919 left Breton with a sense of loss from which he never recovered. "If not for him, I might have become a poet," Breton later eulogized. "He overcame in me the conspiracy of dark forces that makes one believe he can have anything as absurd as a vocation" (*Lost Steps,* p. 2).

The Dada Period

Although Breton's literary ambitions had been put in doubt, he nonetheless continued to write poetry, publishing his first book of verse, *Mont de piété* (*Pawnshop*), in 1919. Rather than composing traditional poems, however, he was now experimenting with new forms, such as using newspaper clippings and scraps of other people's verse to produce a new text (a literary adaptation of the collage technique in art, in which bits of existing images are glued together to form a new image). In one of these, "Counterfeit Coin," Breton reworked an early stanza of his own into a fine piece of absurdity.

At around this time, he also met the writers and artists who would later form the core of the surrealist movement, notably the poets Philippe Soupault, Louis Aragon, and Paul Éluard. These young men had felt sickened by the war and were in revolt against the society that had allowed it to happen—and even more so against the prominent writers who had supported it. Rather than build literary careers as their elders had, they tried to expand poetry, take it to the streets, and use it as a vehicle to "transform the world," in the words of Karl Marx, regarded as the founder of socialism.

Their first chance came in 1920, when they joined the Dada movement. Dada had been founded in Zurich, Switzerland, during the war by a group of refugee artists and writers;

Counterfeit Coin (excerpt)

From the vase of crystal made in Bohemia
From the vase of cry
From the vase of cry
From the vase of
Of crystal
From the vase of crystal made in Bohemia
Bohemia
Bohemia
Hem hem yes Bohemia
From the vase of crystal made in Bo Bo

(Earthlight)

---

*tract a printed political statement, usually containing strong or extreme opinions

*prose poem a poem that is not divided into lines and that does not have rhyme and meter

its aim was to remove art completely from the bonds of logic. "The beginnings of Dada were not the beginnings of an art, but those of a disgust," wrote the group's leader, the Romanian poet Tristan Tzara. "Disgust with the magnificence of philosophers who for 3,000 years have been explaining everything to us" (*Seven Dada Manifestos and Lampisteries,* p. 112). After the war, Tzara brought Dada to Paris, where he was eagerly joined by Breton and friends. They published magazines and tracts* filled with insults for traditional French values and staged wilfully absurd "demonstrations" that left audiences howling in fury. For two years, Breton joined in these demonstrations, enjoying their shock value, but eventually he fell out with Tzara, judging that Dada had "stagnated" (*Conversations,* p. 51).

In the meantime, Breton and his friends experimented with automatic writing, or writing practiced without any conscious guidance. In 1919, inspired by the dream analyses of Sigmund Freud, the founder of modern psychoanalysis, he and Soupault composed the first automatic book, *Les champs magnétiques* (*The Magnetic Fields*), seeking a new voice that would capture the language of dreams and the unconscious. One of Breton's prose poems* from it, "Eclipses," begins "The color of the fabulous salvations darkened until the slightest death-rattle: calm of relative sighs. Despite the smell of milk and coagulated blood, the circus of leaps is full of melancholy seconds" (*Magnetic Fields,* p. 39). In 1924, he made automatic writing the cornerstone of the movement he called surrealism, which he defined as "psychic automatism in its pure state, by which one proposes to express . . . the actual functioning of thought . . . in the absence of any control exercised by reason, exempt from any aesthetic or moral concern" (*Manifestoes of Surrealism,* p. 26).

The Surrealist Revolution

The surrealists attracted public outrage from the outset: they published a broadside* mocking the death of a nationally beloved novelist, disrupted banquets by swinging from the chandeliers, advocated suicide, and pledged their support to the recently founded, and very unpopular, French Communist Party. For Breton, these provocations had a serious aim: surrealism was meant to be not just a literary movement but a way of changing the way people lived and thought. Scandals, political involvement, and even the group's daily meetings around a café table were all part of the public presence Breton wanted it to have.

broadside a large sheet of paper with printing on one or both sides

In this light, even such "interior" activities as automatic writing were given a more external cast. In *Manifeste du surréalisme,* his first surrealist manifesto, Breton pointed out that such writing was within everyone's reach and that anyone could, and would, benefit from tuning in to his or her own unconscious or from studying such irrational manifestations as dreams and insanity. Only in this way, he argued, would people achieve a true revolution and finally do away with the logic and reason that had imprisoned Western thought since the time of the ancient Greeks. "Language has been given to man so that he may make Surrealist use of it," he proclaimed (*Manifestoes of Surrealism,* p. 32).

From the start, Breton was acknowledged as the group's undisputed leader. Not only had he best formulated its principles, but his great personal charisma* managed to hold together some of the most radical minds of the twentieth century, among them the writers Antonin Artaud, Georges Bataille, Michel Leiris, Jacques Prévert, and Raymond Queneau; the artists Leonora Carrington, Salvador Dalí, Marcel Duchamp, Max Ernst, Man Ray, and Yves Tanguy; and the filmmaker Luis Buñuel. The group "loved Breton like a woman," Prévert later recalled, and one historian wrote that "those who enjoyed the moments of his unforgettable friendship . . . were ready to sacrifice everything to him: wives, mistresses, friends" (Nadeau, p. 86).

charisma charm; the ability to draw others to oneself

Love and Other Matters

One of the constants of surrealism was the belief in a single, exclusive passion or "predestined love," though for many surrealists this was more theoretical than real. Breton himself, while never an advocate of promiscuity, was married three times and had a dozen lovers in the course of his life. In nearly every case, he looked to outer signs to show him that the woman in question was, at last, his one predestined lover.

For example, his most famous book, *Nadja,* tells of his meeting in 1926 with a strange and beguiling* young woman and of the ways in which "marvelous chance" reveals life's deeper meaning. In the book (which is based on real events), Breton describes Nadja's unconventional and often disturbing ways of acting, speaking, and living, celebrating her as "the extreme limit of the Surrealist aspiration" (*Nadja,* p. 74). But her true importance for Breton comes in the final section, which is addressed to an unidentified woman (Suzanne Muzard) with whom he has fallen in love. In this section, Nadja becomes the harbinger* of his meeting with Suzanne—all the more so since Breton actually met Suzanne *because* she read the unfinished manuscript of *Nadja.*

Several years later, in May 1934, Breton had a similar experience with the artist Jacqueline Lamba, who became his second wife. In his book *L'Amour fou* (*Mad Love*), he describes the couple's first midnight stroll through the market stalls of Les Halles* and his rediscovery the next day of a forgotten early poem ("Sunflower") that predicted their meeting in remarkable detail:

> The traveler who passed through Les Halles as summer
>   fell
> Walked on her tiptoes
>
> . . . .
>
> A farm prospered in the middle of Paris
>
> > (*Earthlight,* p. 76)

To Breton's mind, these near-mystical coincidences endowed poetry with almost supernatural power, elevating it far above mere "literature."

Just as Breton's love affairs were magnified in his books, so they also had an outsized impact on events in the surrealist group. In 1929, for example, during an especially bitter phase in his romantic relations, he wrote his most vitriolic* work, the

*__beguiling__ mysterious; charmingly deceitful

*__harbinger__ pioneer, precursor

*__Les Halles__ municipal food market of Paris, filled with farmers' and wholesalers' stalls under large cast-iron and glass pavilions

*__vitriolic__ bitter; stinging; harsh

Second manifeste du surréalisme (Second Manifesto of Surrealism), in which he reversed many of the movement's earlier positions. He also violently rejected a number of his old friends for a variety of supposed failings—for instance, wasting their talents on such ordinary pursuits as earning a living. Breton's position was sincere: he rejected the idea that labor is noble, preferring to remain available to life's surprises rather than bury himself in a steady job. "There is no use being alive if one must work," he had written in *Nadja.* "The event from which each of us is entitled to expect the revelation of his own life's meaning . . . *is not earned by work*" (p. 60). At the same time, the rage behind his words and actions that year had as much to do with his troubled love life as it did with his principles.

Given Breton's attitude toward work, it seems almost a contradiction that he spent ten years trying to join forces with the French Communist Party (PCF). It is just that his understanding of politics was a poet's understanding, not a politician's. As Breton saw it, the Communists were fervent revolutionaries who would sweep away the rot of bourgeois values, and he did his best to ignore the grittier aspects of their program, such as wage disputes and political maneuvering. The Communists, for their part, considered the surrealists a bunch of intellectual dilettantes* and refused their offers of help. Finally, after one too many rejections, Breton broke with the PCF in 1935.

*dilettante someone who has a superficial interest in art

He did not entirely abandon politics, however. Disgusted by the PCF, he turned toward the political thinker Leon Trotsky, who opposed the Soviet leader, Joseph Stalin, and was then living in exile in Mexico. In 1938, Breton and Jacqueline Lamba spent three months with Trotsky in Mexico City, where the two men drafted Breton's most overtly political manifesto, "For an Independent Revolutionary Art"; they also laid the groundwork for a political action group that Breton tried to launch when he returned to Paris. But the outbreak of World War II in 1939 put an end to these plans.

Exile

After Paris fell to the Nazis in June 1940, Breton, Jacqueline, and their young daughter, Aube, fled with other refugees to Marseille and from there to New York. While in Marseille, Breton completed his *Anthologie de l'humour noir* (*Anthology of*

Black Humor), based on Jacques Vaché's "joyless and point-less" concept of "umor," but the book, scheduled for publication on the day that the Germans entered Paris, was banned by the Occupation government. He also wrote his longest poem, "Fata Morgana," a song of love for his wife and faith in an eventual victory over Nazi oppression—but this, too, was banned.

Arriving in New York in June 1941, Breton tried to reconstitute the surrealist group with his fellow refugees, including Tanguy, Duchamp, Ernst, and the anthropologist Claude Lévi-Strauss. But he felt disoriented by the frenetic pace of New York and cut off from his beloved Paris, and his attempts to "implant" surrealism in America were largely unsuccessful. During this time, he supported his family (in a rare concession to financial need) by working as an announcer at Voice of America radio—his one condition being that he would read no news items about religion or the pope.

Under the strain of exile, Breton's marriage to Jacqueline fell apart in 1942. The following year, he met Chilean-born Elisa Claro, whom he married in 1945. His book *Arcane 17* (*Arcanum 17*), written in Canada just after the liberation of Paris, compares the rebirth that Elisa had brought to his life with the political rebirth promised by the Nazi defeat.

Exile's Return

When Breton returned to Paris in spring 1946, he found it difficult to pick up where he had left off. For most Europeans, surrealism had died in 1939, and new intellectual currents, such as existentialism (a philosophy concerned with issues of choice and responsibility in human existence) seemed much more relevant to the postwar world. As for Breton's former friends, they were too busy with their own concerns to rejoin him.

Breton did his best to keep surrealism alive through the 1950s and 1960s, however, recruiting new members from the younger generation—many of whom had not even been born when the movement was founded. He maintained the daily café meetings, championed various political causes, and organized several exhibits of surrealist art. He also promoted Native American culture, which he and Elisa had discovered during a trip to Arizona, as well as the theories of the philosopher Charles Fourier, who was an early proponent of communal living and free love. And he continued to write and publish, notably a volume of collected poems in 1948 and a book of interviews in 1952. But his days as a significant intellectual presence were largely over, and by this point he had become something he despised: a grand old man of letters, widely respected but rarely heeded.

Breton died on 28 September 1966, at the age of seventy. Since then, surrealism's ideas and visual innovations have become commonplace in many aspects of daily life, from advertising to fashion design—something of which Breton, had he lived to see it, would not have approved. On the other hand, he would have been gratified by the French student riots of May 1968, when phrases from several of his works were spray-painted as slogans on the walls of Paris buildings.

Selected Bibliography

WORKS BY ANDRÉ BRETON
Poetry in French

Mont de piété (1919).

Les champs magnétiques (with Philippe Soupault) (1920).

Clair de terre (1923).

L'Immaculée conception (with Paul Éluard) (1930).

Ralentir travaux (with René Char and Paul Éluard) (1930).

Le Revolver aux chevaux blancs (1932).

Ode à Charles Fourier (1947).

Poèmes (1948).

Prose in French

Manifeste du surréalisme (1924).

Les pas perdus (1924).

Nadja (1928).

Le surréalisme et le peinture (1928).

Second manifeste du surréalisme (1930).

L'Amour fou (1937).

Anthologie de l'humour noir (1940).

Arcane 17 (1944).

IF YOU LIKE the poetry of Breton, you might also like the poetry of Guillaume Apollinaire or Arthur Rimbaud.

Poetry in English Translation

The Immaculate Conception (with Paul Éluard). Translated by Jon Graham. London: Atlas Press, 1990.

The Magnetic Fields (with Philippe Soupault). Translated by David Gascoyne. London: Atlas Press, 1985.

Ode to Charles Fourier. Translated by Kenneth White. New York: Grossman, 1970.

Ralentir travaux (with René Char and Paul Éluard). Translated by Keith Waldrop. Cambridge, Mass.: Exact Change, 1990.

Young Cherry Trees Secured Against Hares. Translated by Edouard Roditi. New York: View Editions, 1946; new ed., Ann Arbor, Mich., 1969.

Available Collections

Anthology of Black Humor. Translated by Mark Polizzotti. San Francisco: City Lights Books, 1997.

Arcanum 17. Translated by Zack Rogow. Los Angeles: Sun and Moon Press, 1994.

Break of Day. Translated by Mary Ann Caws and Mark Polizzotti. Lincoln: University of Nebraska Press, 1999. Essays.

Communicating Vessels. Translated by Mary Ann Caws and Geoffrey T. Harris. Lincoln: University of Nebraska Press, 1990. An autobiographical "sequel" to *Nadja.*

Conversations: The Autobiography of Surrealism. Translated by Mark Polizzotti. New York: Marlowe, 1995. Radio interviews.

Earthlight. Translated by Bill Zavatsky and Zack Rogow. Los Angeles: Sun and Moon Press, 1993.

The Lost Steps. Translated by Mark Polizzotti. Lincoln: University of Nebraska Press, 1996. Essays.

Mad Love. Translated by Mary Ann Caws. Lincoln: University of Nebraska Press, 1987.

Manifestoes of Surrealism. Translated by Richard Seaver and Helen R. Lane. Ann Arbor: University of Michigan Press, 1969.

My Heart Through Which Her Heart Has Passed: Poems of Love and Desperation. Translated by Mark Polizzotti. Paris and London: Alyscamps Press, 1998.

Nadja. Translated by Richard Howard. New York: Grove Press, 1960.

Poems of André Breton. Edited and translated by Jean-Pierre Cauvin and Mary Ann Caws. Austin: University of Texas Press, 1982.

Selected Poems. Translated by Kenneth White. London: Jonathan Cape, 1969.

Surrealism and Painting. Translated by Simon Watson Taylor. New York: Harper and Row, 1972. Art criticism.

What Is Surrealism? Selected Writings. Edited by Franklin Rosemont. New York: Monad Press, 1978.

WORKS ABOUT ANDRÉ BRETON AND SURREALISM

Aragon, Louis. *Paris Peasant.* Translated by Simon Watson Taylor. Boston: Exact Change, 1994.

Artaud, Antonin. *Selected Writings.* Edited by Susan Sontag and translated by Helen Weaver. New York: Farrar, Straus and Giroux, 1976.

Balakian, Anna. *André Breton: Magus of Surrealism.* New York: Oxford University Press, 1971.

Caws, Mary Ann. *André Breton,* rev. ed. New York: Twayne, 1996.

Caws, Mary Ann. *The Poetry of Dada and Surrealism: Aragon, Breton, Tzara, Éluard, and Desnos.* Princeton, N.J.: Princeton University Press, 1971.

Chénieux-Gendron, Jacqueline. *Surrealism.* Translated by Vivian Folkenflik. New York: Columbia University Press, 1990.

Éluard, Paul. *Letters to Gala.* Translated by Jesse Browner. New York: Paragon House, 1989.

Geshman, Herbert. *The Surrealist Revolution in France.* Ann Arbor: University of Michigan Press, 1968.

Hale, Terry, Paul Lenti, and Ian White, trans. *4 Dada Suicides: Selected Texts of Arthur Cravan, Jacques Rigaut, Julien Torma and Jacques Vaché.* London: Atlas Press, 1995. Includes the complete text of Vaché's "war letters" to Breton.

Lautréamont. *Maldoror and the Complete Works.* Translated by Alexis Lykiard. Boston: Exact Change, 1994.

Levy, Julien, ed. *Surrealism.* New York: Da Capo Press, 1995.

Matthews, J. H. *An Introduction to Surrealism.* University Park: Pennsylvania State University Press, 1965.

Nadeau, Maurice. *The History of Surrealism.* Translated by Richard Howard. Cambridge, Mass.: Harvard University Press, 1989.

Polizzotti, Mark. *Revolution of the Mind: The Life of André Breton.* New York: Farrar, Straus and Giroux, 1995.

Sawin, Martica. *Surrealism in Exile and the Beginning of the New York School.* Cambridge, Mass.: MIT Press, 1995.

Tashjian, Dickran. *A Boatload of Madmen.* New York: Thames and Hudson, 1995.

Thirion, André. *Revolutionaries Without a Revolution.* Translated by Joachim Neugroschel. New York: Macmillan, 1975.

Tzara, Tristan. *Seven Dada Manifestos and Lampisteries.* Translated by Barbara Wright. London: John Calder, 1977.

GWENDOLYN BROOKS

(b. 1917)

by Connie Deanovich

Gwendolyn Brooks writes poetry that looks you in the eye. When you read one of her poems you are confronted. A poem from *Children Coming Home* called "Song: White Powder (Al)" places you, the reader, in the shoes of a young person, Al, who pays the price for not joining in with the neighborhood drug dealers:

> They want me to take the white powder.
> I won't, so they beat me.
>
> They want me to deal the white powder.
> I won't, so they beat me.
>
> They tell me I'll hot-pile the Money.
> They tell me my Power will roll.
> They tell me I'll rule my own runners.
> I'll be Mighty. I'll be
> IN CONTROL.

When I say "Hot at eleven, cold before twelve"
they beat me.

"Hot at eleven, cold before twelve" is an image of death. Although a person who "deals" "white powder" might have it made for a short time, soon he or she will be a cold corpse. This is Brooks's chilling warning. Slang, such as the word "hot-pile" and the phrase "They tell me my Power will roll," adds to the authenticity of the speech used in the poem, creating vivid characters that make the poem come to life. Brooks's achievement as a poet comes from a combination of strong subject matter and a mastery of language that draws readers in close.

Who Is Gwendolyn Brooks?

Brooks was the first African American to receive the Pulitzer Prize (in 1950). The prestigious award was given for her second book, *Annie Allen.* She was honored in 1968 by being named Illinois's poet laureate.* What further distinguishes her writing is that as a whole, it explores what it was like to be black and living in urban America during the entire second half of the twentieth century.

*poet laureate in England, an outstanding poet once appointed as a paid member of the royal household and expected to write poems for certain national occasions. In other countries, the term refers to a poet honored and recognized for his or her achievements.

For most of her life, Brooks lived in Chicago, though she was born in Topeka, Kansas, on 17 June 1917. Brooks attended Englewood High School and Wilson Junior College in Chicago. She received more than seventy honorary degrees and taught at numerous colleges around the country. She was a Consultant in Poetry to the Library of Congress in 1985 (the equivalent of poet laureate) and has her name engraved on the Illinois State Library in Springfield, the capital city. Her poetry has been recognized worldwide. In 1990 she became the first American recipient of the Society for Literature Award, given by the University of Thessaloniki in Athens, Greece. Besides her Pulitzer Prize, she has received numerous other awards, including two Guggenheim Fellowships and the National Medal of Arts, which was presented to her in 1995. Brooks knows that people are curious about what and who made an impact on her life. She writes in the second part of her autobiography, *Report from Part Two,* that her basic influences were her parents, books, the church, and movies.

Parents

Brooks was the first child of Keziah Corinne Wims and David Anderson Brooks. Her brother, Raymond, was born a little more than a year later. *Report from Part Two* begins with Brooks's loving remembrance of her childhood home (p. 10):

> Home always warmly awaited us. Welcoming, endorsing. Home meant a quick-walking, careful, duty-loving, never-surly mother, who had been a schoolteacher, who played the piano, sang in a high soprano, and wrote music to which I wrote the words, made fudge, made cocoa and prune whip and apricot pie, drew tidy cows and trees and expert houses with chimneys and chimney smoke, who helped her children with arithmetic homework. Home meant my father, a janitor for McKinley Music Company. He had kind eyes, songs, and tense recitations for my brother and myself. We never tired of his stories and story poems.

The section of town in which the family made this happy home was Chicago's South Side, which was a destination for blacks moving from the southern United States. Although it had long been an area troubled by crime and poverty, the South Side also served as a cultural center for black writers, musicians, and artists and as a spiritual hub of predominantly Baptist and Catholic churchgoing families. Like New York's Harlem, the South Side of Chicago is seen as an important place in American and, especially, African-American history. The specific region where the Brooks family settled became known as Bronzeville, a term coined by the black newspaper *Chicago Defender* in 1945. Brooks became a lifelong resident of the South Side. Both *A Street in Bronzeville,* her first book, and the children's book *Bronzeville Boys and Girls* take their names from the area. Chicago itself did much to make Brooks the poet she is. She writes about its people, its buildings, the beauty and the ugliness of urban life that is complicated by the special hardships endured by African Americans. Brooks despises the term "inner city" for its limiting power, and she never uses it.

Her parents encouraged her development as a person as well as a writer. When she showed them her writing at about

*intelligentsia intellectual elite

age seven, they cheered her on. Her mother proudly "praised me to Langston Hughes . . . when he came to recite at our church, Metropolitan Community Church, in Chicago," she writes in *Report from Part Two* (p. 11). Much later, when she was a married woman, Brooks hosted Hughes in her home at one of the many artistic parties given for visiting writers and musicians by Chicago's black intelligentsia* in the 1940s. She names him as a major influence on her poetry. In her poem entitled "Langston Hughes," she says he

> Has a long reach,
> Strong speech,
> Remedial* fears.
> Muscular tears.

*remedial healing

Her mother's influence, love, and devotion to her was returned in kind. When Keziah Brooks died at age ninety, it was in her own home under Gwendolyn's care. Besides being a mother of two herself, Brooks is also known as a kind of spiritual mother to younger black writers who came of age during the 1960s— such writers as Amiri Baraka. Her father did much to nurture her as well, including giving her her first desk and instilling in her a love of learning. He had wanted to become a doctor but was cut off from his ambitions after a single year's training. The David Company, a small press publishing house he started, is named after him, the man who filled the family home with books that the young poet-in-the-making read, studied, and loved.

Books

"Home and library taught me that books are bandages and voyages," Brooks writes in *Report from Part Two* (p. 14). "Links to light. Keys and Hammers. Ripe redeemers. Dials and bells and healing hallelujah." Her childhood home was filled with the Harvard Classics (a series of books of classic literature) but also with "Paul Laurence Dunbar's* books, from which my father read to us, in the evening, after dinner." Black magazines, art books, and medical books "in which I loved to dip" (p. 12) were also part of the family's much-valued collection stored in the bookcase that Gwendolyn's father gave to her mother as a wedding gift, and that Gwendolyn inherited and kept in the "southwest corner of my bedroom" (p. 14).

*Dunbar, Paul Laurence (1872–1906) American poet, novelist, and short story writer

Books, for Gwendolyn Brooks, have indeed been voyages, her own books providing a wonderful journey for herself and her readers. In 1939 she married a kindred spirit, a reader and thinker named Henry Blakely, whom she met through involvement with the National Association for the Advancement of Colored People's Youth Council. They had two children. Brooks and Blakely began married life living in a series of kitchenette apartments. The portrait she creates in her poem "kitchenette building," in the opening to her first book, *A Street in Bronzeville,* recalls her less-than-blissful experience and makes reference to Langston Hughes's famous poem "A Dream Deferred":

> But could a dream send up through onion fumes
> Its white and violet, fight with fried potatoes
> And yesterday's garbage ripening in the hall,
> Flutter, or sing an aria* down these rooms

*__aria__ a song sung by a single voice with instrumental accompaniment, often part of an opera

Both poets question again and again the ability of struggling people to keep their dreams alive. It is a common bond between them as well as a cause for celebration. As in the poem "Song: White Powder (Al)," "kitchenette building" rings a cautious note of optimism: "Since Number Five is out of the bathroom now, / We think of lukewarm water, hope to get in it." Life in a "kitchenette building" brought small comforts. Even a warm bath was something for which you waited.

A Street in Bronzeville is divided into four sections. The first, also called "A Street in Bronzeville," comprises twenty vignettes, or little sketches. "The Sundays of Satin-Legs Smith"—five portraits—makes up the second section. The third is called "Negro Hero." The fourth section, a sonnet sequence entitled "Gay Chaps at the Bar," is dedicated to her brother, Raymond, and centers on the return of black American soldiers from World War II.

Although *A Street in Bronzeville* received great reviews and collected awards, the book for which she received the Pulitzer Prize was *Annie Allen,* made up of "Notes from the Childhood and the Girlhood," the mock-epic "The Anniad," "Appendix to the Anniad," and, finally, "The Womanhood." In this volume Brooks experiments with forms and weaves the same theme throughout, the theme of relationships between women and men and how they unravel over time, especially under the strain of war.

Bronzeville Man with a Belt in the Back

In such an armor he may rise and raid
The dark cave after midnight, unafraid,
And slice the shadows with his able sword
Of good broad nonchalance, hashing them down.

And come out and accept the gasping crowd,
Shake off the praises with an airiness.
And, searching, see love shining in an eye,
But never smile.

In such an armor he cannot be slain.

(*The Bean Eaters.* New York: Harper and Row, 1960).

Church

Since Gwendolyn Brooks writes poetry that looks you in the eye, she has to assume a certain level of authority. Besides poetry, she has also written a novel, *Maud Martha;* an autobiography (in two parts); many essays; and several books for children and young adults. Her writing often has a tone of authority, the voice of an experienced adult speaking to inexperienced young people. Brooks displays a spiritual and maternal side when writing for and about children. When she says in "Beulah at Church" that "it feels good to be good" she "carefully describes how [she] felt about church in those early church-going years," as she notes in *Report from Part Two* (p. 14), with its "organ-sound and the sermon / Washing you clean of sin." Beginning in the 1950s, Brooks was raising children of her own as well as teaching poetry workshops for both college students and young children in her community. Well known for her exceptionally deep and rich speaking voice, Brooks's public readings were always well attended, her stage presence that of a wise woman whose melodious voice captivated audiences.

Brooks also sponsored many writing contests and made numerous appearances at schools, reading and talking to children who later appeared in what she calls "her gallery" in *Re-*

port from Part Two (pp. 123–124). This "gallery" can be experienced by reading *Children Coming Home,* a collection of twenty poems that are portraits of twenty children, such as Tinsel, Marie, Al, and Superbe. As time went on, the portraits of children began to darken. Her early children's book *Bronzeville Boys and Girls,* with its portraits of children poor and rich, sick and playing, is very different from *Children Coming Home.* Whereas "Beulah at Church" is a sweet portrait (of Brooks herself, in fact), "Religion (Ulysses)," in *Children Coming Home* has kids who "bring knives pistols bottles, little boxes, and cans" to school, where they stop to "talk to the man who's cool at the playground gate. / Nobody sees us, nobody stops our sin." Although the portraits in the later work are often bleak, they, like the earlier ones, are told the way Brooks sees it.

Movies

During the 1960s and 1970s, Brooks responded to a new generation of black writers writing during the time of the Civil Rights and Black Power movements. Her own work became more political and more suffused with the black idiom.* *In the Mecca: Poems* was nominated for a National Book Award. She traveled twice to Africa "hailed by . . . 'Hey, American,' " (*Report from Part Two,* p. 44) and she started publishing her work in small black-run presses, such as Broadside Press, as well as her own Brooks Press and the David Company. Her departure from mainstream publishing and from mainstream white America can be traced to this period.

> *idiom here, a group of expressions used by a particular group of people at a distinct time and place

Brooks learned that the races were separate and never equal when she was a girl at the movies. In *Report from Part Two* she admits that she "went through early womanhood believing that the glittering white family life on the screen *should* be my model" (pp. 15–17). Blacks in the early days of movies were "ridiculous," "subservient," "masters of stumble-English" of whom "secretly, we were ashamed." Later in life, when the *Chicago Tribune* asked well-known Chicagoans to tell readers about their favorite films, the Illinois poet laureate, Gwendolyn Brooks, submitted the following:

> **"Fiddler on the Roof" and "Roots." If your eyes aren't in trouble when Tevye sings to his sweetly taut and testy wife "Do You Love Me?," if your chest isn't**

chained when he chats with his God, shrugs, jokes with his God, grimaces and finally, in a time of abrupt affliction—affliction that comes across as totally ridiculous and crazily cool—merely spreads his palms at the sky, at his God, WELL, cold brothers, cold sisters, cold cousins, I must title you "Infected," I must title you Terminal. All haters of Blacks, of Blackness, see Alex Haley's "Roots." I believe most cannot experience it and remain haters of Blacks, Blackness (*Chicago Tribune,* 19 March 1995, p. 30).

Brooks is certainly a champion of blacks and blackness. In her *Primer for Blacks* she writes:

> Blackness
> is a title,
> is a preoccupation,
> is a commitment Blacks
> are to comprehend—
> and in which you are
> to perceive your Glory.

When she sees young black men and women who expect to die young, she laments, as in *Report from Part Two* (p. 124), "Today, many such boys—their girl friends, too—EXPECT to 'die soon.' In Chicago. In New York. In Springfield, in Philadelphia. In Whatalotago, Alabama. . . . They do not expect to become twenty-one. They are designing their own funerals. Their caskets will be lined with Kente cloth."* Her most famous poem, "We Real Cool," from her book *The Bean Eaters,* with its young slacker pool players and cool-as-ice rhythm, glows with the magic of the language and keen observation. Brooks has tried to send the message that to be black is to be powerful. By confronting race as a truthful observer and as a poet, Brooks talks eye to eye with her readers, who then must think about what she has to say and delight in the way she says it.

Selected Bibliography

WORKS BY GWENDOLYN BROOKS

A Street in Bronzeville (1945).

Annie Allen (1949).

---

*Kente cloth a type of fabric used in Ghana as a loose-fitting garment

IF YOU LIKE the poetry of Brooks, you might also like the poetry of Amiri Baraka, Lucille Clifton, Robert Hayden, Langston Hughes, or any of the Harlem Renaissance Poets.

Maud Martha (1953). Novel.

Bronzeville Boys and Girls (1956). Children's book.

The Bean Eaters (1960).

In the Mecca: Poems (1968).

Report from Part One: An Autobiography (1972). Includes interviews.

Primer for Blacks (1981).

Selected Poems (1982).

Children Coming Home (1991).

To Disembark (1992). Collects works published by small presses.

Report from Part Two: An Autobiography (1996).

WORKS ABOUT GWENDOLYN BROOKS

Kent, George E. *A Life of Gwendolyn Brooks.* Lexington: University Press of Kentucky, 1990.

Madhubuti, Haki R., ed. *Say That the River Turns: The Impact of Gwendolyn Brooks.* Chicago: Third World Press, 1987.

Mootry, Maria K., and Gary Smith, eds. *A Life Distilled: Gwendolyn Brooks, Her Poetry and Fiction.* Urbana: University of Illinois Press, 1987.

Tate, Claudia, ed. "Gwendolyn Brooks." In her *Black Women Writers at Work.* New York: Continuum, 1983. Interview.

More About Brooks

You can find information about Brooks on the Internet at: http://www.poets.org/LIT/poet/gbrooks.htm

ELIZABETH BARRETT BROWNING

(1806–1861)

by Judith Baumel

The romance between Elizabeth Barrett Moulton Barrett and Robert Browning became legend instantly after they secretly married and moved to Italy in September 1846. She was then a famous, though reclusive, invalid poet. He was a novice poet whose work she had praised long before they met. In her poem "Lady Geraldine's Courtship," published in *Poems* (1844), Elizabeth offered her eponymous* heroine some options for romantic reading. She suggests Spenser and Petrarch, then a "modern volume," perhaps one by Wordsworth, Howitts, Tennyson,

> Or, from Browning some "Pomegranate"
> which, if cut deep down the middle
> Shows a heart within blood-tinctured,*
> of a veined humanity.

eponymous describing a character for whom a literary work is named

"Pomegranate" is a reference to Robert Browning's volume *Bells and Pomegranates*

blood-tinctured bloodstained

Robert Browning's nickname for Elizabeth was "the Portuguese," hence the title *Sonnets from the Portuguese.*

Sonnets from the Portuguese, XLIV

Beloved, thou hast brought me many flowers
Plucked in the garden, all the summer through
And winter, and it seemed as if they grew
In this close room, nor missed the sun and showers.
So, in the like name of that love of ours,
Take back these thoughts which here unfolded too,
And which on warm and cold days I withdrew
From my heart's ground. Indeed, those beds and bowers
Be overgrown with bitter weeds and rue,
And wait thy weeding; yet here's eglantine,
Here's ivy!—take them, as I used to do
Thy flowers, and keep them where they shall not pine.
Instruct thine eyes to keep their colours true,
And tell thy soul, their roots are left in mine.

Browning's response on 10 January 1845 was a now famous letter, which begins, "I love your verses with all my heart, Dear Miss Barrett." The poets corresponded frequently for over four months before he was admitted to Elizabeth's sickroom. The love affair that followed was kept strictly secret from her father, who had forbidden all his adult children to marry. During this time, Elizabeth recorded the progress of her heart in what was to become her remarkable sonnet* sequence, *Sonnets from the Portuguese.* In these poems Elizabeth expands the strategy of love poems, shifting from the conventional male poet's posture of the lover (who finds himself powerless before the force of his love and his distant beloved) to an expression of dual roles (the lover *and* the beloved) and to a concrete expression of the physical experience of love.

*sonnet a fourteen-line poem usually composed in iambic pentameter (each line has five feet, each foot consisting of an unstressed syllable followed by a stressed syllable). There are two dominant sonnet forms in English poetry, the Shakespearean and Petrarchan.

Early Years

Elizabeth Barrett's father, Edward, was raised on his family's sugar plantation in Jamaica. At age seven he was sent far from home to start his education at the rigorous Harrow school in England. Coming from the ease of plantation life and the paradise of the West Indian climate, Edward found England difficult, but he soon fell in love with Mary Graham-Clarke, the daughter of a wealthy merchant who was his host in Newcastle during school vacations. The couple married in May 1805. Elizabeth, the first of twelve children, was born on 6 March 1806 near Durham. Three years later the family moved to Hereford-shire and renovated an estate called Hope End, creating what the father called a "fairy palace" with his own original, oriental-inspired designs.

Elizabeth Barrett, from as early as she could remember, set out to be a poet. In her autobiography, written at age four-teen, she recalled she was four when she "first mounted Pega-sus,* but at six I thought myself privileged to show off feats of horsemanship." She felt she was without female antecedents.* "I look everywhere for grandmothers and see none," she once wrote to an editor. She knew being a female was a handicap, but she also understood that as a woman she had freedom to explore new territory without the constraints male poets felt.

In Elizabeth's mind and with the encouragement she re-ceived from her family, admission to the pantheon* was some-thing more than just a wild dream. Still, there were moments when she had trouble accepting her own ambition, as it was considered an unwomanly trait. She resented the limitations imposed on women of her time—their difficulties in obtaining education and the expectation that their ambitions would be confined to success in the pleasing or serving arts. She be-lieved women could and should live their lives fully in both the private and public spheres, and she challenged herself to create a woman's poetry that was more than purely decorative or merely an imitation of male work. She wanted to respond to the particular female dilemmas of being a daughter, wife, and mother with her whole being—intellectually and politi-cally as well as physically and emotionally.

Elizabeth's mother supported her daughter's ambitions, though the two often debated a woman's prospects and role in marriage. As a young woman, Elizabeth declared she would not marry, and she defended Mary Wollstonecraft's book *A Vindication of the Rights of Woman* against her mother's more mixed response. Years later, as she was contemplating her own marriage with a somewhat altered perspective, Eliza-beth reflected on her parents' marriage and, remembering her mother's death in 1828, wrote, "Scarcely was I a woman when I lost my mother, dearest as she was . . . but of a nature har-rowed up into some furrows by the pressure of circumstances. A sweet, gentle nature which the thunder a little turned from its sweetness, as when it turns milk. One of those women who never can resist, but in submitting, and bowing on themselves, make a mark, a plait, within, a sign of suffering."

*Pegasus a winged horse in Greek mythol-ogy; a symbol for po-etic inspiration

*antecedents exam-ples in the past

*pantheon an elite or distinguished group

*patriarch head of a family

Edward Barrett was devastated by his wife's death. In 1832 the family's financial position deteriorated and he was forced to sell Hope End. Eventually the Barretts moved to Wimpole Street, London, where Edward ruled the family as a firm, Christian patriarch.*

Development of the Poet

*odes lyric poems in an exalted (highly serious) style

Elizabeth was a brilliant and talented child, writing much-appreciated birthday odes* and other occasional verse for her family. Nevertheless, her education was an afterthought. Only after she made a special request was she able to work with the tutor who had been hired for her younger brother Edward. When "Bro" left for boarding school and her access to tutoring ended, Elizabeth, always resourceful in finding ways to educate herself, had her brother send home his school exercises. At twenty-one she began to correspond with and visit her neighbor Hugh Stuart Boyd, a blind scholar with whom she studied Greek and Hebrew.

*voracious hungry

Most of all, Elizabeth read widely, understanding instinctively that the way to become a great writer is to be a voracious* reader. She appreciated the poets of her day—the Romantic poets Wordsworth, Coleridge, Byron, Keats, and Shelley. In addition to reading the acknowledged greats—the Greeks and Romans, Dante, Shakespeare, and Milton, she had high regard for the Augustan poets,* Pope and Dryden in particular. Avoiding traditionally feminine domestic and romantic subjects, her early poems evoked their style as well as their subject matter—translations and reconsiderations of the classics and didactic* and philosophical meditations. Elizabeth's "Essay on Mind" was a deliberate recollection of Pope's "Essay on Criticism." Her first long poem was "The Battle of Marathon," and at twenty-six she translated Aeschylus's *Prometheus Bound* from ancient Greek.

*Augustan poets in England, poets who flourished at the turn of the eighteenth century

*didactic intended to teach or instruct

Overcoming Adversity

In 1821, when Elizabeth was fifteen and just beginning to publish in magazines, she and her sisters Henrietta and Arabella became ill. Though the other girls quickly recovered, Elizabeth did not. Her symptoms included pain in her "swollen" spine and back and severely weakened lungs. She was given a common remedy of her time, laudanum (a liquid made from opium), and thus she began a lifelong dependence on the drug, as well as a life of suffering opium's side effects: headaches, insomnia, lack of appetite, constipation, and fatigue.

In 1838, after *The Seraphim and Other Poems* was published to good reviews, Elizabeth experienced a flare-up of her illness and went to Torquay in the south of England for recuperation. Throughout her illness she was depressed and lonely. The depression worsened with the news that her brother Sam, who had been managing the family estates in Jamaica, had died of fever. Afterwards she begged that her favorite brother, Bro, be permitted to stay with her in Torquay, and when he drowned in a boating accident there, her grief and guilt were nearly unbearable.

Periods of intense writing alternating with breakdowns in her health became a pattern. Her symptoms were severe but unexplained by her doctors. The suspicions that her ill health was caused by nervous exhaustion—and therefore somehow in her control—combined with the experience of real physical ailment confounded* Elizabeth all her life. Yet despite her long periods of confinement, she was always able to find the strength to read and write, supervise her publishing, and correspond with the literary world as well as with her extended family and friends.

*confounded troubled

One important support for the poet was her independent income. Her grandmother's death in 1830, and later her uncle Sam's, provided an annual income. Later still, an inheritance from the family friend and patron, John Kenyon, who had encouraged Robert Browning to meet Elizabeth, maintained the couple. These stipends allowed Elizabeth the freedom to pursue her writing.

Courtship and Marriage

By the time she was forty Elizabeth was a published and recognized poet. For years her poetry had touched on what she believed to be her own imminent death. The headstrong and passionate Robert Browning changed Elizabeth's world. The changes started with a simple step—leaving her sickroom for the first time in years—and ended with her new life with Browning in Italy. Because Elizabeth was in many ways sophisticated and sensitive to the nuances of human relations and because she loved her father, she tried to be cautious throughout the affair. She was practical enough to ask for moderation at times, and for action at others. Her thoughtful nature balanced her emotional nature and sustained and nurtured her deep connection to Browning.

Even in the very last moments before their secret marriage, Elizabeth was considering whether she could or should make such a drastic and risky choice. She knew that her marriage would alienate her from her father. Indeed, father and daughter never spoke again.

Many have wondered what caused Edward Barrett to be so hostile to the marriage of his adult children, when he himself had had a happy marriage and twelve children. The scholar and novelist Julia Markus suggests that Edward's decision might have been a by-product of the family's complicated Jamaican heritage, which included a number of Creole* members. The uncertain relationship between the illegitimate, though acknowledged, members of the family and the legal heirs appears to have weighed more heavily on Edward as he aged. One fear may have been the possibility of the appearance of a black child in the direct line of inheritance in the future.

In her letters Elizabeth openly referred to her own dark skin, flat nose, and wide mouth. Before she married Browning she revealed her family history. She had dropped Moulton from her name because she believed that through her grandfather Charles Moulton she possessed a mixed "lineage . . . the blood of the slave! Cursed we are from generation to generation." That this lineage was cursed morally and socially may have preyed on Edward's mind.

It most likely was on Elizabeth's mind during the early days of her honeymoon, when she wrote "The Runaway Slave at Pilgrim's Point" in support of American abolitionists.* The story can be seen as an allegory* of her own escape from the "slavery" of her family, but it can also be understood as an exorcism* of her family heritage, which included black slaves and a cousin who was speaker of the House of Assembly in Jamaica and a famous defender of slavery.

Florence

After a yearlong honeymoon spent mostly in Pisa, Italy, the couple moved into a palazzo in Florence, named Casa Guidi,

*Creole a person of European descent, or of mixed European and black descent, born in the West Indies

*abolitionists those who advocate ending slavery

*allegory a story in which the fictional objects, characters, and actions are equated with meanings that lie outside the narrative itself

*exorcism cleansing

where they established a home base for the rest of their marriage. In 1847 Elizabeth saw a parade celebrating the grand duke's promise of civil liberties to the Florentines and quickly began the first section of *Casa Guidi Windows,* an optimistic account of the beginning of the Italian Risorgimento.* The second section, written later, is a more sober analysis of the disappointments, struggles, and aspirations of modern Italy lurching toward freedom and national unity.

> **Risorgimento* a political movement in nineteenth-century Italy for national unity

During the early years of her marriage Elizabeth Barrett Browning felt as well as she ever had since her childhood. The union was a happy, cooperative, and unusually equal one, and it became a source of the inspired complexity of her mature work. Elizabeth found a pleasure in the physical world; she also found the inspiration to explicitly connect her intellectual pursuits to those of wife and mother. After two miscarriages, she gave birth to a son, Robert Weidemann Barrett Browning (nicknamed Pen), on 9 March 1849. Elizabeth adored Pen and raised him in a liberal manner, encouraging his curiosity and avoiding imposed rules and rote study. In her letters to her sister Henrietta she often quoted his wit and insight, part in English, part in Italian, and full of childish pronunciations and phrasing.

Mature Work

For many years Elizabeth Barrett Browning had planned a long work, possibly a novel in verse, that would address a central concern of her life—the necessity for a woman to be fulfilled in a purposeful life. In *Aurora Leigh* she imagined an unconventional heroine, smart and powerful, something like a character in a George Sand novel, or perhaps like George Sand herself. Elizabeth admired and defended this free-thinking woman, her friend, who wore men's pants, smoked cigars, had many lovers, and wrote freely about sex. Aurora's name is an homage* to George Sand's given name, Aurore Dupin.

> **homage* tribute; honor

Aurora is a modern heroine—an independent woman, a writer, a fighter for social and political causes, and finally, a woman who finds happiness in love. Readers from Queen Victoria to important poets and politicians of the day considered *Aurora Leigh* a moving and important book. The American suffragette Susan B. Anthony gave her personal copy of the book to the Library of Congress with a note indicating its particular significance to her work. Just after *Aurora Leigh* was published in 1857, Robert, Pen, and Elizabeth traveled to England. It turned into a stressful and disappointing stay during which Elizabeth argued with her brothers and was refused a visit to her father. Soon afterward, Edward died, unreconciled with his daughter, and the sadness Elizabeth felt pervaded the rest of her life.

Final Years

In 1860, while in Rome finishing *Poems Before Congress,* her book about the continuing political difficulties in Italy, Elizabeth became ill. The Brownings spent the summer in Siena and the next winter in Rome, hoping the warmer weather would improve her health. There she and Pen posed for a photograph for her family in England. She was "vain," she wrote, about Pen's bright good looks, but inwardly she felt herself in decline and was unable to go out for more than a few outings in six months. Recent news of her sister Henrietta's death had been an additional blow. It was compounded, on her return to Florence in the spring of 1861, by the death of the great Italian statesman Camillo di Cavour. On 29 June, Elizabeth Barrett Browning died in her bed, Robert Browning reported, after holding him and repeating, "God bless you, God bless you."

*cortege funeral procession

In death this Anglo-Italian patriot was accorded a rare honor. The city of Florence gave permission for her funeral cortege* to proceed through the streets of the city to the Protestant cemetery. Robert Browning collected Elizabeth's late work—including "The North and the South," written just a month before her death—in *Last Poems,* published in March 1862. It is a collection that continues her philosophical, political, and feminist themes and one that, despite her condition at the time of writing, weakened by grief and pain, is as forceful and brilliant as anything she had done.

*caricature exaggeration; distortion

At the time of her death in 1861, it would have been hard to imagine how the next generations would view Elizabeth Barrett Browning. Her work was largely unread (except perhaps for the first line of the forty-third sonnet in *Sonnets from the Portuguese*: "How do I love thee? Let me count the ways"), her career was compared unfavorably to other Victorian women writers, and the rich story of her accomplishments was reduced to a caricature* of a weak lady rescued from a tyrannical father by her robust and talented husband. Fluctuations in fame and appreciation are common in literary history. Rankings often reflect the concerns of those doing the ranking or the shifting fashions of literary style and theme. In the case of Elizabeth Barrett Browning, her own strong, often radical positions may have threatened Edwardian readers and undermined what had been, through her entire publishing life, a very high bold place in "the mansion of literature."

In her 1933 essay on Elizabeth Barrett Browning, the novelist Virginia Woolf sarcastically dismissed the prevailing literary opinion that placed Elizabeth in "the servants' quarters, where, . . . she bangs crockery about and eats vast handfuls of peas on the point of her knife." Despite Woolf's assessment, it was not until the last quarter of the twentieth century that Elizabeth began to regain her previous position.

Selected Bibliography

WORKS BY ELIZABETH BARRETT BROWNING
Poetry

Prometheus Bound, Translated from the Greek of Aeschylus, and Miscellaneous Poems (1833)

The Seraphim and Other Poems (1838)

Poems (1844)

Sonnets from the Portuguese (1850)

Casa Guidi Windows (1851)

Aurora Leigh (1857)

Poems Before Congress (1860)

Last Poems (1862)

Letters

Letters of Elizabeth Barrett Browning. Edited by Frederic Kenyon. London: Macmillan, 1894.

The Brownings Correspondence 1806–1846. Edited by Philip Kelley, Ronald Hudson, and Scott Lewis. Winfield, Kans: Wedgestone Press, 1984–1993.

Diary by E. B. B.: The Unpublished Diary of Elizabeth Barrett Browning 1831–1832. Edited by Philip Kelley and Ronald Hudson. Athens: Ohio University Press, 1969.

Available Collections

Aurora Leigh. Norton Critical Edition. Edited by Margaret Reynolds. New York: W. W. Norton, 1996.

Casa Guidi Windows. Edited by Julia Markus. New York: Browning Institute, 1977.

The Poetical Works of Elizabeth Barrett Browning. With a new introduction by Ruth M. Adams. Boston: Houghton Mifflin, 1974.

Selected Poems. Introduction by Margaret Forster. Baltimore: Johns Hopkins University Press, 1988.

WORKS ABOUT ELIZABETH BARRETT BROWNING

Forster, Margaret. *Elizabeth Barrett Browning: A Biography.* New York: Doubleday, 1988.

Markus, Julia. *Dared and Done: The Marriage of Elizabeth Barrett and Robert Browning.* Athens: Ohio University Press, 1995.

Mermim, Dorothy. *Elizabeth Barrett Browning: The Origins of a New Poetry.* Chicago: University of Chicago Press, 1989.

Radley, Virginia L. *Elizabeth Barrett Browning.* New York: Twayne, 1972.

Stephenson, Glennis. *Elizabeth Barrett Browning and the Poetry of Love.* Ann Arbor, Mich.: UMI Research Press, 1989.

Woolf, Virginia. *The Second Common Reader.* London: Harcourt Brace, 1932.

ROBERT BROWNING
(1812–1889)

by Karen Odden

Some poetry readers think of Robert Browning mainly as the man for whom Elizabeth Barrett Browning wrote the lovely *Sonnets from the Portuguese,* the most famous of which begins, "How do I love thee? Let me count the ways." Elizabeth published these poems in 1850, four years after their marriage, but their love and the works they wrote were intertwined from the very beginning, for their affair had begun when Robert read her collection *Poems* (published in 1844) and started writing to her. The Brownings' marriage united two astonishingly talented and industrious poets. During their time together, she completed the long verse *Aurora Leigh,* which many consider her masterpiece, as well as political poems and lyrics; he wrote the poems for his collections *Christmas-Eve and Easter Day* and *Men and Women* and gathered the material for his masterpiece, *The Ring and the Book.* Sadly, though, the marriage lasted only fifteen years; Elizabeth died in Robert's arms in 1861, in Italy. At that time, her poetry was more popular than his, but by the 1870s his

*Victorian characteristic of the era of Queen Victoria (1837–1901)

reputation was rapidly surpassing hers. He is now hailed as one of the most entertaining Victorian* poets.

Beginnings

Browning was born to Robert Browning and Sarah Anne Wiedemann on 7 May 1812, and his only sibling, Sarianna, was born exactly twenty months later. Their home was in Camberwell, a suburb south of London but still close enough that they could see the tall buildings. Sarah Browning, who was ten years older than her husband, was of Scottish descent. A religious woman, she regularly attended the Congregationalist church near their home, and she was a talented musician. The poet's father had originally wanted to be an artist—he had a real talent for painting—but his father (also named Robert) refused to support him financially, so he was forced to work as a clerk in the Bank of England, which he disliked. He earned a good salary, however, and the family was quite affluent.* In his spare time, the elder Browning read avidly: he knew half a dozen languages, both ancient and modern, and during his lifetime he assembled an extraordinary library of more than six thousand books.

*affluent abundantly wealthy

Young Robert was deeply influenced by the spirituality of his mother and the artistic leanings of both his parents. When he was quite young, he attended a local dame school,* then a boarding school, and then the nearby Peckham School, where he was forced to memorize the rules of Latin and Greek grammar. While he enjoyed learning, he disliked discipline and preferred to approach it in his own way. He spent hours devouring the books in his father's library, reading everything from classical works in Latin and Greek to the English Romantic poets Lord Byron, John Keats, and Percy Bysshe Shelley, who would later have a deep effect on him. By the time he was twelve, Browning wrote his first volume of poetry, *Incondita,* which he later destroyed. At fourteen, he left the Peckham School and studied under tutors at home for two years, during which time he continued learning Latin and Greek, became proficient in French, and studied a variety of subjects, including music theory and fencing. He idolized the poet George Gordon, Lord Byron, who had died young supporting the Greeks in their battle for independence from the Turks. He even adopted some of Byron's personal mannerisms and bor-

*dame school a school where a woman taught children reading and writing in her own home

rowed Byron's style for one of his own earliest poems. Later, he began to think Byron a bit too egotistical; at age fourteen, as a result of reading Percy Bysshe Shelley's *Miscellaneous Poems,* he transferred his loyalty to him. During this time, Browning himself did not write much poetry, but, influenced by Shelley—and much to the distress of his mother—he experimented with atheism and became a vegetarian.

After having been tutored at home, Browning wanted more education. Because he had been raised as a Congregationalist, he could not attend Oxford or Cambridge, which were closed to religious dissenters, so in 1828 he enrolled in the newly founded University of London. But he left shortly afterward because—true to his childhood form—he found the classes dull and uninspiring. For the next few years, he simply read works from his father's library, still uncertain whether he wanted to become a poet.

In 1832, however, inspired by seeing Shakespeare's play *Richard III,* Browning began to write poems in earnest. First, he wrote *Pauline: A Fragment of a Confession,* a somewhat autobiographical lyrical* narrative in a style unlike Shelley's. While traveling through continental Europe in 1834, he wrote "Johannes Agricola in Meditation," based on the life of the sixteenth-century Protestant Reformer, and the creepy poem "Porphyria's Lover," about a man who strangles his lover with her own hair. In these two poems Browning raised questions that he would continue to address in many of his later works: First, how do we perceive historical figures? Second, what different kinds of relationships exist between men and women?

His first major poem was *Paracelsus* and his first play was *Strafford.* Each was a moderate success, but his poem *Sordello* was a dismal failure—the reviewers treated it as a standing joke. Undaunted, Browning threw himself into social life. In 1844, he read a copy of Elizabeth Barrett's *Poems* and wrote her a letter praising it. Their correspondence flourished, and he met her the following year. She was nearly forty years old, an invalid, and still living at home, in great part because her tyrannical father disapproved of marriage for any of his children. Despite this, Elizabeth and Robert eloped on 12 September 1846. They went to Italy and, after a short stay in Pisa, took up residence in Florence.

As a result of his extensive reading and travels, Browning was incredibly knowledgeable. It has been said that in order to understand his poetry, one should—like him—be fluent in

"Religious dissenters" were people who were not members of the Church of England, (also called the Anglican Church). Congregationalists, Baptists, and Methodists were all considered religious dissenters and were not allowed the same rights and privileges as Anglicans.

*lyrical having a musical quality

seven or eight languages and literatures and be highly familiar with music and art, Greek and Roman mythology, the Bible, classical plays, historical works, biographies, and the works of many of the major English authors going back to Shakespeare. This is a tall order, but the depth of Browning's scholarship is one reason why it is so rewarding to reread his works over time, as our own knowledge increases.

Time in Italy

Browning was deeply influenced by Italy and by his study of Italian culture. He had first visited Italy in 1838, and while Elizabeth was alive they and their son, Robert Wiedemann Browning (known as Penini and nicknamed "Pen"), lived in Italy. Many of Browning's most famous poems have Italian settings and themes: in *Pippa Passes* (no. 1 of *Bells and Pomegranates*), a young girl wanders through the small town of Asolo, near Venice: "The Statue and the Bust" tells the story of a young woman who falls in love at first sight with the duke of Florence; "Fra Lippo Lippi" describes the lascivious* nighttime adventures of an Italian painter; "Andrea del Sarto" is about another Italian painter; and the work that many regard as Browning's masterpiece, *The Ring and the Book,* was based on a real-life seventeenth-century murder of an Italian woman named Pompilia and the trial of her husband, Count Guido Franceschini.

Many of these poems are dramatic monologues, in which the speaker of the poem is a character, like an actor in a play. For example, "Fra Lippo Lippi" begins with the speaker, a monk, identifying himself and then defending his right to go to a brothel if he wants:

> I am poor brother Lippo, by your leave!
> You need not clap your torches to my face.
> Zooks,* what's to blame? you think you see a monk!
> What, 'tis past midnight, and you go the rounds,
> And here you catch me at an alley's end
> Where sportive ladies leave their doors ajar?
> *(Poems of Robert Browning)*

The poem is written in what is called blank verse—unrhymed iambic pentameter.* Many poets, including Shakespeare, have

*__lascivious__ sexually lustful

*__Zooks!__ a mild oath; the equivalent of "Wow!" or "Oh my!" Originally "God's hooks," meaning the nails that held Christ on the cross.

*__iambic pentameter__ verse that has five metrical feet to a line, with two syllables in each foot and the accent (stress) on the second syllable (example: da DA)

Meeting at Night

I

The grey sea and the long black land;
And the yellow half-moon large and low;
And the startled little waves that leap
In fiery ringlets from their sleep,
As I gain the cove with pushing prow,
And quench its speed i' the slushy sand.

II

Then a mile of warm sea-scented beach;
Three fields to cross till a farm appears;
A tap at the pane, the quick sharp scratch
And blue spurt of a lighted match,
And a voice less loud, through its joys and fears,
Than the two hearts beating each to each!

Parting at Morning

Round the cape of a sudden came the sea,
And the sun looked over the mountain's rim:
And straight was a path of gold for him,
And the need of a world of men for me.

(Pettigrew, *The Poems,* vol. 1)

used blank verse because it provides a poetic structure but at the same time is thought to approximate natural speech.

Other poems by Browning have to do with the relationship between men and women and between love and art; they often present a particular situation. In one pair of poems— "Meeting at Night" and "Parting at Morning"—he is concerned with the lengths to which lovers will go to be together and the necessity for parting. Some of his poems are quite sensational in topic: in "Porphyria's Lover," for example, a man strangles his lover on the night of her engagement party because she is upper-class and he cannot possess her. In "Count Gismond," a woman explains how she was seduced and betrayed; in "The Glove" a woman throws her glove into a lion's cage as a dare— she expects her lover to retrieve it, but he despises her for forcing him to prove his love in this way. In one of Browning's most famous poems, "My Last Duchess," the duke of Ferrara has poisoned his first wife after having her portrait painted—and now he wants to marry another unsuspecting young woman. This poem opens with the duke addressing a listener (commonly called the silent auditor), in this case an ambassador who is arranging the marriage between his employer's daughter and the duke:

> That's my last duchess painted on the wall,
> Looking as if she were alive. I call
> That piece a wonder, now: Frà Pandolf's hands
> Worked busily a day, and there she stands.
> Will't please you sit and look at her?
> (Poems of Robert Browning)

When lines are enjambed, the meaning of one line runs over to the next one. By contrast, end-stopped lines have a firm stop at the end (usually marked by a comma, period, or an exclamation point).

Note that this is not blank verse but rhymed iambic pentameter. The rhyme scheme is not very noticeable, however, because some of the lines are enjambed; the duke still seems to be talking normally, just as anyone might talk. Of course, the duke is anything *but* normal. He is proud of the painting, but when his "last duchess" was alive, he was exceedingly jealous because her "smiles went everywhere" instead of only toward him. The poem suggests that he has turned her into an art object because that way she is easier to control. Of course, the ambassador becomes a bit suspicious that the duke may try to poison his next wife as well. The final lines of the poem suggest the duke's desire to tame and control all kinds of living things—wives, Greek mythological figures, sea horses, and ambassadors—by turning them into art or directing their physical movements:

*Neptune in Roman mythology, the god of the sea

> . . . Will't please you rise? We'll meet
> The company below, then. . . . .
> . . . Nay, we'll go
> Together down, sir. Notice Neptune,* though,
> Taming a sea-horse, thought a rarity,
> Which Claus of Innsbruck* cast in bronze for me!
> (Poems of Robert Browning)

*Claus of Innsbruck a fictional artist. Innsbruck, Austria, was famous for its bronze sculpting in the sixteenth century.

*aristocratic upper-class

Readers should note Browning's use of repetition because it often points to a central theme: the Duke's two questions, "Will't please you . . . ?" suggest that he disguises his manipulation of people with aristocratic* courtesy—but his comment "Nay, we'll go down together" (so that the ambassador can't warn the count that his daughter might be in danger) hints that the duke is used to getting his way.

Return to England

After Elizabeth died in 1861, Robert returned to London with Pen, and they rented a house near Elizabeth's sister Arabel. Browning joined a men's club, Athenaeum, where he spent many evenings; he oversaw Pen's education; and he was offered the editorship of the *Cornhill* magazine in 1862 (he declined). He also found time to complete his collection *Dramatis Personae* in 1864. The Latin title of this work means "persons of the drama"—that is, a cast of characters—and it suggests that the poems are monologues spoken by actors in the "play" of life. The two most famous poems from this collection are "Caliban upon Setebos," alluding to Shakespeare's play *The Tempest,* in which the character Caliban is a half-man, half-monster, and "Rabbi Ben Ezra," which refers to *The Rubáiyát of Omar Khayyám,* an eleventh-century Persian work translated by the English poet Edward FitzGerald. "Rabbi Ben Ezra" begins with the famous words "Grow old along with me! / The best is yet to be." But while it celebrates the present as a time to be enjoyed, it represents change as inevitable (stanza 15):

> Youth ended, I shall try
> My gain or loss thereby;
> Leave the fire ashes, what survives is gold:
> *(Poems of Robert Browning)*

In 1869, Browning completed his longest work, *The Ring and the Book.* He found the material for this work in an old, yellowed notebook that he bought at a market stall in Florence not long before Elizabeth's death. *The Ring and the Book* is like a modern criminal trial. A "ring" of ten different witnesses (or groups of people) give their testimony about the murder of a woman named Pompilia, but none of the accounts match up perfectly. This poses questions: Who is telling the truth? Is "truth" somewhere in the middle of the ring of accounts? Is there any real truth? (*The Ring and the Book* is long and complex, but if you enjoy Browning, a good place to start is with Pompilia's sad story in Book Seven.) The poem opens with a description of Elizabeth's gold wedding ring and compares it to the old yellow notebook. Also, the artistry of the ring is compared to the artistry of the poem itself:

> Do you see this Ring?
>   'T is Rome-work,*
> . . . .
> Gold as it was, is, shall be evermore:
> Prime nature with an added artistry—
> No carat* lost, and you have gained a ring.
> What of it? 'T is a figure, a symbol, say;
> A thing's sign: now for the thing signified.
> Do you see this square old yellow Book. . . ?

Here, gold suggests the transformation from crude facts to literary art, but in "Rabbi Ben Ezra" Browning uses the same symbol—gold—to stand for the transformation from youth to age. One of the most intriguing aspects of Browning's poetry is the way he reuses metaphors, but each time with a different meaning.

With *The Ring and the Book,* Browning's reputation was secure. His sister, Sarianna, returned to England from Paris and became his constant companion after their father died in 1866. There were many rumors that Browning was on the verge of being engaged, but he never remarried. He published collections of poems every year or two for the rest of his life, and his standing as a poet continued to grow. Cambridge University gave him an honorary degree in 1879, and the Browning Society was founded in 1881. Still, many of his later poems are now less famous than those in *Men and Women* and *Dramatis Personae.* His last collection of poems, *Asolando,* was published on 12 December 1889, the day of his death. Browning died of natural causes at his son's home in Venice, but his body was brought back to London and buried in the Poets' Corner in Westminster Abbey.

Selected Bibliography

WORKS BY ROBERT BROWNING
Poetry, Plays, and Translations

Pauline: A Fragment of a Confession (1833). A poem.

Paracelsus (1835). A poem.

Sidebar notes:

***Rome-work** made in Rome by jewelers in the Castellani firm

***carat (karat)** a unit used to measure the weight of precious stones or the purity of gold

IF YOU LIKE the poetry of Browning, you might also like the poetry of Lord Byron, Percy Bysshe Shelley, or Alfred Lord Tennyson.

Strafford (1837). Plays.

Sordello (1840). A poem.

Bells and Pomegranates (1841–1846). Poetry and plays. Includes *Pippa Passes.*

Christmas-Eve and Easter Day (1850).

Men and Women (1855). A collection of poems.

Dramatis Personae (1864). A collection of poems.

The Ring and the Book (1868–1869). A poem.

Balaustion's Adventure (1871).

Prince Hohenstiel-Schwangau (1871).

Fifine at the Fair (1872).

Red Cotton Night-Cap Country (1873).

Aristophanes' Apology (1875).

The Inn Album (1875).

Pacchiarotto and How He Worked in Distemper; with Other Poems (1876).

The Agamemnon of Aeschylus (1877). Translation.

La Saisiaz (1878).

The Two Poets of Croisic (1878).

Dramatic Idyls (1879).

Dramatic Idyls, Second Series (1880).

Jocoseria (1883).

Ferishtah's Fancies (1884).

Parleyings with Certain People of Importance in Their Day (1887).

Asolando (1889).

Prose

Essay on Chatterton (1842).

Essay on Shelley (1852).

Letters

The Brownings' Correspondence. Edited by Philip Kelley, Ronald Hudson, and Scott Lewis. Winfield, Kans.:

Wedgestone Press, 1894–. 40 vols. planned, of which 14 were published as of 1999.

The Brownings to the Tennysons. Edited by Thomas J. Collins. Waco, Tex.: Armstrong Browning Library, Baylor University, 1971.

The Letters of Robert Browning and Elizabeth Barrett, 1845–1846, 2 vols. Edited by Elvan Kintner. Cambridge, Mass.: Harvard University Press, 1969.

Letters of Robert Browning Collected by Thomas J. Wise. Edited by Thurman L. Hood. New Haven, Conn.: Yale University Press, 1933.

New Letters of Robert Browning. Edited by William Clyde DeVane and Kenneth Leslie Knickerbocker. New Haven, Conn.: Yale University Press, 1950.

Twenty-two Unpublished Letters of Elizabeth Barrett Browning and Robert Browning. Edited by W. R. Benét. New York: United Feature Syndicate, 1935.

Diaries and Memoirs

The Diary of Alfred Domett 1872–1885. Edited by E. A. Horsman. London: Oxford University Press, 1953.

Gosse, Edmund. *Robert Browning: Personalia.* Boston: Houghton Mifflin, 1890.

Ritchie, Anne. *Records of Tennyson, Ruskin and Browning.* New York: Harper and Brothers, 1892.

William Allingham, a Diary. Edited by H. Allingham and D. Radford. London: Macmillan, 1907.

Available Collections

The Complete Works of Robert Browning, 14 vols. Edited by Roma A. King, Jr. Columbus: Ohio University Press, 1969–.

The Plays of Robert Browning. Edited by Thomas J. Collins and Richard J. Shroyer. New York: Garland, 1988.

The Poems. 2 vols. Edited by John Pettigrew. New York: Penguin, 1993.

Poems of Robert Browning. Edited by Donald Smalley. Boston: Houghton Mifflin, 1956.

Poetical Works of Robert Browning, 17 vols. London: Smith, Elder, 1888–1894.

The Ring and the Book. Edited by Richard D. Altick. New York: Penguin, 1990.

WORKS ABOUT ROBERT BROWNING

Altick, Richard D., and James F. Loucks, II. *Browning's Roman Murder Story; A Reading of* The Ring and the Book. Chicago: Chicago University Press, 1968.

Berdoe, Edward. *The Browning Cyclopaedia.* New York: Macmillan, 1949.

DeVane, William Clyde. *A Browning Handbook.* New York: Appleton-Century-Crofts, 1955.

Griffin, W. Hall, and Harry Christopher Minchin. *The Life of Robert Browning.* Hamden, Conn.: Archon, 1966.

Irvine, William, and Park Honan. *The Book, the Ring, and the Poet: A Biography of Robert Browning.* New York: McGraw-Hill, 1974.

Jack, Ian. *Browning's Major Poetry.* Oxford, U.K.: Clarendon, 1973.

Karlin, Daniel. *The Courtship of Robert Browning and Elizabeth Barrett.* London: Oxford University Press, 1985.

Maynard, John. *Browning's Youth.* Cambridge, Mass.: Harvard University Press, 1977.

Miller, Betty. *Robert Browning: A Portrait.* London: Murray, 1952.

Orr, Alexandra. *A Handbook to the Works of Robert Browning.* London: Bell, 1937.

Orr, Alexandra. *Life and Letters of Robert Browning.* Revised by Frederick G. Kenyon. London: Smith, Elder, 1908.

Ryals, Clyde de L. *The Life of Robert Browning: A Critical Biography.* Oxford, U.K.: Blackwell, 1993.

Ward, Maisie. *Robert Browning and His World,* 2 vols. New York: Holt, Rinehart and Winston, 1967.

Whiting, Lilian. *The Brownings: Their Life and Art.* Boston: Little, Brown, 1911.

Woolford, John, and Daniel Karlin. *Robert Browning.* New York: Longman, 1996.

More About Browning

You can find information about Robert Browning on the Victorian website at: http://www.lamp.ac.uk /victoria/vctrnlnk.htm

ROBERT BURNS

(1759–1796)

by Angus R. B. Cochran

As the national poet of Scotland, Robert Burns is one of the few poets whose birthday is celebrated annually by thousands. At Burns suppers around the world on 25 January, Burns's poetry is recited, whisky is drunk, and haggis (a mixture of lamb, suet, and oatmeal packed in a sheep's stomach) is served. On these festive evenings, Burns is remembered as the people's poet, the failed farmer who turned his personal experience of love and loss into a body of poetry that celebrates human appetites and ridicules human follies. The highlight of the evening occurs as the haggis is carved and Burns's poem, "To a Haggis," is read. The poem begins grandly, with an ornate tribute to this king of puddings:

> Fair fa'* your honest, sonsie* face,
> Great Chieftan o' the Puddin-race!
> Aboon* them a' ye tak your place,
>   Painch,* tripe, or thairm:*
> Weel* are ye wordy* of a *grace*
>   As lang's* my arm.

Burns's poetry is easier to understand if you read it aloud.

Quotations from Burns's work throughout are taken from Kinsley, ed., *The Poems and Songs of Robert Burns* (1969).

*__fa'__ lay claim to
*__sonsie__ jolly
*__aboon__ above
*__painch__ paunch
*__thairm__ intestines
*__weel__ well
*__wordy__ worthy
*__lang's__ long

Thereafter, the poem praises the haggis as the heartiest of dishes and the basis for Scotsmen's health and strength. The address to the haggis is typical of much in Burns's poetry, particularly its patriotism, its wit, and its use of a dignified poetic form for humorous effect. The poem also illustrates the difficulty modern readers encounter with Burns's eighteenth-century Scottish diction.*

*diction choice of words

In addition to writing poetry, during the last twelve years of his short life Burns collected traditional Scots folksongs and composed new lyrics to traditional tunes. The most famous of these is "Auld Lang Syne" (literally "Old Long Ago"), the song sung each New Year's Eve as the new year is rung in. It is nearly impossible to tell whether Burns composed the words to "Auld Lang Syne" himself or collected them from an existing song, but critics agree that he did add original elements to the song, particularly in the evocation of childhood friendship. The song describes the reunion between two long-separated friends, and the narrator recalls their early days together as boys.

Auld Lang Syne

We twa* hae run about the braes,*
  And pou'd* the gowans* fine;
But we've wander'd mony* a weary fitt,*
  Sin auld lang syne.*
We twa hae paidl'd* in the burn,*
  Frae morning sun till dine;
But seas between us braid* hae roar'd,
  Sin auld lang syne.

---

*twa two
*braes riverbanks
*pou'd pulled
*gowans flowers
*mony many
*fitt foot
*syne ago
*paidl'd paddled
*burn creek
*braid broad

Around Burns's birthday and New Year's Eve, a Burns cult has sprung up that sentimentally commemorates Robert Burns in the image of the peasant poet, a literary wonder of nature who loved to drink and seduce women. Yet, more than this, the historical Burns was a political radical who harbored unusually democratic ideas for his time and a serious poet intent upon crafting his poetry from eighteenth-century English poetic conventions and Scottish literary traditions.

Early Years

In 1759 Robert Burns was born to Agnes Brown and William Burnes (the poet later modernized the spelling of his surname) in a cottage in Alloway, a village in the southwest of Scotland. Burns grew up poor, the eldest of seven children in a farming family, and he spent most of his childhood and teenage years helping to cultivate the land that the family rented. Although there was little time or money for schooling, Burns did have some formal education between the ages of six and seven, when a teacher was hired to teach the sons of local farmers. But most of his learning, other than a few more weeks' schooling in his early teens, was gained independently through his father's tutoring in history, religion, and mathematics, and through Burns's own reading in English literature. He learned French and a little Latin and read many Renaissance and eighteenth-century writers, including Shakespeare, John Milton, and John Dryden. In addition to this training, Burns received an informal introduction to Scottish folk culture through servants and relatives in the house who sang folk songs and told stories and legends drawn from Scots myths.

The cottage where Burns was born is open to the public, as are many of his later houses.

At home, Burns's upbringing was apparently strict but fair, an attitude reflecting the pervasive influence of the Church of Scotland in eighteenth-century Scots society. As a Presbyterian denomination that preached the inherent evilness of humanity, the Church of Scotland emphasized that religion was the one permissible consolation in lives filled with hard work and self-denial. This puritanism was difficult for Burns to support, and he found himself in conflict with his father when, for example, he took Scottish country dance lessons.

In 1777 the family moved to Lochlie Farm, near Tarbolton, where William Burnes hoped the land would be more productive. Burns stayed mostly on his parents' farm, although in 1781–1782 he tried setting himself up in business in nearby Irvine. But the venture failed and Burns was forced to return penniless to Lochlie. Around the same time, Burns began the first of his many romantic relationships, which yielded nine illegitimate children in all. Much has been made of this record, but by the standards of his time it was not unusual, even if it did shock the pious. For each of these children Burns accepted responsibility and provided an upkeep.

In 1784, Burns's father died prematurely, leaving the family deeply in debt. Burns and his younger brother, Gilbert, took the family to another farm, Mossgiel, which they rented from a friend who admired Burns's poetry. For the rest of his life, Burns recalled bitterly how hard his father had worked and how little he had received in return. High rents and poor land were only two of the social and economic inequalities that Burns blamed for his father's early death.

Poetry

Robert Burns composed his first poem in 1774, at age fifteen, for a girl with whom he went harvesting. For the next twelve years, until the publication of his poems in 1786, Burns wrote with increasing conviction and originality. Initially, his juvenile poems copy the style of eighteenth-century sentimental poetry from England; but his later poetry starts to look more toward Scots poetry for its form and vocabulary. Throughout his writing career, Burns read avidly, primarily in English literature, but in Scots writing too. The eighteenth century saw a remarkable revival in Scottish writing, after a long period in which it looked as though Scots English might disappear as a literary language. After Burns studied Scots literature, his poetry began to show distinct Scottish characteristics, both in subject matter and in vocabulary.

The culmination* of the eighteenth-century Scots literary revival is often considered to be the publication in 1786 of Burns's *Poems, Chiefly in the Scottish Dialect,* the so-called Kilmarnock edition. Most of the poems in this volume were written between 1784 and 1786, a period of great turbulence in Burns's life. A year after his father's death, Burns's first child was born to Betty Paton, a former servant. In the following year, Burns fell in love with Jean Armour, a local woman, who soon became pregnant. When Armour's parents heard that Burns had offered to marry their daughter, they forbade her marriage to the poor farmer and instead sent Jean off to live elsewhere. Burns was very distressed and contemplated emigrating to Jamaica, where he had been promised a job. Instead he published the Kilmarnock volume, and his fame, if not his fortune, was ensured. Upon publication, the collection of poems became an instant hit among critics and country folk

*culmination peak; completion

alike. Amid great adulation,* Burns traveled to Edinburgh at the end of 1786 to introduce himself to his admiring public.

*adulation** praise

The poems themselves range from the sentimental to the satirical, and most contain a moral, frequently drawn from nature. In one of the most famous of Burns's poems, "To a Mouse," the poetic voice describes the regret he feels at breaking up a field mouse's nest with his plough. Burns claims that humanity is both part of nature, in being subject to the whims of fortune, and yet separate, in trying to subjugate nature for human purposes:

Satire is a literary form in which an author mocks the social fashions of his or her time.

> I'm truly sorry Man's dominion
> Has broken Nature's social union,
> An' justifies that ill opinion,
>   Which makes thee startle,
> At me, thy poor, earth-born companion,
>   An' *fellow mortal*!

In the poem, the farmer and the field mouse share a similar perspective; both are "earth-born" and live close to the land. While in the eighteenth century many philosophers argued that humanity was responsible for taking care of the land, the poem suggests that man's main effect has been to break the bonds of nature rather than strengthen them. As the poet notes, because of the farmer, the mouse is left exposed and homeless, with winter not far off. But then at the end of the composition, Burns remakes the rift between nature and humankind in an analogy* that connects the mouse's vulnerability with the farmer's:

analogy comparison based on similarity

> But Mousie, thou art no thy-lane,*
> In proving *foresight* may be vain:
> The best laid schemes o' *Mice* an' *Men,*
>   Gang aft agley,*
> An' lea'e us nought but grief an' pain,
>   For promis'd joy!
>
> Still, thou art blest, compar'd wi' *me*!
> The *present* only toucheth thee:
> But Och! I *backward* cast my e'e,
>   On prospects drear!
> An' *forward,* tho' I canna *see,*
>   I *guess* an' *fear*!

thy-lane on your own

These lines are the source of John Steinbeck's title of his 1937 novel, *Of Mice and Men.*

gang aft agley go often wrong

In the end, Burns points out that the mouse's lack of a memory and an imagination give it an advantage over humans, for it knows trouble only in the present.

The companion piece to "To a Mouse" is "To a Louse," which is considerably more satirical. In this second poem, the poet describes watching a louse crawl up the bonnet of a fashionable young woman sitting in front of him at church. As the louse advances, the poet notes the extreme contrast between the woman's elegance and the louse's grotesqueness. The woman thinks everyone is looking at her because of her beauty, but in reality they are following the louse's progress. The poem ends by ridiculing human vanity, a fault that the poet finds in himself:

> O wad some Pow'r the giftie* gie* us
> *To see oursels as others see us!*
> It wad frae* monie a blunder free us
>   An' foolish notion:
> What airs in dress an' gait wad lea'e* us,
>   An ev'n Devotion!

*giftie gift

*gie give

*frae from

*lea'e leave

Both of these poems were written using a three-hundred-year-old Scottish verse form called "standard Habbie." Each six-line stanza in the Habbie is composed of four lines of iambic pentameter* (lines one through three and five) and two lines of iambic dimeter* (lines four and six); the rhyme scheme is *aaabab.*

In Edinburgh, Burns met many of the leading literary figures of his time, and in 1787, a revised edition of *Poems, Chiefly in the Scottish Dialect* was published there. Feeling that his newfound fame was a safeguard against public opinion, Burns added poems that he had omitted from the original Kilmarnock edition. But some of his poetry he still thought too irreligious or bawdy to publish. The most famous of these suppressed compositions is "Holy Willie's Prayer," a verse satire that attacks the Church of Scotland's emphasis on predestination. Many Presbyterians believed that to be saved from damnation, one had to be chosen by God, and that no matter how virtuously one lived, one's fate was predetermined. In "Holy Willie's Prayer," the speaker assumes that he is one of the saved:

> Yet I am here, a chosen sample,
> To shew thy grace is great an' ample;

*iambic pentameter verse that has five metrical feet to a line, with two syllables in each foot and the accent (stress) on the second syllable (example da DA da DA)

*iambic dimeter verse that has two metrical feet to a line, with two syllables in each foot and the accent (stress) on the second syllable

I'm here, a pillar in thy temple
    Strong as a rock,
A guide, a ruler and example
    To a'* thy flock.

***a'** all

He then proceeds to enumerate all his sins and to curse his enemies. Wrapped up in his complacent monologue, Holy Willie completely misses the hypocrisy that the reader is intended to catch.

Songs

Burns left Edinburgh in mid-1788 and returned to farming, this time on a farm in Dumfriesshire. He reconciled with Jean Armour, and finally they married. Once again, however, Burns was faced with the difficulties of trying to support a family by working the land, and he managed to secure extra income by winning a position as an excise-tax collector. At the time, many goods were taxed and excisemen would travel around assessing the tax due. In 1791, with a promotion in the Excise, Burns moved his family into an apartment in the town of Dumfries itself. Now that he had a more secure source of income, he had more time to write. But he produced very little poetry after his trip to Edinburgh. The narrative poem written in rhyming couplets, "Tam O' Shanter," is the most notable piece from this period.

Instead, Burns turned his talents to collecting, and writing lyrics for, traditional Scottish folk songs. With James Johnson, a song publisher he had met in Edinburgh, Burns gathered and edited songs for several volumes of Johnson's *Scots Musical Museum,* published posthumously between 1787 and 1804. He also collaborated with George Thomson, another music publisher, in his multivolume collection, *Select Collection of Scottish Airs.* For all his composing and editing in these two collections, Burns accepted no payment; he thought that reclaiming the musical heritage of his country was a patriotic duty. For many critics, Burns's contribution to songwriting stands as his greatest and most influential achievement. He worked on hundreds of songs, sometimes simply transcribing* the music and lyrics, sometimes writing new lyrics for old tunes, and sometimes combining fragmentary lyrics with words of his own. Many of the songs are love songs, such as "I Love My Jean," which was written to Jean Armour. It ends:

transcribing copying

There's not a bony* flower, that springs
  By fountain, shaw,* or green;
There's not a bony bird that sings,
  But minds* me o' my Jean.

Connecting the subject of the poem with the beauty of nature is standard Burns, of course, but it is a common device in folk songs as well. At the beginning of "A Red, Red Rose," Burns again uses a natural simile to describe his sweetheart: "My luve's like a red, red rose, / That's newly sprung in June."

In other poems, Burns treats social and historical topics, frequently depicting the struggle for Scottish independence as a heroic battle against English oppression. Best-known of these nationalist songs is Burns's "Scots Wha Hae,"* which is set to the tune of an old drinking song. While the subject is the fourteenth-century Battle of Bannockburn, Burns's contemporaries would also have associated the song with the eighteenth-century national struggle for Scottish independence. The poem finishes with a call to arms against the English:

Wha* for Scotland's king and law
Freedom's sword will strongly draw,
Freeman stand or freeman fa',*
  Let him follow me!

After working for twelve years on the songs, Burns became ill at the end of 1795 and died of rheumatic fever on 21 July 1796. Jean gave birth to their last child four days later, on the day Burns was buried. Because Burns's life was so short and his exploits were so colorful, it is perhaps not surprising that he became enshrined as a national figure so soon after his death. Not only did he restore Scots as a poetic language capable of articulating the pleasures and traditions of ordinary life, but he also refurbished and extended Scottish folk music for generations to come.

Selected Bibliography

WORKS BY ROBERT BURNS

Poetry

Poems Chiefly in the Scottish Dialect (1786).

Letters

Roy, G. Ross, and J. De Lancey Ferguson, eds. *The Letters of Robert Burns.* 2 vols. Oxford, U.K.: Clarendon, 1985.

Available Collections

The Kilmarnock Poems (Poems, Chiefly in the Scottish Dialect, 1786). Edited by Donald A. Low. London: Dent, 1985.

The Poems and Songs of Robert Burns. 3 vols. Edited by James Kinsley. Oxford, U.K.: Clarendon Press, 1968.

The Poems and Songs of Robert Burns. Edited by James Kinsley. Oxford, U.K.: Oxford University Press, 1969.

The Poetical Works of Robert Burns. Edited by Raymond Bentman. Boston: Houghton Mifflin, 1974.

Robert Burns: Selected Poems. Edited by Carol McGuirk. Harmondsworth, U.K.: Penguin, 1993.

The Scots Musical Museum. 6 vols. Edited by James Johnson. Edinburgh, U.K.: James Johnson, 1787–1803.

A Select Collection of Original Scottish Airs for the Voice. 5 vols. Edited by George Thomson. London: Preston and Son, 1793–1818.

Songs of Robert Burns. Edited by John Ashmead and John Davison. New York: Garland, 1988. Musical score.

WORKS ABOUT ROBERT BURNS

Bentman, Raymond. *Robert Burns.* Boston: Twayne, 1987.

Bold, Alan. *A Burns Companion.* New York: St. Martin's Press, 1991.

Carswell, Catherine. *The Life of Robert Burns.* Edinburgh, U.K.: Canongate, 1930.

Crawford, Robert, ed. *Robert Burns and Cultural Authority.* Iowa City: University of Iowa Press, 1997.

Crawford, Thomas. *Burns: A Study of the Poems and Songs.* Stanford, Calif.: Stanford University Press, 1960.

Daiches, David. *Robert Burns.* 3d rev. ed. New York: Macmillan, 1967.

Daiches, David. *Robert Burns and His World.* London: Thames and Hudson, 1971.

Jack, R. D. S., and Andrew Noble, eds. *The Art of Robert Burns.* London: Vision Press, 1982.

Low, Donald A., ed. *Robert Burns: The Critical Heritage.* London: Routledge and Kegan Paul, 1974.

Low, Donald A., ed. *Critical Essays on Robert Burns.* London: Routledge and Kegan Paul, 1975.

Mackay, James. *RB: A Biography of Robert Burns.* Edinburgh, U.K.: Mainstream, 1992.

McGuirk, Carol. *Robert Burns and the Sentimental Era.* Athens: University of Georgia Press, 1985.

McGuirk, Carol, ed. *Critical Essays on Robert Burns.* New York: G. K. Hall, 1998.

Noble, Andrew. "Burns, Blake, and Romantic Revolt." In *The Art of Robert Burns.* Edited by R. D. S. Jack and Andrew Noble. London: Vision Press, 1982. Pages 191–214.

Simpson, Kenneth, ed. *Love and Liberty. Robert Burns: A Bicentenary Celebration.* Edinburgh, U.K.: Tuckwell Press, 1997.

RECORDINGS OF ROBERT BURNS'S SONGS

Mclean, Dougie. *Tribute to Robert Burns, Neil Gow, and Robert Tannahill.* Dunkeld Records, 1995.

McColl, Ewan. *Songs of Robert Burns.* Folkways, 1959.

Redpath, Jean. *The Songs of Robert Burns.* Philo, 1996.

GEORGE GORDON, LORD BYRON

(1788–1824)

by Ange Mlinko

Although the term "rock star" was not in anyone's vocabulary in 1812, it would have been useful to describe the English poet George Gordon, Lord Byron, when his long work *Childe Harold's Pilgrimage* made him a sensation at age twenty-four. In certain ways, Byron was like today's rock musicians, who not only compose their music but actually live what they sing about. Byron created exciting art and lived an exciting life. Today, our songs are still dominated by the "Byronic hero"—a handsome, aloof, misunderstood youth.

The Byrons were rakes,* gamblers, and adventurers. They included the poet's uncle "Wicked Lord Byron" and "Mad Jack," the poet's father (Captain John Byron), who married Catherine Gordon for her money and then financially ruined her and fled to France. With their baby son, Catherine had to beg shelter from relatives. This unstable, lonely life changed dramatically when, at the age of ten, the future poet

Quotations from Byron's poetry throughout are taken from *The Works of Lord Byron* (Wordsworth Editions, 1994).

*__rake__ someone who is rebellious or unrestrained

185

inherited a vast estate, Newstead Abbey, along with the title of baron. Little George Gordon became Lord Byron.

Byron relished his aristocratic status—it added to both his abundant charm and his excessive narcissism.* But although he always felt privileged, he also felt tortured. He gave himself airs because of his rank but was deeply in debt; he was handsome but had to diet strictly to avoid getting fat; and, most of all, he struggled with the shame of having been born with a clubfoot.* He walked with a limp (which kept him from dancing the fashionable waltz at society balls), and even swam in his trousers to hide his deformity.

*narcissism obsession with oneself

*clubfoot a twisted, deformed foot—an inherited condition

Early Poems and Adventures

Byron was born in London on 22 January 1788. He attended Harrow and then Trinity College, Cambridge, where he took his baccalaureate. In school, he read and loved the poems of Alexander Pope and the ancient Roman Horace, but it was not until later that their public-minded, satirical poems would influence his own. Byron's first book, *Hours of Idleness* contained simple lyrics. He had written them at Cambridge University, where his periods of depression alternated with extravagant partying. The book was savaged in a prominent magazine, the *Edinburgh Review,* and this prompted Byron to write his first satire,* *English Bards and Scotch Reviewers,* a vicious rebuttal. Luckily for him, he was out of the country when it was published: in 1809, at the age of twenty-one, he left for a two-year tour of southern Europe.

*satire sarcastic, ironic criticism

At this point it was not yet clear to Byron that he would devote himself to writing poetry. He made fun of poets in several letters, and, truth be told, he did not like to revise, polish, and perfect his own verses. For him there was nothing more inspiring than getting on a ship bound for a warm, exotic climate; having a series of infatuations with inappropriate people; and engaging in wild, debauched behavior far away from home. Nevertheless, Byron kept writing. One poem was "Written After Swimming from Sestos to Abydos," and he did indeed swim across the Hellespont Strait, like the ancient mythical hero Leander. Another poem, "Hero and Leander," was based on that myth—Leander swims across this channel every night to visit his forbidden bride, and every dawn he swims back. In his poem, Byron regrets that his motive for swimming

The Hellespont Strait, also called the Dardanelles, divides Europe and Asia Minor and averages three to four miles in width.

the Hellespont was glory, which is not as noble as Leander's motive, love. But the outcome of Leander's nobility is death—in the myth, he finally drowns—whereas Byron only catches a cold! While this is a humorous poem, showing Byron's sophisticated wit, it also shows a more serious aspect of his personality: a taste for self-mythologizing.

Another poem Byron wrote during this time made him famous when he published it on his return to England. This was *Childe Harold's Pilgrimage,* which hinted at autobiography:

> Whilome* in Albion's isle* there dwelt a youth,
> Who ne in virtue's ways did take delight;
> But spent his days in riot most uncouth,
> And vex'd with mirth the drowsy ear of Night.
> Ah, me! in sooth* he was a shameless wight,*
> Sore given to revel and ungodly glee;
> Few earthly things found favour in his sight
> Save concubines and carnal companie,
> And flaunting wassailers of high and low degree.
>
> (Canto I, stanza 2)

***Whilome** once upon a time
***Albion's isle** England
***sooth** truth
***wight** creature

In London society of that day poetry was popular, but it had to be suitably genteel.* A poet could be blackballed* by the admission that nothing gave him pleasure but "concubines" (prostitutes) and "wassailers" (drunkards). Yet by saying these things about a persona,* Childe Harold, Byron could escape personal blame. The poem follows Harold through the same landscapes that Byron visited: Portugal, Spain, Albania, Greece. The travelogue, though, was not what made the poem a sensation. It was the persona that fired readers' imagination.

***genteel** polite; refined
***blackballed** shunned; excluded
***persona** a fictional character who may or may not be the author's voice

At first glance Harold is cynical and self-destructive, wallowing in vice, but the narrator assures us that he is suffering from a secret torment. The suggestion is that, despite all the depraved women he makes love to, he is driven by the memory of one who "could ne'er be his." (Canto I, stanza 5). Seeing the happiness of ordinary people around him only isolates him more; he plays sad songs to relieve his pain, just like a troubled boy with a guitar today.

Women were enchanted by Childe Harold. When the poem was published, Byron found himself receiving a flood of invitations to dinners and balls. Everyone assumed that, in some measure, Byron was Harold. It helped that he was a beautiful man, with chestnut curls falling over his forehead and pale, delicate features; he was a perfect stand-in for his creation. Girls wrote him passionate letters, flocked around him at social gatherings, and schemed to attract him by any means.

"Mad, Bad, and Dangerous to Know"

Byron responded as many stars do—he had one stormy love affair after another. His most persistent mistress was Lady Caroline Lamb, famous for her wild exploits. It was Lamb who, in her diary, coined the phrase most associated with Byron: "Mad, bad, and dangerous to know" (reprinted in *Lady Caroline Lamb,* by Elizabeth Jenkins, 1932). He was dangerous indeed—at one gala, a matron* forbade her daughter to even look at him.

> ***matron** married woman; mother

One particular love affair proved his greatest passion and his downfall. As a child, he never knew his half-sister, Augusta Leigh. When they met as adults, he was struck by her likeness to him—the same features, the same egotistic but charming personality. He thought of her as a female alter ego. But as the mother of several children, she probably also represented something he never had—a warm, bustling family life in a stable home. In fact, he said as much in his "Epistle to Augusta," written after he had left her for good: "There yet are two things in my destiny,— / A world to roam through, and a home with thee." Their forbidden love affair, and her pregnancy with a child that may have been his, pushed him to marry a woman he did not love, the extremely proper and religious Annabella Milbanke. Byron regretted his marriage at once and lashed out at Annabella. She left him within the year, taking their newborn daughter, Ada, with her.

> ***pariah** outcast

For London society, this was the last straw. There had been explosive affairs, rumors of incest, outrageous debts— and now this scandalous divorce. A poetic hero can easily become a pariah:* unconventional behavior may be envied at first, but then it is punished. Byron's only choice was to flee England once again, and he set sail in April of 1816. Although he did not know it then, he would never return.

Exile and *Don Juan*

The difference between the spoiled youth of 1812 and the damaged man of 1816 can be gauged by comparing the first

So We'll Go No More A-Roving

So we'll go no more a-roving*
  So late into the night,
Though the heart be still as loving,
  And the moon be still as bright.

For the sword outwears its sheath,
  And the soul wears out the breast,
And the heart must pause to breathe,
  And Love itself have rest.

Though the night was made for loving,
  And the day returns too soon,
Yet we'll go no more a-roving
  By the light of the moon.

*a-roving roaming

part of *Childe Harold's Pilgrimage* and the last part, written after his exile. Cantos I and II made Byron famous, but cantos III and IV show real genius. This is the poetry of a broken-hearted man. He had lost Augusta and Ada—his only biological family—and had "grown aged in this world of woe, / In deeds, not years" (Canto III, stanza 5). To be old in deeds, not years, evokes a certain horror; although Byron was now only twenty-seven, his emotions were wrung out, leaving him numb and weary. How could life show him anything new?

Byron composed the final cantos of *Childe Harold's Pilgrimage* under the influence of the poet Percy Bysshe Shelley, who became a friend while they were both spending the summer in Geneva, Switzerland. Shelley was also in exile for challenging English society—among other things, he preached atheism and free love. But Shelley was more of an idealistic intellectual than a man of the world, so he was a perfect foil for Byron. Their passionate debates stirred them to deeper creativity. Meanwhile, the English poet laureate,* Robert Southey, called Shelley and Byron the "Satanic school." Byron had another daughter, Allegra, with Clare Claremont (the stepdaughter of William Godwin, who was the father of Shelley's wife, Mary).

Byron moved on to Italy for a couple of years, settling in Venice in 1816. In Venice, he wore himself out partying and

*poet laureate in England, an outstanding poet once appointed for life as a paid member of the royal household and expected to write poems for certain national occasions. In other countries, the term refers to a poet honored and recognized for his or her achievements.

*contemplative fo-
cused on deep
thought rather than ac-
tion*

*carousing partying;
drinking*

*ironic characterized
by a contrast between
our expectations and
reality, or between
what words say and
what they actually
mean*
*epic a long poem
that tells the story of a
hero's deeds*
*ottava rima a stanza
of eight lines of verse
with the rhyme
scheme abababcc*

*guilelessly inno-
cently*

*piety orthodox reli-
gious belief*

Boobies and noddies are types
of seabirds, but both terms can
also be insults whose meaning
is close to "fool" or "idiot."

then writing until sunrise. Soon Byron's poetry became more
worldly again. The man who once wrote "The great object of
life is Sensation" would never remain contemplative* for long.
During this time, he wrote perhaps his most perfect short
poem "So We'll Go No More A-Roving," in which he describes
the feelings of someone whose heart is exhausted by too
much nighttime carousing.* The tone is wistful but not regretful; the heart may be exhausted, but it is not extinguished.

In fact, Byron's mature poetic gift was satirical, as it was
for his favorites, Pope and Horace. A satirist is a social com-
mentator, who uses ironic* wit to make readers aware of their
own contradictions as social creatures. "Satire" comes from a
Latin word meaning "a full plate" or a plateful of fruits—a mixture or medley. And this, more than anything, describes
Byron's greatest poem, *Don Juan,* a sixteen-canto epic.*
Byron started *Don Juan* in Venice with the aim "to giggle and
make giggle" (*Selected Letters,* p. 214). He had discovered his
proficiency with the ottava rima,* whose triple rhyme has a
built-in comical quality while the final couplet has the timing
of a punch line. Using this bouncy stanza for the great themes
of sex, war, and money guaranteed a lighthearted tone and a
mischievous rebelliousness.

This time Byron did not create a hero in his own image:
Don Juan is his opposite, a passive innocent boy who is drawn
into love affairs, survives a shipwreck, is sold into slavery,
fights in a war, and becomes an ambassador. Unlike traditional
heroes, though, Juan has no quest; he merely reacts to situa-
tions so guilelessly* that he throws the workings of society
into unflattering relief wherever he goes. The conventional
framework of hero and quest is turned into an antihero and an
antiquest—making *Don Juan* a "mock" epic.

As the poem progresses, Byron emerges at its center. As
the narrator, a worldly and hilarious character who upsets our
pieties* with his comments, he wins us over to his charming,
cynical point of view. In the shipwreck scene, the survivors resort to cannibalism, but instead of being outraged, Byron tells
the tale in relentless detail: First the survivors seize Juan's father's spaniel to eat. Then they draw lots to see who will be
sacrificed, using a love letter of Juan's for paper. Next they
start to eye the fattest sailor, but they think better of it because
he has venereal disease! In the couplet "At length they caught
two boobies, and a noddy, / And then they left off eating the
dead body" (Canto II, stanza 82), the rhyme of "noddy" and

"body" chimes mockingly, but what is it mocking—the dead or the survivors? This ambiguity enraged Byron's public, who all but boycotted *Don Juan*.

Some of the poem's best qualities—humor, irreverence, natural speech rhythms—are not qualities that we normally associate with poetry of the Romantic period. Neither Shelley nor the Romantic poet John Keats, for instance, would have written, "There's not a sea the passenger e'er pukes in / Turns up more dangerous breakers than the Euxine"* (Canto IV, stanza 5). Nor had any other ambitious poet dared to depict himself as a drunkard, poking fun at the impulse to be "poetic":

> I would to Heaven that I were so much clay,
>   As I am blood, bone, marrow, passion, feeling—
> Because at least the past were passed away,
>   And for the future—(but I write this reeling,
> Having got drunk exceedingly to-day,
>   So that I seem to stand upon the ceiling)
> I say—the future is a serious matter—
>   And so—for God's sake—hock* and soda water!
>
> (Canto I, fragment)

The tone of the first two lines seems earnest and sentimental: Byron is saying something like Shelley's "I fall upon the thorns of life, I bleed!" (in "To a Skylark"). But then he loses his train of thought and admits that he is intoxicated. He tries to pick up the thread again but impatiently gives up and calls for more wine. This time, there would be no persona; Byron would speak as himself—polite society be damned!

Another innovation is the way he calls attention to the fact that he is writing a poem. Describing someone's heartbreak, he writes, "Below his window waved (of course) a willow," mocking romantic earnestness with the droll* interjection "of course." Byron's chattiness disarms us: he digresses constantly, remarking on a variety of subjects, like this hymn in praise of speed:

> Now there is nothing gives a man such spirits,
> Leavening his blood as cayenne doth a curry,
> As going at full speed—no matter where its
> Direction be, so tis but in a hurry,
> And merely for the sake of its own merits;

*Euxine the Black Sea

*hock a type of white wine. A mixture of hock and soda-water was a popular cure for a hangover

*droll oddly humorous

Cayenne is an extra-hot pepper added to a sauce called curry. Byron points out that both spicy foods and fast driving make our hearts beat faster.

> For the less cause there is for all this flurry,
> The greater is the pleasure in arriving.
> The greater *end* of travel—which is driving.
>
> (Canto X, stanza 72)

The poem casually veers off into commentary on as many things as cross his mind, expansive as his love of the real world, real things. ("Are not words *things?*" he insisted in a letter; *Selected Letters,* p. 85.) *Don Juan* could have continued endlessly. As an epic, it paralleled Byron's life and thought, and it has no dominating structure. When he died, it was still ongoing, and it remains a great poetic cliff-hanger.

It is interesting to see how Byron took habits that might have been flaws—like his distaste for revision and his short attention span—and turned them into virtues by finding the right form. By taking on a large project, he could let himself stretch out; writing a battle scene, then a satire, then an essay on poetry, then a travelogue. And at a time when intellectual, introspective poetry was in favor, Byron stayed true to his outgoing, satirical self. He wrote to a friend that *Don Juan* "may be bawdy, but is it not good English? It may be profligate* but is it not *life,* is it not *the thing?* Could any man have written it who has not lived in the world?" (*Selected Letters,* p. 220).

Tiring of domestic life with his last love, an Italian countess, Byron threw his energies and his wealth behind the struggle of Greece to win independence from Turkey. Before he could fight, however, he died of fever in Missolonghi, Greece, on 19 April 1824. The last entry in his notebook included a poem written some weeks before his illness, "On This Day I Complete My Thirty-Sixth Year." Its last lines—"Then look around, and choose thy ground, / And take thy rest"—show how close Byron's life and art really were. He had written his epitaph* without knowing it.

*profligate extravagant; undisciplined

*epitaph the writing on a tombstone—can be used to mean any words written in memory of one who is deceased

IF YOU LIKE the poetry of Byron, you might also like the poetry of Geoffrey Chaucer, Alexander Pope, W. H. Auden, Gregory Corso, Kenneth Koch, Frank O'Hara, or Ron Padgett.

ᏍᏟ

Selected Bibliography

WORKS BY GEORGE GORDON, LORD BYRON
Poetry

Hours of Idleness (1807).

English Bards and Scotch Reviewers (1809).

Childe Harold's Pilgrimage (1809–1817).

The Vision of Judgment (1822).

The Prisoner of Chillon (1816).

Beppo (1818).

Don Juan (1818–1824).

Available Collections

Byron's Poetry. New York: W. W. Norton, 1978. A selection of poetry, letters and journals, and criticism.

Complete Poetical Works. Edited by Jerome J. McGann and Barry Weller. London: Oxford University Press, 1981.

Don Juan. Edited by T. G. Steffan and E. Steffan. New York: Penguin, 1988.

The Works of Lord Byron. England: Wordsworth Editions, 1994.

Letters

Lord Byron: Selected Letters and Journals. Edited by Leslie A. Marchand. Cambridge, Mass.: Belknap Press of Harvard University Press, 1982.

WORKS ABOUT LORD BYRON

Bloom, Harold, ed. *George Gordon, Lord Byron (Modern Critical Views).* New York: Chelsea House Publishers, 1986.

Gleckner, Robert F., ed. *Critical Essays on Lord Byron.* New York: G. K. Hall, 1991.

Grosskurth, Phyllis. *Byron: The Flawed Angel.* Boston: Houghton Mifflin, 1997.

Jump, John D. *Byron: A Symposium.* London: Macmillan, 1975.

Marchand, Leslie. *Byron: A Biography,* 3 vols. New York: Knopf, 1957.

Marchand, Leslie. *Byron's Poetry: A Critical Introduction.* Cambridge, Mass.: Harvard University Press, 1968.

Ridenour, George M. *The Style of "Don Juan."* New Haven, Conn.: Yale University Press, 1960.

More About Byron

You can write to:
The Newstead Abbey Byron Society
Hon. Secretary, Maureen Crisp
The White Lady Restaurant
Newstead Abbey Park
Nottingham, NG15 8GE
United Kingdom

fax: (01623) 796856
http://www.fujisan.demon.co.uk.

C. P. CAVAFY

(1863–1933)

by Edmund Keeley

Unless otherwise indicated, quotations from Cavafy's poetry throughout are taken from Savadis, ed., *C. P. Cavafy: Collected Poems*.

A poet who grows up in several foreign countries has both advantages and disadvantages. Constantine Peter Cavafy was born on 29 April 1863 to Greek parents (Peter John and Hariclea Cavafy) in Alexandria, Egypt. He attended school in London and Alexandria, though few details of his formal education survive. As a young man he lived for three years in Constantinople (now Istanbul, Turkey) before returning to Egypt to spend all of his adult life in Alexandria as a member of the city's Greek community. His early years in England gave him a chance to read the English poets, who became an important influence on his work, and it is said that he always spoke his native Greek with a slight English accent. Also, his distance from the Greek mainland encouraged his imagination to explore the ancient Hellenic* world of the Greek diaspora:* along with Alexandria, other cities such as Antioch in Syria and Beirut and Sidon in Phoenicia (now Lebanon) were part of the world that Alexander the Great had conquered and Hellenized in the fourth century B.C.

*Hellenic Greek, usually with reference to ancient Greece and its heritage

*diaspora dispersion; the scattering of a group of people to areas outside of their homeland

The Poet's Small Corner of the World

In Cavafy's early adulthood, the modern city of Alexandria posed problems for him. His family, once socially and financially prominent, lost its fortune through unwise business speculations shortly after his father's death, when Cavafy was only seven. To support himself, Cavafy worked for more than thirty years as a clerk in the Egyptian Irrigation Service run by the British, with no chance of joining the permanent staff because of his Greek citizenship. As a homosexual, he also felt restricted by the puritanical* society that surrounded him in the "small corner" of the world—as his 1910 poem "The City" puts it—that he had chosen for his life's work. From a journal note that he wrote in 1907 we see that even in his forties he had not quite managed to resolve his love-hate relationship with his home city:

> By now I've gotten used to Alexandria, and it's very likely that even if I were rich I'd stay here. But in spite of this, how the place disturbs me. What trouble, what a burden small cities are—what lack of freedom. I'd stay here (then again I'm not entirely certain that I'd stay) because it is like a native country for me, because it is related to my life's memories. But how much a man like me—so different—needs a large city. London, let's say. . . (Keeley, p. 19).

Alexandria as the Sensual City

The resolution came some four years later, after Cavafy had moved into the second-floor apartment on rue* Lepsius that was to be his residence for the rest of his life. From the age of forty-seven until his death at seventy, he lived alone, not as a recluse but as a man of letters devoted first of all to his poetry yet also to the encouragement of younger poets and foreigners, such as English fiction writer E. M. Forster, who visited him for literary talk and advice. During his later years he also began to distribute his work to friends and admirers in folders that allowed him to clip together offprints of his poems from magazines and individual poems published as broadsheets;* the folders were kept continually up-to-date year in and year out. He

puritanical narrow-minded or austere, especially regarding sexuality

rue French word for street

broadsheet a newspaper page

Ionic

That we've broken their statues,
that we've driven them out of their temples,
doesn't mean at all that the gods are dead.
O land of Ionia, they're still in love with you,
their souls still keep your memory.
When an August dawn wakes over you,
your atmosphere is potent with their life,
and sometimes a young ethereal* figure,
indistinct, in rapid flight,
wings across your hills.

ethereal other-worldly

never published a collected edition of his work during his lifetime because he apparently never considered his life's work complete enough for that purpose, and in his last days he was reported to have said: "I still have twenty-five poems to write."

At the time Cavafy moved into his rue Lepsius apartment, he decided to make use of his "life's memories" in poems that gradually revealed the city under his balcony window to be the setting of an intense eroticism, of the lovers he had known and the sensual pleasures he had experienced in his youth, as we see in a 1917 poem entitled "In the Evening":

It wouldn't have lasted long anyway—
the experience of years makes that clear.
Even so, Fate did put an end to it a bit abruptly.
It was soon over, that wonderful life.
Yet how strong the scents were,
what a magnificent bed we lay in,
what pleasure we gave our bodies.

An echo from my days given to sensuality,
an echo from those days came back to me,
something of the fire of the young life we shared.
I picked up the letter again,
and I read it over and over till the light faded away.

Then, sad, I went out on to the balcony,
went out to change my thoughts at least by seeing
something of this city I love,
a little movement in the street and the shops.

Alexandria as a Poetic Myth

The poet's accommodation* with his city and his imaginative transformation of it into an erotic backdrop for remembered sensations also encompassed ancient Alexandria, a city that became a central poetic myth in Cavafy's work from 1910 on. The myth had a basis in the long history of Alexandria, from the time of the first rulers, the Ptolemies, through the Arab conquest in A.D. 642 and beyond, but the poet used this history to create an imaginary city that offered a special way of life consistent with the poet's image of both an ideal possibility and a fated reality. The way of life allowed for the worship of physical beauty, the devotion to poetry and art, the enjoyment of theater, the promotion of the Greek language, and the celebration of feeling, but the poet was also aware that this mode of living could be costly if carried to excess and that, in any case, it was subject to the intervention of fate. A number of his poems that present his portraits of ancient Alexandrians are epitaphs for those who died young after a life given over entirely to pleasure, though there is redemption in the memory of what has passed and in its preservation in poetry:

> Raphael, they're asking you to write a few lines
> as an epitaph* for the poet Ammonis:
> something very tasteful and polished. You can do it,
> you're the one to write something suitable.
> For the poet Ammonis, our Ammonis.
>
> Of course you'll speak about his poems—
> but say something too about his beauty,
> about his subtle beauty that we loved.
>
> Your Greek is always excellent and musical.
> But we want all your craftsmanship now.
> Our sorrow and our love move into a foreign language.
> Pour your Egyptian feeling into the Greek you use.
>
> Raphael, your verses, you know, should be written
> so they contain something of our life within them,
> so the rhythm, so every phrase clearly shows
> that an Alexandrian is writing about an Alexandrian.
>
> "For Ammonis, Who Died at 29, in 610"

Images of the Man in the Street and of the Mighty

An important characteristic of Cavafy's ancient Alexandrians is that they are a mixture of different races, religions, and languages that live together comfortably. Raphael is a Christian Copt* and Ammonis an ancient Egyptian in the poem we have just seen, with Greek rather than Egyptian as their language of choice. Cavafy was a writer who promoted tolerance and communal harmony among people of different backgrounds and beliefs. As the English author E. M. Forster said of him in an early comment on his work, "racial purity bored him. . . . The civilization he respected was a bastardy* in which the Greek strain prevailed, and into which, age after age, outsiders would push, to modify and be modified" (E. M. Forster, *Two Cheers for Democracy,* 1951, pp. 249–250).

Copt an Egyptian Christian

bastardy a mixture of different races or nationalities

The speaker in the poem "Ionic" identifies himself with the Christians who came into Ionia in Asia Minor during the early centuries after Christ to break the statues of the ancient Greek gods and to drive them out of their temples. But he suggests that the souls of the gods are so in love with what they lost that they still hover over the landscape, and sometimes one of them returns as an "ethereal figure" to fly rapidly over the Ionian hills.

Another characteristic of his ancient Alexandrians, of the man and woman in the street, is their political shrewdness, sometimes bordering on cynicism,* and their suspicion of the mighty who think they have command of the people's destiny. When Antony and Cleopatra go out to the new Alexandrian Gymnasium to award kingdoms they do not actually posess to their three children, their gathered subjects are charmed by the spectacle, as they are by the warm, poetic day, but we are told that "they knew of course what all this was worth, / what empty words they really were, these kingships" ("Alexandrian Kings").

cynicism distrust; dismissal as untrue

Mark Antony, ruler of the Roman Empire, was the father of three of Cleopatra's children.

Less knowing in Cavafy's world are those in power who earn the disfavor of the gods because of their arrogant belief in their own invincibility,* what the Greeks call "hubris." We learn in the poem "The Footsteps" (1909), for example, that the evil Roman emperor Nero, in the prime of his strength, lies asleep "callous, peaceful, happy," quite unconscious of the deadly footsteps of the Furies* climbing the stairs to do him in. And the

invincibility indestructibility

Furies Spirits that avenge wrongdoing, especially murder

*ascendancy rise to the top. In this case, the culture's rise to the pinnacle of power and prestige.

speaker in the poem entitled "In the Year 200 B.C.," who criticizes the Spartans' earlier loss of power and superiority while praising the "far-flung supremacy" of Alexander's later empire in his day, remains fatally unaware that Alexander's empire is shortly doomed to be conquered by the Roman legions.

Cavafy came to see, as his work matured, that any individual success and any moment of historical ascendancy* was subject to reversal by the gods—in the end a tragic perspective. But it is also a perspective that warns us against arrogance, self-deception, and complacency, while showing us that wisdom and courage are found in those who see things as they are and who recognize their limitations, especially when confronted by the inevitable end that awaits all things human. That is part of the advice in "The God Abandons Antony" that the poet offers Mark Antony at the time he faces defeat at the hands of Octavius Caesar, in the battle of Actium, when the god Dionysus—or, in Shakespeare's version, the god Heracles—abandons him to his fate. The other part of his advice is that Antony should recognize that the true god abandoning him in his final moments is the city of Alexandria, the gift and source of pleasure that this great Roman general and lover of Cleopatra proved worthy of receiving:

> When suddenly, at midnight, you hear
> an invisible procession going by
> with exquisite music, voices,
> don't mourn your luck that's failing now,
> work gone wrong, your plans
> all proving deceptive—don't mourn them uselessly.
> As one long prepared, and graced with courage,
> say goodbye to her, the Alexandria that is leaving.
> Above all don't fool yourself, don't say
> it was a dream, your ears deceived you:
> don't degrade yourself with empty hopes like these.
> As one long prepared, and graced with courage,
> as is right for you who were given this kind of city,
> go firmly to the window
> and listen with deep emotion, but not
> with the whining, the pleas of a coward,
> listen—your final delectation*—to the voices,
> to the exquisite music of that strange procession,
> and say goodbye to her, to the Alexandria you are losing.

*delectation delight

The Poet's Unique Voice

In a commentary on his own poetry, Cavafy once said that his work could be divided into poems that are erotic, historical, or philosophical, though he stressed that these categories frequently overlap. This is clearly so in the poems about Ammonis's epitaph and Antony's last hours. But sometimes Cavafy offers the reader advice directly, without speaking to or through a character. Several of these "philosophical" poems have become among his best-known and most frequently quoted poems, such as the one entitled "As Much as You Can," in which he tells the reader to try not to degrade his or her life by "taking it around and exposing it so often / to the daily silliness / of social events and parties" until life comes to seem a boring stranger or hanger-on. But poems of this kind were most often early work. In his maturity, Cavafy usually preferred to express himself through short poems that tell a story or through dramatic monologues* in which a character clearly identified in the poem expresses his thoughts. Whether his emphasis is erotic, historical, or philosophical, Cavafy succeeded in creating a poetic world that is original in both its perspective and its mode of expression—what W. H. Auden called his "unique tone of voice" (*The Complete Poems of Cavafy,* p. viii). It is a voice often rich in irony* and humor, only occasionally lyric, that almost always uses distinct speakers.

    It is also a voice that is consistently crafted in its diction* and rhythm. During his early years, the poet frequently wrote his poetry not in the spoken language (known as "demotic") but in the artificial "purist" language (known as "Katharevusa"), a language modeled on ancient Greek that had been created at the end of the eighteenth century and that became the official language of the country into the mid-twentieth century, though most poets had long since chosen to write in demotic. As Cavafy developed his mature style, his poetry became dominated by the spoken language and its conversational expressions, though he still made use of purist elements and he sometimes offered "Katharevusa" for purposes of irony or to represent the pretensions of some of his characters. To the end the language of his poetry remained close to the relatively formal language spoken by the Alexandrian community to which he belonged.

*dramatic mono-logue a poem written as a speech for one character

*irony saying the opposite of what you mean to make your point even more strongly

*diction choice of words

*homophonous rhymes pronounced alike but with different meanings or spellings. The words *to, too,* and *two* are an example.

In terms of form, his early poetry was often strictly rhymed, sometimes by way of homophonous rhymes,* as in "Teichi" (Walls):

Chōris periskepsin, chōris lypēn, chōris aidō
megala k'hypsēla trigyrō mou ektisan teichē.

Kai kathomai kai apelpizomai tōra edō.
Allo den skeptomai: ton noūn mou trōgei aūti hē tychē;

dioti pragmata polla exō na kamō eichon.
A hotan ektizan ta teichō pēs na mēn prosexo.

All ōden akousa pote kroton ktistan ē ēchon.
Anepaisthētōs m'ekleisan apo ton kosmon exō.

The English translation by Rae Dalven reads:

Without consideration, without pity, without shame
they have built great and high walls around me.

And now I sit here and despair.
I think of nothing else: this fate gnaws at my mind;

for I had many things to do outside.
Ah why did I not pay attention when they were building
   the walls.

But I never heard any noise or sound of builders.
Imperceptibly they shut me from the outside world.

*free verse poetry that does not follow traditional forms, rhythmic patterns, or rhyme schemes

But in his maturity Cavafy turned more and more to free verse* that was complex in meter if always carefully shaped; in some instances, he offered poems with elaborate or very loose rhyme schemes (as are illustrated by George Savidis's notes in *C. P. Cavafy: Collected Poems*).

What Cavafy's mature voice tells us was ahead of its time. In his tolerance of the unconventional and of a mixed society, in his political skepticism and his tragic sense of life, he speaks to the contemporary reader as much as he did to the few who recognized his genius during his lifetime, and his capacity for remaining current is what justifies his constantly expanding popularity and his growing reputation as a major poet of the twentieth century.

Selected Bibliography

WORKS BY C.P. CAVAFY

The Complete Poems of Cavafy. Translated by Rae Dalven with an introduction by W. H. Auden. New York: Harcourt, Brace, and World, 1961.

C. P. Cavafy: Collected Poems. Translated by Edmund Keeley and Philip Sherrard. Edited by George Savidis. Rev. ed. Princeton: Princeton University Press, 1992.

The Essential Cavafy. Translated by Edmund Keeley and Philip Sherrard. Edited by George Savidis. Introduction by Edmund Keeley. Hopewell, N. J.: Ecco Press, 1995.

WORKS ABOUT C.P. CAVAFY

Bien, Peter. *Constantine Cavafy.* Columbia Essays on Modern Writers, no. 5. New York: Columbia University Press, 1964.

Keeley, Edmund. *Cavafy's Alexandria.* Revised edition. Princeton, N. J.: Princeton University Press, 1996.

Liddell, Robert. *Cavafy: A Biography.* New York: Schocken Books, 1976

The Mind and Art of C. P. Cavafy: Essays on His Life and Work. Athens, Greece: Denise Harvey and Co., 1983.

Special Issues of Periodicals

Grand Street 2 (spring 1983). Edited by Ben Sonnenberg.

Journal of the Hellenic Diaspora 10, nos. 1–2 (spring–summer 1983). Guest edited by Margaret Alexiou.

✍️
More About Cavafy:
You can find the website of the Cavafy Archive and Library at:
http://www.snhell.gr/english.html

BLAISE CENDRARS

(1887–1961)

by Jay Bochner

I was barely sixteen but my childhood memories were
    gone
I was 48,000 miles away from where I was born
I was in Moscow, city of a thousand and three bell tow-
    ers and seven train stations
And the thousand and three towers and seven stations
    weren't enough for me
Because I was such a hot and crazy teenager

Quotations from Cendrars's po-
etry throughout are taken from
Padgett, trans., *Complete
Poems*.

C endrars opens his epic* poem *La prose du transsi-
bérien et de la petite Jeanne de France* (*The Prose of
the Trans-Siberian and of Little Jeanne of France*) by
looking at himself as a teenage boy, when he ran away from his
home in a small Swiss town, through Germany, Poland, and all
the way to Russia. He could hardly have predicted that ten
years later he would find himself at the center of the artistic
avant-garde,* having a drink in a café in Montmartre, a section

*epic a long poem
that tells the story of a
hero's deeds. The
most famous Western
epic is *The Odyssey*, by
Homer.
*avant-garde ad-
vanced or cutting-
edge; experimental

of Paris, France, known for its cultural life, with some of the most famous artists, musicians, and writers of the century:

> I'm going to the Lapin Agile* to remember my lost
>   youth again
> Have a few drinks
> And come back home alone
>
> (p. 29)

***Lapin Agile** An inexpensive restaurant frequented in the early 1900s by poor artists. Translated, the name means "Nimble Rabbit."

As these lines suggest, he would soon be on his way again. One of Cendrars's great contributions to French modernist* poetry was to be forever on the run, always returning to literary circles with work that was original and new. Another long poem of this period, *La Paname; ou, Les aventures de mes sept oncles* (*Panama; or, The Adventures of My Seven Uncles*), roams the wide world only to end in another famous Paris café, this time in Montparnasse, a section of the city traditionally associated with the arts and located on the left bank of the Seine River.

***modernist** modernist poets rejected the ornamentation of much late nineteenth and early twentieth century poetry, and tried to infuse their work with the immediacy and energy of contemporary life.

> A seltzer bottle sneezes
> The literary tittle-tattle keeps moving
> Very low
> At the Rotonde*
> As if at the bottom of a glass
>
> (pp. 49–50)

***Rotonde** a famous cafe in Paris

Here, Cendrars would meet with the poet Guillaume Apollinaire, the artists Pablo Picasso and Marc Chagall, and the composer Igor Stravinsky, as well as his best friends Fernand Léger (an artist with whom Cendrars wrote three books) and Amedeo Modigliani (who painted Cendrars's portrait six or seven times). It was a period, just before the devastation of World War I, when artists, writers, and musicians intermixed in what the American novelist John Dos Passos called a "creative tidal wave," an "explosion" that produced "the best work in the arts in our time." Cendrars's part in this explosion was to bring poetry out of the nineteenth century and into modernity, making it reflect the everyday changes brought into people's lives by industry, mechanization, and modern travel and communication. His poetry exhibits both optimism about the possibilities of modern life and a sadness about its failures and dislocations. He managed to stay true to his own ideas by departing from the "literary tittle-tattle," taking his friend Léger off to an obscure, working-class bar, for example, or disappearing altogether to the other end of the world. As the title of one memoir about him expressed it, *Cendrars Is Never Here*.

Starting Out

Cendrars was born Frédéric Sauser in the watchmaking Swiss town of La Chaux-de-Fonds on 1 September 1887. He gave various versions of the story of his youth, so we do not really know just how frequently his family moved. They lived in Paris, London, and probably Egypt, where his father may have managed a hotel. More to the point is how these changes affected Cendrars's poetry, in which we read of him, in this untitled poem collected in *To the Heart of the World* (1919), wondering about his allegiances* and origins in a world in which travel and immigration are so common.

> Am I pelagic* like my Egyptian nanny or Swiss like my
> father
> Or Italian, French, Scottish, and Flemish like my grand-
> father or
> whichever of my great-grandfathers was an organ-maker
> in the
> Rhineland and in Burgundy. . . .
>
> (p. 225)

From the ages of eight to ten he lived in Naples, Italy, then went to school back in Switzerland, in Basel and Neuchâtel. According to Cendrars, it was from Neuchâtel that, at sixteen, after pilfering his sister's piggy bank and sliding down the drainpipe, he took off. His father had locked him in his room after discovering that he had accumulated some three hundred hours of absences from the commerce school he had been enrolled in. The boy no doubt did run away, but perhaps not without help from his family—once in Russia he worked for a Swiss jeweler in Saint Petersburg, a job his father may have found for him in the community of Swiss exiles,* as a way of compromising with his fiery and footloose son.

In Russia, the government was just finishing the construction of the Trans-Siberian Railroad, which would link western Russia to the Pacific Ocean, a monumental undertaking to help the country into the twentieth century. The route

*allegiance loyalty

*pelagic from the ocean

*exile forced absence from one's homeland. The word is also used to mean a person who is in exile.

was forged over five thousand miles (more than double the track that linked the American West with the rest of the nation) through six time zones. "The Trans-Siberian" recounts Cendrars's three-week ride along this line, during which the hospital trains full of soldiers wounded in the Russo-Japanese War rushed in the opposite direction after the Japanese defeated the Russians at Port Arthur, where Russia had hoped to have a port on the Pacific. Many have wondered if Cendrars ever really made this Homeric* (long and extensive, like the journeys in Homer's epic poems) voyage; his response to questions about his truthfulness was to remind readers of what he alone had enabled them to see:

> I deciphered all the garbled texts of the wheels and
>   united the scattered elements of a violent beauty
> Which I possess
> And which drives me
>
> (p. 28)

Cendrars was still in Saint Petersburg during the beginnings of the Russian Revolution—Bloody Sunday in January of 1905; the assassination of the Grand Duke Sergei, the governor general of Moscow; the general strike in October—and aspects of these events found their way into his novel *Moravagine*, published in 1926. In 1907 he studied medicine in Switzerland; a year later he was raising bees in a small town in France, and later he was an actor in Brussels, Belgium. In 1910 he tried his luck in Paris, then returned to Saint Petersburg. From there he traveled, for the first time, to America, arriving in steerage* like a new immigrant. It was in New York that he wrote his first long poem of note, *Les Pâques à New York* (Easter in New York), and where, before he departed in June of 1912, he created his pen name (Blaise from the French *braise*, "embers"; Cendrars from *cendres*, "ashes"). While New York City in 1912 was hardly the center of cultural activity that Paris was, it nevertheless opened his eyes to the extremes of modern life—the soaring skyscrapers (there were none yet in Europe) contrasted with the severe poverty of immigrants.

> Lord, the poor masses for whom you made the Sacrifice
> Are here, penned in, heaped up, like cattle, in
>   poorhouses.

> Huge dark ships come in around the clock

The Russo-Japanese War (1903–1904) occurred when Japan attempted to prevent Russian expansion into the Pacific Ocean. Russian troops arrived via the Trans-Siberian Railroad, as the Russian naval fleet had been partially destroyed, then bottled up by the Japanese at Port Arthur.

Russian Revolution of 1905: prompted by Russian military defeats at the hands of the Japanese, the populace increasingly pressured the tsar, Nicholas II, to form a constitutional government. Nicholas made concessions, then arrested many workers, and dispersed or exterminated what remained of the movement. The Revolution was successful only in 1917.

*steerage The lowest, windowless part of a ship.

And dump them off, pell-mell, onto the dock.

. . . .

They're circus animals that leap the meridians.*
They're thrown a piece of rotten meat, like swine.

. . . .

Lord, cold as a shroud the dawn slipped away
And left the skyscrapers naked in the day.

(pp. 6, 11)

*meridian the geographer's lines of longitude, running North-South on the globe, used to measure one's position on the earth

This was not the American dream as advertised, and almost no one, American or European, was writing of such contrasts between the haves and the have-nots in a spiritually deficient and commercialized world, certainly not in such straightforward language.

Paris and the Avant-Garde

In July of 1912 Cendrars returned to Paris, linking up with various figures in the avant-garde. Apollinaire, for one, published his poems, which quickly found a European public interested in new ways of writing. Many of these poems are dedicated to painter friends, and some are even about them, such as this one about Marc Chagall, collected in *Dix-neuf poèmes élastiques* (Nineteen Elastic Poems):

He's asleep
He wakes up
Suddenly, he paints
He takes a church and paints with a church
He takes a cow and paints with a cow
With a sardine

(p. 60)

Cendrars also published, in his own small book cooperative, the two long poems "Easter in New York" and "The Trans-Siberian." This latter poem was printed on a single seven-foot sheet, accompanied by a seven-foot painting by the artist Sonia Delaunay. The lettering is in colored inks and of many different shapes and sizes. He finished *Panama,* longest of the three poems, but it was not published until 1918. Each of these works is an epic presentation of the individual searching for a footing in the new worlds of the twentieth century, and in each of them the printed words and lines on the page appear to skip, slide, and explode in imitation of the hero's dangerous balancing acts:

> The Milky Way around my neck
> The two hemispheres on my eyes
> At top speed
> There are no more breakdowns
> . . . .
> Earth Earth Seas Oceans Skies
> I'm homesick
> I follow every face and I'm scared of mailboxes
> The cities are wombs
> I don't follow the roads anymore
> Lines
> Cables
> Canals
> Nor suspension bridges!
>
> (p. 49)

The publication of these poems confirmed Cendrars's growing reputation as a great adventurer-traveler of the modern world, but just as great an adventure is taking place on the page, in the actual writing, which is full of verve,* inventiveness, bluntness, strangeness, often enough, and unsentimental intimacy. As in much modernist poetry, thought here is fragmented and appears to change direction from line to line. This style reproduces the disruption felt by a person bombarded with sensations. But whereas in most modernist writing disruption seems mainly internal to the hero's mind, in Cendrars's verse the speaker is sensitized to innumerable sights of people and things in a fast-moving world. And if the adventures are not his personal ones, then the writing is all the more remarkable for its appearance of being eyewitness reality. In fact, exoticism* in the poem may not be the author's at all, but that of others, as in *Panama,* where most of the events are narrated by means of letters from Cendrars's seven uncles to their sister, Cendrars's mother:

> Papeete,* September 1, 1887
> My dear, dear sister
> I've become a Buddhist, a member of a political sect*
> I'm here to buy dynamite

*verve spirit; character; "spunk"

*exoticism appeal gained from being foreign or strange

*Papeete the capital of Tahiti

*sect a group of people held together by common religious or political beliefs

You can buy it here at grocery stores the way you buy
    chicory* in France
In little packets
Then I'll go back to Bombay and blow up the English
Things are getting hot
I'll never see you again . . .

(p. 39)

*chicory a plant. Its roots were used as a cheap substitute for coffee.

World War I and the 1920s

When France declared war in August 1914 Cendrars and two friends drafted a call to all foreigners to enlist, and Cendrars was first to do so himself. Before leaving for the front he married Fela Poznanska, with whom he already had two sons (a daughter was born in 1921). He joined the Foreign Legion* and within a few months found himself in the trenches. He escaped injury for about a year, but in September 1915 his right forearm was blown off. Back in Paris, he taught himself to write with his left hand, and, with so many men at the front, found all sorts of odd jobs, harvesting watercress in a small village, for example. He lived for a while with gypsies, getting to know the impoverished suburbs of Paris and their bustling underground economies.

*Foreign Legion a French military force made up of foreign volunteers

When the war came to an end in November 1918, cultural activities resumed in Paris and Cendrars found old friends and new ones, who saw him as a legendary survivor of the prewar art scene. As the assistant to the French film director Abel Gance for the movie *J'accuse* (1919), he recruited soldiers mutilated in the war to play an ending scene in which the dead rise from the battlefield (Cendrars acted in the scene as well). He worked with Gance on his next film, *La roue* (1923), some of which was shot in an isolated cabin Cendrars found high in the Alps* and later used for the setting of his novel *Dan Yack*. He directed his own film in Rome, wrote scenarios for ballets, and ran a publishing house. Meanwhile, his poetry had taken a remarkable turn: *Kodak (documentaires)* is mostly a volume of what is now called "found poetry," poems assembled from nonpoetic texts written by others. (In 1914 he had produced "News Flash," probably the first found poem.) In strictly legal terms, *Kodak* is one massive plagiarism;* on the other hand, it is the discovery of poetic wonder and sensuality in what

*Alps a European mountain range

*plagiarism the publishing of someone else's writing as if it were one's own

transatlantic across the Atlantic Ocean. Here, the term may refer to radio communications that come from across the Atlantic Ocean, or to steamships.

Paris-Midi A popular Parisian newspaper

Intransigeant a Paris newspaper

futurism an artistic movement that embraced, and even glorified, new machines and mechanization.

simultaneity the occurrence of two or more events at the same time; here, probably a reference to a movement in the arts, simultaneism, concerned with conveying the sense of many unrelated things happening all at once

Bodin, Jean (1530–1596) Early Renaissance French philosopher and magistrate who wrote a book on the proper punishment of witches and Satanists.

acetylene fuel for a welder's blowtorch

Crackling (excerpt)

Sparks
Chrome yellow
We're in contact
The transatlantics* are coming in from every direction
Going away
Every watch is set
And the bells are ringing
*Paris-Midi** announces that a German professor was eaten
    by cannibals in the Congo
Well done
This evening's *Intransigeant** includes poems for postcards
It's stupid when all the astrologers burglarize the stars
You can't see anymore
I question the sky
The Weather Bureau is forecasting bad weather
There is no futurism*
There is no simultaneity*
Bodin* burned all the witches
There is nothing
There are no more horoscopes and you have to work
I'm upset
The Spirit
I'm going to take a trip
And I send this stripped-down poem to my friend R . . .

(*Dix-neuf poèmes élastiques,* Nineteen Elastic Poems)

appeared to be the most unimaginative of places: the dull prose of menus and newspapers, out of which he produced such poems as "Work."

    Some crooks have just blown up the railway bridge
    The coaches caught fire at the bottom of the valley
    The injured swim in the boiling water from the
        disemboweled locomotive
    Living torches run among the debris and spewing steam
    Other coaches stay hanging 60 yards up
    Men with flashlights and acetylene* torches follow the
        trail down the valley
    And the rescue is organized quietly and quickly

Under the cover of rushes of reeds of willows the
    waterfowl make a nice rustling noise
Dawn is long in coming
But already a team of a hundred carpenters called by
    telegraph and come by special train is busy
    rebuilding the bridge
Bang bang-bang
Pass me the nails

                        (p. 104)

Kodak, rather than a series of snapshots of the real world, is a tour through the world of print and the minds of unknown, or unsung, writers.

In Cendrars's next volume, *Feuilles de route* (Travel Notes), he reported on his own voyages to and from South America. These poems take the shape of short postcards or radiograms* back to a woman in France. "Travel Notes" goes perhaps as far as any collection of poems could in the direction of making poetry out of the simplest events and the simplest language, as here in "Letter":

You said to me if you write me
Don't just use the typewriter
Add a line in your own hand
A word a nothing oh a little something

.   .   .   .

But my Remington* is beautiful

.   .   .   .

Still to please you I add in ink
Two or three words
And a big blot of ink
So you can't read them

                        (p. 143)

*radiogram an old-fashioned predecessor of the radio cassette recorder, combining a record player (gramophone) and a radio

*Remington a brand of typewriter, which, in the 1920s, was still new technology

The Poet Turns to the Novel

Somewhat suddenly after these two volumes of 1924, Cendrars ceased to write poetry altogether. He had already published a volume of African folk tales in 1921; in the later 1920s he wrote two adventure novels, the brutal *Moravagine* and the wrenching *Dan Yack,* and a fictionalized biography of a

*levitation the act of rising in the air without visible means of support, so that it appears to be supernatural

forgotten John Sutter, called the "Emperor of California," on whose vast holdings of land in California gold was discovered in 1848, causing the gold rush. In the 1930s Cendrars concentrated on journalism, writing a book on French crime gangs; a report on the first crossing of the Atlantic Ocean by a French luxury liner, the *Normandie;* a translation of a biography of American gangster Al Capone; a book on Hollywood; and newspaper accounts of the civil war in Spain. The start of World War II found him as a reporter on a British submarine, and shortly later traveling in a baggage car with the evacuated gold reserves of the French national bank; he spent the war years in a sort of internal exile in the South of France. Here, in Aix-en-Provence, and after three years with his silenced Remington, he began to write the four massive, complex, interrelated novels of his later years. In these works the adventures and obsessions of his very full life are telescoped and magnified, assembled and reconstructed. The last, published in 1949 and translated as *Sky: Memoirs,* makes all his life's adventures appear airborne and, in fact, one of its main topics is levitation.*

After the war, Cendrars eventually returned to Paris, to write one more novel, *To the End of the World* (1956), and to spend his last years with Raymonde, an actress he had been in love with since 1917 and married in 1949. (His first wife had died several years earlier.) Until Cendrars's death in Paris on 21 January 1961, they lived within sight of the Eiffel Tower. This landmark had been a recurring topic in his work, as in his 1914 poem about the radio antenna atop the tower, which captured news from around the world.

Selected Bibliography

WORKS BY BLAISE CENDRARS
Poetry in French

> *Les Pâques à New York* (1912; Easter in New York).
>
> *La prose du transsibérien et de la petite Jeanne de France* (1913; Prose of the Trans-Siberian and of Little Jeanne of France).
>
> *Le Paname; ou, Les aventures de mes sept oncles* (1918; Panama; or, The Adventures of My Seven Uncles).
>
> *Dix-neuf poèmes élastiques* (1919; Nineteen Elastic Poems).

Kodak (documentaires) (1924; *Kodak*).

Feuilles de route (1924; Travel Notes).

Fiction

African Saga (1921). Translated by Margery Bianco. New York: Negro University Press, 1969.

Shadow (from *The African Saga*). Translated and illustrated by Marcia Brown. New York: Scribner's, 1982.

Gold (1925). Translated by Nina Rootes. New York: Michael Kesend, 1984.

Moravagine (1926). Translated by Alan Brown. New York: Penguin Classics, 1979. Reissued with introduction by Henry Miller. New York: Blast Books, 1990.

Dan Yack (1927). Translated by Nina Rootes. New York: Michael Kesend, 1987.

Confessions of Dan Yack (1929). Translated by Nina Rootes. London: Peter Owen, 1990.

Hollywood (1936). Translated with an introduction by Garrett White. Berkeley: University of California Press, 1995.

The Astonished Man (1945). Translated by Nina Rootes. London: Peter Owen, 1970.

Sky: Memoirs (1949). Translated by Nina Rootes. Introduction by Marjorie Perloff. New York: Paragon Books, 1992.

To the End of the World (1956). Translated by Alan Brown. Introduction by Margaret Crosland. London: Peter Owen, 1991.

Available Collections

Complete Poems. Translated by Ron Padgett. Introduction by Jay Bochner. Berkeley: University of California Press, 1992.

Complete Postcards from the Americas: Poems of Road and Sea. Translated and with an introduction by Monique Chefdor. Berkeley: University of California Press, 1976.

Kodak. Translated by Ron Padgett. New York: Adventures in Poetry, 1976.

Modernities and Other Writings. Translated by Esther Allen with Monique Chefdor. Edited and with an introduction by Monique Chefdor. Lincoln: University of Nebraska Press, 1992.

Panama; or, The Adventures of My Seven Uncles. Translated by John Dos Passos. New York: Harper, 1931.

Selected Writings of Blaise Cendrars. Edited by Walter Albert. New York: New Directions, 1966. Repr. Westport, Conn.: Greenwood Press, 1978.

WORKS ABOUT BLAISE CENDRARS

Bochner, Jay. *Blaise Cendrars: Discovery and Re-creation.* Toronto, Canada: University of Toronto Press, 1978.

Caws, Mary Ann. "Blaise Cendrars: A Cinema of Poetry." In her *The Inner Theater of Recent French Poetry.* Princeton, N.J.: Princeton University Press, 1972.

Chefdor, Monique. *Blaise Cendrars.* Boston: Twayne, 1980.

Miller, Henry. "Blaise Cendrars." In *The Books in My Life.* New York: New Directions, 1952.

Perloff, Marjorie. "Profond Aujourd'hui." In her *The Futurist Moment: Avant-Garde, Avant Guerre, and the Language of Rupture.* Chicago: University of Chicago Press, 1986.

More About Cendrars

You Can Write to:
Centre d'étude Blaise Cendrars
Swiss National Library
Unitobler, 49
Langgasstrasse, CH-3012
Berne, Switzerland

AIMÉ CÉSAIRE
(b. 1913)

by Clayton Eshleman

In America, we have never had a great artist who was also an important politician. However, on the island of Martinique, in the West Indies, the poet Aimé Césaire was elected mayor of the capital, Fort-de-France, in 1945, and deputy for Martinique (then a French colony) to the Constituent Assembly in Paris. Besides inventing twentieth-century Martinican poetry and refocusing French surrealism,* Césaire served as mayor and deputy (the equivalent of a U.S. congressman) until his retirement in the early 1990s.

Césaire brought his political and artistic visions together in a concept that he coinvented and explored in his poetry: *negritude*. For Aimé Césaire, this term expresses a renewed awareness and acceptance of being black, and pride in laying claim to one's African roots.

Quotations of Césaire's work throughout are taken from Eshleman and Smith, trans., *Aimé Césaire: The Collected Poetry.*

*surrealism an artistic movement that aimed (chiefly during the 1920s and 1930s) to express the workings of the unconscious or subconscious mind

Early Life

Aimé Césaire was born on 25 June 1913 in Basse-Pointe, a town on the northern coast of Martinique. He was the second of seven children. His father was a local tax inspector and his mother a dressmaker. While his family did not belong to the class of illiterate agricultural laborers that made up the vast majority of black Martinicans, they were poor. In Césaire's *Cahier d'un retour au pays natal* (*Notebook of a Return to the Native Land*), he depicts how it was to grow up in a home whose roof was patched with pieces of gasoline cans and whose bed legs were old kerosene cans:

> **At the end of the wee hours, another little house very bad-smelling in a very narrow street, a minuscule house which harbors in its guts of rotten wood dozens of rats and the turbulence of my six brothers and sisters, a cruel little house whose demands panic the ends of our months and my temperamental father gnawed by one persistent ache, I never knew which one, whom an unexpected sorcery could lull to melancholy tenderness or drive to towering flames of anger; and my mother whose legs pedal, pedal, night and day, for our tireless hunger, I was even awakened at night by these tireless legs which pedal the night and the bitter bite in the soft flesh of the night of a Singer* that my mother pedals, pedals for our hunger and day and night (p. 41).**

In this prose poetry* passage, Césaire writes long, winding phrases with repetitions that build up momentum. Notice how the phrase "the bitter bite in the soft flesh of the night" associates the stabbing motion of the sewing-machine needle with his mother's pained and weary body, as she works incessantly with the foot pedal of an old-style sewing machine.

When Aimé was eleven, his family moved to Fort-de-France where he was able to attend the Lycée Victor Schoelcher, at that time the only secondary school for all of Guadeloupe, French Guiana, and Martinique.

Martinican Nature

One feature of Césaire's poetry is its abundance of Martinican fauna and flora,* probably a result of the influence of one of his secondary school teachers. Eugène Revert took his students out to the local countryside to interest them in its unique geographical characteristics at a time when standard

*Singer a brand of sewing machine

*prose poetry poetry that is not divided into lines and that does not have rhyme and meter

*fauna and flora the animal (fauna) and plant (flora) life in a particular area

examination questions were based on mainland French history and geography. Many years later, Césaire discussed the poetic and political reasons for his careful observation of Martinican nature in an interview (cited and translated in *The Collected Poetry*, p. 405):

> I must name Martinican things, must call them by their names. The cañafistula mentioned in [the poem] "Spirals" is a tree; it is also called the drumstick tree. It has large yellow leaves and its fruit are those purplish bluish black pods, used here also as a purgative.* The balisier resembles a plantain, but it has a red heart, a red florescence at its center that is really shaped like a heart. The cecropias are shaped like silvery hands, yes, like the interior of a black's hand. All of these astonishing words are absolutely necessary, they are never gratuitous. . . .*

***purgative** a medicine that clears out one's digestive system

***gratuitous** extra and unnecessary

Sometimes Césaire identifies plants and creatures by their genus or scientific names instead of their popular names. Thus instead of "big centipede" we find "scolopendra," or instead of "destructive beetle" he writes "cockchafer."

Paris, *Negritude,* and Surrealism

Césaire's outstanding performance at Lycée Schoelcher earned him a scholarship to the Lycée Louis-le-Grand in Paris (1931). In 1935 he gained entrance to France's highest liberal arts institute, the École Normale Supérieure in Paris. In all, Césaire spent eight years in Paris, before returning to Martinique in 1939. While in Paris, he met the poets Léon-Gontran Damas from French Guiana and Léopold Senghor from Senegal, who helped him work out his concept of *negritude*. This concept was in part made possible by the twentieth-century "discovery" of African civilizations and cultures, the news of which was just arriving in western Europe from travelers and anthropologists. *Negritude* was a major attempt to correct the centuries-old problem of the alienated* position of blacks in history. In ancient times the blacks inhabited their homeland: a whole continent. Then the diaspora* scattered blacks across the world, leaving them enslaved or colonized with neither a present nor a future nor even a language of their own.

***alienated** excluded

***diaspora** dispersion; the scattering of a group of people to areas outside of their homeland *vernacular the language or dialect commonly spoken in a particular region

The colonial system refers to the economic and political relationship that existed between Martinique and France. The island was settled by the French in 1635 and African slave labor was brought in starting in 1664. Slavery was ended in 1848, but the island remained part of France.

In this regard, Césaire's relation to the French language is complex. Illiterate Martinicans spoke Creole—an oral vernacular* that, though evolved from French, had a limited vocabulary and lacked a literary tradition. Césaire was pointed away from Creole when he was a child, as his father used to read the children French prose classics instead of telling them stories in Creole. However, French is not a native Martinican language in the same way that Wolof and Bambara are native African languages. French was imposed upon Martinicans in the past by their slave masters and, in Césaire's day, by the colonial system.

Since Césaire found Creole inadequate for creating poetry with his worldview, he was faced with working out his poetic destiny in a language of which he was essentially a prisoner. But his situation turned out to be much less grim than it sounds. In Paris, he discovered the great nineteenth-century French poets, including Charles Baudelaire, Arthur Rimbaud, and Lautréamont, who were also in revolt against the kind of thinking that created French colonialism.

During the same years, Césaire also explored possibilities raised by surrealism, a radical movement in the arts that placed a tremendous value on dreams and on accessing those aspects of the mind involved in dreaming. He was particularly interested in the surrealist technique of "automatic writing." The idea here was that by writing spontaneously, without correcting oneself or even insisting that the writing make sense, it was possible to break up conventional patterns in language and approximate the state of dreaming, as well as to get below one's rational mind into the deep recesses of oneself. It has been said that when the poet-leader of the surrealists, André Breton, went to bed at night, he hung a sign on his door that said, "Man at Work." This was a witty way of expressing the surrealist belief that one worked on one's poetry while one dreamed. In his subconscious mind Césaire could discover a world that was not a product of colonial society and education. Surrealism thus offered Césaire a chance to rid himself of the alienation most black Martinicans experienced and to begin to discover the authenticity that had been denied him.

Notebook of a Return to the Native Land

Césaire began his long poem *Notebook of a Return to the Native Land* in 1936, after returning from a trip to Yugoslavia, where he spent some time on an island called Martinska in the Aegean Sea. The story goes that the name of the island and certain of its aspects recalled Césaire's homeland so vividly to him that he began to confront for the first time in writing what it meant to be a black Martinican. The first drafts of the poem were written in a student notebook—thus the first word of the title.

The *Notebook* is more of an extended lyric poem than an epic. It opens with a brooding,* static overview of the psychology and geography of Martinique. A second movement* begins with the speaker's desire to go away: suddenly the lifeless present is sucked into a whirlpool of abuses and horrors suffered by blacks throughout their colonized history. The second movement reaches its low point in a passage where the speaker discovers himself mocking an utterly degraded old black man on a streetcar. The final, rushing third movement is ignited by the line: "But what strange pride suddenly illuminates me!" (p. 67). In a series of shifts between the emergence of a future hero giving new life to the world and images from the slaves' "middle passage" of the past, the "sprawled flat" passivity of the first movement is changed into a standing insurrection* on a slave ship. In this poem Césaire must (metaphorically) conceive and give birth to himself while exorcising* his inner and collective image of the black. The language and images in *Notebook*—considered to be Césaire's masterpiece—are quite wild and amazing.

Politics

In his role as the Martinican representative for the French Communist party, Césaire was responsible for the 1946 bill that transformed Martinique's status from a French colony into a department with full rights of French citizenship for all its inhabitants. He left the Communist party in 1956 after the sinister character of the Stalinist regime in the Soviet Union was exposed. He then founded his own party, the Martinican Progressive Party (1958), which he led until his retirement in the early 1990s.

POLITICAL POETRY

Imaginative political poetry is difficult to write well, because if you have a cause that you want to support, you risk simply repeating what others have said. Your agenda may be more

*brooding gloomy

*movement a section within a poem or song

The middle passage was the route that slave ships took from Africa across the Atlantic Ocean to the Americas.

*insurrection revolt against authority

*exorcising purifying; getting rid of bad or evil parts

Joseph Stalin was the general secretary of the Communist party, who as a virtual dictator led the Soviet Union from 1924 until his death in 1953. His policies included centralization of agriculture and industry and the brutal suppression of political opponents.

Mississippi

Too bad for you men who don't notice that my eyes
    remember
slings and black flags
which murder with each blink of my lashes

Too bad for you men who do not see who do not see
    anything
not even the gorgeous railroad signals
formed under my eyelids by red and black discs of
the coral snake that my munificence* coils in my tears

Too bad for you men who do not see that in the depth
    of the reticule*
where chance deposited our eyes
there is, waiting, a buffalo sunk to the very hilt of the
swamp's eyes

Too bad for you men who do not see that you cannot
    stop me from building for him plenty
of egg-headed islands out of the flagrant sky
under the calm ferocity of the immense geranium of
    our sun.

munificence gen-
erosity

reticule a drawstring
bag

dense crowded or
highly concentrated.
Dense literature is lit-
erature that takes a lot
of effort and concen-
tration to read because
there is a lot to under-
stand in each short
passage

solidarity unity or
sympathy

*dramatic mono-
logue* a poem written
as a speech by one
character

powerful than anything you can do with it. The poet Kenneth
Koch has written: "The problem in writing poetry about a
cause is how to remain yourself, how to be personal enough so
that your own thoughts and feelings can get into the poem—
feelings which may be contradictory and which may include
questions and doubts—how to be free enough to remain open
to inspiration and original perceptions" (pp. 281–282).

"Mississippi" is a typical, dense,* political poem by Césaire written in the mid-1940s. It is written out of solidarity*
with African Americans in the southern United States, significantly before the civil rights movement. It is a dramatic monologue,* in which the speaker, an African American Mississip-
pian, is aware on one hand of an inner, insurrectional vitality,
and on the other hand of how ignorant white racists are of this
vitality. Notice how in each stanza Césaire injects his own sur-
real images so that the reader receives his personal response
as well as his politics. Also notice the mysterious and foreboding animal powers of the speaker.

The word "him" in the fourth stanza refers to the "buffalo" in the third. This buffalo represents the suppressed African American dynamism* just waiting to burst forth. Although the second stanza is complicated, it is not nonsense. The speaker proposes that the whites do not pick up the warning signals that the venom and grief in his eyes give off. The fact that his venom is coiled in his sorrow represents a great generosity on his part toward the whites. Stripped of his sorrow, the implication goes, he would become a mass of unmitigated revenge. Notice how Césaire has associated the black and red rings of a coral snake with the circular warning lights of a railroad signal.

The act of comprehending a complex poem like "Mississippi" is almost like writing a poem of your own. Césaire asks you to go halfway with him, to imagine what he has imagined. In a way, he is offering you a challenging half poem. For it to be a whole poem you must complete it in your imagination as you read.

> *dynamism force or energy

Conclusion

As a person from Martinique, where no one is indigenous* but where to be educated is to have one's identity consumed by models imported from Europe, Césaire began with the greatest disadvantages. His initial move in poetry was to take a step backward as he took a step forward, to ground his work in, as he later put it, "the first days of the species," as he assimilated Rimbaud, Lautréamont, and French surrealism. This ability to be at the same moment in the deep past suffering black slavery and in the present anticipating a liberated future is extraordinary, and is the main reason that Césaire is difficult—and also a great poet. For these forces are not just subjects of poems, but rather, elements in a molten* substance, rising to the surface and descending.

> *indigenous relating to the earliest human inhabitants of a place

> *molten in a hot, liquid form

Selected Bibliography

WORKS BY AIMÉ CÉSAIRE
Poetry

Cahier d'un retour au pays natal (1939).

Les armes miraculeuses (1946).

> IF YOU LIKE the poetry of Césaire, you might also like the poetry of André Breton, Blaise Cendrars, or Guillaume Apollinaire.
>
> ❣

Soleil cou coupé (1948).

Corps perdu (1949).

Ferrements (1960).

Cadastre (1961).

Moi, laminaire (1982).

Prose

Discours sur le colonialisme (1950).

Lettre à Maurice Thorez (1956).

Toussaint Louverture (1960).

Plays

La tragédie du roi Christophe (1963).

Une saison au Congo (1965).

Une tempête (1969).

Available Collections and Translations

Aimé Césaire: The Collected Poetry. Translated by Clayton Eshleman and Annette Smith. Berkeley: University of California Press, 1983. With extensive introductions and detailed notes on the poems.

Lyric and Dramatic Poetry, 1946–1982. Translated by Clayton Eshleman and Annette Smith. Charlottesville: University Press of Virginia, 1990. With extensive introductions and detailed notes on the poems.

Discourse on Colonialism. Translated by Joan Pinkham. New York: Monthly Review Press, 1972. Césaire's most important political essay.

Non-Vicious Circle: Twenty Poems of Aimé Césaire. Translated by Gregson Davis. Palo Alto, Calif.: Stanford University Press, 1984. Translation, with notes and commentary, of twenty representative Césaire poems.

WORKS ABOUT AIMÉ CÉSAIRE

Arnold, A. James. *Modernism and Negritude: The Poetry and Poetics of Aimé Césaire.* Cambridge, Mass.: Harvard University Press, 1981. The first full-scale critical study of Césaire in English.

Koch, Kenneth, and Kate Farrell. *Sleeping on the Wing: An Anthology of Modern Poetry with Essays on Reading and Writing.* New York: Random House, 1981. An introduction to twenty-three American and foreign-language poets. See especially Koch's "Note on Translation" (pp. 67–70) and his comments on political poetry (pp. 281–283).

GEOFFREY CHAUCER

(ca. 1342–1400)

by Gary Lenhart

Although he was not born into nobility, the ambitious and resourceful Geoffrey Chaucer made a career of service to the English monarchy. He rose rapidly in rank from court page to soldier to customs collector to diplomat. His diplomatic missions took him to Spain, Flanders (most of which is now part of Belgium), France, and Italy. Everywhere he went, he listened to the local stories and poems, which he brought back home and wrote down in English. He was particularly struck by the French *Roman de la rose* (Romance of the Rose) and the Italian poems of Dante, Francesco Petrarch, and Giovanni Boccaccio. Indeed, large parts of Chaucer's poems consist entirely of translation from these French, Italian, or Latin originals. But it was the homely strokes—his plain language—with which he adapted the exotic stories for his audience that have placed them at the center of English literature. Chaucer's language may sound old and strange to us, but he is the first modern European poet to write in English. After six hundred years, he remains one of the most entertaining and inspiring of all English poets.

The language of Chaucer, called Middle English, was used from the twelfth century until the fifteenth century, when it was replaced by Modern English.

Life

Chaucer's father was a prosperous London wine merchant and his mother the daughter of a wealthy London moneylender. The precise date of Chaucer's birth is uncertain, though scholars place it about 1342. Chaucer first appears on record in 1357, when he was attached to the household of King Edward III's son Prince Lionel and the prince's wife, the countess of Ulster, who bought him a short cloak, a pair of shoes, and tight red and black breeches. Chaucer next appears in historical records as a soldier in Edward's army that invaded France in 1359, where he was captured by the enemy and later ransomed by the king. Apparently he remained in the service of either the king or Prince Lionel during the next ten years, during which he married Philippa Pan, the daughter of a knight. Her sister was the longtime mistress and eventually the wife of John of Gaunt, another of the sons of King Edward. Chaucer's in-laws were all closely attached to the royal family.

Beginning in 1366, Chaucer served the monarchy on diplomatic missions that took him to the court of Peter the Cruel in Spain; to Genoa, Florence, Milan, and Padua in Italy; and many times to France. In 1374 he was appointed a collector of customs at the Port of London, a post that required full and close bookkeeping, the drudgery of which Chaucer complained about in the *House of Fame*. During this time the Chaucers had at least one son, Thomas; and possibly another son (Lewis) and two daughters.

In 1385, Chaucer received permission to perform his duties as customs collector through a permanent deputy. He moved from London to Kent, where he was elected to attend Parliament. It was during this time of disengagement from London and his customs duties that Chaucer began to compose his major poems, *Troilus and Criseyde,* the *Legend of Good Women,* and the *Canterbury Tales.* In 1387 Philippa Chaucer died, and with her death the income of the Chaucer household decreased markedly. Two years later Chaucer was appointed a clerk of the king's works, a post that paid him well for managing royal business. But Chaucer had to carry money for the many ventures he supervised and he was robbed several times. After two years of service he was replaced as clerk of the works and appointed a forester of the king's parks. At the end of 1399, Chaucer leased a house in the garden of Westminster Abbey, where he spent the last months of his life.

On 25 October 1400, Chaucer died and was buried in the abbey, the first tomb in what has since become the Poets' Corner, where many famous English poets have been buried.

Minor Works

As noted, large parts of many of Chaucer's poems are translations from poems in French, Italian, or Latin. Because of his poetic ambition, he sometimes projected and often began works that remained unfinished or survive in fragments. Where feasible, he incorporated his early poems or some of these fragments into later works. It has been as difficult for scholars to attribute the dates and order of his poems as it has been for them to sketch the poet's biography. But today most scholars agree to the following rough outline of Chaucer's poetic output. It should be noted that the poems grouped in most editions of Chaucer under "short poems" were written throughout his life.

Only the *Book of the Duchess,* "An ABC," and some of Chaucer's early "complaints" (stories in which a rejected lover argues his case or expresses his sorrow) were composed before 1372. Most editions of Chaucer also include the translation of the *Roman de la rose,* which may also belong to this period. However, many scholars now debate how much of that translation was actually written by Chaucer. The *Book of the Duchess* is an allegorical* love vision after the style of the popular French ballads* of Chaucer's day and reveals his knowledge and appreciation of that poetry. It was written upon the death in 1369 of Blanche, the duchess of Lancaster and the first wife of John of Gaunt. "An ABC" is a free translation of a French poem supposedly made at the request of the same duchess of Lancaster that the poet supply her with a prayer for her devotions. "The Complaint unto Pity," "Complaint to His Lady," and "Complaint of Mars" were probably written during this same period. These complaints were likely also modeled on French poems.

Between 1372 and 1380 Chaucer wrote the *House of Fame* and early versions of several tales he later revised for the *Canterbury Tales.* The *House of Fame* is a dream vision that resembles the *Book of the Duchess* in form but that expresses Chaucer's dissatisfaction with the tedium of his customs calculations and his yearning for fame. The poem is notable for the author's familiarity with Dante's *Divine Comedy* and his summary of Virgil's *Aeneid* (it is supposed that reading

*__allegorical__ having a story in which the fictional objects, characters, and actions are equated with meanings that lie outside the story itself

*__ballad__ rhythmic poem that tells a story and is often meant to be sung

*purgatory in the Roman Catholic religion, a place where souls go after death to be punished, and thereby made worthy of heaven

The Peasants' Revolt occurred in the summer of 1381 in response to the enforcement of tax laws.

*heresy dissenting opinions from official church dogma or, in this case, from the god of love

Dante's poem inspired Chaucer to read Virgil, Dante's guide through hell and purgatory*). The *Parliament of Fowls,* written for Valentine's Day, is also a dream vision, but the mocking, satirical edge that characterizes so much of Chaucer's later work first becomes prominent in this long poem. The parliament described in the author's dream includes a range of birds that parodies the social classes of fourteenth-century England, from the eagles at the top of the social hierarchy to the seed fowl at the bottom. Although the poem was written at about the time of a Peasants' Revolt in England, when everyone must have been edgy about class conflicts, Chaucer seems content to make merry at everyone's expense.

From 1380 to 1387, Chaucer wrote *Troilus and Criseyde,* the *Legend of Good Women,* and some of the Italian stories that would later be incorporated into the *Canterbury Tales;* he also worked on his translation of the *Consolation of Philosophy,* by the Roman philosopher Boethius. The poet's projects were becoming more ambitious, and he was beginning to turn from the creaky dream vision style that he had employed so often to the more fluent and realistic narrative method used by his Italian contemporaries. *Troilus and Criseyde* is the only major poem that Chaucer ever finished. According to the prologue in the *Legend of Good Women,* Cupid, the god of love, commanded Chaucer to atone for the heresies* he had expressed against love in *Troilus and Criseyde* and in his translation of the *Roman de la rose* by writing this poem about women who were famous faithful lovers. The *Legend of Good Women* begins with the tales of Cleopatra, Thisbe, and Dido and sketches six other heroines, but the poem was left in fragments.

After 1387, Chaucer devoted himself to the *Canterbury Tales,* interrupting that work only to write a few short poems (including "The Complaint of Chaucer to his Purse" and the fragmentary *Treatise on the Astrolabe,* allegedly composed to explain the astrolabe, an instrument used to observe celestial bodies, to his son Lewis).

Troilus and Criseyde

In *Troilus and Criseyde,* Chaucer adapted the story of two ill-fated lovers from Boccaccio's *Filostrato.* Indeed, a good deal of Chaucer's version is a free translation of Boccaccio's tale, in which Troilus pines for the unattainable Criseyde, enlists the services of his friend and her relative Pandarus to help him, and swears his undying fealty* to her. By a quirk of fortune, however, the Trojan leaders suddenly negotiate with the Greeks an exchange of Criseyde for the captured Antenor. Although Criseyde vows to Troilus that she will return to him as soon as possible, she soon switches her love from Troilus to the Greek Diomedes and remains among the Greeks. Troilus fights vengefully against Greek troops but is wounded and dies in despair.

    Chaucer changes Troilus very little. His disappointed protagonist remains a model of thirteenth-century chivalry,* a noble victim of his own lofty ideals. Chaucer, however, makes a few major changes that render his version a little harder on Criseyde and Pandarus than Boccaccio's. In both versions, Troilus falls hopelessly in love with the widowed Criseyde but is intimidated by her beauty, social status, and apparent indifference to him. He confides his love only to his friend Pandarus, who convinces him that his suit is not hopeless and agrees to be the go-between who will approach Criseyde. But in Boccaccio's poem, Pandarus is a young soldier of Troilus's generation, cousin to Criseyde, and distracted by his own unsuccessful love. Chaucer makes Pandarus an older man, Criseyde's uncle, and a more comic figure. By removing Pandarus from the arena of young love, Chaucer makes him a figure who should know better than to act as a facilitator in this secret affair.

    In subsequent English poetry Chaucer's Criseyde became a synonym for faithless women. Although she seems sincere in her protestations of love for Troilus, she also seems to be aware of the manipulations that prepare her meeting with him. Nor does she hold out long against the suit of Diomedes. By our standards, she appears to be a realistic young woman who constantly makes the best of the difficult situations in which she is placed. One suspects even that Chaucer is sympathetic to her realism, but she betrays the standards of fourteenth-century romance by refusing to give all, even her life, for love.

Canterbury Tales

Chaucer's *Canterbury Tales* is one of the great unfinished poems in English literature. A party of twenty-nine pilgrims to the shrine of Saint Thomas à Becket in Canterbury arrive at

*__fealty__ fidelity

*__chivalry__ a code of behavior that developed among medieval knights and emphasized manners, Christianity, courage, and honor

General Prologue to the Canterbury Tales
(excerpt)

Whan that Aprill with his shoures soote
The droghte of March hath perced to the roote,
And bathed every veyne in swich licour
Of which vertu engendred is the flour;
Whan Zephirus eek with his sweete breeth
Inspired hath in every holt and heeth
The tendre croppes, and the yonge sonne
Hath in the Ram his halve cours yronne,
And smale foweles maken melodye,
That slepen al the nyght with open ye
(So priketh hem nature in hir corages);
Thanne longen folk to goon on pilgrimages,
And palmeres for to seken straunge strondes,
To ferne halwes, kowthe in sondry londes;
And specially from every shires ende
Of Engelond to Caunterbury they wende,
The hooly blisful martir for to seke,
That hem hath holpen whan that they were seeke.

(*The Complete Works of Geoffrey Chaucer*)

---

the Tabard Inn in Southwerk. There they are joined by Chaucer and the host of the inn. The latter proposes that the party pass its time by telling stories. The plan of the poem was to include two tales by each member of the party. But as Chaucer left it, the poem comprises only one tale each by twenty-four of the pilgrims, and many of those are incomplete. The only member of the party who tells two is Chaucer himself, only because he is stopped midway through his tale of Sir Thopas by the host, who deplores his "drasty rymyng"* and insists that he continue in prose. Chaucer accommodates him with a "litel thyng in prose" about a man named Melibeus, whose wife and daughter are assaulted by his enemies.

The subjects of the tales range widely across thirteenth-century English society, as might be expected from the range of pilgrims in the band. The first tale belongs to a knight, its most eminent member in social status, who relates the lofty chivalric tale of Palamon and Arcite, virtuous young cousins and knights of Thebes who become mortal enemies over their

*__drasty rymyng__ filthy or worthless rhyming

Modern English Translation

As soon as April pierces to the root
The drought of March, and bathes each bud and shoot
Through every vein of sap with gentle showers
From whose engendering* liquor spring the flowers;
When zephyrs* have breathed softly all about
Inspiring every wood and field to sprout,
And in the zodiac the youthful sun
His journey halfway through the Ram* has run;
When little birds are busy with their song
Who sleep with open eyes the whole night long
Life stirs their hearts and tingles in them so,
Then people long on pilgrimage to go,
And palmers* to set out for distant strands
And foreign shrines renowned in sundry* lands.
And specially in England people ride
To Canterbury from every countyside
To visit there the blessed martyred saint
Who gave them strength when they were sick and faint.

(*The Portable Chaucer*)

engendering life-giving

zephyr a breeze, especially one from the west

Ram Aries, the zodiac sign for 21 March through 21 April

palmer a person wearing two crossed palm leaves as a sign of a pilgrimage made to the Holy Land

sundry various

love for the fair Emily, daughter of the king of Athens. In style, form, and subject, the story resembles *Troilus and Criseyde*, though the characters may be even more unblemished in their devotion to the code of chivalric love. A drunken miller* among the pilgrims responds to this long highbrow tale of idealistic heroism with a bawdy story about a young student boarder and the attractive young wife of a wealthy old carpenter. The elevated tone of the "Knight's Tale" is countered wholly by the raunchy cynicism of the "Miller's Tale," the humor of which centers on sexual infidelity, anal cavities, and slapstick cruelties. A reeve* in the party, who is a carpenter by trade, takes offense at the miller's tale and responds with an equally bawdy story about a miller, his wife and daughter, and, this time, two lusty young scholars. A cook follows the "Reeve's Tale" with a story that promises to be in the same vein but remains unfinished.

So the tales proceed, balancing romantic tales of virtue with bawdy comic stories. The first are usually told by pilgrims

miller a person whose job is to grind grain into flour (using a mill)

reeve an administrative official on a medieval English manor

prioress a nun of relatively high rank

of social eminence or uncommon integrity, such as a lawyer, a wealthy merchant, a prioress,* a country parson, and an admirable young scholar. These stories are often allegorical and frequently exotic and usually isolate an admirable virtue from realistic human expectations. For example, the young clerk recounts from Petrarch the tale of Walter, prince of Lombardy, and the poor but beautiful village girl Grisilde, whom Walter chooses for his wife. Walter decides to test the love of his wife by commanding her to give up the children she bears him. Although he secretly sends them to relatives for upbringing, he hides that from Grisilde, who for twelve years believes her children have been slain. Despite her incomprehensible but abiding absolute devotion to Walter, he decides to test her further. He informs her that he has decided to marry a young girl nearer his social station and that she should leave all the belongings that he has given her as his wife and return to the humble home of her father. Then he asks her to prepare the palace for her replacement. Grisilde submits readily to Walter's will in everything. The young girl that Walter brings to Lombardy to wed is his daughter, who is now a young lady. Finally assured of Grisilde's unparalleled devotion, Walter reveals to her his deception, returns her now adolescent children, and welcomes her back as his wife. Somewhere in this horrendous story is a lesson about patience and obedience to one's master's will.

The tales of comic realism are often in the vein of the miller's and reeve's tales mentioned earlier, and the tellers include several lustful church officials. Perhaps the most memorable and surprising figure in the *Canterbury Tales* is the Wife of Bath, a woman whose prologue and tale span both romance and realism. Despite the fact that she has no special beauty or grace, the Wife of Bath has wed and buried five husbands. Informed by this ample experience, her discussion of marriage extends to more pages than the tale she eventually tells. Her tale, set at the time of King Arthur, involves knights and ladies of the courts and a good deal of enchantment. At first glance it would seem that the Wife of Bath's tale, unlike her lusty prologue, is an idealistic medieval romance. But in her story, a handsome knight is forced by circumstance to wed an old crone, who offers him the choice of a "foul and old" but faithful wife or a wife "yong and fair" who is unfaithful to him. Only when the knight has submitted entirely to the mastery of his wife does the old crone transform into a fair and faithful young

King Arthur, who may or may not have been an actual person, is the central figure in the Arthurian legends, set in the sixth century.

woman. This lesson provides the common ground between the Wife of Bath's worldly prologue and her romantic tale. She is perhaps the only pilgrim to be wise in both realms.

The characters in the *Canterbury Tales* are types familiar to us even today, but the world of the tales has changed considerably. Because of the different ways we think about human life, readers are often uncertain about when Chaucer is being ironic and when he is being direct. He often sets side by side stories that contradict each other or appeal to contrasting values. Unlike modern poets, Chaucer never has to suspend his readers' disbelief in the unlikely, irrational, or miraculous events that he relates. Chaucer lived at a time when scientific proof was valued less than today and anything seemed possible. He could tell any story that struck his fancy, whether he heard it at the French court, from Italian humanists,* or at a London tavern. The richness and breadth of experience that results may be unequaled among English poets.

*humanist one who is devoted to the general welfare of humankind

IF YOU LIKE the poetry of Chaucer, you might also like the poetry of Dante or Shakespeare's comedies.

Selected Bibliography

WORKS BY GEOFFREY CHAUCER

The Canterbury Tales. Rev. ed. Translated into modern English by Nevill Coghill. Baltimore, Md.: Penguin, 1962.

The Complete Works of Geoffrey Chaucer. 2d ed. Edited by F. N. Robinson. London: Oxford University Press, 1957.

The Portable Chaucer. Selected, translated, and edited by Theodore Morrison. New York: Penguin Books, 1977.

Troilus and Cressida. Rendered into modern English verse by George Philip Krapp. New York: Random House, 1932.

WORKS ABOUT GEOFFREY CHAUCER

Elbow, Peter. *Oppositions in Chaucer.* Middletown, Conn.: Wesleyan University Press, 1975.

French, Robert Dudley. *A Chaucer Handbook.* 2d ed. New York: F. S. Crofts, 1947.

Gardner, John. *The Life and Times of Chaucer.* New York: Knopf, 1977.

More About Chaucer

You can find information about Chaucer on the Internet at:

http://www.unc.edu/depts/chaucer/

http://geoffreychaucer.org/

Gardner, John. *The Poetry of Chaucer.* Carbondale: Southern Illinois University Press, 1977.

Howard, Donald R. *Chaucer: His Life, His Works, His World.* New York: Dutton, 1987.

Lowell, James Russell. "Chaucer." In his *My Study Windows.* Boston: Houghton, Mifflin, 1899.

Pearsall, Derek A. *The Life of Geoffrey Chaucer: A Critical Biography.* Oxford: Blackwell, 1992.

Williams, George. *A New View of Chaucer.* Durham, N.C.: Duke University Press, 1965.

Woolf, Virginia. "The Pastons and Chaucer." In her *Common Reader.* New York: Harcourt Brace, 1925.

LUCILLE CLIFTON

(b. 1936)

by Carol Howard

When we think of poets, we do not imagine them working in offices from nine to five or getting up in the early morning hours to make breakfast for their children before packing them off to school. The reality, however, is that most poets have bills to pay and families to care for. Some poets find these responsibilities a hindrance to their writing; others consider it a boon. Lucille Clifton—who had six children during the decade before publishing her first collection of poems in 1969 at age thirty-three—is one poet whose writing complements, but does not take precedence over, her busy life with family, friends, and work. "[M]y life as a human," she declares in an autobiographical note, "A Simple Language" (*Black Women Writers*), "only includes my life as a poet, it doesn't depend on it."

Yet Lucille Clifton has emerged as one of the finest American poets of our era, as her many prestigious awards and honors attest. When crafting poems—which she does with equal readiness in her office or in the kitchen—she writes of African American communities and traditions, of history and

*precocious mature
at an early age

spirituality, and of herself and her family. Over the past thirty years, she has published eight collections of poems, a prose memoir, and a score of children's books that focus chiefly upon the lives of young African Americans. In addition to writing and caring for her family, Clifton has taught at several colleges and universities and holds the title of Distinguished Professor of Humanities at St. Mary's College in Maryland, the state that honored her as poet laureate from 1979 to 1982.

The daughter of Samuel Sayles, who was employed in the steel mills, and Thelma Moore Sayles, a homemaker who worked in a laundry, Lucille Sayles (later Clifton) was born in Depew, New York, on 27 June 1936 and raised there and in nearby Buffalo. A precocious* young woman, she won a scholarship to Howard University in Washington, D.C., where she studied drama and met some of the other great black writers and intellectuals of her generation, including the novelist Toni Morrison and the poet and dramatist Amiri Baraka. At Howard, Lucille also met her future husband, Fred Clifton, whom she married in 1958. In 1955, three years before her marriage, she transferred to Fredonia State Teachers College (now the State University of New York at Fredonia) in upstate New York. At the time, she was working as an actor and beginning to develop her distinctive poetic style.

*enjambment the
running over of a sentence from one line to another

*caesura a pause in
the flow of sound that
occurs in the middle of
a line

*vernacular the language or dialect commonly spoken in a particular region

Although her poems are short and their language simple, Clifton's skillful use of rhythm and repetition creates remarkably complex effects. Most striking are the unspoken ideas, as well as the majestic silences, that Clifton produces through such poetic techniques as enjambment* and caesura,* a sparse yet dramatic use of punctuation and capital letters, and the expressive spaces that stretch between the printed words and across the page. She leaves many of her poems untitled. Clifton most often works with standard English; when she wants to evoke oral tradition or a sense of the spoken word, however, she deftly shifts into North American black vernacular* and, occasionally, into Caribbean English.

Family and Heritage

Many of Clifton's poems and her prose memoir describe a deep sense of connection to family and ancestors. A number of poems explore feelings of loss and admiration for family members who have died. These include exquisite, moving tributes to Clifton's mother, who died suddenly in 1959, when Clifton was only twenty-three and pregnant with her first child. Other poems are addressed to Clifton's father, whom she alternately honors and reproaches. Perhaps the most poignant verses are those dedicated to the memory of her husband, Fred, who succumbed to cancer in 1984 at forty-nine. Despite her personal losses, Clifton's poetry demonstrates an unshakable sense of optimism and faith in the stability of the bonds of kinship. To the Irish poet William Butler Yeats's bleak declaration in "The Second Coming" about the modern world that "things fall apart; the centre cannot hold," Clifton, in her 1976 memoir, *Generations,* responds with conviction: "Things don't fall apart. Things hold" (p. 275).

Thus, even as Clifton acknowledges human vulnerability, her writing often centers on human strength, survival, and even triumph. Nowhere is this fortitude announced with more gusto than in the stout words of advice "Get what you want, you from Dahomey* women" (p. 223), which Clifton attributes in her memoir to her African-born great-great-grandmother, Caroline Donald Sale. Because it is recorded in African American vernacular, this ancestral counsel feels immediate and supportive and has special authority coming from a woman who survived decades of slavery in the United States, but who, as Clifton emphasizes, died a free woman. That fact is of utmost importance to Clifton, who believes that one must strive to overcome the effects of oppression.

Clifton's sense of family and personal history encompasses a broad spectrum of African American history. She therefore weaves together poems about her immediate family and lineage with those of a broader historical and political scope. The result is that incidents in the life of her own great-great-grandmother become testimony in the telling of American history. At the same time, a personal, intimate voice describes characters and events of wide-ranging historical and political significance. For example, several poems in Clifton's second collection, *Good News About the Earth,* pay tribute to the strength and the sacrifices of some of the leaders of the revolutionary movements and organizations for black empowerment in the 1960s: Malcolm X, Eldridge Cleaver, Bobby Seale, and Angela Davis. Yet these reflections appear alongside poems about family members, who are also her "heroes," as this section of the volume is called.

She has, in addition, written many other tributes and elegies* to persons famous and forgotten. An untitled poem

*__Dahomey__ country in west Africa, now called Benin

*__elegy__ a poem of sorrow and reflection, usually about one who is dead

*legacy effect of something done in the past
*abolitionist an advocate for ending slavery

*apartheid the legal policy of segregation of and discrimination against non-European ethnic groups, especially blacks, in South Africa. Apartheid was a legal institution from 1948 until 1993.

(identified by its first line "harriet") appearing in her third collection, *An Ordinary Woman,* finds Clifton's autobiographical narrator evoking the lives of strong black women in history and considering the chance that she might be a reincarnation of one of them; "if i be you" is the poem's speculative refrain. Here the narrator prays that she may do justice to the legacy* of Harriet Tubman and Sojourner Truth (two legendary nineteenth-century abolitionist* spokeswomen) and to her own less famous, but nevertheless industrious, devout, and nurturing grandmother. Another poem of broad historical and political scope, "poem beginning in no and ending in yes," from the volume *Quilting,* laments the loss—and celebrates the spirit—of Hector Peterson, a thirteen-year-old casualty of the 1976 Soweto uprising against apartheid* in South Africa. Still another, later poem, which appears in *The Terrible Stories* and begins "the son of medgar," marks the occasion of the retrial and conviction of the murderer of Civil Rights leader Medgar Evers, slain in 1963 in the driveway of his home in Jackson, Mississippi.

Clifton's sense of continuity between the personal and the political also colors her appreciation of an African American artistic tradition. Although a formal and public recognition of the centrality of African American art forms in American history and culture appears in the influential early twentieth-century essays of African American leader W. E. B. Du Bois, it was the 1960s and 1970s that witnessed a wide-scale, politically engaged Black Arts movement, of which Clifton was a participant. Her celebration of traditional African American art is readily apparent in the volume *Quilting,* in which poems are clustered together under such headings as "log cabin" and "eight-pointed star," commemorating traditional quilt patterns. Quilting—often a collective enterprise—is now recognized as an art form to which African American women have contributed many significant innovations and accomplishments. It is also a form that defies the outdated notion that creative work that has household value does not count as art or that art is the product only of solitary genius.

Self and Community

Many of Clifton's poems focus on her personal experiences. In *The Terrible Stories,* Clifton recounts the loss and fear she has endured living with breast cancer. Other poems, from *Quilting,* applaud menstruation and describe menopause and hysterectomy in alternately solemn and wistful tones. Others record life as a poet: the drive to write, the bustle and exhaustion associated with travel to poetry readings. Still other, earlier poems of the 1970s describe how Clifton learned to appreciate herself and her body. In the untitled closing poem ("the thirty eighth year") of *An Ordinary Woman,* for instance, Clifton's narrator announces that

> i had expected to be
> smaller than this,
> more beautiful,
> wiser in afrikan ways,
> more confident,
> i had expected
> more than this.

By the end of the poem, however, the same woman who takes stock of herself so critically makes her own ordinariness seem quite extraordinary. To her dead mother she declares:

> i have taken the bones you hardened
> and built daughters
> and they blossom and promise fruit
> like afrikan trees.
> i am a woman now.
> an ordinary woman.

Continuing the theme of self-appreciation, poems that appear in the 1980 collection *Two-Headed Woman* exalt "nappy" African American hair and "big hips," and one poem entitled "what the mirror said" congratulates a big womanly body that commands attention:

> listen,
> you a wonder.
> you a city
> of a woman.
> you got a geography
> of your own.

Such poems offered a welcome alternative to the Euro-American concept of beauty that had led many African Americans to straighten their hair and bleach their skin.

For Clifton, the importance of a healthy self-image extends to the neighborhood and the surrounding community as well. Consider the untitled opening poem ("in the inner city") of her first collection, *Good Times,* a poem that remains one of Clifton's two or three most famous:

in the inner city
or
like we call it
home
we think a lot about uptown
and the silent nights
and the houses straight as
dead men
and the pastel lights
and we hang on to our no place
happy to be alive
and in the inner city
or
like we call it
home

The narrator might at first appear to be painting a gloomy, desolate* picture of her neighborhood by describing it as an unimportant "no place" that residents "hang on to" from necessity rather than choice. The bleak simile* "houses straight as dead men" reinforces this image. But the lights of this place are a soft "pastel," not a glaring neon, and the closing reprise* of the opening lines establishes a comforting rhythm in the poem. The narrator, in fact, refuses the white, middle-class outsider's perspective; she refuses to distance herself from this place and thus, she substitutes for the impersonal and distancing phrase "the inner city," the much more personal and appreciative insider's word "home."

The importance of a sense of self-worth and of community is also readily apparent in Clifton's books for children. For instance, the series of seven books of stories written in verse that chronicle the life and formative experiences of Everett Anderson, a six-year-old African American boy growing up poor in the city, celebrates the joy of self-discovery and the importance of strong ties to family and friends. Even as they portray scenes of happiness, however, these books confront the diffi-

*__desolate__ lifeless; deserted; run-down

*__simile__ a comparison using "like" or "as": "Your face is like the sunshine."

*__reprise__ return of the main theme of a song or poem

cult realities of life, including poverty and death. An especially touching book is *Everett Anderson's Goodbye,* which relates the young hero's experience of learning how to cope with the loss of his father. The principal message of Clifton's children's books is clear: "When I write, especially for children, I try to get . . . across . . . that being poor or whatever your circumstance, you are capable of being the best of people and that best, as a human, does not come from the outside in, it comes from the inside out" ("A Simple Language").

A Sense of Spirit

Clifton's sense of the importance of human connection manifests itself not only in the world of the living but also in the spiritual realm. Some poems allude* to her belief in the power of automatic writing, a form of contact between the natural and supernatural worlds in which spirits are thought to guide human hands to spell out a message. Clifton has, in fact, traced her spiritual awakening to a 1975 session at the Ouija board, thought by some to be a vehicle for communicating with the dead. On this occasion, she believes that she and her daughters received a communication from her deceased mother. These occult experiences form the subject of an untitled poem ("the light that came to lucille clifton") in *Two-Headed Woman* that describes a scene of automatic writing:

> the light that came to lucille clifton
> came in a shift of knowing
> when even her fondest sureties*
> faded away. . . .
>
> .   .   .   .   .   .
> but the light insists on itself in the world;
> a voice from the nondead past started talking,
> she closed her ears and it spelled out in her hand
> "you might as well answer the door, my child,
> the truth is furiously knocking."

What is most startling in this proclamation is that the scene of automatic writing ("a voice . . . spelled out in her hand") is no idle game or casual contact with the spirit world, but a moment of true revelation—hence the repeated reference to "the

---

". . . Best . . . does not come from the outside in, it comes from the inside out."

__allude__ refer indirectly

__surety__ certainty

light." That the poet's full name is solemnly announced in the opening line indicates that this poem bears witness to a life-altering experience.

Clifton writes of her personal experience of mystical connection to family past, but many of her poems signal an interest in more widely accepted religious traditions. Poems with biblical themes are sometimes cast in African American vernacular in order to revise the Judeo-Christian tradition in a distinctly African American setting. Such is the case with several of the sixteen poems that fall under the heading "some jesus" in *Good News About the Earth.* In *An Ordinary Woman,* Clifton also draws upon the Hindu religious tradition. A number of poems focus on the autobiographical narrator's alternating feelings of dread and sympathy as she beholds the Hindu goddess Kali, who is associated with both destruction and creativity: "it is the black God, Kali, / a woman God and terrible." These poems are among the few of Clifton's that use capital letters, a signal of Clifton's reverence for this goddess. Clifton's repeated identification of Kali as a "black God," moreover, directs our attention to the Hindi meaning of her name, "the Black One," which suggests just how awe-inspiring she is. Clearly, though, Clifton's use of the adjective "black" resonates* for an African American audience.

The wide-ranging scope of Clifton's spirituality matches the broad-mindedness of her political, historical, and artistic interests. Her concerns spring from her sense of herself as an African American woman, as a citizen of the world, and as a poet: "I am a woman and I write from that experience. I am a Black woman and I write from that experience. I do not feel inhibited or bound by what I am" ("A Simple Language"). In a short poem entitled "the poet," from *An Ordinary Woman,* Clifton succinctly expresses the sense of urgency she brings to her vocation as a poet and the joyous inspiration that has characterized her career:

> i beg my bones to be good but
> they keep clicking music and
> i spin in the center of myself
> a foolish frightful woman
> moving my skin against the wind and
> tap dancing for my life.

*resonate to "ring true" or have relevance

testament

in the beginning
was the word.

the year of our lord,
amen. i
lucille clifton
hereby testify
that in that room
there was a light
and in that light
there was a voice
and in that voice
there was a sigh
and in that sigh
there was a world.
a world a sigh a voice a light and
i
alone
in a room.

(*Two-Headed Woman*)

Selected Bibliography

WORKS BY LUCILLE CLIFTON
Poetry

Good Times (1969).

Good News About the Earth (1972).

An Ordinary Woman (1974).

Two-Headed Woman (1980).

Next: New Poems (1987).

Quilting: Poems 1987–1990 (1991).

The Book of Light (1993).

The Terrible Stories (1996).

Prose

Generations: A Memoir (1976).

IF YOU LIKE the poetry of Clifton, you might also like the poetry of Gwendolyn Brooks or Sonia Sanchez.

Children's Books

The Black BC's (1970).

Some of the Days of Everett Anderson (1970).

Everett Anderson's Christmas Coming (1971).

All Us Come Across the Water (1973).

The Boy Who Didn't Believe in Spring (1973).

Don't You Remember (1973).

Good, Says Jerome (1973).

Everett Anderson's Year (1974).

The Times They Used to Be (1974).

My Brother Fine with Me (1975).

Everett Anderson's Friend (1976).

Three Wishes (1976).

Amifika (1977).

Everett Anderson's 1–2–3 (1977).

Everett Anderson's Nine Month Long (1978).

The Lucky Stone (1979).

My Friend Jacob (1980).

Sonora Beautiful (1981).

Everett Anderson's Goodbye (1983).

Dear Creator: A Week of Poems for Young People and Their Teachers (1997).

Available Collection

Good Woman: Poems and a Memoir 1969–1980 (1987).

WORKS ABOUT LUCILLE CLIFTON

Anaporte-Easton, Jean. "Healing Our Wounds: The Direction of Difference in the Poetry of Lucille Clifton and Judith Johnson." *Mid-American Review* 14, no. 2 (1994): 78–87.

Hull, Akasha (Gloria). "Channeling the Ancestral Muse: Lucille Clifton and Dolores Kendrick." In *Feminist Measures: Soundings in Poetry and Theory.* Edited by Lynn

Keller and Cristanne Miller. Ann Arbor: University of Michigan Press, 1994.

Johnson, Dianne. "The Chronicling of an African-American Life and Consciousness: Lucille Clifton's Everett Anderson Series." *Children's Literature Association Quarterly* 14, no. 3 (1989): 174–178.

Johnson, Joyce. "The Theme of Celebration in Lucille Clifton's Poetry." *Pacific Coast Philology* 18, no. 1–2: 70–76.

Lazer, Hank. "Blackness Blessed: The Writings of Lucille Clifton." *The Southern Review* 25, no. 3 (1989): 760–770.

Madhubuti, Haki. "Lucille Clifton: Warm Water, Greased Legs, and Dangerous Poetry." In *Black Women Writers (1950–1980): A Critical Evaluation.* Edited by Mari Evans. New York: Anchor-Doubleday, 1984. Includes "A Simple Language."

McCluskey, Audrey T. "Tell the Good News: A View of the Works of Lucille Clifton." In *Black Women Writers (1950–1980): A Critical Evaluation.* Edited by Mari Evans. New York: Anchor-Doubleday, 1984.

Ostriker, Alicia. " 'Kin and Kin': The Poetry of Lucille Clifton." In *Literary Influence and African-American Writers.* Edited by Tracy Mishkin. New York: Garland Publishing, 1996.

White, Mark Bernard. "Sharing the Living Light: Rhetorical, Poetic, and Social Identity in Lucille Clifton." *College Language Association Journal* 40, no. 3 (1997): 288–304.

Worsham, Fabian Clements. "The Poetics of Matrilineage: Mothers and Daughters in the Poetry of African American Women, 1965–1985." In *Women of Color: Mother-Daughter Relationships in Twentieth-Century Literature.* Edited by Elizabeth Brown-Guillory. Austin: University of Texas Press, 1996.

SAMUEL TAYLOR COLERIDGE

(1772–1834)

by Anselm Berrigan

The youngest of thirteen children, Samuel Taylor Coleridge developed a fascination with stories of the supernatural at an early age. So much so, in fact, that his father felt compelled to burn some of his books, including *Arabian Nights,** when he realized that young Samuel was regularly reading himself into states of terror. From the beginning of Coleridge's life he had a unique sense of imagination—one that would later propel some of his greatest poems, including "The Rime of the Ancient Mariner" and "Kubla Khan."

As you might expect of the youngest child of such a large family (his father, Reverend John Coleridge, had married twice, with three children from the first marriage and ten from the second), Coleridge was a mature and active boy, often running all around the countryside near Devon, England, where he was born on 21 October 1772. One day, in an episode he recalled in a letter to a friend some years later, Coleridge got into a fight with his brother Frank, ran at him with a knife, and was

**Arabian Nights* a series of Arabic stories of unknown origin; includes stories of Ali Baba, Sinbad the Sailor, and Aladdin

restrained by their mother. He was so alarmed by his own behavior that he ran out of the house and hid in the meadows by the river Otter all night until a search party came and found him just as he was beginning to catch a cold. Coleridge's health was shaky for most of his life, and it is possible that in that incident the origins of his later attacks of rheumatism and, by extension, his opium addiction, can be found, not to mention his bent for impulsive behavior and dashes across the land.

rheumatism a disease marked by inflammation and pain of the joints

Education and Imagination

Much of Coleridge's personality and interests, both in life and in writing, can be traced back to his childhood. Coleridge's father recognized his talents early on, and encouraged his education, despite the book-burning incident, until his own death in 1781, when Coleridge was nine. Coleridge had a quick mind and a love of conversation. The poet John Keats once described a short discussion he'd had with Coleridge as they took a walk together. Coleridge, Keats said, went on about "a thousand things"—nightingales, poetry, dreams, nightmares, metaphysics,* monsters, mermaids, even ghost stories—all subjects related to nature and the human mind, two of Coleridge's chief poetic subjects. After the death of his father, Coleridge was placed in Christ's Hospital, a school in London, where the headmaster was very strict. His years at this school became the source of many nightmares over the course of his life. In his poem "Frost at Midnight," written in 1798, Coleridge made reference to these school days:

metaphysics the study of such concepts as being, substance, essence, time, space, and identity

> For I was reared
> In the great city, pent 'mid cloisters* dim,
> And saw nought lovely but the sky and stars.
> *(Selected Poetry and Prose)*

Despite the severity of conditions at Christ's Hospital (beatings were routine), Coleridge began to read and write extensively there. His earliest writings were charms, spells, and chants to ward off sickness. He read and absorbed works by the ancient poets Homer and Virgil, and the French philosopher Voltaire, among many others, and began to develop the philosophical side of his mind. Coleridge, during his entire life, kept numerous journals and notebooks, revised endlessly,

cloister a walkway on the side of a building usually having one side walled and the other side open to the outdoors; a secluded area within a monastery or convent

and wrote countless short poems and fragments, as well as essays on all sorts of topics, breathlessly moving from one project to another, often leaving many of his undertakings incomplete. He was a rigorous scholar with a large appetite for learning, but he could shift his attention from one project to another without a moment's notice.

Coleridge is known primarily as a Romantic* poet, and, along with William Wordsworth, Robert Southey, and others, as one of the Lake poets.* But he was also a journalist, translator, literary critic, lecturer, playwright, and philosopher. Much the same way he moved rapidly from one project to another in his writing, he moved rapidly from one venture to another in his life. When he could finally leave Christ's Hospital in 1791, Coleridge entered Cambridge University and began to gain some notice for his poetry. Two years later, however, debt forced Coleridge to leave Cambridge, and he enlisted in the army under the name Silas Tomkyn Comberbacke. His army stint did not last long, for he was a terrible soldier, and by 1794 Coleridge was back in Cambridge working as a journalist and beginning to meet many of the people who became his lifelong friends. At one point in the summer of 1794, Coleridge and Robert Southey hatched a plan to move to America, settle on the Susquehanna River with their friends and families, and start an ideal society that they would call Pantisocracy. The plan never got off the ground, though it did help in Coleridge's engagement and marriage to Sarah Fricker, Southey's sister-in-law. However, the marriage was never a completely happy one, as it was forged as much out of idealism as it was out of mutual love, and was a source of guilt for Coleridge for many years.

Conversational and Supernatural Poetry

In 1795 Coleridge met William Wordsworth, and they embarked on a friendship that gave birth to some of the most well known and loved poetry in the English language. It was not until 1797 that Coleridge and Wordsworth became really close, moved into nearby houses in the Lake District, and wrote much of the poetry for which they became known. Coleridge and Wordsworth were both deeply influenced by their study of psychology, nature, and the ideals of the French Revolution. They set out to write poems that would be free of

Romantic committed to individual expression of emotions and imagination. Opposed to classical forms and social conventions.

Lake poets Romantic poets who resided in England's Lake District. They included Coleridge, William Wordsworth, and Robert Southey.

The French Revolution was aimed at creating natural human rights based on reason rather than tradition. Those rights included equality before the law for everyone and a fairer distribution of land and wealth. The Revolution also sought to limit the power of the Catholic monarchy.

the forms and subject matter of the previous century, with Wordsworth investigating common speech and human psychology and Coleridge taking on visionary and spiritual concerns, the movement of the mind into unknown spaces.

Over the next couple of years, Coleridge composed many of his most famous poems. He adopted two particular styles, one conversational and another visionary, that allowed him to break free of the influences (especially that of the seventeenth-century poet John Milton) that had marked much of his earlier work. "Frost at Midnight" and "This Lime Tree Bower My Prison" are prime examples of the first style. They are poems that start with natural description, recognize an interaction between the mind and what it perceives, and take on the belief that nature and experience can help strengthen and educate a person in times of trouble. "This Lime Tree Bower My Prison," written in 1797, is an especially vivid example of these beliefs, as Coleridge imagines a walk that Wordsworth and other friends are taking without him because he has injured his leg. Coleridge imagines the path they follow (a walk he had taken himself countless times), and focuses on his friend, writer Charles Lamb, in order to channel himself into the picture, as shown in these lines from the poem:

> Now, my friends emerge
> Beneath the wide wide heaven—and view again
> The many-steepled tract* magnificent
> Of hilly fields and meadows, and the sea,
> With some fair bark, perhaps, which lightly touches
> The slip of smooth clear blue betwixt two isles
> Of purple shadow! Yes, they wander on
> In gladness all; but thou, methinks, most glad,
> My gentle-hearted Charles! For thou hadst pined
> And hungered after nature many a year
> In the great city pent, winning thy way,
> With sad yet patient soul, through evil and pain
> And strange calamity!*

> (*Romanticism: An Anthology,*
> edited by Duncan Wu, Blackwell, 1994, p. 511–512).

tract a plot of land

calamity distress; misery

It is a poem full of exuberance for nature, and friendship as well—Coleridge was the type of person who makes a strong impact on other people's lives, and friendship represented a major part of his personal philosophy and poetic content. Coleridge goes on in the poem to recognize nature as "a living thing / Which *acts* upon the mind" and, toward the poem's end, declares "Henceforth I shall know / That nature ne'er deserts the wise and pure" (p. 513). Although Coleridge wrote "This Lime Tree Bower My Prison" at the end of the eighteenth century, it is interesting to compare it, and his other "conversational poems" to poetry written by twentieth-century authors—Frank O'Hara* comes to mind—who also used themes of friendship and nature in their work in lively, conversational language.

Coleridge's other mode of poetry can be described as supernatural. "Kubla Khan," written in 1798, is a dream vision, a fragment of a longer poem Coleridge saw in a dream but could not remember in its entirety (he claimed in the preface to the poem that it dissolved from his memory when someone knocked on his door as he was trying to transcribe the poem; Coleridge also wrote that the dream came about while he was under the influence of laudanum, a form of opium that was legal in England at the time). "Kubla Khan" is more about the creative and imaginative processes and a mystical view of nature than any conventional subject matter, and was likely influenced by Coleridge's infatuation with fairy tales as a child, as the first five lines of the poem can attest:

> In Xanadu did Kubla Khan
> A stately pleasure-dome decree:
> Where Alph, the sacred river, ran
> Through caverns measureless to man
>   Down to a sunless sea.
>
> (*Selected Poetry and Prose*)

> Xanadu is an imaginary place created by Coleridge in this poem. The word is now used to mean an idyllic, exotic, or luxurious place.

It was also during this period of composition in the years just before 1800 when Coleridge began writing "Christabel," a haunting, seductive, Gothic* ballad* about evil and guilt that he worked on for years before finally publishing it in 1816, and "The Rime of the Ancient Mariner," Coleridge's best-known poem. "The Rime of the Ancient Mariner" unfolds over seven parts in 625 lines, told largely in recollection by the mariner* to a wedding guest. Its central drama concerns the outcast, isolated sailor, who violated the laws of hospitality by killing an albatross,* and underwent a redemptive period of drifting and hallucination. The poem's narrative structure allowed Coleridge to explore many of his deepest concerns: the relationship between humankind and nature, shifting psychological states

> **Gothic* characteristic of the medieval or Romantic periods, as opposed to the classical period
> **ballad* rhythmic poem that tells a story and is often meant to be sung
> **mariner* a sailor
> **albatross* a type of seabird.

exile forced absence from one's homeland.

(especially isolation and madness), themes of exile* and return, dream states, and spiritual symbolism. The poem is strikingly easy to read despite its many themes and moves crisply through its ballad form, which Coleridge spices up with shifting rhythms and perspectives. At times it is also apparent that Coleridge is using the voice of the sailor to express his own sense of himself in the world, as in this stanza from the last section:

> I pass, like night, from land to land;
> I have strange power of speech;
> That moment that his face I see,
> I know the man that must hear me:
> To him my tale I teach.

(Selected Poetry and Prose)

Later Years: Poetry, Journalism, and Lecturing

Over the years, Coleridge's reputation as a poet and scholar went through nearly as many changes as his own life and writing did. Some critics maintain that Coleridge was a failed genius who never lived up to the promise of his early poetry.

prolific producing many works; fertile; productive

But Coleridge remained a prolific* writer after the magical years of 1797–1799, although his focus turned to other projects. He traveled through Germany with Wordsworth and Wordsworth's sister, Dorothy, also a strong influence on his writing, and took on translation projects and lecturing. In

ode a lyric poem in an exalted manner

1802, after writing "Dejection: An Ode"* a sad, troubled poem in which Coleridge finds himself questioning his motivations, abilities, and capacity for joy, his health began to fail due to rheumatism, and his opium addiction became a steadily growing dilemma. Because his marriage had all but failed, Coleridge took any opportunity to be away from his family. When, in 1804, he left England for Malta, many of his friends believed he was going off to die.

However, in 1806 Coleridge returned to England somewhat revitalized (though he never managed to shake his opium addiction) and eventually went to work as a columnist for an evening paper, the *Courier,* while also launching his own periodical, *The Friend.* The range of subjects Coleridge took on in his columns is extremely wide, issues central to England at the

This Lime-Tree Bower My Prison (excerpt)

Well, they are gone, and here must I remain,
This lime-tree bower* my prison! I have lost
Such beauties and such feelings, as had been
Most sweet to have remembered, even when age
Had dimmed mine eyes to blindness! They, meanwhile,
My friends, whom I may never meet again,
On springy heath, along the hilltop edge,
Wander in gladness, and wind down, perchance,
To that still roaring dell* of which I told;
The roaring dell, o'erwooded, narrow, deep,
And only speckled by the midday sun;
Where its slim trunk the ash from rock to rock
Flings arching like a bridge; that branchless ash,
Unsunned and damp, whose few poor yellow leaves
Ne'er tremble in the gale, yet tremble still,
Fanned by the waterfall! And there my friends
Behold the dark green file of long lank weeds,
That all at once (a most fantastic sight!)
Still nod and drip beneath the dripping edge
Of the dim clay-stone.

(*Romanticism: An Anthology,* edited by Duncan Wu,
Blackwell, 1994)

*__bower__ a shelter made of tree boughs or vines; an arbor

*__dell__ a secluded valley or clearing

time: child labor in factories, the rights of women, and other divisive political and religious issues. Coleridge's political and social philosophies as conveyed by these writings were largely humanitarian,* liberal,* and levelheaded. He also began to lecture across England in 1811, and in 1815 dictated his *Biographia Literaria,* a long, autobiographical prose work that contains a great deal of analysis of his own poetry, methods of writing, and sources of inspiration and education. Charges of plagiarizing ideas from German writers (the philosopher Immanuel Kant, in particular) were leveled at Coleridge during the latter part of his life, and have some merit insofar as his prose writing is concerned, but should not be seen as detracting from his poetic accomplishments.

Although not nearly as well known as his earlier work, some of Coleridge's poems written in the second half of his life are worth reading. His poetry on his advancing age and

*__humanitarian__ devoted to the general welfare of humankind

*__liberal__ open to new ideas or proposals of political and social reform

failing health can be extremely moving, and works such as "A Tombless Epitaph,"* written in 1811, which finds Coleridge in stages of reflection very different from the type seen in poems such as "Frost at Midnight," have moments of elegiac,* strong-willed beauty, as in these last seven lines:

> O framed for calmer times and nobler hearts!
> O studious Poet, eloquent for truth!
> Philosopher! contemning wealth and death,
> Yet docile,* childlike, full of Life and Love!
> Here, rather than on monumental stone,
> This record of thy worth thy Friend inscribes,
> Thoughtful, with quiet tears upon his cheek.
>
> *(Complete Poems)*

Coleridge, in his last years, wrote extensively on religion and the relationship between church and state, mostly in prose tracts. He settled in with friends at Highgate, a section of London, and engaged in Thursday-evening "classes," in which he lectured on philosophy to five or six young students. Although his friendship with Wordsworth had cooled over the years, the two did take a trip to continental Europe together in 1828, and one notable visitor to Coleridge's home in his last years was the American writer Ralph Waldo Emerson. Coleridge died on 25 July 1834, relatively at peace with himself and his life, despite the many difficult years and failed projects. Coleridge's own lines were used as an epitaph for his grave in Highgate Cemetery:

> Beneath this sod
> A poet lies, or that which once seem'd he.
> O, lift one thought in prayer for S.T.C.;
> That he who many a year with toil of breath
> Found death in life, may here find life in death!

Selected Bibliography

WORKS BY SAMUEL TAYLOR COLERIDGE
Poetry
The Eolian Harp (1796).

The Rime of the Ancient Mariner (1798). Published in *Lyrical Ballads,* a collection of poems by Coleridge and William Wordsworth.

Fears in Solitude (1798).

France, an Ode (1798).

Frost at Midnight (1798).

This Lime-Tree Bower My Prison (1800).

Dejection: an Ode (1802).

Kubla Khan (1816).

Christabel (1816).

Available Collections

Collected Letters of Samuel Taylor Coleridge. 6 vols. Edited by Earl Leslie Griggs. Oxford, U.K.: Clarendon, 1971.

The Collected Works of Samuel Taylor Coleridge. Princeton, N.J.: Princeton University Press, 1984.

The Complete Poems. Edited by William Keach. New York: Penguin, 1997.

Selected Poetry and Prose of Coleridge. Edited by Donald A. Stauffer. New York: Random House, 1951.

WORKS ABOUT SAMUEL TAYLOR COLERIDGE

Ashton, Rosemary. *The Life of Samuel Taylor Coleridge: A Critical Biography.* Cambridge, Mass.: Blackwell, 1996.

Chambers, E. K. *Samuel Taylor Coleridge: A Biographical Study.* Oxford, U.K.: Clarendon, 1938.

Fruman, Norman. *Coleridge, the Damaged Archangel.* New York: Braziller, 1971.

Holmes, Richard. *Coleridge: Early Visions.* New York: Viking, 1990.

More About Coleridge

You can find information about Coleridge on the Internet at:
http://etext.lib.virginia.edu /stc/Coleridge/stc.html
http://www.geocities.com /Athens/4017/

GREGORY CORSO

(b. 1930)

by Nelly Reifler

Juvenile Delinquent

The young man from New York City sat in the tiny, cold prison cell studying books by such great writers as Homer, Ovid, Fyodor Dostoyevsky, Christopher Marlowe, Stendhal, and Percy Bysshe Shelley. It was 1947 and the seventeen-year-old prisoner with the fiery eyes and shock of black hair was Gregory Corso. He was serving a three-year sentence for theft. Even though he was just a teenager, it was his third time in prison.

Gregory Corso was born on 26 March 1930 in the Little Italy neighborhood of New York City. His mother and his father, Fortunato Corso, separated shortly after he was born, and soon after his mother suddenly returned to Italy, leaving the baby Gregory behind. Between that time and the age of ten, little Gregory lived with eight sets of foster parents. When he was eleven his father took him in, hoping that having a child would keep him from having to fight in World War II. Fortunato was drafted into the navy, however, and Corso wound up living on the streets, a tough and streetwise ragamuffin.

One cold night when he was twelve, Corso was so hungry that he kicked in the windows of a restaurant just to get food. He was caught on the way out and sent to jail. Shortly after his release a year later, he was back out on the streets, alone and hungry again, with nowhere to go. He broke into a youth center to sleep, but he was caught and sent to jail again. There he became sick and was transferred to Bellevue Hospital, where he wound up spending months in a ward for the mentally ill. All the while he was building up the individualistic character, keen observations, and sharp sense of humor that came out in his writing years later.

In his poem "Dialogues from Children's Observation Ward" (from *The Vestal Lady on Brattle*) written when he was in his early twenties, Corso captures the darkness of being a child with few resources in the world:

> —You don't paint nice. You paint faces on window
> shades
> and you don't make them look nice—
> —Window shades is all I got,
> and faces is all I got—

The final time he landed in jail, at Clinton Prison in northern New York State, Corso decided to use his time there wisely. "Don't serve time; let it serve you," some of the kinder, older prisoners told him, and so he spent his sentence educating himself in the great classics of poetry. It was also in Clinton Prison that he started to write, although he never wrote about his experiences in jail. Later he explained his choice not to reflect on that time this way: "If one must climb a ladder to reach a height and from that height see, then it were best to write about what you see and not about how you climbed. Prison to me was such a ladder" (*Contemporary Authors*, Detroit, Gale).

Adopted by the Beats

When he was released in 1950, Corso found employment as a manual laborer in New York City, but he worked seriously on his poetry every day. One evening, as he was sitting alone in a bar in Greenwich Village reading over his poems, he was approached by Allen Ginsberg, the brilliant young poet who was at the center of a group of writers who soon became known as

---

One cold night when he was twelve, Corso was so hungry that he kicked in the windows of a restaurant just to get food.

the "Beats." Ginsberg asked to read Corso's poems and was amazed by their quality. He found them unique, grounded in the whole range of poetic history but with an added edge of street talk and slang. They were also unabashedly sentimental at times. Ginsberg and Corso became fast friends, and soon Corso found himself part of a community of writers, artists, and bohemians that also included, at various points, Jack Kerouac, William Burroughs, Neal Cassady, Gary Snyder, Lawrence Ferlinghetti, Diane di Prima, and others.

When he was twenty-four, Corso moved to Boston. Although he was not a student, he spent most of his time around Harvard University. He loved the library there and continued his studies of classics and poetry sitting in its calm and quiet halls— a far cry from the cramped prison cell where he had started his education. Corso became known on campus, and his first published poems appeared in the Harvard *Advocate.* Students from Harvard and Radcliffe raised the funds to publish Corso's first book of poetry, *The Vestal Lady on Brattle,* in 1955. The poems in this collection show their influences, some clearly displaying Corso's admiration of classical and Romantic poetry and others employing "hipster" lingo and the rhythms and noises of bebop jazz.* Whatever the style, many of the poems in this first book have a melancholy air and contain eerie images of death. "Sea Chanty" recalls timeless sailors' songs:

> My mother hates the sea,
> my sea especially,
> I warned her not to;
> it was all I could do.
> Two years later
> the sea ate her.
> Upon the shore I found a strange
> yet beautiful food;
> I asked the sea if I could eat it,
> and the sea said that I could.
> —Oh sea, what fish is this
> so tender and so sweet?—
> —Thy mother's feet—was its answer.

The book was criticized by some as disjointed and scattered, while others praised its use of conversational rhythms. Some critics could not separate Corso from the Beat movement, which was quickly growing and gaining in popularity.

The Beat Generation of writers, including Allen Ginsberg, Jack Kerouac, and William Burroughs, began publishing their books during the 1950s. From "beat" came the term "beatnik," a person whose affinity for jazz, uninhibited poetry, physical and spiritual intoxication, and free love, as well as a highly casual style of dress, amounted to a rejection of conventional American social values.

*bebop jazz a style of jazz that uses dissonant notes, unusual rhythms, and fast tempos

*vocative direct address meant to get someone's attention

Reuel Denney wrote in the October 1956 issue of *Poetry* magazine, "All of the poems have the air of having been preceded immediately by the hipster vocative,* 'Man!' . . . Bopster Corso simply digs one thing and another as he goes along" (p. 48). Denney quotes only the most jazz-influenced poems in his review, however, and does not mention the more formally restrained ones.

A Talent Blooms

In 1956, Gregory Corso moved to San Francisco, joining Allen Ginsberg, who had been living there for two years. During those two years the poetry scene had exploded, with Ginsberg at the center. Corso arrived shortly after a landmark event in the Beat movement, a poetry reading at the Six Gallery, a converted auto-repair shop on Fillmore Street. Ginsberg organized the reading, and the postcard that he sent out to publicize it read: "Six Poets at the Six Gallery . . . Remarkable collection of angels all gathered at once in the same spot. Wine, music, dancing girls, serious poetry, free satori*" (Miles, p. 195). Ginsberg gave the first public reading of his poem "Howl" that night, and he electrified the audience. It was a festive night, full of wine and excitement, and all the poets who participated were instantly famous in the San Francisco Bay Area. It was into this energized literary atmosphere that Gregory Corso arrived. He moved into an apartment in North Beach, an old Italian neighborhood with winding streets and steep hills where young artists and writers had started to settle. Corso soon stood out for his sharp, individualistic point of view, and sardonic, sometimes abrasive, New York humor.

*satori a state of sudden enlightenment or spiritual awakening in Zen Buddhism

In North Beach, Gregory met the poet Lawrence Ferlinghetti, who owned City Lights Bookstore and published a series of paperbacks called the Pocket Poets. Gregory's second book, *Gasoline,* was number eight in the Pocket Poets series. From the time that this book was published until the early 1960s, Corso's fame remained steady.

Gasoline is a much more personal and original book than *The Vestal Lady on Brattle.* During the three years between the two publications Corso had been strengthening his poetic voice, and the poems in *Gasoline* are more weighty than his earlier work, demonstrating Corso's rich vocabulary.

I cross the street and enter the building.
The garbage cans haven't stopped smelling.
I walk up the first flight; Dirty Ears
aims a knife at me . . .
I pump him full of lost watches.

"Birthplace Revisited"

Geoffrey Thurley, in his essay "McClure, Whalen, Corso," praises Gregory Corso's use of non sequitur* (as in the lines just quoted), pointing out that the odd juxtaposition* of images is "meant to throw light on things, to illuminate the experiences of which they are severally composed" (Bartlett, p. 177). "The Mad Yak," another poem in *Gasoline,* illustrates how Corso's use of the unexpected is both jarring and poignant. The animal has seen family members slaughtered and turned into mundane, utilitarian objects. The Yak's voice is full of both pathos and humor.

*non sequitur a statement that does not logically follow from what comes before it

*juxtaposition placing side by side

Much of the work in *Gasoline* was written in Paris, where Corso lived from 1957 to 1958. Corso found the city to be wonderfully conducive to his work. In his poem "Paris," Corso invokes the spirits of the French writers Charles Baudelaire, Antonin Artaud, Arthur Rimbaud, Guillaume Apollinaire, Victor Hugo, and Émile Zola.

At about the same time that *Gasoline* was published, another poem of Corso's was released as a broadside* by City Lights. It was called "Bomb," and it is still one of his most well known and controversial works. Written in the shape of a mushroom cloud, it is a darkly witty ode* to the hydrogen bomb. It starts at the top of the cloud:

*broadside a large sheet of paper with printing on one or both sides

*ode a lyric poem in an exalted manner

Budger of history   Brake of time   You   Bomb
Toy of universe   Grandest of all snatched-sky   I cannot hate you

It continues by declaring love for the bomb and then adds lists of wild words that bombs might shout, ending with a strange and chilling image of the future bombs that people will build:

*ermine a type of fur

magisterial bombs wrapped in ermine*   all beautiful
and they'll sit plunk on earth's grumpy empires
fierce with moustaches of gold

(*The Happy Birthday of Death*)

The poem had an extremely strong effect on people, both conservative and liberal. When Corso read the poem in England at Oxford University, angry pacifist students booed him off the stage. They threw shoes at him and accused him of being a fascist. In his typically abrasive, street-kid way, Corso called the students a "bunch of creeps." Ginsberg, who was there with him, tried to explain the subtleties of the poem, but the students would have none of it. Finally, Ginsberg and Corso had to leave the auditorium.

Twenty years later Corso reflected on "Bomb" in his short poem "Many Have Fallen" (from *Herald of the Autochthonic Spirit*). This poem does not apologize for the humor of "Bomb," but it does add a note of sobriety and sadness to the subject matter, ending:

> Well, 20 years later
> not one but 86 bombs, A-Bombs, have fallen,
> We bombed Utah, Nevada, New Mexico,
> and all survived
> . . . until two decades later
>
> when the dead finally died.

The Sixties

In the early 1960s the Beat Generation became part of popular culture, with "beatnik" characters, sporting goatees and berets, becoming common on television and in movies. Jack Kerouac, whose novel *On the Road* was a huge success, and Allen Ginsberg became cultural celebrities. Corso, however, did not receive mass recognition. Part of this was by choice: Corso always preferred not to be considered a member of any organized movement.

Corso continued to be prolific throughout the early 1960s, producing six books of poetry alone, three collaborative books, and a novel, all between 1960 and 1965. The first book of the sixties was *The Happy Birthday of Death,* published by New Directions, a publishing house supportive of experimental writers. The poems in this book, as the title indicates, approach mortality with humor and lucidity. The cover of the book bore a black-and-white photo of a mushroom cloud, with the "i" in "Birthday" a lit birthday candle.

The Mad Yak

I am watching them churn the last milk
        they'll ever get from me.
They are waiting for me to die;
They want to make buttons out of my bones.
Where are my sisters and brothers?
That tall monk there, loading my uncle,
        he has a new cap.
And that idiot student of his—
        I never saw that muffler before.
Poor uncle, he lets them load him.
How sad he is, how tired!
I wonder what they'll do with his bones?
And that beautiful tail!
How many shoelaces will they make of that!

(*Gasoline*)

In the early 1960s Corso moved often, spending time in Paris, Tangiers (Morocco), and New York. Although he was writing and publishing all the time, he had very little money. Besides this financial instability, he had problems with drinking and gambling. Ginsberg often had to help out Corso with money, knowing that Corso might take it all to the racetrack and lose it in a day.

Corso also had volatile relationships with women. He married and divorced three times between 1960 and the early 1970s, and he had three children during this time. The State University of New York at Buffalo hired Corso to teach, but this job did not last long because he refused to sign a loyalty oath, required by the state of New York from all the university employees.

His poetry during the 1960s grew increasingly personal and serious, more heartfelt, and less sardonic.* The existential* attitude toward life and death in his earlier work was replaced by a questioning voice that yearns for a fuller life. In the poem "The Mutation of the Spirit" (from *Elegiac Feelings American*), he says:

It's no longer When will I break through this dream
suddened upon me by questioning life

*__sardonic__ mocking, sarcastic

*__existential__ skeptical, absurdist

> no longer is it A life unquestioned
> did well enough unquestioned

The Troubled Youth Grows Up

In 1969 Corso was at Ginsberg's farm in upstate New York when they got the news that Jack Kerouac had died, and they went to the funeral together. The death of his friend, the most popular writer of his generation, affected Corso deeply. Kerouac's passing was, in some ways, the passing of an era—the freshness and excitement of the music, art, and literary changes that the Beats were part of had become history. Corso's poems started to reflect more on his personal past as well as his current addictions and on his conflicted feelings about bringing children into the world. In "Columbia U Poesy Reading—1975," he lists the accomplishments and deaths of his peers and then says, "Me—I'm still considered an unwashed beatnik sex commie dope fiend." Later in the poem he is summoned by his muse, who tells him he must choose between her and his vices. In contrast to his productivity in the 1960s, eight years of poetry (1973–1981) are gathered into one book, the 1981 collection *Herald of the Autochthonic Spirit*. The language is simple and elegant, with shorter lines than in some of the earlier work, and the line breaks seem natural. Throughout the book Corso refers to his addictions and regrets, opening his heart to the reader:

> I feel there is an inherent ignorance in me
> deep in my being
> to the very core

These lines are from the poem "Wisdom"—the title implying that perhaps it is only when the poet becomes wise that he is able to recognize his ignorance. Corso also incorporates poems for and about his children, including "A Guide for My Infant Son," which, in its brevity and clarity, encapsulates the tension between beauty and death that exists in all his poems:

> Simple perfection
> Perfect simplicity
> It's easy

like painting a flower
or
snapping it dead.

Selected Bibliography

WORKS BY GREGORY CORSO

The Vestal Lady on Brattle (1955).

Gasoline (1958).

The Happy Birthday of Death (1960).

The American Express (1961). A novel.

Long Live Man (1962).

The Mutation of the Spirit: A Shuffle Poem (1964).

There Is Yet Time to Run Back Through Life and Expiate All That's Been Sadly Done (1965).

Elegiac Feelings American (1970).

Herald of the Autochthonic Spirit (1981).

Mindfield (1989).

WORKS ABOUT GREGORY CORSO

Allen, Donald M., ed. *The New American Poetry, 1945–1960.* New York: Grove, 1960.

Bartlett, Lee, ed. *The Beats: Essays in Criticism.* Jefferson, N.C.: McFarland, 1981.

Cook, Bruce. *The Beat Generation.* New York: Charles Scribner's Sons, 1971.

Miles, Barry. *Ginsberg: A Biography.* New York: Simon and Schuster, 1989.

Nemerov, Howard. *Poets on Poetry.* New York: Basic Books, 1966.

Rexroth, Kenneth. *Assays.* Norfolk, Conn.: J. Laughlin, 1961.

Schumacher, Michael. *Dharma Lion: A Critical Biography of Allen Ginsberg.* New York: St. Martin's Press, 1992.

IF YOU LIKE the poetry of Corso, you might also like the poetry of Allen Ginsberg or Gary Snyder. You may also want to look at the poetry of Percy Bysshe Shelley, whose work had a tremendous influence on Corso.

ROBERT CREELEY

(b. 1926)

by Lisa Jarnot

A New England Childhood

Robert Creeley had little time to think about poetry when he was a young man. Growing up in the small New England town of West Acton, Massachusetts, he spent his days with other children in the neighborhood, playing outdoor games, swimming at nearby ponds during the summer, and ice-skating on those same ponds during the wintertime. He especially enjoyed games involving the imagination, pretending to be Tarzan or Robin Hood. Later in life he would recall, "In the summer we swam a lot and fished. Played knights and joust. We'd use the lids of grain barrels as shields and cut saplings for lances and we would charge at each other full tilt" (Terrell, p. 201). In the area surrounding his parents' home there were farms and wooded areas, and the young Creeley had many opportunities to explore his environment.

He was born in Arlington, Massachusetts, on 21 May 1926, into a comfortable middle-class family. His father, Oscar Slade Creeley, was a doctor, and his mother, Genevieve Jules

Creeley, was a nurse. In his poetry there are often references to his memories of childhood places. Here is an example from a poem called "The Picnic" (in *The Collected Poems of Robert Creeley*, 1945–1975):

> Ducks in the pond,
> icecream & beer,
> all remind me
> of West Acton, Mass—
>
> where I lived when young
> in a large old house
> with 14 rooms
> and woods out back . . . .
>
> Time we all went home,
> or back,
> to where it all was,
> where it all was.

Me, Myself, and I

The loss of his eye changed the way he perceived objects and people.

Not only does Creeley's work concern itself with ideas of the poet's physical location in the world, but it also addresses his perception of himself in relationship to communities and friends. Certain events that took place when he was a boy became important to Creeley's life in this way. The first occurred when he was two years old. While Creeley was riding in a car, the side window broke in an accident, and his left eye was so badly injured that it had to be removed. The loss of his eye changed the way he perceived objects and people. Sometimes Creeley makes use of a pun, presenting the words "I" and "eye" interchangeably in poems. His work shows preoccupation with vision—of looking at the world through one eye and of being alone, or being a single "I."

Creeley's contemplations about being alone in the world are partly a result of another major event of his childhood. When he was four years old, his father got pneumonia and died unexpectedly. This death also became a subject of Creeley's poetry. His mother and many of her relatives who lived nearby helped raise him. He was close to his older sister,

Helen, but had few male role models when he was a boy. Like another great New England poet, Emily Dickinson, Robert Creeley inherited what might be described as a "puritan" sense of the world: that one should be careful of excess and reserved in one's social manners. Out of this sense Creeley developed a preoccupation in his poems with the dilemmas of the mind in relation to a physical world of desires. His work also came to be characterized by short precise lines, often reserved in their expression of emotion.

From Harvard to the Chicken Farm

When Creeley was fourteen, he began attending a private high school in Plymouth, New Hampshire, called the Holderness School. It was during this time that he decided that he wanted to be a writer. He attended Harvard University during the years 1943–1946. As a student there, Creeley met other young men and women who would go on to become writers. He also met musicians who introduced him to jazz music and painters who introduced him to the visual arts. At Harvard, Creeley read the work of such poets as Wallace Stevens, Hart Crane, and Marianne Moore. Another group of poets that interested him were the English poets of the seventeenth century known as the Metaphysical poets. Many of the Metaphysical poets wrote about love and God. Emotions and ideas of love are very important in Robert Creeley's poems, though they are also a point of conflict. He sometimes speaks of the "human condition" in his writing, of the various inevitable dilemmas and facts that are a part of our everyday life. Many of his poems record such everyday events. One of the projects of Creeley's poems is to create a sense of clarity about basic human emotions—love, fear, hatred, and anger. Here is an excerpt from a poem called "The Crisis" (in *The Collected Poems of Robert Creeley*):

> Let me say (in anger) that since the day we were married
> we have never had a towel
> where anyone could find it,
> the fact.
>   Notwithstanding that I am not
> simple to live with, not
> my own judgement, but no
> matter. . .

In this poem, as in many of his works, Creeley takes a simple moment of his personal life and incorporates it into a meditation on human relationships and feelings.

The War Years

Robert Creeley dropped out of school during World War II and became an ambulance driver for the American Field Service in the India-Burma theater.* In 1945 he returned to Harvard but left school the following year without completing his undergraduate degree. One of the reasons he left was to start a family. He was married to Ann Mackinnon in 1946, and in 1948 the couple had their first son. For three years, Creeley and his new family lived in Littleton, New Hampshire, where Creeley started a farm and raised chickens and pigeons. When asked in a 1995 interview what his interests were besides poetry, Creeley answered, "Children and animals and people I've loved like family, friends" (Luttrell).

Creeley and his wife had two more children while living in New Hampshire, a son in 1950 and a daughter in 1952. Another important thing happened in 1952: Creeley's first book of poetry, *Le Fou,* was published. He and his family soon moved to southern France and then to the island of Majorca, near the coast of Spain. It was in Majorca that he became the editor of the Divers Press and started to publish books by other people. As a publisher, he began to meet new poets and other artists from the United States and Europe.

Black Mountain and Beyond

In 1950, Creeley began a correspondence with a poet from New England named Charles Olson. That year Olson had written an important essay about free-verse* poetry called "Projective Verse." Olson included in the essay something that Robert Creeley had said: "Form is never more than an extension of content" (Robert Creeley, ed., *Selected Writings,* 1966, p. 16). This idea became very important to American poets during the second half of the twentieth century. In traditional poetry, standard forms of rhyme and meter are used as a framework through which ideas and stories are developed. Olson's "Projective Verse" essay encouraged poets to write in a

The Conspiracy

You send me your poems,
I'll send you mine.

Things tend to awaken
even through random communication.

Let us suddenly
proclaim spring. And jeer

at the others,
all the others.

I will send a picture too
if you will send me one of you.

(*Selected Poems*)

more "free" form, and he pointed out that the form of a poem could evolve out of the ideas, emotions, or images expressed in it. He believed that the form of a poem and the arrangement of lines might be dictated by the poet's breathing patterns, heartbeat, or normal speech patterns.

It was through Charles Olson that Creeley became involved with Black Mountain College, an experimental arts school in North Carolina. From 1953 through 1957, Creeley edited a poetry magazine called the *Black Mountain Review,* through which he became more familiar with the poetry of Robert Duncan, Denise Levertov, Cid Corman, Joel Oppenheimer, John Weiners, Edward Dorn, and Paul Blackburn. Black Mountain College was important in many ways. It was a place where some of the twentieth-century's significant painters, musicians, and poets came together to work and study. For the duration of its existence (1933–1956), it was a vibrant place where artists exchanged ideas, and the poets who went there subsequently moved on to establish communities in various cities across the United States.

Robert Creeley never expected to become a teacher, but he left Spain and went to Black Mountain in 1954 to teach poetry. He was a shy young man, and during his first semester the students sometimes could not understand what he was saying because his nervousness caused him to mutter. While at Black Mountain, Creeley taught a class about one of his favorite writers, the American modernist poet William Carlos Williams. Creeley also attended classes at Black Mountain and received a bachelor of arts degree there in 1956. It was there that he met many writers who would be important to his life, among them Olson, Duncan, and Levertov, and they became his closest friends.

One of Creeley's interests in poetry is how it allows the poet to find his or her home in the world. The world might be imaginary, as in the games of Tarzan he played as a child. It might also be a real world inhabited by other poets. As he said in an autobiographical essay, "It is the pleasure and authority of writing that it invents a life to live in the first place" (*Autobiography,* p. 10).

Finding the Beat

The Beat Generation of writers, including Allen Ginsberg, Jack Kerouac, and William Burroughs, began publishing their books during the 1950s. From "beat" came from the term "beatnik," a person whose affinity for jazz, uninhibited poetry, physical and spiritual intoxication, and free love, as well as a highly casual style of dress, amounted to a rejection of conventional American social values.

In 1956, after leaving Black Mountain, Creeley briefly went to San Francisco, where he met the emerging Beat writers Allen Ginsberg and Jack Kerouac. There are elements of Beat writing in Creeley's work, particularly as he shared with these poets similar interests in jazz music and the counterculture of 1950s America. Another thing that Creeley liked about Beat writing was that it expressed emotions candidly and directly. Like many early Beat poems, Creeley's verse is sharp and clear. His poems are characterized by short lines and simple images. Look at the following poem, "Sad Advice" (in *Selected Poems*) and the ways in which it is composed of simple, everyday language, as if being spoken to a friend:

> If it isn't fun, don't do it.
> You'll have to do enough that isn't.
>
> Such is life, like they say,
> no one gets away without paying
>
> and since you don't get to keep it
> anyhow, who needs it.

While Creeley's poems at times seem simple, they are carefully structured. Sometimes the lines are formed out of an attention to music and sometimes out of an attention to the way people speak. As a young person, Creeley had visited New York City and there became interested in jazz. Many of his poems are composed of fragments of phrases similar to musical phrases in jazz. As the critic Tom Clark writes, "The imagination of a cool, angular, driving jazz, punctuated with anxious, staccato* accents and playing at moderated volume somewhere off in the backdrop, is an important element in the existential ambiance* of much of Creeley's earliest serious writing" (p. 47).

Similarly, his work is often composed of fragments of phrases of emotions and of "stuttered" lines. Here is an example from a poem called "For W.C.W.," a tribute to William Carlos Williams:

> The rhyme is after
> all the repeated
> insistence.
>
> There, you say, and
> there, and there,
> and *and* becomes
>
> just so. And
> what one wants is
> what one wants. . . .

> (*Collected Poems of Robert Creeley*)

Notice how Creeley breaks the lines in unexpected places, as in the first stanza, where the phrase "after all" is split onto two separate lines. Creeley often makes such unusual breaks in his lines, especially when reading his poems in public. There are different ways to think about these line breaks. They might be seen in relation to Creeley's puritan (morally strict) upbringing, because they show the poet's self-conscious hesitation to say too much too quickly. The unusual line breaks are also indicative of the poet's feeling that sometimes our thoughts are fragmented, that it is not always easy to say what we would like to, and that when our emotions enter into the poem, they create a tension or restriction of line as we try to decide what to say next.

*staccato short, quickly cut off

*ambiance the feeling, or atmosphere, of a work

Poet and Teacher

After Creeley left San Francisco, he moved to New Mexico. He and Ann had divorced in 1955, and in 1957 he married Bobbie Louise Hawkins, with whom he had two daughters. He also attended the University of New Mexico and in 1960 received a master of arts degree. While attending classes, he became a teacher at a local high school in order to earn a living. While he settled into family life and teaching, he also spent a good deal of time writing. The 1960s were crucial to Creeley's career as a poet. It was in 1960 that an important anthology, *The New American Poetry,* was published. This anthology gathered together the work of young poets from various parts of the country for the first time. It included the work of the Black Mountain poets alongside the Beat poets, San Francisco Renaissance poets, and New York school poets. Then, in 1962, Creeley's book *For Love: Poems 1950–1960* was published, and he became a nationally known poet. He traveled to give poetry readings and took part in poetry conferences. One important conference took place in 1963, in Vancouver, British Columbia, where Creeley was teaching at the time. At the Vancouver poetry conference, Black Mountain school and Beat poets converged to give readings and lectures. Then, in 1965, a similar conference was held at the University of California at Berkeley. Throughout the 1960s and 1970s, Robert Creeley played an important role in shaping the culture and poetry of the time.

The San Francisco Renaissance refers to the gathering of young poets and artists in the mid-1950s in San Francisco, where they exchanged ideas about art and politics. The New York school is a group of poets, including Frank O'Hara, John Ashbery, and Kenneth Koch, that began during this same time period and that found connections to the music and art scenes of the time.

The Island

While Creeley is best recognized as a poet, he is also a fiction writer. In 1963 his novel, *The Island,* was published. As he said later, "I had wanted, in fact, to write prose, novels, as I imagined, which might support myself and family in a modest but specific manner. . . . Nothing of the sort ever happened, and by the time I was thirty, I'd contrived to teach as a means of living, which I've done ever since" (*Selected Poems,* p. xx). One of the schools at which Creeley began to teach during the late 1960s was the State University of New York at Buffalo. In 1973, he moved to the Buffalo area permanently. Creeley's second marriage ended in divorce in 1976, and he was married for the third time to Penelope Highton, with whom he had two children. He continued teaching at the State University of New York at Buffalo and became a well-known poet all over the world. From 1989 through 1991 he served as the state poet of New York.

A Life's Work

In an autobiographical essay Robert Creeley said, "We believe in a world or have none" (*Autobiography,* p. 98). For Creeley, poetry is a form of writing that allows people of all kinds to connect to each other. In his poem "The Conspiracy" he encourages his reader to enter into the realm of the poem and to conspire with him in inventing a world.

Throughout his life Creeley has created a world of people and places through his poems, stories, and novels. He has traveled over much of the world. He has lived in such diverse places as France, Spain, Guatemala, and Finland, and his work has been translated into many languages. Creeley has also been awarded two Guggenheim Fellowships, a Rockefeller grant, the Bollingen Prize, the Shelley Memorial Award, and the Robert Frost Medal. Robert Creeley found his way into poetry through the use of his imagination as a child, and poetry became a permanent part of his life. In the introduction to his *Selected Poems* he wrote: "Why poetry? Its materials are so constant, simple, elusive, specific. It costs so little and so much. It preoccupies a life, yet can only find one living. It is a music, a playful construct of feeling, a last word and communion" (p. xxi).

Selected Bibliography

WORKS BY ROBERT CREELEY
Poetry

Le Fou (1952).

All That Is Lovely in Men (1955).

The Whip (1957).

A Form of Women (1959).

For Love: Poems 1950–1960 (1962).

Words (1965; enlarged ed., 1967).

IF YOU LIKE the poetry of Creeley, you might also like the poetry of Edwin Arlington Robinson or William Carlos Williams.

The Charm: Early and Uncollected Poems (1967; enlarged ed., 1969).

Pieces (1968).

A Day Book (1972).

Thirty Things (1974).

Hello: A Journal, February 29–May 3, 1976. (1978).

Later (1979).

Mirrors (1983).

Memory Gardens (1986).

The Company (1988).

Windows (1990).

Selected Poems (1991).

Echoes (1994).

Life and Death (1993; enlarged ed., 1998).

Prose

The Island (1963). A novel.

The Gold Diggers and Other Stories (1965).

A Quick Graph: Collected Notes and Essays (1970).

Mabel: A Story and Other Prose (1976).

Presences: A Text for Marisol (1976).

Autobiography. Contemporary Authors, Autobiography Series, vol. 10. (1989). Reprinted as *Autobiography* (1990).

Correspondence

Charles Olson and Robert Creeley: The Complete Correspondence. 10 vols. Edited by George Butterick. Santa Barbara: Black Sparrow Press, 1980–1996.

Irving Layton and Robert Creeley: The Complete Correspondence, 1953–1978. Edited by Ekbert Faas and Sabrina Reed. Montreal, Canada: McGill-Queen's University Press, 1990.

Interviews

Allen, Donald, ed. *Contexts of Poetry: Interviews 1961–1971*. Bolinas, Calif.: Four Seasons Foundation, 1973.

Faas, Ekbert. Interview. In *Towards a New American Poetics: Essays and Interviews.* Santa Barbara, Calif.: Black Sparrow Press, 1978.

Luttrell, Steve. "An Interview with Robert Creeley." *Café Review* 6 (spring 1995).

Riach, Alan. "Robert Creeley in Conversation with Alan Riach." Hamilton, New Zealand. 26 July 1995. Online: http://wings.buffalo.edu/epc/authors/creeley/interview .html.

Available Collections

The Collected Essays of Robert Creeley. Berkeley: University of California Press, 1989.

The Collected Poems of Robert Creeley, 1945–1975. Berkeley: University of California Press, 1982.

The Collected Prose of Robert Creeley. New York and London: Marion Boyars, 1984; corrected ed., Berkeley: University of California Press, 1988.

WORKS ABOUT ROBERT CREELEY

Altieri, Charles. "Robert Creeley's Poetics of Conjecture: The Pains and Pleasures of Staging a Self at War with Its Own Lyrical Desires." In his *Self and Sensibility in Contemporary American Poetry.* Cambridge, U.K.: Cambridge University Press, 1984.

Clark, Tom. *Robert Creeley and the Genius of the American Common Place.* New York: New Directions, 1993.

Conte, Joseph M. "One Thing Finding Its Place with Another: Robert Creeley's Pieces." In his *Unending Design: The Forms of Postmodern Poetry.* Ithaca, N.Y.: Cornell University Press, 1991.

Foster, Edward Halsey. "Robert Creeley: Poetics of Solitude." In his *Understanding the Black Mountain Poets.* Columbia: University of South Carolina Press, 1995.

Fox, Willard. *Robert Creeley, Edward Dorn, and Robert Duncan: A Reference Guide.* Boston: G. K. Hall, 1989.

Tallman, Warren. *Three Essays on Creeley.* Toronto, Canada: Coach House Press, 1973.

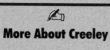

More About Creeley

You can write to:
Robert Creeley
c/o New Directions Books
80 Eighth Avenue
New York, NY 10011

Terrell, Carroll F., ed. *Robert Creeley: The Poet's Workshop.* Orono: National Poetry Foundation, University of Maine, 1984.

von Hallberg, Robert. "Robert Creeley and John Ashbery: Systems." In his *American Poetry and Culture, 1945–1980.* Cambridge, Mass.: Harvard University Press, 1985.

Wilson, John, ed. *Robert Creeley's Life and Work: A Sense of Increment.* Ann Arbor: University of Michigan Press, 1987.

VICTOR HERNÁNDEZ CRUZ
(b. 1949)

by Herbert Kohl

Victor Hernández Cruz was born in Aguas Buenas, Puerto Rico, on 6 February 1949. He described his birthplace like this:

> I was born in a barrio* with the name of a Taino* fruit: El Guanabano. Located in the central or urban area of the town of Aguas Buenas, Puerto Rico, some 35 minutes from San Juan. The streets of El Guanabano were not yet paved. When it rained everything became a mess, the downpour created a small river flowing down to the town plaza, the red dirt making the stream appear to be guava juice. Kids would jump outside to play in the torrential tropical showers.

Hernández Cruz's early life in Aguas Buenas was full of song and poetry and had a lasting influence on his work. His grandfather was a *tabaquero,* a cigar maker. He was also a legendary singer who sang romances and love songs. According to Hernández Cruz,

*barrio a Spanish-speaking neighborhood

*Taino relating to the Tainos, an aboriginal people native to the Caribbean islands

Autobiographical quotations throughout are taken from "Home Is Where the Music Is," pp. 53–55 of *Homeground.*

It was within the *chin-chals* [the gathering places of young social activists and artists] of Aguas Buenas that my imagination first heard poetry declaimed, thrown outloud in coordination with head and hands weaving. I was only a child amidst the tobacco leaves, taken there by my grandfather or my uncle Carlos who used to go and recite poetic standards like "El Brindis Del Bohemio." My uncle continued this tradition of declaiming into the frozen zones of New York's lower East Side tenements.

The Move to New York

Hernández Cruz and his family moved to the Lower East Side of New York in the late 1950s. By the 1960s his neighborhood had become a center of intellectual and social ferment. This was a time of social change and hope for all peoples. The Civil Rights movement was changing people's lives. New voices were being heard, voices of people who had previously been silent or marginalized.* Such writers as Allen Ginsberg, Ishmael Reed, LeRoi Jones (Amiri Baraka), David Henderson, and Diane DiPrima were part of the predominantly Puerto Rican neighborhood. Beat poetry, feminist poetry, protest poetry, modernist poetry, and black poetry were germinating in that community. Every night people came to share ideas and poems in clubs and cafés. One of those places was called Slugs, whose house band was Sun Ra and His Celestial Arkestra, a famous jazz group that played what they called "planetary music." In that café, poets, musicians, novelists, and political activists took in the jazz and talked about their work and their dreams of an America in which poverty would not exist and all people would be respected. It was a romantic time, a time of hope and promise. The young poet Hernández Cruz was immediately recognized as a person with an exceptional gift for languages. Many people who know him assert that he speaks poetry in everyday life. His words can be funny, ironic, profound, or casual, but they are always crafted in a way to which an ear tuned to poetry will immediately respond. It is no accident that, later in life, he became the World Heavyweight Poetry Champion at a contest of poets held each year. During the contest, poets spontaneously respond to themes

marginalized given an almost outsider status within a group; not central they choose themselves. Hernández Cruz, like his grandfather, was born to that poetic challenge.

First Publication

As a teenager, Hernández Cruz chose to be part of the multicultural artistic community where he grew up and chose poetry as his way of life. At the age of seventeen, he self-published his first book, *Papo Got His Gun.* The book was produced in an edition of 260 copies by Calle Once Publications (Eleventh Street Publications), set up by Hernández Cruz and some friends. It was the press's only publication. Hernández Cruz and his friends made a color print for the cover, mimeographed* the poems, stapled the volume, and sold it in the community for seventy-five cents a copy.

One of the poems in that book, "A Letter to José," announced Hernández Cruz's commitment to poetry:

> Joe i been fighting
> not the way we used to fight with the Sportsmens
> but with words that must be as sharp as blades

Eight poems from *Papo* were published in the well-known magazine *Evergreen Review* (August 1967), and Hernández Cruz had become a respected poet while still in high school.

Hernández Cruz was—and still is—a voracious reader and student of poetry in English and Spanish. A major influence on his work has been William Carlos Williams, a poet whose mother was Puerto Rican and whose first language was Spanish. Two aspects of Williams's work seem to be particularly important in Hernández Cruz's development: his experiments with the "variable foot" and his commitment to create a true American vernacular* that would give poetic voice to the rhythms and images of the diverse peoples that make up the United States.

The variable foot allowed for breaking lines in a poem to create a visual and sound structure that challenges the formal regularity of traditional poetry: a two-word line might be followed by a seven-word line. Line breaks were determined by the flow of language and the look of the poem on the page, not by a predetermined line and syllable structure. One can see both of these influences in the following selection from "If

mimeographed duplicated with a machine that uses stencils to make copies. The mimeograph machine was replaced by the photocopier.

The "Sportsmens" was a Puerto Rican street gang of the period.

vernacular the language or dialect commonly spoken in a particular region

Tiny," in Hernández Cruz's second book, *Snaps,* published by a major publisher, Random House, when he was only twenty:

> If Tiny
> shines like gold
> & moves like storms
> & brings down walls
> (i help her out
> i scream in halls
> i smoke all day
> the man gets scared
> he thinks we loud
> that is the truth
> we bass & hip & cool
> we crazy anyway)

The spirituality and wild flights of language and imagination in the poetry of Allen Ginsberg also influenced Hernández Cruz's work. Ginsberg was a friend and a mentor. The generosity of Ginsberg, Ishmael Reed, June Jordan, and other poets also shaped Hernández Cruz's sense of the poet as belonging to a diverse community of writers whose work overflows the usual boundaries of genre and style. There are few forms of writing that Hernández Cruz has not attempted.

The Move to Berkeley

In 1969, Hernández Cruz moved to Berkeley, California, just at the time when the *nuyoriqueño* (Nuyorican, or New York/ Puerto Rican) poetry movement was beginning to flourish. At the age of twenty he became poet-in-residence at the University of California, Berkeley, despite the fact that he had never received his high school diploma. At that time such poets as Miguel Algarín, Pedro Pietri, and Piri Thomas, who had been born in Puerto Rico but had grown up in New York City, infused the bilingual, bicultural sounds and rhythms of the New York Puerto Rican experience into their poetry. Hernández Cruz, who was bicoastal as well as bilingual, traveled between New York and the San Francisco Bay Area and was a central part of this movement. It is ironic that some of his poems most identified with the *nuyoriqueño* movement were written in California. This selection from the poem "From the Secrets I," from his third volume of poetry, *Mainland,* is an example:

> Thoughts in Spanish run through
> the mind
> The buildings speak broken English

In the same volume he has a short poem that embodies the spirit of much of his work: "Think with your body/And dance with your mind."

Interestingly, Hernández Cruz never called himself a *nuyoriqueño* poet, though he was part of the movement. He drew on poets as diverse as Walt Whitman and Shakespeare and considered the realm of poetry, as he puts it, as large as the planet. The vision projected in his poetry is of a culturally rooted, yet universal sense of the world as a complex puzzle whose pieces have yet to fall together. In the course of his development, he began to write both in English and in Spanish. In some poems the languages are mixed. Hernández Cruz is one of the few poets who writes equally well in more than one language. Here's an example ("side 24") from his fourth poetry book, *Tropicalization,* that crosses the boundaries of language:

> Walk el cement
> Where las chinas* roll
> illuminating my path
> Through old streets
> With ancient tales

***las chinas** Puerto Rican Spanish for oranges, here meaning sweet and beautiful

In his next book, *By Lingual Wholes,* some poems are printed simultaneously in English and Spanish. Although they are similar, one version is not a direct translation of the other. The two poems are crafted in two languages:

Version	Versíon
EACH LITTLE	CADA
PORE	PORO
HAS A LIGHT	TIENE UNA LUZ
AND OUTSIDE	Y AFUERA
DARKNESS	OBSCURIDAD
YOU SHINE	TU BRILLAS

The Bay Area Influence

The San Francisco Bay Area also had a profound effect on Hernández Cruz's development. During the 1960s, 1970s, and early 1980s, it was a gathering place for many poets and artists from throughout the Americas. There were artists from Chile and Nicaragua, from Panama and El Salvador, from Mexico and Columbia, and from Peru and Venezuela who gathered to share poetry and ideas. Many of these people were in political exile from countries with harsh dictatorships who dreamed of using the arts to help free their people. Like all poets, they also wrote love poetry and poems that celebrated a special moment of life or honored a death. Such poets as Fernando Alegria from Chile and Roberto Vargas from Nicaragua helped transform Hernández Cruz from an American poet into a poet for all of the English- and Spanish-speaking world. He became fluent in the many idioms of the Spanish language as they are spoken and written in Latin America and Spain. Typically, he read as voraciously in Spanish as he had in English.

In addition, the poet and novelist Ishmael Reed, who had moved to the Bay Area a bit before Hernández Cruz, continued to be a friend and mentor. Reed's determination to produce literature from all of the cultures of the Americas, as manifested in the magazine *Yardbird Reader* and in the publications of the Before Columbus Foundation, introduced Hernández Cruz to Asian American, Native American, and ethnic European American writing. The literary circle in the Bay Area at the time was very large, and few writers could be unaffected by the multiplicity of passionate, crafted, and diverse voices that were emerging.

Back to Puerto Rico

In 1989, Hernández Cruz moved back to Aguas Buenas, the community where he was born and lived as a young child. There he is surrounded by relatives and old friends, by people who never left Puerto Rico and those who have returned from New York, New Jersey, Chicago, and other cities where Puerto Ricans once went to escape poverty. The Spanish and English he hears is compounded by the regional accents of American English, an element he relishes and at times works into his poetry.

Although Hernández Cruz travels to teach in universities throughout the United States and to read his poetry all over the world, returning to Puerto Rico has had a major effect on his development as a poet. In Puerto Rico he came into closer touch with the cultural traditions that led to his grandfather's poetic declamations* and to the development of modern Afro–Puerto Rican music. His work has focused increasingly on developing the rhythms and spiritual and social tradition of the Taino heritage on the island, as it interacted with African traditions and with Spanish-Moorish-Sephardic (Jewish) traditions. It is from these streams of culture that modern Puerto Ricans have sprung, and these are the forces that flow in Hernández Cruz's poetry. He is clear about this, as the following selection from the poem "Root of Three," first published in his volume *Islandis* and reprinted in his collected poems, *Rhythm, Content, and Flavor,* indicates:

> I walk in New York with a mountain
> in my pocket
> I walked in Puerto Rico with a guitar
> in my belly
> I walked in Spain with Mecca*
> in my sandals
> I invented the theory of guayaba*
> Humacao* turned it into a seed
> Gave it to a woman
> Who dove into a hole in the ground
> with it
> She came back in seven days
> with a round yellow fruit
> In Ifa* land I was a cane for
> the poets of divination
> I saw blood cells
> moonlight as drum beats

A Larger Vision

Hernández Cruz's relationships with these writers connected him to the literature and the life of the writer in Latin America as well as Spain. In that context he began to write for a Spanish-speaking audience as well as for an English-speaking or bilingual audience. His vision of the wholeness of things became

declamations highly ornate formal statements

Mecca a city in Saudi Arabia that is considered the center of the Islamic world

guayaba a tropical fruit

Humacao a town in Puerto Rico named for a Taino hero who resisted the Spanish

Ifa the West African community and ancestral home of Puerto Rican black people

*campesino a farm worker

*plantain a small banana-like fruit

Problems with Hurricanes

A campesino* looked at the air
And told me:
With hurricanes it's not the wind
or the noise or the water.
I'll tell you he said:
it's the mangoes, avocados
Green plantains* and bananas
flying into town like projectiles.

How would your family
feel if they had to tell
The generations that you
got killed by a flying
Banana.

Death by drowning has honor
If the wind picked you up
and slammed you
Against a mountain boulder
This would not carry shame
But
to suffer a mango smashing
Your skull
or a plantain hitting your
Temple at 70 miles per hour
is the ultimate disgrace.

The campesino takes off his hat—
As a sign of respect
towards the fury of the wind
And says:
Don't worry about the noise
Don't worry about the water
Don't worry about the wind—

If you are going out
beware of mangoes
And all such beautiful
sweet things.

(Red Beans)

merged with his sense of being part of many poetic worlds beyond the borders of the continental United States and the island of Puerto Rico. What he says about music in *Red Beans,* his 1991 collection of poems and essays, could equally apply to his own poetry: "It seems to be the center of the musician to translate, rearrange, to give personal flavor to a variety of rhythms and melodies."

The same sentiment is expressed in this excerpt from "Corsica," a poem in the same volume:

> Underneath with the geologic plates
> Puerto Rico and Corsica
> Are holding hands
>
> . . . .
> Puerto Rico is in the Mediterranean
> All the eyes are the same.

Victor Hernández Cruz has been working on several long poems in Spanish that trace the history of Puerto Rico from prehistoric times to the early native Taino settlements and the African diaspora* and Spanish settlements up to the present "Americanization" of the island. He also continues to write poems in English. He still lives in Aguas Buenas in the same neighborhood he grew up in, and reads his poetry from New York City to San Francisco, from Mexico City to Madrid.

Hernández Cruz is an extraordinary performer of poetry. When he reads, one can hear the African rhythms, the Spanish and Moorish tones and inflections,* the Native American recitations and chants, and the New York chatter that have gone into the making of his poems. As he wrote in an early pamphlet titled *Doing Poetry:* "poems are songs. poems cry & laugh, a poet is in the world / the world is in the poet."

*diaspora dispersion; the scattering of a group of people to areas outside their homeland

*inflection a change in the volume or pitch of the voice

Selected Bibliography

WORKS BY VICTOR HERNÁNDEZ CRUZ
Poetry

Papo Got His Gun (1966).

Snaps (1969).

Doing Poetry (1969).

Mainland (1973).

Tropicalization (1976).

By Lingual Wholes (1982).

Islandis (1989).

Prose

"Home Is Where the Music Is." In *Homeground.* Edited by Kathryn Trueblood and Linda Stovall. Hillsboro, Ore.: Blue Heron, 1996.

Video Recording

Victor Hernández Cruz. Lannan literary series, no. 12. Los Angeles: The Lannan Foundation, 1989.

Available Collections

Red Beans. Minneapolis: Coffee House Press, 1991.

Rhythm, Content, and Flavor. Houston: Arte Publico Press, 1989.

WORKS ABOUT VICTOR HERNÁNDEZ CRUZ

Aparicio, Frances. "Salsa, Maracas and Baile: Latin Popular Music in the Poetry of Victor Hernández Cruz." *MELUS* 16 (spring 1989–1990): 43–58.

Turner, Faythe E. "Puerto Rican Writers on the Mainland: The Neoricans: A Thematic Study." Ph.D. dissertation, University of Massachusetts, 1978.

Wallenstein, Barry. "The Poet in New York: Victor Hernández Cruz." *Bilingual Review* 1 (September–December 1974): 312–319.

E. E. CUMMINGS

(1894–1962)

by Loren Goodman

When the poet William Carlos Williams said, "E. E. Cummings means my language," he was referring not to the English language but to the language of poetry (Bloom, p. 905). The Mexican writer and Nobel laureate Octavio Paz referred to Cummings's work as "a perfection . . . incandescent . . . freshness itself . . . a springtime of flames" (Bloom, p. 909).

After a long and productive poetic and artistic career, the iconoclastic* poet E. E. Cummings was asked to return to Harvard, his alma mater, in 1952–1953 to accept the prestigious Charles Eliot Norton Professorship. The only requirement was that he deliver six lectures over the course of the year. True to form, Cummings wrote *i: six nonlectures.* He had great difficulty putting them together, but with hard work and rehearsal, he succeeded, and his lectures were very popular. Cummings gave some insight into his unique aesthetic* in his second lecture, stating, "Poetry and every other art was and is and forever will be strictly and distinctly a question of individuality. . . . Poetry is being, not doing" (p. 24).

Quotations from Cummings's poetry throughout are taken from *Complete Poems 1923–1962.*

iconoclastic attacking established beliefs or institutions

aesthetic a set of ideas about art or beauty

Early Life

Edward Estlin Cummings was born on 14 October 1894 in a huge three-story house at 104 Irving Street in Cambridge, Massachusetts. His family spent summers (and sometimes winters) in the country, near Silver Lake, New Hampshire. His father, Edward, was an assistant professor of sociology at Harvard and a Unitarian minister. His mother, Rebecca, devoted herself to the care of Estlin (as he was called) and his little sister, Elizabeth. Rebecca Cummings often sang and read to them, and she taught Estlin to write and keep a diary. Cummings's paternal grandfather was an inventor who lost most of his wife's money devising a pedal for piano practice and a toilet paper dispenser. On his mother's side of the family were many literary and adventuresome ancestors, including Susanna Rowson, the author of *Charlotte Temple,* the first American novel, published in 1791.

Cummings—whose first word was "Hurrah!"—had a strong literary upbringing. He was given letter blocks for his second birthday, knew the alphabet four months later, and said his first rhyme at the age of three. Cummings was strongly influenced by the wordplay, puns, and metaphors of his father's sermons (for example, "Wordliness is next to Godliness"). Cummings's mother wanted him to be a poet; she even kept a book of verses he composed at the age of six. Cummings grew up happy in a loving family with a strong sense of individualism, community, and tradition. He loved music and drew from an early age, illustrating his diary entries. He enjoyed the circus so much that he made up programs and tickets to see "Edward Estlin Cummings and his matchless group of 32 elephants little and big" (Kennedy, p. 23).

Cummings was educated at home until he was eight, when he was sent to Miss Webster's School, a private grade school. In 1904 his parents sent him to Agassiz Public School, and when he was only nine, he was placed in the seventh grade because of his reading skills. Here he was required to memorize many poems, mainly by New England poets, with an emphasis on patriotism, duty, and brotherhood, such as Henry Wadsworth Longfellow's "Legend Beautiful." In ninth grade at the Peabody School he read more Longfellow, whose poems he parodied* throughout his career.

*parody to imitate in a humorous way, intending to ridicule

In 1907, at the age of twelve, Cummings went to Cambridge Latin School, a college prep school. There he embarked on a rigorous course of study centered on Greek, Latin, and French. He studied no sciences but gained a deep understanding of the way languages work—especially the etymology* and syntax* of English. Although he tried rowing, he was more interested in writing and art than in sports, and he edited and wrote fantasies for the school literary magazine, *Cambridge Review*.

At Harvard

Cummings entered Harvard in 1911 at the age of sixteen. In 1915 he graduated magna cum laude* with a degree in literature (Greek and English), and then stayed on another year to earn a master's degree in English in 1916. Cummings loved language but not philosophy, as evidenced by his D− in Greek philosophy. As he once said to a friend, quoting the French poet Stéphane Mallarmé: "One doesn't write poetry with ideas: one writes poetry with words" (Kennedy, p. 53). He liked the art of putting words together and disliked the intellectualism of taking texts apart; instead of writing critical papers, Cummings often turned in parodies.

Because Cummings lived at home for his first two years of college, his social life at Harvard developed slowly. His first real friend there was his Greek teacher, Theodore Miller, who introduced him to the works of the ancient Latin and Greek poets Catullus, Horace, Sappho, and Anacreon. Cummings translated many Greek and Latin poems. He liked Dante and drew detailed diagrams of Dante's Hell, Purgatory, and Paradise. He read Shakespeare under the famous Shakespeare scholar George Lyman Kittredge, who scoured each line for its linguistic* origins. Cummings also studied German and read Russian novels. Creative writing was encouraged at Harvard, and Cummings wrote for literary magazines such as the *Harvard Monthly*. He began experimenting with lowercase and capital letters after noticing that capitals were used for emphasis even in the middle of sentences in *Krazy Kat,* his favorite comic (he later preferred to see his entire name in lowercase letters). Some of his college poems, which later appeared in his

*etymology the history of a word or linguistic form, shown by tracing its historical occurrence in language

*syntax the structure of a sentence

*magna cum laude with great honor

*linguistic relating to language

books, were written in more traditional poetic form, including "All in green went my love riding," which begins:

> All in green went my love riding
> on a great horse of gold
> into the silver dawn.
>
> four lean hounds crouched low and smiling
> the merry deer ran before.
>
> Fleeter be they than dappled dreams
> the swift sweet deer
> the red rare deer.

Cummings made several friends with whom he shared literary interests, including S. Foster Damon, John Dos Passos, and Scofield Thayer. Damon took him to see the Armory Show of modern art in 1913 in New York, where Cummings was excited by the works of the Romanian sculptor Constantin Brancusi. Cummings also greatly enjoyed Damon's copies of Gertrude Stein's *Tender Buttons* and Ezra Pound's anthology *Des imagistes*. At his commencement Cummings delivered a speech entitled "The New Art" on the works of Claude Monet, Paul Cézanne, Marcel Duchamp, Amy Lowell, and Gertrude Stein.

Cummings & Goings

After graduating in 1916, Cummings spent three months at home, working on his art and poems. During this time he hung out at bars in Boston and started incorporating into his poems street language, accents, and dialects, which most poets at the time avoided, a practice illustrated in this section of "Gert" from "Five Americans" in *is 5*:

> Her voice?
> gruesome: a trull*
> leaps from the lungs "gimme uh swell fite
>
> like up ter yknow, Rektuz, Toysday nite;
> where uh guy gets gayn troze uh lobstersalad

trull prostitute

Beginning on 1 January 1917, he worked in New York for less than two months in an office at *Collier's* magazine. There, while reading the *New York Sun* obituary of Buffalo Bill, he was inspired to write:

> Buffalo Bill's
> defunct
>   who used to
>   ride a watersmooth-silver
>
>   stallion
> and break onetwothreefourfive pigeonsjustlikethat
>   Jesus
>   he was a handsome man
>   and what i want to know is
>   how do you like your blueeyed boy
>   Mister Death
>
>   (p. 60)

After quitting his job, Cummings experimented with poetry and devoted himself to becoming an artist. Unemployed in New York, he received help from his parents and his patron, Scofield Thayer. Cummings lived a satisfying self-involved existence as a writer-artist. He became known as a great conversationalist and social presence, mingling till the wee hours with Greenwich Village social sets. This lifestyle took a sharp turn on 7 April 1917, when Cummings volunteered to be an ambulance driver for a Red Cross unit assigned to the French army during World War I. Cummings quickly became good friends with another volunteer, William Slater Brown, who had studied journalism, English, and French literature at Columbia University.

Cummings and Brown were pacifists and did not get along well with the rest of the Americans in their unit. In a letter requesting transfer to a French aviation unit, they made the mistake of stating that they were reluctant to kill Germans. French intelligence agents were already inspecting their mail, since Cummings tried to trick the censors by writing his letters home in code, and Brown teased the censors directly. Thus, Brown and Cummings were arrested—Brown for being a spy and Cummings for his association with Brown. They were taken to an internment center* in Normandy. When Cummings's parents found out what had happened, they tried to

"Buffalo Bill," born William F. Cody, was a scout for military units fighting American Indians. He was also an actor and showman and a rider for the Pony Express.

*internment center
a place of confinement or imprisonment, usually for prisoners of war, enemy aliens, and political prisoners

get him released, but the French were uncooperative. Cummings actually seemed to enjoy being imprisoned, since it gave him plenty of time to think about and discuss the "greatest of all sciences—Art" (Kennedy, p. 156).

Cummings was released on 19 December 1917. He returned in February 1918 to New York, where he resumed his bohemian* lifestyle, painting, writing, and going to vaudeville and strip shows. In July he was drafted into the army. Selected to go to officer training school, Cummings refused, wanting neither responsibility nor rank. At training camp in Massachusetts, Cummings read the works of the Irish novelist and poet James Joyce and worked on new poetic methods. During this time he met a soldier who inspired him to write one of his best-known poems, which begins:

> i sing of Olaf glad and big
> whose warmest heart recoiled at war:
> a conscientious object-or

Cummings was discharged from the army in January 1919 and returned to New York. As early as the spring of 1918, Cummings had fallen in love with Elaine Thayer, the wife of his friend and patron. Cummings wrote many love poems for Elaine, including "Puella Mea" (My Girl). By May or June 1919, Elaine was pregnant with Cummings's child. Although they married on 19 March 1924—the Thayers having been divorced in 1921—Elaine and Cummings never lived together and were themselves divorced later that year. It was a terrible psychological blow to Cummings, who contemplated suicide. Bitter struggles over the divorce, custody, and visitation ensued, and their daughter, Nancy, grew up believing Scofield Thayer was her father. Thayer, Elaine, and Cummings remained "the best of friends" (Kennedy, p. 189).

After a brief and rocky marriage to Anne Barton ended in 1932, Cummings met Marion Morehouse, a tall, slender fashion model and actress. They were soon married and enjoyed a lasting relationship, living in New York's Greenwich Village. Over the years, with the help of an agent, Cummings made his living by reading for college audiences and became one of the best-known poets among college students. In 1957, two thousand people crammed into an auditorium at the University of Michigan to see Cummings, while another thousand waited outside. On 3 September 1962, after splitting wood in a barn

*bohemian unconventional

one hot afternoon in New Hampshire, Cummings died of a brain hemorrhage.

Poet & Painter

Many people thought that Cummings was a much better writer than painter, including William Carlos Williams, who stated, "He paints—but I don't like his painting. . . .Words are his proper medium" (Bloom, p. 906). Cummings replied that since it was harder for him to paint, it was artistically more meaningful to succeed in that medium. In 1919 he met the American painter Joseph Stella, who inspired him to enter two paintings—*Sound* and *Noise*—in the spring 1919 New York Society of Independent Artists Exhibition. Cummings continued to enter his paintings in exhibitions throughout the 1920s and held his first one-person exhibition in 1931 at the Painters and Sculptors Gallery. The same year he published an autobiographical collection of artwork entitled *CIOPW,* standing for "charcoal, ink, oil, pencil, and watercolor." The book contained renderings of the comic actor Charlie Chaplin, burlesque shows, Coney Island, and various friends.

Cummings traveled to and lived in Europe for brief periods throughout his life. During one of his early trips, in 1921, with John Dos Passos, he met Ezra Pound, whom he admired. They began a lifelong friendship. In 1945, when Pound was in the hospital, Cummings—despite being in debt himself—used a check for one thousand dollars from the sale of his painting *Mt. Chocorua* to pay for Pound's medical bills. In addition to Dos Passos and Pound, Cummings was a friend of other writers: Hart Crane, who Cummings said was "what a poet should be like" (Kennedy, p. 268); the poet and critic Allen Tate; and the homeless bard Joe Gould, who claimed to be composing "The Oral History of Our Time," which he said was already eleven times longer than the Bible. Gould was the inspiration for at least one Cummings poem, "27," from the collection *No Thanks:*

> little joe gould has lost his teeth and doesn't know where
> to find them(and found a secondhand set which
>   click)little
> gould used to amputate his appetite with bad brittle
> candy but just (nude eel)now little joe lives on air.
>
> (p. 410)

"Nude eel" is a play on the words "New Deal," President Franklin Delano Roosevelt's legislative program designed to bring about economic recovery after the Great Depression.

Four (excerpt)

you being in love
will tell who softly asks in love,

am i separated from your body smile brain hands merely
to become the jumping puppets of a dream?   oh i mean:
entirely having in my careful how
careful arms created this at length
inexcusable,this inexplicable pleasure—you go from sev-
        eral
persons:believe me that strangers arrive
when i have kissed you into a memory
slowly,oh seriously
—that since and if you disappear

solemnly
myselves
ask "life,the question how do I drink dream smile

and how do I prefer this face to another and
why do i weep eat sleep—what does the whole intend"
they wonder.   oh and they cry "to be,being,that i am alive
this absurd fraction in its lowest terms
with everything cancelled
but shadows
—what does it all come down to?   love?   Love
if you like and i like,for the reason that i
hate people and lean out of this window is love,love
and the reason that i laugh and breathe is oh love and the
        reason

that i do not fall into this street is love."

Cummings received many awards for his poetry through-out his career, including two Guggenheim grants (1933 and 1950). His proposal for the first grant was probably the briefest in history: "a book of poems." In 1944 he won the Shelley Memorial Award for *1×1;* 1950 also brought the Academy of

American Poets Prize, and in 1958 he received the prestigious Bollingen Prize.

Prose

Although Cummings is most famous for his work as a poet, his first book was written in prose. *The Enormous Room,* an experimental account of his three-month internment in France during World War I, came out in 1922. The American novelist F. Scott Fitzgerald was one of its many admirers, and John Dos Passos wrote that although the book was "written in the guise of prose," it was a form of poetry similar in its uniqueness to new flavors of gum and Eskimo pies (Bloom, p. 909).

Cummings's second major prose work, *Eimi* ("I am" in Greek), was not praised so highly. It was an experimental work derived from Cummings's travels in Russia in 1931. Sometimes likened to James Joyce's *Ulysses* or *Finnegan's Wake* because of its obscurity and length, the work is based in form on Dante's *Inferno*. The main character, a wanderer of sorts, is "Kem-min-kz." One reviewer gave it the "Worst Book of the Month" award, but Marianne Moore called the "entire book a poem" (Kennedy, p. 360).

Poems

In New York during the fall of 1919, Cummings put together his first book of poems, "Tulips & Chimneys." It contains many poems he wrote while in college, which he revised by breaking up the lines. The section "Sonnets—Actualities" contains mostly love poems for Elaine. The book was published as *Tulips and Chimneys,* with the ampersand* spelled out. Most reviews were hostile. Since the publishers refused to print the title with the ampersand, Cummings privately printed a book called *&* in 1925, the same year *XLI Poems* was published.

Cummings's poems received a great deal of attention because of their unusual typographic* and syntactic structures. Although he was influenced by painting, he was also inspired by French experimental poetry, as these lines from *XLI Poems* demonstrate:

***ampersand** the character "&"

***typographic** relating to the font, style, or arrangement of typeset words or letters

French experimental poetry is discussed in the articles "Calligramatic and Concrete Poetry" and "Twentieth-Century Modernist Poetry" in these volumes.

```
un der,
 a lo
co
mo
   tive   s pout
              ing
                vi
                o
              lets
```
(p. 179)

"Portraits—III, " from *&* is almost like ancient hieroglyphic in-
scriptions—picture writing:

```
ta
ppin
g
toe

hip
popot
amus Back

gen
teel-ly
lugu-
bri ous

                    eyes
LOOPTHELOOP

as

fathandsbangrag
```

One reviewer said that Cummings's poems looked "like
the ruins of a typecasting establishment" (Bloom, p. 907). Yet
his techniques were infectious. Whether their reaction was
positive or negative, critics often peppered their reviews with
Cummings-esque concoctions, such as "hiddenly" (James
Dickey) and "uninterfering" (Marianne Moore) (Bloom pp.
912–917). Cummings's books were elaborate constructions. For
instance, *ViVa,* published in 1931, was based on the number
seven. It contains seventy poems; every seventh poem is a son-

net,* and the last seven poems are sonnets. *No Thanks*—so named because no one wanted to publish it (the names of the publishers appear at the beginning of the book in the shape of a funeral urn)—is written in complex "schema." In other words, the poems were not simply written and gathered but were assembled according to a carefully planned framework.

Cummings's *Collected Poems* was more popular than his previous books. It was well marketed, along with a phonograph recording of some of the poems, and—like *is 5*—included a quirky introduction for the reader. In 1944, *1×1* (One times one) came out; it was well reviewed and went through second and third printings. *Xaipe*—pronounced "Kyereh" (the Greek command "Rejoice")—appeared in 1950. Although Cummings received the Academy of American Poets Award for it, there was a negative reaction to some of its apparently anti-Semitic content. The last of Cummings's books published during his life, *95 Poems,* contains perhaps his most beautiful poem, a sort of modern haiku.* The silence of its parentheses marks the passage of a falling leaf in space:

I

l(a

le
af
fa

ll

s)
one
l

iness

Selected Bibliography

WORKS BY E. E. CUMMINGS
Poetry

Tulips and Chimneys (1923).

& (1925).

---

*sonnet a fourteen-line poem usually composed in iambic pentameter (each line has five feet, each foot consisting of an unstressed syllable followed by a stressed syllable). There are two dominant sonnet forms in English poetry, the Shakespearean and Petrarchan.

*haiku a Japanese poetic form, usually unrhymed, consisting of three lines of seventeen syllables. A haiku often focuses on a single moment. See also discussion of haiku in the essay on Poetic Forms in these volumes.

IF YOU LIKE the poetry of Cummings, you might also like the poetry of Guillaume Apollinaire or Robert Creeley.

XLI Poems (1925).

is 5 (1926).

ViVa (1931).

No Thanks (1935).

50 Poems (1940).

1×1 (1944).

Xaipe (1950).

95 Poems (1958).

73 Poems (1963).

Prose

The Enormous Room (1922). Account of Cummings's three-month internment in France during World War I.

Eimi (1933). Experimental prose.

i: six nonlectures (1953). Lectures as Charles Eliot Norton Professor at Harvard, 1952–1953.

Other Works

CIOPW. New York: Covici Friede, 1931. Artwork.

Him. New York: Boni and Liveright, 1927. Play.

The Red Front, by Louis Aragon. Chapel Hill, N.C.: Contempo, 1933. Translation by Cummings.

Audio Recording

E. E. Cummings Reads His Collected Poetry, 1943–1958. Caedmon TC 2081.

Available Collections

Complete Poems 1923–1962. 2 vols. New York: MacGibbon and Kee. Rev. ed. in 1 vol. New York: Harcourt Brace Jovanovich, 1972.

Selected Letters of E. E. Cummings. Edited by F. W. Dupee and George Stade. New York: Harcourt Brace Jovanovich, 1969.

WORKS ABOUT E. E. CUMMINGS

Baum, S. V., ed. *EETI: E. E. Cummings and the Critics.* East Lansing: Michigan State University Press, 1962.

Bloom, Harold, ed. "e. e. cummings." In *Twentieth Century American Literature*. vol. 2. New York: Chelsea House, 1986.

Breit, Harvey. *The Writer Observed*. New York: World, 1956. Interviews.

Cohen, Milton A. *Poet and Painter: The Aesthetics of E. E. Cummings's Early Work*. Detroit: Wayne State University Press, 1987.

Friedman, Norman. *E. E. Cummings: The Art of His Poetry*. Baltimore: Johns Hopkins University Press, 1964.

Friedman, Norman. *E. E. Cummings: The Growth of a Writer*. Carbondale: Southern Illinois University Press, 1964.

Kennedy, Richard S. *Dreams in the Mirror: A Biography of E. E. Cummings*. New York: Liveright, 1980.

Norman, Charles. *E. E. Cummings: The Magic Maker*. New York: Duell, Sloan and Pearce, 1964.

Rotella, Guy. *Critical Essays on E. E. Cummings*. Boston: G. K. Hall, 1984.

More About Cummings

You can find information about Cummings on the Internet at: http://www.poets.org/lit/ poet/eecumfst.htm

DANTE

(Dante Alighieri)
(1265–1321)

by Jeffrey T. Schnapp

In the year 1274 an event took place that shaped the whole of Dante Alighieri's subsequent career as a poet. He encountered Beatrice, the radiant young woman to whom he dedicated most of his love lyrics. From the start, Dante felt that Beatrice was no ordinary being. Mysterious signs accompanied her every appearance and movement. He first spotted her on the verge of her ninth year in the streets of Florence, she first greeted him at the ninth hour of the same day nine years later (1283), and she died in the ninth decade of the thirteenth century (1290) on the ninth hour of the the ninth day of the ninth month. For Dante these nines were no coincidence. They marked Beatrice as a creature at once natural and supernatural, a messenger between this world and the next. Angel-like when she walked the streets of Florence in a body of flesh and blood, Beatrice joined the angels in the celestial paradise after her death. And from that heavenly perch she continued to lead her beloved from vice to virtue, sin to salvation, by inspiring a body of poetry deeply imbued with the Christian faith. Such, at least, is the story that Dante unfolds, from *La vita nuova* (The new life), his first major work, to the masterpiece he completed near the end of his life, the *Divina commedia* (known in English as *The Divine Comedy*).

Dante's Life

Born in Florence in May 1265, Dante was the son of Alighiero di Bellincione d'Alighiero and Donna Bella, both of whom died by the time Dante was seventeen. The thirteenth century was a tumultuous time in northern Italy. Florence was in the midst of a commercial boom that had transformed it into one of Europe's richest cities and established its coin, the florin, as one of Europe's standard currencies. But supporters of the papacy (known as Guelfs) battled it out with supporters of the Holy Roman Emperor (known as Ghibellines) in the streets of such cities as Siena, Pisa, and Florence. Cities allied with one party or the other regularly squabbled among themselves. Even when one party triumphed, there were internal splits, more like the dynastic battles within Mafia families than like the conflicts between modern political parties—splits, for instance, like that between the "Black" and "White" Guelfs.

At the time of Dante's birth, the city was firmly in Guelf hands. The Alighieri were minor members of the Guelf aristocracy, and Dante was probably educated by private tutors and later at the University of Bologna, one of the oldest universities in the world.

Dante rose to a number of high public offices through his membership in the guild of physicians and apothecaries,* being elected prior* and serving as ambassador on at least two occasions. In 1302, during the second of these ambassadorships (to the pope), the Black Guelfs seized absolute power, accused Dante and several prominent White Guelfs of subversion and corruption, and sentenced them to perpetual exile.* Never again did Dante return to Florence or embrace his wife, Gemma (whom he had wed in 1285 and with whom he had two sons and a daughter). The decades of exile were bitter. Dante, a White Guelf with Ghibelline leanings, never tired of proclaiming his innocence or his hopes for a resurgence of the Roman Empire and for the papacy's reform. Most of his time was spent wandering about northern Italy, with extended stays in the Veronese court of Cangrande della Scala, to whom he dedicated *Paradiso* (Paradise), the third and final part of *The*

The Holy Roman Empire controlled much of central Europe from 962 to 1806. It imagined itself as the Christian successor to the Roman Empire but found itself at odds with the Roman Catholic Church's territorial and political claims.

*apothecary a druggist

*prior a religious official

*exile forced absence from one's homeland

Divine Comedy, and with Guido Novello da Polenta in Ravenna, where he died on 13 or 14 September 1321. To this day, Dante's bones remain buried in Ravenna, despite repeated efforts on the part of Florence to secure their transfer to the empty tomb located in the church of Santa Croce.

La Vita Nuova

Written between 1292 and 1295, *La vita nuova* tells the story of Beatrice's life and death and their impact upon Dante. Beatrice's appearance marks a new phase in Dante's life—a "new life" that is as much a love story as it is the story of Dante's maturation as a poet. While alive, Beatrice inspired lyrics that alternately trace the effects of love upon the lover or appeal directly to her or the god of love. The following sonnet, "Many a time the thought returns to me," is typical:

> Many a time the thought returns to me:
>   What sad conditions Love on me bestows!
>   And moved by Pity I say frequently:
>   "Can there be anyone who my state knows?"
>   For Love takes hold of me so suddenly
>   My vital spirits I am near to lose.
>   Only one of them all survives in me,
>   Staying to speak of you, as Love allows.
> To aid me then my forces I renew
>   And pallid,* all my courage drained long since,
>   I come to you to remedy my plight;
>   But if I raise my eyes to look at you
>   So vast a tremor in my heart begins
>   My beating pulses put my soul to flight.
>
> (Reynolds, p. 52)

*__pallid__ pale

Framed by a prose narrative in which each poem is analyzed and situated within the unfolding story of Dante and Beatrice's romance, sonnets like this one exemplify what Dante himself called the *dolce stil nuovo* (the "sweet new style"). They sing about the torments and ecstasies of love within the framework of a celebration of love's ennobling power. Love raises humankind above animal urges. It civilizes, it gives rise to an appreciation for art and poetry, and it tames the savage heart. The embodiment of love's ennobling effect is a beloved

To find out more about the *dolce stil nuovo,* see the article on Troubadours in these volumes.

Purgatorio (excerpt)

I have at times seen all the eastern sky
becoming rose as day began and seen,
adorned in lovely blue, the rest of heaven;
and seen the sun's face rise so veiled that it
was tempered by the mist and could permit
the eye to look at length upon it; so,
within a cloud of flowers that were cast
by the angelic hands and then rose up
and then fell back, outside and in the chariot,
a woman showed herself to me; above
a white veil, she was crowned with olive boughs;
her cape was green; her dress beneath, flame-red.
Within her presence, I had once been used
to feeling—trembling—wonder, dissolution;
but that was long ago. Still, though my soul,
now she was veiled, could not see her directly,
by way of hidden force that she could move,
I felt the mighty power of old love.
As soon as that deep force had struck my vision
(the power that, when I had not yet left
my boyhood, had already transfixed me),
I turned around and to my left—just as
a little child, afraid or in distress,
will hurry to his mother—anxiously,
to say to Virgil:* "I am left with less
than one drop of my blood that does not tremble:
I recognize the signs of the old flame."

(canto 30, verses 22–48; Allen Mandelbaum translation)

who summons the poet to ever higher callings. She is the *donna gentile,* or gentle lady: "gentle" because she is noble not by birth but by natural inclination and because she is filled with angelic grace.

By the midpoint of the *La vita nuova,* the young poet has turned away from lyrics that directly address Beatrice (and thereby imply her bodily presence) to a poetry of praise that proclaims her virtues to other lovers. The true turning point arrives, however, with Beatrice's death, which discloses the deeper meaning of her existence—to lead Dante and his poetry from mortal to immortal love, from earthly loves to the love of God. Mourning and melancholy pervade the next few poems. Then comes the temptation to forget, when a living woman momentarily eclipses the memory of Beatrice. But Beatrice triumphs in the end, and *La vita nuova* concludes with Dante's promise "to compose concerning her what has never been written in rhyme of any woman" (Reynolds, p. 99).

The Philosophical Works and Stony Rhymes

Dante's early output as a poet is not restricted to the celebration of Beatrice. Along with the poems in *La vita nuova,* Dante composed lyrics on topics ranging from beauty to human folly. He was also an active participant in poetic duels—so-called *tenzoni*—in which poets swapped sometimes combative sonnets like the salty one in *Rime* in which Dante accuses his friend Forese Donati of being a bastard* by birth and a glutton* by inclination: "Bicci my boy, you son of God-knows-who / . . . Your goods diminish as your belly grows / And stealing now must keep it full for you" (Diehl, p. 157). Perhaps the high point of Dante's writings after *La vita nuova* are the *rime petrose,* or "stony rhymes," dating from about 1296. These four lengthy songs portray the cruelty of a "stony lady" toward a lover whose poems are at once pleas for compassion and gestures of vengeance:

> My song, go straight up to that certain lady
> Who pierced my heart and yet will not concede*
> What I in hunger need,
> And send an arrow home into her breast:
> For great revenge, great honor crowns one's quest.
> (Diehl, p. 187)

For all his brilliance as a composer of love lyrics, Dante was also an accomplished philosopher, whose interests included cosmology,* theology, poetics, the natural sciences, and political theory. During his first decade in exile, he composed two important (though unfinished) treatises:* *Convivio* (The banquet) and *De vulgari eloquentia* (On vernacular eloquence). The first, written in Italian, takes the form of a commentary on his own philosophical songs: songs in which Beatrice is remembered but overshadowed by Lady Philoso-

*__bastard__ a person who was born out of wedlock

*__glutton__ someone who eats too much

*__concede__ to yield; to give up reluctantly

*__cosmology__ the general science and philosophy of the universe

*__treatise__ a written argument

In the Middle Ages, all important documents were composed in Latin, the language of the courts and the church. Yet Latin was spoken only by educated members of society. So the "vernaculars" were used by the great majority of people in their everyday lives.

Cantos and canticles are sections within a large work.

*terza rima rhymes made up of eleven-syllable lines, organized into "tercets" (units of three lines of verse) that rhyme according to the pattern aba bcb cdc ded, and so on

phy (symbol of the love of wisdom). The second treatise, written in Latin, sets out to define the relationship between Latin and Greek—the scholarly languages of Dante's era—and the so-called vulgar Latin tongues. These were the vernaculars, varying from town to town and region to region, out of which arose modern languages like French, Spanish, Portuguese, and Italian. By means of a survey of the fourteen major dialects spoken in Italy and of the poetic forms associated with each, Dante sets forth his dream of an "illustrious vernacular," a modern Italian counterpart to ancient Latin, a courtly language that would combine the best features of each dialect and rise above regional differences. (In much the same spirit, his later political treatise, *Monarchia* [On monarchy], argues that the Roman Empire should rise up anew and restore peace and harmony to northern Italy.)

The Divine Comedy

In a very real sense, the fulfillment of every one of Dante's projects and promises comes about in the *Comedy*—his dream of a new vernacular that might rival ancient Latin and Greek as a means of literary expression, his desire to promote the church's turn away from secular concerns to its spiritual calling, and his promise to sing of Beatrice like no other woman had been sung about before.

Although Dante's poem is usually referred to as *The Divine Comedy,* the adjective "divine" was added to the title in the late fifteenth century, long after the poet's death. He himself called it his *comedía* (comedy) and *sacro poema* (sacred poem). The *Comedy* is a work of vast ambition, scope, and proportion. Composed between 1308 and 1321, it is divided into one hundred cantos in three canticles (*Inferno, Purgatorio,* and *Paradiso*). It is written in a new verse form (*terza rima**) that emphasizes the symbolic properties of the number three (associated in Catholicism with the Holy Trinity, the object of Dante's final vision in *Paradiso*). Its title bears a double meaning. On the one hand, "comedy" describes the poem's plot, which begins unhappily and ends happily for its pilgrim-hero. On the other hand, "comedy" points both to the varied character of what the poem contains, from farting devils in the pit of Hell to singing angels in Celestial Paradise, and to the humble language that Dante chose to express this variety—Italian. For Dante, "comedy" implies not humor but humility.

The *Comedy* is autobiographical, and the events that it describes—always as if they actually took place, not as dreams or fictions—take place during Easter week of the year 1300. It tells the story of how, midway in the course of his life, Dante underwent a spiritual crisis and of how that crisis was overcome. As the poem opens, he finds himself lost in a dark wood, wallowing in sin and on the brink of damnation. He is saved thanks to the ancient Roman poet Virgil, who, prompted by Beatrice, sets him back on the straight and narrow road that leads to salvation. The means to Dante's regeneration is a guided trip: first a descent into Hell, then a climb up Mount Purgatory, and finally an ascent into Celestial Paradise, in the course of which Dante bears witness to the consequences of sin, the rewards of virtue, the nature of divine justice, and the structure of a universe that God created in his own image.

Virgil serves as a guide in *Inferno* and *Purgatorio* because of the admiration that Dante felt for his *Aeneid,* the epic poem in which Virgil described the wanderings of the Trojans, the foundation of Rome, and the rise of the Roman Empire. For Dante, Roman history was tied to Christian history to such an extent that he believed that even the timing of Christ's crucifixion depended upon the end of Rome's civil wars. So he viewed Virgil's poem as a kind of Book of Exodus of the Trojans, a non-Christian book secretly inhabited by Christian truth. In cantos 20–21 of *Purgatorio,* the first-century poet Statius recounts a tale (made up by Dante) of how reading Virgil prompted his conversion to Christianity. "You did as he who goes by night and carries / the lamp behind him," Dante tells Virgil, "—he is of no help / to his own self but teaches those who follow" (2.22.67–69; Mandelbaum, p. 194). But Virgil's words do not ensure their author's own salvation. Rather, a rebel unto God's law, Virgil is relegated to Limbo, a place located just inside the gate of Hell, where he will reside for all eternity amidst other unbaptized souls.

Virgil's job is to lead Dante to Beatrice. The road to Beatrice, however, is paved with experiences of sin. On his journey through Hell, Dante encounters several individuals, from ancient heroes like Ulysses (also known as Odysseus, the hero of Homer's epic poem the *Odyssey*) to contemporary charac-

Medieval Christians imagined Purgatory as a place where souls who were eventually going to be saved did penance for the sins they had committed while they were alive.

Exodus, a book in the Hebrew Bible (referred to by Christians as the Old Testament), tells the story of the Jews' crossing of the desert and arrival in the promised land. Dante saw a parallel with the Trojans' finding of their own "promised land": the site where the city of Rome was founded.

ters like Ciacco (the Hog), each of whom exemplifies a particular sin: lust, gluttony,* avarice,* prodigality,* anger, heresy,* violence, deceit, or treachery. During his climb up Mount Purgatory, Dante sees how the damage wrought by sin can be undone through penance, repentance, punishment, and prayer. Virgil oversees Dante's step-by-step turn against sin and embrace of virtue until the two pilgrims reach the summit of the mountain, where, on the edge of the Garden of Eden, Dante is set free, baptized anew, and reunited with Beatrice.

The triumph of Beatrice in canto 30 of *Purgatorio* marks one of the high points in a poem that abounds in high points. Beatrice emerges from a shroud of flowers atop a magnificent chariot, in the midst of an extravagant allegorical* parade that links her arrival to the Second Coming of Christ. Her role as savior, already foreshadowed in *La vita nuova,* now consists in lifting her lover from planet to planet, heaven to heaven, up to the Court of Heaven, where he will be granted a privilege usually reserved for the blessed alone—a face-to-face vision of God. *Paradiso* tells the story of this final ascent, of the beatific* souls (including the thirteenth-century Italian philosopher and theologian Thomas Aquinas, the apostle Paul, and Adam) who come down to welcome Dante so as to ease his passage, and of the challenges faced by Dante as he struggles to describe heaven's glory to mortal readers. Abounding in extravagant imaginings and in invented verbs—like *trasumanar,* or "passing beyond the human" (3.1.70)—the final canticle reaches its climax with a mystical vision that transforms Dante, making him one with God. But the union is momentary. In order to someday rejoin the blessed, he must return to earth and endure the harsh realities of exile. He must tell his story, even if it means risking further persecution, so that, just as Virgil served him as a guide, his *Comedy* may guide its readers on their earthly journeys.

"Dante and Shakespeare divide the modern world between them," declared the poet T. S. Eliot (p. 225), thinking of the *Comedy*. Like no other work of medieval literature, the *Comedy* immediately gave rise to a tradition of line-by-line commentaries (an honor usually reserved for sacred books) that began with Dante's own sons and continues into the present. Its enduring impact upon literature has been powerful, from Chaucer's *Canterbury Tales* to John Milton's *Paradise Lost* to Ezra Pound's *Cantos.*

Selected Bibliography

WORKS BY DANTE

Poetry in English Translation

The Banquet. Translated by Christopher Ryan. Saratoga, Calif.: Anma Libri, 1989.

Dante's Lyric Poetry, 2 vols. Translated with commentary by Kenelm Foster and Patrick Boyde. Oxford, U.K.: Clarendon Press, 1967.

The Divine Comedy. Translated by Charles S. Singleton. Princeton, N.J.: Princeton University Press, 1970–1975.

The Divine Comedy. Translated by Allen Mandelbaum. Berkeley: University of California Press, 1980–1982.

La Vita Nuova. Translated by Barbara Reynolds. Baltimore: Penguin, 1969.

A Question of the Water and of the Land. Translated with commentary by Charles Hamilton Bromby. London: D. Nutt, 1897.

Rime. Translated by Patrick S. Diehl. Princeton, N.J.: Princeton University Press, 1979.

Vita Nuova. Translated by Mark Musa. Oxford, U.K., and New York: Oxford University Press, 1992.

Prose in English Translation

De vulgari eloquentia. Edited and translated by Steven Botterill. Cambridge, U.K.: Cambridge University Press, 1996.

Epistolae. Translated with commentary by Charles Sterrett Latham. Cambridge, Mass.: Riverside Press, 1891.

Literary Criticism of Dante Alighieri. Translated and edited by Robert S. Haller. Lincoln: University of Nebraska Press, 1973.

Monarchia. Edited and translated by Prue Shaw. Cambridge, U.K., and New York: Cambridge University Press, 1995.

Available Collections

The Portable Dante. Edited by Paolo Milano. Rev. ed. New York: Viking Press, 1969.

IF YOU LIKE the poetry of Dante, you might also like the poetry of Virgil. ❧

A Translation of the Latin Works of Dante Alighieri. Translated with commentary by Philip H. Wicksteed and Alan G. Ferrers Howell. London: J. M. Dent and Sons, 1940.

The Vita Nuova and Canzoniere of Dante Alighieri. Edited and translated by Thomas Okey and Philip H. Wicksteed. London: J. M. Dent and Sons, 1906.

WORKS ABOUT DANTE

Auerbach, Eric. *Dante: Poet of the Secular World.* Translated by Ralph Manheim. Chicago: University of Chicago Press, 1961.

Barbi, Michele. *Life of Dante.* Edited and translated by P. Ruggiers. Berkeley: University of California Press, 1960.

Barolini, Teodolinda. *Dante's Poets: Textuality and Truth in the Comedy.* Princeton, N.J.: Princeton University Press, 1984.

Boyde, Patrick. *Dante Philomythes and Philosopher: Man in the Cosmos.* Cambridge, U.K.: Cambridge University Press, 1981.

Chiarenza, Marguerite Mills. *The Divine Comedy: Tracing God's Art.* Boston: Twayne, 1989.

Davis, Charles Till. *Dante and the Idea of Rome.* Oxford, U.K.: Clarendon Press, 1957.

Durling, Robert, and Ronald Martinez. *Time and the Crystal: Studies in Dante's Rime Petrose.* Berkeley and Los Angeles: University of California Press, 1990.

Eliot, T. S. *Selected Essays.* New York: Harcourt, Brace, and World: 1960.

Freccero, John. *Dante: The Poetics of Conversion.* Edited by Rachel Jacoff. Cambridge, Mass.: Harvard University Press, 1986.

Freccero, John, ed. *Dante: A Collection of Critical Essays.* Englewood Cliffs, N.J.: Prentice-Hall, 1965.

Gardner, Edmund G. *Dante and the Mystics: A Study of the Mystical Aspect of the Divina Commedia and Its Relations with Some of Its Mediaeval Sources.* London and New York: J. M. Dent and Sons, 1913.

Hawkins, Peter. *Old and New Parchments: Vision and Revision in Dante.* Stanford, Calif.: Stanford University Press, forthcoming.

Hollander, Robert. *Allegory in Dante's Commedia.* Princeton, N.J.: Princeton University Press, 1969.

Jacoff, Rachel, ed. *The Cambridge Companion to Dante.* Cambridge, U.K.: Cambridge University Press, 1993.

Jacoff, Rachel, and Jeffrey T. Schnapp, eds. *The Poetry of Allusion: Virgil and Ovid in Dante's Commedia.* Stanford, Calif.: Stanford University Press, 1991.

Mazzotta, Giuseppe. *Dante, Poet of the Desert: History and Allegory in the Divine Comedy.* Princeton, N.J.: Princeton University Press, 1979.

Moore, Edward. *Studies in Dante.* Oxford, U.K.: Clarendon Press, 1896–1903.

Schnapp, Jeffrey T. *The Transfiguration of History at the Center of Dante's Paradise.* Princeton, N.J.: Princeton University Press, 1986.

Singleton, Charles S. *Dante Studies I: "Commedia": Elements of Structure.* Cambridge, Mass.: Harvard University Press, 1954.

Singleton, Charles S. *Dante Studies II: Journey to Beatrice.* Cambridge, Mass.: Harvard University Press, 1958.

Thompson, David. *Dante's Epic Journeys.* Baltimore: Johns Hopkins University Press, 1974.

Took, J. F. *Dante, Lyric Poet and Philosopher: An Introduction to the Minor Works.* Oxford, U.K.: Clarendon Press, 1990.

✍

More About Dante

You can read Dante's *Comedy* on the Internet at: http://www.divinecomedy.org/

EMILY DICKINSON

(1830–1886)

by Jordan Davis

When Emily Dickinson died, her sister, Lavinia, found a box containing dozens of little handmade books and stacks of papers. Lavinia knew that her sister, who preferred not to leave the family house, had been writing witty and daring poems all her life, but just how many poems came as a surprise. Although Emily had tried to find a publisher when she was younger, she lived to see only seven poems in print, and editors had even changed the words to some of those few poems. But here were about nine hundred poems—poems that tried to explain unexplainable subjects like death, change, secrets, and truth—written in hard-to-read handwriting, many words marked with alternate choices, and usually in a challenging tone:

> I like a look of agony,
> Because I know it's true—
> Men do not sham Convulsion
> Nor simulate, a Throe—

Quotations of Dickinson's poetry throughout are taken from Franklin, ed., *The Manuscript Books of Emily Dickinson: A Facsimilie.*

The Eyes glaze once—and that is Death—
Impossible to feign
The Beads upon the Forehead
By homely Anguish strung.

This strange idea, that death and pain should be respected because they are honest, sounds even stranger because it is written in the rhythm of Dr. Isaac Watts's* church hymns. These hymns, when they mention death, usually suggest that people's souls are immortal and therefore death is dishonest and something to be passed through. Dickinson's poems, with their difficult style, unusual word choice, and unpleasant subject matter, presented a rough task to the editor. It was not going to be easy to bring the poems of Emily Dickinson into the world!

Her Family

Emily Dickinson spent almost all her life in Amherst, Massachusetts, where she was born on 10 December 1830. Her paternal grandfather founded Amherst College, though to raise the money to keep the college going he gave so much of his own money that he had to sell the family homestead and take a job teaching at what was little better than an outpost in the Ohio wilderness. His eldest son, Edward, grew up to be a successful lawyer, buying back the homestead, becoming president of Amherst College, serving as a U.S. representative, and almost running for governor of Massachusetts.

Edward and his wife, Emily, had three children: Austin, Emily, and Lavinia, in that order. The children were well educated and were competitive readers and writers. Emily won prizes in school for her essays but also reported in a letter that their father thought that Austin's letters were sometimes as good as Shakespeare. At one point in their early twenties, Austin sent Emily some of his poems to read, provoking Emily to write back: "Now Brother Pegasus,* I'll tell you what it is— I've been in the habit *myself* of writing some few things, and it rather appears to me that you're getting away my patent, so you'd better be somewhat careful, or I'll call the police!"

She had little to fear. Austin went on to become not a poet but a lawyer like his father, taking the job of treasurer of Amherst College. He married Susan Gilbert, a beloved friend

Watts, Dr. Isaac English religious thinker and hymn writer of the late seventeenth and early eighteenth centuries

Pegasus a winged horse in Greek mythology; a symbol for poetic inspiration

and correspondent of Emily's. It fell to Lavinia, the youngest child (Emily called her the "practical" child in the family), to take care of the household. Neither daughter married, though both saw suitors.

Velvet Masonry

The chief surprising effect in Emily Dickinson's poetry is the jarring combination of two words, sometimes next to each other, sometimes with "of" between: "Inebriate of Air," "world cashmere," "Pendulum of snow," "Different Peru," "Bright Absentee," "Satin Cash." Particularly striking are familiar phrases with substituted words: "the Golden Same," "A Swelling of the Ground," "the Favorite of Doom."

Some of her poems extend the effect of these combinations into entire definitions, drawing unfamiliar connections that seem right, as in this poem, which may have influenced the poet Wallace Stevens:

> There is a Zone
> whose even Years
> No Solstice interrupt—
> Whose sun constructs
> perpetual Noon
> Whose perfect Seasons
> wait—
>
> +Whose Summer set
> in Summer, till
> The Centuries of
> June
> And Centuries of
> August +cease
> And consciousness—is
> Noon.
>
> +Where +fuse—lapse—
> blend

Emily Dickinson's poetry is studded with words from math, science, and geography, often applied to emotions and ideas about religion, in elaborate metaphor. In this Dickinson followed the tradition of the metaphysical poets, a group of seventeenth-century English poets including John Donne, who wrote of his beloved, "She is all states," and George Herbert, who wrote that man "is a brittle, crazy glass." In the following poem, she crosses the fable of the goose that laid the golden egg with the dissection of a singing bird:

> Split the Lark—and you'll find the Music—
> Bulb after Bulb, in Silver rolled—
> Scantily dealt to the Summer Morning
> Saved for your Ear when Lutes* be old.
>
> Loose the Flood—you shall find it patent*—
> Gush after Gush, reserved for you—
> Scarlet Experiment! Sceptic* Thomas!
> Now, do you doubt that your Bird was true?

lute a handheld stringed instrument, similar to a guitar

patent spreading, free-flowing

sceptic skeptic; a person who doubts

Certain words come back again and again in Emily Dickinson's poetry. In her early poetry she writes often of "morning," "summer," "roses," "cashmere," "purple," and "cocoon." These early poems frequently end with exclamation points, and the general tone is of luxury and defiance.* Later, these pretty words appear less often than technical words like "disc," "oxygen," "orchards," "phosphors," "heart," "lens," and "ratio." In these later poems the exclamation points alternate with question marks, and the tone of the poems changes to match the increasing unfamiliarity. In 1862, in the middle of the Civil War, when her writing accelerated to a poem a day, her vocabulary changed again to include words both pretty and technical, like "desert," "solid," "yellow," "zero," "liquor," "sparks," and "telegraphic." After the war her vocabulary changed less frequently, though she did introduce the word "electric" in the late 1870s and used it often in her later poems. "Birds," "bees," "snakes," and "guns" occur throughout her work.

defiance an unwillingness to give in

Secrets

A recurring theme in Emily Dickinson's poetry is secrecy. From about the time she started keeping her poems in her little books, Emily withdrew from social life in Amherst, staying home and tending her garden, helping take care of her mother, and reading and writing. Gradually this withdrawal came to be extreme; from her thirties on, whenever visitors came to the house Emily would go up to her room, and she would often speak to people only through closed doors. Her strange behavior led people to speculate as to what had caused her to want to hide so much. Some said it was because her father had been very severe with her about a love affair she may have had with a minister in Philadelphia. Others said it was simply out of respect for her father's wish that she not marry.

Still others said that Emily knew that she loved women and did not want to cause any scandal for her successful family. One such theory was published in a Boston magazine a few years after Emily's death. Lavinia wrote a letter to the editor to refute the speculation: "Emily's so called 'withdrawal from general society,' for which she never cared, was only a happen. Our mother had a period of invalidism, and one of her daughters must be constantly at home; Emily chose this part and, finding the life with her books and nature so congenial, continued to live it." This explanation was not enough to stop people from wondering, though, and the speculation continues today. In the late twentieth century some scholars repeated the suggestion that Emily withdrew because of a "love disaster," this time identifying her lover as Susan Gilbert, the woman who married her brother, Austin. "Big my Secret but it's *bandaged*—," Emily wrote. "It will never get away."

Paradox* and Spirituality

*paradox a statement that seems to be a contradiction but may be true

In the Dickinson household, novels and popular poetry were met with some disapproval. Edward Dickinson did approve of the Bible and Shakespeare, however, and Emily quickly found the books of the Bible she liked, such as Revelation. She wrote in her letters that she especially liked the writing of the British novelists George Eliot and the Brontë sisters and the poets John Keats and Robert and Elizabeth Barrett Browning. She knew the work of American writers Ralph Waldo Emerson and Henry David Thoreau, but she did not read the poet Walt Whitman because she had heard that he was "disgraceful." She may have belonged to a Shakespeare Club when she was at Amherst Academy; like his poetry, her work contains many paradoxes and riddles, such as tasting a liquor that was never

The farthest Thunder that I heard
Was nearer than the Sky
And rumbles still, though torrid Noons
Have lain their missiles by—
The Lightning that preceded it
Struck no one but myself—
But I would not exchange the Bolt
For all the rest of Life—
Indebtedness to Oxygen
The Happy may repay,
But not the obligation
To Electricity—
It founds the Homes and decks the Days
And every clamor bright
Is but the gleam concomitant*
Of that waylaying Light—
The Thought is quiet as a Flake—
A Crash without a Sound,
How Life's reverberation
Its Explanation found—

brewed, a load that becomes impossible to carry only when you put it down, and the company of solitude.

Emily did prefer to be different from the rest, and when, in 1847, she went to Mount Holyoke Female Seminary for college, a few miles from home, she was among the thirty of 230 students in the school who did not have a religious conversion experience that year. After only one year her father decided not to send her back. Why he made this decision is not clear. However, no known letter from Emily says that she was less than pleased to be back in Amherst, and she had experienced severe homesickness much of her time away.

In the mid-nineteenth century, America was in the midst of a series of Christian religious upheavals, called the Great Awakening. Popular Protestant preachers would come to town and call on people to make a personal commitment to Jesus Christ; in recent times, this is called being "born again." Regular church attendance was a matter of great importance in that society, as it had been since the settling of the first Puritans in Massachusetts. There are many poems by Emily Dickinson in which she confronts this call to make a public declaration of her faith, saying exactly how she felt about religion, Christian and otherwise, which she saw as a beautiful way of talking about death with which she sometimes agreed and sometimes did not. She seems to have agreed with the theory of being born again but not with the practice of public declaration. Intensely private, she wrote to God directly, having heard that God "replies in person / When the cry is meant." Ironically, these private declarations have turned out to be more public and persistent than if she had shouted them in a crowded church or revival tent.

Fame

In her late twenties Emily Dickinson started keeping her poems in the little books her sister was to discover thirty years later. At the same time she began to seek readers, hoping for an editor who would like and understand her poems and would want to publish them. She gave some poems to her brilliant friend and sister-in-law Sue, and she seems to have changed the poems to reflect Sue's comments. She began a long correspondence with Charles Wadsworth, a very successful minister (Mark Twain wrote about hearing him preach) whom she may have heard speak in Philadelphia. For many years people thought that Wadsworth was the (married) man Emily was not allowed to love, but scholars have slowly come to agree that her affection for him was platonic.* A close friend of the family was Samuel Bowles, the editor of the *Springfield Republican,* a newspaper printed not far away. While he liked Emily and thought highly of her intelligence, he printed only five of her poems.

*platonic usually used to describe relationships that are close but without sexual desire

Emily Dickinson's ambition for her poems was bigger than the local newspapers. In 1862, on reading an article in the *Atlantic Monthly* by a young poet, Thomas Wentworth Higginson, Emily decided to try for a very big publisher indeed. Higginson's article was a letter to prospective young writers, and Emily wrote to him to see whether he would consider her a talented writer. Although he was not an editor of the *Atlantic Monthly,* Higginson had set himself up in his article as an authority, an influential figure, someone who could help a young writer. Emily's poems and her strange introductory letter caught his attention at once. Although he wrote to his family of his ambivalence* about the work of this new hopeful writer, he did seek out a meeting with her and corresponded with her for the rest of her life. He put Emily back in touch with her

*ambivalence uncertainty or indecisiveness

childhood acquaintance, the successful writer Helen Hunt Jackson (who then tried to persuade Emily to put together a book of poems; why Emily declined remains unclear, although it is possible she felt too proud to receive help from her old friend). Higginson wrote to Emily about her poems, recommending that she make them more formally regular, like the popular poetry of the day. But it was not until after Emily's death that he helped see her poems into print, and even then he remained unsure that they were poetry.

The attempts to find a publisher unsuccessful, Emily continued to write poems, but at a slower rate. She made two trips to Boston to see doctors about her eyes, but aside from that she spent nearly all her time at home. After the death of her father in 1874, she was reported to wear only white.

Familiarity and Strangeness

After Emily Dickinson's death in Amherst on 15 May 1886, Lavinia took the box of poems next door to her brother's house, a house Emily had not visited for many years. She gave the poems to Susan Gilbert Dickinson to read, as Emily had done thirty years before. Sue kept the poems for two years, sorting them into categories (W for Wind, D for Death, N for Nature) in an attempt to decide which poems were publishable. Lavinia, hoping to speed things along, took the poems back from Sue and gave them to Mabel Loomis Todd, a writer and scholar who loved Austin (and whose love was returned) and whose husband was an astronomy professor at the college. Todd, with Higginson, put together a book of 115 of the 1,775 manuscript poems, which was published in 1890 to enormous success by Roberts Brothers of Boston. The fame of the poet-recluse of Amherst grew as a second series of poems, a collection of letters, and a third series of poems were all published in the following six years.

Selected Bibliography

WORKS BY EMILY DICKINSON
Poetry
  Poems by Emily Dickinson (1890).

Poems by Emily Dickinson, second series (1891).

Poems by Emily Dickinson, third series (1896).

Letters

Emily Dickinson Face to Face: Unpublished Letters with Notes and Reminiscences. Edited by Martha Dickinson Bianchi. Boston: Houghton Mifflin, 1932.

Letters of Emily Dickinson. 2 vols. Edited by Mabel Loomis Todd. Boston: Roberts Brothers, 1894.

The Letters of Emily Dickinson. 3 vols. Edited by Thomas H. Johnson. Cambridge, Mass.: Harvard University Press, 1958.

Open Me Carefully: Emily Dickinson's Intimate Letters to Susan Huntington Dickinson. Edited by Martha Nell Smith and Ellen L. Hart. Ashfield, Mass.: Paris Press, 1998.

Available Collections

Bolts of Melody: New Poems of Emily Dickinson. Edited by Mabel Loomis Todd and Millicent Todd Bingham. New York: Harper and Brothers, 1945.

The Complete Poems of Emily Dickinson. Boston: Little, Brown, and Company, 1924.

The Complete Poems of Emily Dickinson. Edited by Thomas H. Johnson. Boston: Little, Brown, 1960.

Further Poems of Emily Dickinson. Boston: Little, Brown, 1929.

The Manuscript Books of Emily Dickinson: A Facsimile. 2 vols. Edited by R. W. Franklin. Cambride, Mass.: Belknap Press, 1981.

New Poems of Emily Dickinson. Edited by William H. Shurr with Anna Dunlap and Emily Grey Shurr. Chapel Hill: University of North Carolina Press, 1993.

The Poems of Emily Dickinson: Including Variant Readings Critically Compared with All Known Manuscripts. 3 vols. Edited by Thomas H. Johnson. Cambridge, Mass.: Harvard University Press, 1955.

The Single Hound: Poems of a Lifetime. Boston: Little, Brown, and Company, 1914.

Unpublished Poems of Emily Dickinson. Boston: Little, Brown, and Company, 1935.

WORKS ABOUT EMILY DICKINSON

Danly, Susan, ed. *Language as Object: Emily Dickinson and Contemporary Art.* Amherst: University of Massachusetts Press, 1997.

Doriani, Beth Maclay. *Emily Dickinson: Daughter of Prophecy.* Amherst: University of Massachusetts Press, 1996.

Eberwein, Jane Donahue, ed. *An Emily Dickinson Encyclopedia.* Westport, Conn.: Greenwood Press, 1998.

Farr, Judith. *The Passion of Emily Dickinson.* Cambridge, Mass.: Harvard University Press, 1992.

Howe, Susan. *My Emily Dickinson.* Berkeley, Calif.: North Atlantic Books, 1985.

Lease, Benjamin. *Emily Dickinson's Readings of Men and Books: Sacred Soundings.* New York: St. Martins Press, 1990.

Leyda, Jay. *The Years and Hours of Emily Dickinson.* 2 vols. New Haven, Conn.: Yale University Press, 1960.

Oberhaus, Dorothy Huff. *Emily Dickinson's Fascicles: Methods and Meaning.* University Park: Pennsylvania State University Press, 1995.

Sewall, Richard B. *The Life of Emily Dickinson.* 2 vols. New York: Farrar, Straus and Giroux, 1974.

Smith, Robert McClure. *The Seductions of Emily Dickinson.* Tuscaloosa: University of Alabama Press, 1997.

Whicher, George Frisbie. *This Was a Poet: A Critical Biography of Emily Dickinson.* New York: Charles Scribner's Sons, 1938.

JOHN DONNE

(ca. 1572–1631)

by Lewis Warsh

Very few of John Donne's poems were published during his lifetime. The subject matter of his poetry—especially his early love poems and those that attack Queen Elizabeth I—was considered too scandalous to make public. Given the conservative attitudes of his time, Donne knew he would be imprisoned if he tried to publish them. For most of his life he was content to circulate his poems in manuscript among his friends.

An edition of his poems, edited by his son, finally appeared in 1633, two years after he died. But few people appreciated his poetry or acknowledged his greatness until the early part of the twentieth century. Why, you might ask, did it take almost three hundred years for Donne's poems to enter the mainstream? Compare him to Shakespeare, for instance, who died fifteen years earlier than Donne and who was considered one of the most famous playwrights of his day. Shakespeare's reputation became enormous, while Donne virtually disappeared from the map of world literature. Not until 1912, when a new edition of his poems was published, did Donne's reputation begin to rise. In fact, he became so well known that his prose writings were published as well. These consist mostly of sermons that he delivered during the last two decades of his life.

Another question you might ask is why Donne speaks so clearly to us now, while readers in the eighteenth and nineteenth centuries found his work difficult and harsh. One possible answer is that many of the conflicts Donne experienced—mostly religious and worldly issues—are conflicts we experience. His attitude toward love was also ahead of its time. Donne tried to resolve his conflicts by writing poetry. Like many poets, he achieved in his work a clarity and insight that often eluded him in life.

Early Years and First Poems

Little is known about Donne's childhood. He was born in London, England, in either 1571 or 1572 to a wealthy family. His father, also named John, was warden of the Company of Ironmongers, a position comparable to that of the head of a labor union today. He died when Donne was four. Three of Donne's sisters died in infancy, but a younger brother and an older sister survived. Both of Donne's parents were practicing Catholics, which was considered a crime by the Protestant establishment. Donne's mother, in fact, was a descendant of the English statesman and author Sir Thomas More, who—after a long trial—was executed in 1535 for refusing to give up Catholicism.

Donne entered Oxford University at the age of twelve, even at that time a young age to enter college. He stayed at Oxford for three years and then transferred to Cambridge, but did not graduate. In 1591, he decided to study law and enrolled in Thavies Inn in London. The next year he was admitted to Lincoln's Inn to study law. (The Inns were law schools associated with the court.) When Donne turned twenty-one, he inherited the money that his father had left him. This gave him the freedom to follow his true inclinations. Instead of concentrating on legal studies, he began to study languages—French, Spanish, and Italian—and medicine. And he gained a reputation as a "ladies' man." He spent most of his nights at the theater or visiting his various women friends. Studying law taught him how to shape an argument, and his relationships with women taught him about human nature. The combination of these two influences—law and love—is something to keep in mind when you read Donne's early poems, especially the book *Songs and Sonnets* (written 1601–1605).

In 1596, Donne found employment in the foreign service under the earl of Essex. Donne accompanied Essex on a successful expedition to intercept the Spanish fleet threatening England's shores. A year later he went with Essex to intercept ships sailing from India. One reason for taking these voyages was to escape his romantic involvements in England. He also composed verse-letters* describing his travels. "The Storm" and "The Calm" are remarkable for their precise notations of a hurricane that almost destroyed his ship.

The playwright Ben Jonson, a friend and contemporary of Donne's, is quoted as saying that Donne wrote "all his best pieces before he was twenty-five years old" (Hughes, 1968, p. 18). This is debatable, but it is true that his poetic genius began to flower during the years 1593–1598. His first poems were a series of satires, modeled on ancient Greek and Latin poems. A satire is a kind of playful criticism, and Donne used this form to make fun of lawyers, priests, people in high society, and judges who took bribes. Donne was rebellious by nature, and it is no accident that he chose to write in a form that set him off from the poetry of his contemporaries.

*verse-letters letters written in verse form, usually addressed to a specific person

Songs and Sonnets

Satire was just one of the many forms in which Donne experimented. He also wrote elegies,* verse-letters, epigrams,* and epithalamiums.* He liked to write poems on occasions—a birth, a death, a marriage. The style of his *Songs and Sonnets,* which he finished in 1605, was quite original. Donne is often referred to as a "metaphysical" poet—a poet who attempts to understand the world through contemplation, not by action. Although Donne's own love life forms the basis of many of the poems in this book, he wrote not simply love poems but meditations on love and all its complications and possibilities.

In 1601 he wrote his first major poem, *The Progress of the Soul.* The poem was originally called "Metempsychosis," which refers to a theory of reincarnation—according to this theory, after death a person's soul can enter any living being, whether animal or vegetable. In this poem, Donne had an

*elegy a poem of sorrow or reflection, usually about someone who is dead

*epigram a short poem dealing with a single, sharply observed thought or event

*epithalamium a song or poem in honor of a bride and groom

ambitious plan to trace the life of a soul from paradise to the present. Although the soul passes from one body to another down through time, it never changes. There are traces of autobiography in the poem as well. Donne, at age thirty, was trying to come to terms with his own life, which up till then had been filled with distractions and romantic adventures. He was wondering whether he would ever create anything that might last. He was also experiencing a religious crisis. He had lost his faith as a Catholic but was reluctant to adopt the Protestant faith, the state religion of his time. The basic idea of "Metempsychosis" was distinctly non-Christian. Later in his life, when he became a priest, he attempted to destroy this poem.

Also in 1601, he secretly married Anne More. At the time, Donne was private secretary to Sir Thomas Egerton, lord keeper of the privy seal. Anne was the seventeen-year-old niece of Egerton's wife. Donne was imprisoned for almost a year for marrying someone so young. Anne's father, Sir George More, knew about Donne's earlier reputation as a ladies' man and disapproved of him as a husband for Anne. Donne expressed his frustration at being separated from his wife by writing a poem, "The Canonization," which begins with the line, "For God's sake, hold your tongue, and let me love" (*Songs and Sonnets*).

Little is known about Anne More except that she remained faithful to her husband when he was in prison. Donne was truly in love with her. It was during the early years of their marriage that he wrote most of the poems in *Songs and Sonnets,* some of which obviously refer to his wife. "Love's Growth," for instance, begins with these lines:

> I scarce believe my love to be so pure
> As I had thought it was,
> Because it doth endure
> Vicissitude,* and season, as the grass
> Methinks I lied all winter, when I swore
> My love was infinite, if spring make it more.

Yet many of the poems in this book treat the subject of love with an air of cynicism. Ideal love is impossible, according to Donne, and can lead only to confusion and suffering. He makes fun of husbands who have been deceived by their wives. He boasts of his conquests with married women. From

---

The lord keeper of the privy seal presided over the upper house of Parliament, much as the Speaker presides over the U.S. House of Representatives, and was also an intermediary between Parliament and the crown.

*vicissitude natural change

Death Be Not Proud

Death be not proud, though some have called thee
Mighty and dreadful, for, thou are not so,
For those whom thou think'st, thou dost overthrow,
Die not, poor death, nor yet canst thou kill me.
From rest and sleep, which but thy pictures* be,
Much pleasure, then from thee, much more must flow,
And soonest our best men with thee do go
Rest of their bones, and soul's delivery.
Thou art slave to Fate, Chance, kings, and desperate men,
And dost with poison, war, and sickness dwell,
And poppy,* or charms can make us sleep as well,
And better than thy stroke; why swell'st* thou then?
One short sleep past, we wake eternally,
And death shall be no more; death, thou shall die.

*picture here, an image or copy

*poppy a drug extracted from a plant of the same name. This drug induces vivid dreams.

*swell'st to "swell" from being filled with pride

these poems you gain the impression that Donne distrusted women. "You can't live with them," he seems to be saying, "but you can't live without them." One reason his marriage to Anne More lasted so long may have been that his wife gave him the impossible love he describes in one of his most famous poems, called "Song" (*Complete Poetry and Selected Prose*):

> Go, and catch a falling star,
>   Get with child a mandrake root,*
> Tell me, where all past years are,
>   Or who cleft the Devil's foot,
> Teach me to hear Mermaids singing,
>   Or to keep off envy's stinging,
>   And find
>   What wind
> Serves to advance an honest mind.

> If thou be'st born to strange sights,
>   Things invisible to see,
> Ride ten thousand days and nights,
>   Till age snow white hairs on thee,
> Thou, when thou return'st, will tell me
> All strange wonders that befell* thee,
>   And swear

*mandrake root a plant said to have magical powers. It has a branched root that resembles the human body.

The devil is traditionally pictured as having cloven (cleft) hooves, like a goat. Who "cleft" them is an unanswerable question.

*befell happened to

Nowhere
Lives a woman true, and fair.

If thou findst one, let me know,
    Such a Pilgrimage* were sweet;
Yet do not, I would not go,
    Though at next door we might meet,
Though she were true, when you met her,
And last, till you write your letter,
    Yet she
    Will be
False, ere I come, to two, or three.

Donne had the rare ability to be humorous and profound at the same time. Finding a woman "true and fair," he writes, is as impossible as catching a falling star or living a life free of envy. Yet there is also a melancholy quality about the poem, a longing for the impossible. Although Donne's way of writing at first seems complicated, his voice also has a natural tone, as if he were talking to you directly.

Donne's marriage to Anne More was a major influence on his poetry and on the rest of his life as well. His young wife's wealthy father refused to give the couple any assistance. When Donne was released from prison in 1602, he had neither a university degree nor a job. Anne eventually gave birth to twelve children, seven of whom survived to adulthood. For many years the family depended on the kindness of friends and relatives. Despite this help, Donne and his family spent the years 1603–1610 in poverty.

Middle Years

In 1605, Donne and his family moved to a small house in the English town of Mitcham. He earned a meager living by writing pamphlets about the religious and political controversies of the time. In his letters, Donne describes how the lack of heat in the house was undermining his health and the health of his family. An essay he wrote during this time, *Biathanatos,* indicates that he was contemplating suicide. Finally, Anne's father agreed to help them. Donne had been living in a kind of retirement, since he did not have enough money to buy presentable new clothes. But when Anne's father began giving them an allowance, Donne was once again free to mingle with London society in an attempt to seek out new patrons. It was at this time that he met Lucy Russell, countess of Bedford, and she became one of his main sources of support. Many of his poems written during this time, most notably "Twickenham Gardens," were addressed to Lady Bedford. Because of her support of Donne and other poets, she was known as the "Lady of the Muses."

Death was the main subject of Donne's poems at this time—not only suicide, but also the way death was connected to rebirth and resurrection. Donne did a great deal of soul-searching during these years. He became more scholarly and introspective* and began to question the Catholic religion in which he had been raised. The years 1609–1611 were the most critical of his life.

*introspective examining one's own thoughts and feelings

In retrospect, it seems as though he was preparing himself for the years to come. Donne was a man of many identities. In his first life he lived as a man-about-town. In his second life, which we see here, he was a father and scholar, the penniless head of an ever-growing household. He was not quite forty when his life changed again.

"Anniversaries"

In 1610, Donne wrote an elegy on the death of fourteen-year-old Elizabeth Drury and sent it to her father, Robert. Donne hoped that Drury would become his patron. In those days it was common for wealthy patrons to give money to artists whom they favored, and Robert Drury did generously provide Donne with a house. The location was Drury Lane in London, where Donne and his family lived for the next ten years.

In gratitude to Robert Drury, Donne composed two more poems for Elizabeth, "The First Anniversary" and "The Second Anniversary." These poems are not simply elegies for the dead girl but attempts by the poet to evaluate his own life. Up until this time, he was torn between two impulses: the religious life and the worldly life. The *Songs and Sonnets* reflected his worldly experience. The *Holy Sonnets* (1609–1631) mirror his intense religious feelings and his fear that because of his life as a sinner, he had no chance of salvation. In the two "Anniversary" poems, he attempts to resolve this conflict.

Think of the two "Anniversary" poems as if they were prayers or meditations. Donne had an intense and complicated inner life, and in these poems, it took all his powers of concentration to express what he was feeling. One of the main themes of his earlier poems had been the connection between love and death. One of the themes of the "Anniversary" poems—as well as many of the sermons he later preached—was how worldly love can be converted to love of God. The "First Anniversary"— the first poem that he published in his lifetime—marked the end of his inner conflict between the worldly and the spiritual life.

Many of Donne's poems were addressed to people of wealth or position who might help him. In 1613 he wrote a wedding poem to the earl of Somerset with the hope that the earl could get him a job as a clerk. This was a key moment in Donne's life. He had spent many years meditating on spiritual matters, yet he had been hesitant about committing himself wholeheartedly to a religious life. In 1615, however, he made a choice. On 23 January of that year he entered the priesthood of the Church of England and soon afterward was appointed chaplain to King James I.

Last Years

Although his poetry was neglected during his lifetime and for centuries afterward, Donne was considered one of the greatest preachers of his day. Ironically, in 1616 he was appointed preacher at Lincoln's Inn in London, where years before he had studied law. Now his congregation consisted of young law students. No doubt the experience made him reflect on his own days as a young man in London and everything that had happened in the intervening years.

In 1617 his wife died. Donne expressed his grief in one of his greatest sonnets:

> Since she whom I lov'd hath paid her last debt
> To Nature, and to hers, and my good is dead,
> And her Soul early into heaven ravished,
> Wholly on heavenly things my mind is set.
> Here the admiring her my mind did whet
> To seek thee, God; so streams to show the head;*
> But though I have found thee, and thou my thirst
>   hast fed,

*head source

A holy thirsty dropsy* melts me yet.
But why should I beg more Love, when as thou
Dost woo my soul, for hers offering all thine:
And dost not only fear lest I allow
My Love to Saints and Angels things divine,
But in thy tender jealousy dost doubt
Lest the World, Flesh, yea* Devil put thee out.
"Holy Sonnet XVII" (*Divine Poems*)

*dropsy accumulation of liquids in bodily tissues

*yea yes

The poem is about grief but also acceptance. For years Donne was torn between worldly love and love of God. In "Holy Sonnet X," Donne tries to come to terms with his own fear of dying. He speaks to Death as another person. In this way, he hopes to diminish Death's power over him. One of Donne's greatest themes is the conflict between the secular and the religious life. After Anne's death, he committed himself to a religious life without reservation.

In 1619 Donne traveled on a peace mission to Germany as chaplain to Viscount Doncaster. It was on this trip that his health began to fail. In 1621 he was appointed dean of St. Paul's Cathedral in London, and it was there that he preached his greatest sermons. In 1624 he was appointed vicar of St. Dunston's, another church in London. Izaak Walton was a member of his congregation and became Donne's first biographer. Much of what we know of John Donne as a preacher comes from Walton's firsthand observations.

The illness that he developed while traveling abroad (stomach cancer) continued to plague him. In 1631 he delivered his last sermon, "Death's Duel," which many consider a sermon on his own death. He died shortly afterward, on 31 March 1631, famous as a preacher but barely acknowledged as a poet.

Selected Bibliography

WORKS BY JOHN DONNE

Poetical Works. 2 vols. Edited by H. J. C. Grierson. London: Oxford, 1912.

John Donne: Complete Poetry and Selected Prose. Edited by Charles M. Coffin. New York: Random House, 1952.

The Sermons of John Donne. 10 vols. Edited by George R. Potter and Evelyn M. Simpson. Berkeley: University of California Press, 1953–1962.

IF YOU LIKE the poetry of Donne, you might also like the poetry of Andrew Marvell or George Herbert.

Complete Poetry of John Donne. Edited by John T. Shaw-cross. New York: Doubleday, 1967.

WORKS ABOUT JOHN DONNE

Bennet, Joan. *Four Metaphysical Poets.* Cambridge, U.K.: Cambridge University Press, 1934.

Coffin, Charles M. *John Donne and the New Philosophy.* New York: Columbia University Press, 1937.

Eliot, T. S. "The Metaphysical Poets." In *Selected Essays.* New York: Harcourt Brace, 1950.

Gardner, Helen, ed. *John Donne: A Collection of Critical Essays.* Englewood Clifffs, N.J.: Prentice Hall, 1962.

Gosse, Edmund. *The Life and Letters of John Donne.* 2 vols. London and New York: Dodd, Mead and Heinemann, 1899.

Hughes, Richard E. *The Progress of the Soul.* New York: Morrow, 1968.

Leishman, James B. *The Metaphysical Poets.* Oxford, U.K.: Clarendon Press, 1934.

Marotti, Arthur, ed. *Critical Essays on John Donne.* New York: G. K. Hall, 1994.

Rugoff, Milton. *Donne's Imagery.* New York: Corporate, 1939.

Spencer, Theodore, ed. *A Garland for John Donne.* Cambridge, Mass.: Harvard University Press, 1931.

Tuve, Rosemond. *Elizabethan and Metaphysical Imagery.* Chicago: University of Chicago Press, 1947.

Unger, Leonard. *Donne's Poetry and Modern Criticism.* Chicago: Henry Regnery, 1950.

Walton, Izaak. *Life of Dr. Donne.* London, 1640.

White, Helen. *The Metaphysical Poets.* New York: Macmillan, 1936.

✍ More About Donne

You can find information about Donne on the Internet at http://www.island-of-freedom.com/DONNE.HTM
http://www.luminarium.org/sevenlit/donne/

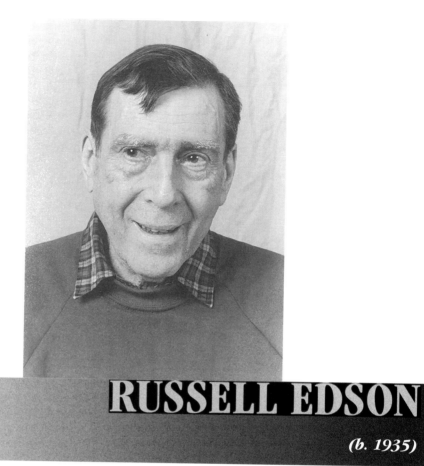

RUSSELL EDSON
(b. 1935)

by Connie Deanovich

Grass can grow in the living room. You can get upstairs to your bedroom in a canoe. You can have a son who is a toad and a wheelbarrow made from a cow. True or false? If you are reading the poetry of Russell Edson, the answer is "true." A man's body can fall apart in a road, and he can pick part of it up and put it in his pocket. A person in Russell Edson's poetry can ask, "how did this castle get into my car?" People can also marry cars, eat rats and apes, and have dining rooms that float in space. The world in Edson's poetry is not the normal world.

Also, Edson writes his poetry using an unusual form called the prose poem. This form requires poets to write in sentences instead of lines. He has also written highly regarded plays, essays, and novels.

While Edson's writing is well known, not much is known about his life. Edson is quoted in *Contemporary Authors* about why so little is known about him:

> Take it or leave it, I make it a point not to be a celebrity, most of whom are uncreative scum feeding

on the public attention; if I have any public value, it is in my published works, not in my secret dreams. Information as to how I scratched, and where, will make interesting twitterings after I'm dead; not while I still live, and still scratch (p. 271).

From this statement it is clear that he is an opinionated person ("uncreative scum") and that he doesn't want to talk about his personal history. Being alive, to Russell Edson, is being able to scratch—not a very flattering image. Flattery is not often found in his poetry, in which mothers are decidedly ugly people, your family does not care for you, and dining is disastrous. In "The Ox" (from *The Childhood of an Equestrian*) father becomes an ox who "would stand over his newspaper, turning the pages with his tongue, while he evacuated on the rug."

Born on 9 April 1935, Russell Edson spent most of his life in Stamford, Connecticut, before moving to the neighboring town of Darien. He is the son of the cartoonist who created the Andy Gump comic strip, and he is married to Frances Edson. His formal education stopped at tenth grade, though he also studied as an adult at Columbia University in New York and at the experimental Black Mountain College in North Carolina. In 1974 he received a Guggenheim Fellowship. However, Edson wants people to read his writing, not to read about him. For the last several decades of his life he has not been formally photographed. His life is a private one. His life's work is his wonderful and bizarre writing.

> What we want is a poetry of miracles—minus the "I" of ecstasy! A poem that as many people who read it each reads a different poem. A poetry freed from its time. A poetry that engages the Creation, which we believe is still in process, and that it is entirely an imaginative construction, which our creative acts partake of, and are necessary to. We are all helping to imagine the Universe ("Portrait of the Writer as a Fat Man," p. 297).

"Dinner Time"

Almost all of the action in Edson's poetry takes place at home. A man can ride the roof of his house like a horse. In "Father Father, What Have You Done?" this action causes the house to

> Flattery is not often found in his poetry, in which mothers are . . . ugly . . . and dining is disastrous.

collapse. "The house rears up on its back porch and all its bricks fall apart and the house crashes to the ground." But the man and his wife survive, and the poem simply ends "His wife cries from the rubble, father father, what have you done?" Humor and understatement lessen Edson's tragedies. This poem is from his first book *The Very Thing That Happens,* in which Edson begins exploring the themes he will use throughout his career. Two major themes of Edson's are that places can come to life and that people can have bodies that are pliable, or able to change and be molded to suit the action of the poem. Usually his people are family members, and the place is the family home.

Since home is the center of action for Edson, it is no wonder that houses and the rooms in houses can take part in the action. In his poem "Dinner Time," a husband and wife—characters he uses often—bicker with each other and fight, using their own bodies and the things in their kitchen. The wife, who has destroyed all the dishes by throwing them against the wall, says, "You know I have to subdue the kitchen every night, otherwise it'll cook me and serve me to the mice on my best china. And you know what small eaters they are; next would come the flies, and how I hate flies in my kitchen." Flies, of course, come when there is a decaying body, the wife's body. She is not worried about being dead, however, but about flies in her kitchen. Our expectations are overturned in the work of Edson, and the result is that his poems are ironic* and fun to read. Readers can imagine the stove, with arms, setting out dinner for a family of mice. The image is somewhat appealing rather than gruesome. Edson writes, "Writing is the joy when all other joys have failed. Else, but for the unsavory careerists,* why write? It is good fun to ruin the surface of a piece of paper; to, as it were, run amuck. One hurts no one, and paper is cheap enough" ("Portrait of a Writer," p. 299).

Edson served up some particularly grotesque imagery in "Ape," which was published in *The Childhood of an Equestrian*. It begins, "You haven't finished your ape, said mother to father, who had monkey hair and blood on his whiskers." Apes and monkeys appear often in Edson's work, as beautiful silver creatures as well as things to kill. Dark notes sound regularly, and during their foul dinner the man and wife in "Ape" bicker rather than converse. Father cries, "I'm damn sick of ape every night," and it sounds as if he is complaining about the meatloaf. Mother tries to entice him, "Break one of the ears off,

*ironic** having an actual outcome that is opposite or contrary to what was expected

*careerist** a person (in this case a writer) willing to sacrifice creative or moral principles to gain career advancement

*postmortem after death

they're so crispy." The imagery, which more resembles a postmortem* dissection than a dinner, makes the reader see an ape as a huge piece of meat with "onion rings" on its fingers rather than as a fascinating creature most people see in the zoo. It is chilling to read "I stuffed its nose with garlic," or, "Try a piece of its gum, I've stuffed its mouth with bread." Edson turns mealtime into a horror show, but a fun horror show for all but the most unforgiving temperaments. His characters are not fully fledged people, which helps keep the poems entertaining. They are the universally despised "Mother" and the disgusting, mean "Father" he portrays over and over.

If eating at home is a terrible thing, then perhaps it is no surprise that kitchens themselves run away, as in "Through the Woods" from *What a Man Can See* (1969), or that dining rooms vomit, as in "Vomit" from *The Clam Theater. The Intuitive Journey and Other Works* contains "The Abyss," in which the entire "dining room floats out into space." Rooms and the people occupying them disappear throughout Edson's poetry. The same book contains "The Terrible Angel," in which a baby has turned to wood and its mother is "taken into the carpet." In "The Dog," the ceiling eats the family pet. In "The Old Woman's Breakfast," the woman "can't tell if she spoons the porridge into herself, or herself into the porridge." Eventually "she begins to spill over the edge of the table." This is the kind of imagery surrealist* artists like Salvador Dali and René Magritte used in their paintings, in which huge watches bend over mountainsides and steam locomotives charge out of fireplaces. Dream imagery and that of comic books, music videos, and experimental films also resemble the fantastic sights in Russell Edson's poetry. "A good prose poem is a statement that seeks sanity whilst its author teeters on the edge of the abyss," he says. "The language will be simple, the images so direct, that oftentimes the reader will be torn with recognitions inside himself long before he is conscious of what is happening to him" ("Portrait of a Writer," p. 301). The prose poet stretches reality in the poem and the reader's own sense of reality.

Sometimes rooms and houses are quiet places. Although it is no less fantastic for its sense of calm, "The Pilot," also from *The Intuitive Journey,* has an old man sitting in a dirty room and looking at a star, which is "an electrical freckle that has fallen out of his head and gotten stuck in the dirt on the window." He spends the night telling himself to "Be brave, my

*surrealist an artist or poet involved in the art movement surrealism, which aimed (chiefly during the 1920s and 1930s) to express the workings of the unconscious or subconscious mind

Captain." "And all night the old man steers his room through the dark." The ship's wheel is a chair. Night is sometimes a difficult time for people. Here Edson shows sympathy for the old man, even though the old man is slightly disgusting. The sea imagery gives the poem timelessness and the sense of a journey. Since the man is old and afraid, the journey is the trip toward death. Edson suggests all of this through his use of image-rich language. He never tells; he shows. In *The Wounded Breakfast,* the poem "How Things Will Be" has the bedrooms "awake at night, blank-eyed." The idea that night is a tough time to get through, rather than a restful time to enjoy, comes across here even without a person's being in the poem.

"The Feet of the Fat Man"

People in Russell Edson's hands are like sophisticated puppets with pliable bodies. Pull the legs off a man, and he can keep on going, for a while anyway ("Oh My God, I'll Never Get Home" in *The Clam Theater*). Every night a man and wife can be eaten, because they are professional duck dinners ("Mr. & Mrs. Duck Dinner" in *The Intuitive Journey*). Like puppets, the people inhabiting the strange and marvelous world created by Edson die in action but return the next day to be used again. Imagination and invention are hallmarks* of Edson's character creations in his poetry, which is often rich in dialogue; in his novels; and in his plays, such as those in *The Falling Sickness.*

    The poem "The Ancestral Mousetrap" (in *The Clam Theater*) inventively shows the gestures of the body by suggestion and reflection. The physical action of setting a trap has been saved by the very existence of the trap itself. It is as if a tossed ball has been frozen in midair. "We are left a mousetrap, baited with cheese. . . . in this mousetrap is caught the thumb print of his pressure." The dead relative's gesture was trap setting, and now it is kept in a "jewel box . . . to keep it from the robber-mouse." It is not the trap or the cheese that is precious, of course; it is the "ancestor's gesture . . . the thumb print of his pressure." Furthermore, the whole scene is ridiculous. Who cares about a mousetrap, or a "thumb print of pressure"? What kind of person sets a trap, then leaves it to relatives? Edson's humor is subtle and bold at the same time. A mousetrap is a

***hallmark** a distinguishing feature

small thing, yet it stands for death with all its enormities. Much is left to the imagination in "The Ancestral Mousetrap."

"The Feet of the Fat Man," however, is not made up of wispy gestures. This poem, from *The Intuitive Journey*, contains one of Edson's most pliable bodies. "This man is so fat that his head suddenly slips down into his neck. His face looks up out of his neck." The top of his body slips down into his stomach, and then he folds down into his calves. At the end his "foot is full of hair." The fat man's body funnels into his feet like a huge hairy soap bubble sucked down a drain. In "Conjugal" (in *The Childhood of an Equestrian*) a "man is bending his wife" in a private act of lovemaking that takes the pair directly into the wallpaper in their room. Some couples are depicted as sexual beings in Edson's poetry; not all of them are the bickering Mother and Father figures. The difference between real puppets and Edson's puppetlike characters is that he can do much more with his language creatures than a puppeteer can with puppets.

He can turn a woman into a radio where the "voice came out from between her breasts" ("The Further Adventures of Martha George" in *The Childhood of an Equestrian*). He can make tiny sheep that fit in a test tube and that might be "used as a substitute for rice, a sort of wooly rice" ("Counting Sheep" in *The Intuitive Journey*). In "The Wheelbarrow" (from *The Wounded Breakfast*) a cow is made into a wheelbarrow. Objects, too, are mutilated. In "The Autopsy," from *The Reason Why the Closet-Man Is Never Sad,* an autopsy is performed on an old raincoat. A candle-clutching wife says,

> I just wanted to know if you found any blood clots?
> Blood clots?!
> For my necklace. . . .

Somehow Edson is able to make a reader think that it is possible for a coat to have blood clots and for those blood clots to be necklace material, like rubies. In the same book a "cluster of canaries" forms a yellow taxi in the magical poem "The Taxi."

Part of Edson's technique is to leave things up to his reader's imagination. First he decides how things will be, and then his readers decide how they get to be that way—the canaries become a taxi through the efforts of the reader's imagination. The result is a brilliant display of the possibilities of

---

"This man is so fat that his head suddenly slips down into his neck."

> ## The Ancestral Mousetrap
>
> We are left a mousetrap, baited with cheese. We must not jar it, or our ancestor's gesture and pressure are lost, as the trap springs shut.
>
> He has relinquished his hands to what the earth makes of flesh. Still, here in this mousetrap is caught the thumb print of his pressure.
>
> A mouse would steal this with its death, this still un-spent jewel of intent.
>
> In a jewel box it is kept, to keep it from the robber-mouse; even as memory in the skull was kept, to keep it from the robber-worm, who even now is climbing a thief in the window of his eyes.
>
> *(The Clam Theater)*

language. The language in a prose poem can be especially liberating for the poet. As Russell Edson comments in his essay "Portrait of the Writer as a Fat Man," "To come back to the prose poem. What makes us so fond of it is its clumsiness, its lack of expectation or ambition. Any way of writing that isolates its writer from worldly acceptance offers the greatest creative efficiency." Through poetry, a prose poet is free to reinvent the world. Humor, abundant imagination, the creative use of language, and strange domestic events are hallmarks of the unique prose poems of Russell Edson, a private writer whose efforts to write within the freedom of isolation have been rewarded by widespread admiration.

Selected Bibliography

WORKS BY RUSSELL EDSON

The Very Thing That Happens (1964).

What a Man Can See (1969).

The Childhood of an Equestrian (1973).

The Clam Theater (1973).

The Falling Sickness: A Book of Plays (1975).

The Intuitive Journey and Other Works (1976).

IF YOU LIKE the poetry of Edson, you might also like the poetry of Ron Padgett, Charles Simic, or James Tate.

The Reason Why the Closet-Man Is Never Sad (1977).

The Wounded Breakfast (1985).

The Song of Percival Peacock: A Novel (1992).

The Tunnel: Selected Poems (1994). A good place to start.

Essay

"Portrait of the Writer as a Fat Man: Some Subjective Ideas or Notions on the Care & Feeding of Prose Poems." In *A Field Guide to Contemporary Poetry and Poetics*. Edited by Stuart Friebert, David Walker, and David Young. New York: Longman, 1980.

WORKS ABOUT RUSSELL EDSON

Bryfonski, Dedria, ed. *Contemporary Literary Criticism*. Vol. 13. Detroit: Gale Research, 1980. Pp. 190–191.

Evory, Ann, ed. *Contemporary Authors*. Vol. 33–36. Detroit: Gale Research, 1978. Pp. 270–271.

Friebert, Stuart, and David Young, eds. *The Longman Anthology of Contemporary American Poetry*. 2d ed. New York: Longman, 1989. Pp. 398–399.

Riggs, Thomas, ed. *Contemporary Poets*. Detroit: St. James Press, 1996.

Upton, Lee. *The Muse of Abandonment: Origin, Identity, Mastery, in Five American Poets*. London and Lewisburg, Pa.: Bucknell University Press, 1998.

✍️

More About Edson:

You can find information about Russell Edson on the Internet at: http://www.msu.edu/user/forddavi/edson/edson.html

T. S. ELIOT

(1888–1965)

by A. Michael Matin

Although best known as the poet who wrote "The Waste Land," T. S. Eliot was also a major playwright, critic, and publisher. In these last two roles, he guided the artistic judgments of two generations of writers and readers. Eliot was a central figure of literary modernism, a movement that became dominant in the years following World War I. His poetry was influenced by his strong convictions not only about aesthetics,* but also about culture, politics, and religion. He defined his point of view as that of a "classicist in literature, royalist in politics, and anglo-catholic in religion" (*For Lancelot Andrewes,* p. ix). Yet he was not born into any of these roles, and the story of his life and intellectual development largely consists of his efforts to recast himself into them.

Quotations of Eliot's poetry throughout are taken from *The Complete Poems and Plays 1909–1950.*

*****aesthetics** the study of the nature of art or beauty

Early Life: From America to England

The youngest of seven children, Thomas Stearns ("Tom") Eliot was born in Saint Louis, Missouri, on 26 September 1888, to

*egalitarianism belief in equality

*Unitarianism a Protestant denomination that stresses individual belief guided by the use of reason

*prefiguring foreshadowing; predicting

*oscillation fluctuation between two extremes

*bohemian unconventional

Henry Ware Eliot and Charlotte Champe Stearns Eliot, members of old New England families. He ultimately rejected the egalitarianism* of his family's Unitarianism* and embraced the formality and ritual of the Anglican Church, as he would exchange his American citizenship to become a British subject. Still, the Unitarian ethic stayed with him. He especially credited the legacy of his paternal grandfather, William Greenleaf Eliot, a Unitarian minister, for having instilled in him a reverence for religious and educational institutions and the precept "that personal and selfish aims should be subordinated to the general good" (*To Criticize the Critic,* p. 44).

Although Eliot was afflicted from birth with a double hernia that kept him from participating in rigorous sports, he loved the outdoors. During his childhood, his family summered regularly in Massachusetts, where he learned to sail and developed a lifelong love for the sea. Prefiguring* the later and deeper ambiguities of his dual national affiliations, this oscillation* between Missouri and Massachusetts led him to consider himself neither a midwesterner nor a northerner but rather a "resident alien" in both places. In 1905, at the age of seventeen, he enrolled in Milton Academy, a college preparatory school near Boston.

Eliot entered Harvard in 1906 and completed his bachelor's degree in only three years, distinguishing himself among his peers and his professors. He edited the school's literary magazine, the *Harvard Advocate,* to which he also contributed some of his own poems. Increasingly drawn to literature, he returned to Harvard for another year and in 1910 received a master's degree in English literature. After a trip to Europe on a traveling fellowship, spent mostly in Paris, where he attended lectures at the Sorbonne and absorbed the artistic, bohemian* culture, he returned to Harvard in the fall of 1911 to begin doctoral work in philosophy with the intention of pursuing a career as an academic philosopher. By this time he had already written some of the finest of his early poems, including "The Love Song of J. Alfred Prufrock" and "Portrait of a Lady," although they were not published until several years later. He returned to England in 1914 to continue his doctoral studies at Oxford University.

In England in 1915 he met and quickly married Vivien Haigh-Wood, an Englishwoman. (An uncharacteristically impulsive move for the cautious and conservative Eliot, the marriage proved to be an unhappy one. Both were chronically afflicted with physical and mental disorders, and Vivien became increasingly unstable as the years passed. At his insistence, they ultimately separated in 1933, although his religious convictions prohibited the possibility of divorce.) Eliot completed his doctoral dissertation in 1916 and sent it to Harvard, where it was enthusiastically received by the philosophy department. But he did not return to America for a formal defense* and consequently never received his doctorate, for he had made up his mind to stay in England to pursue a career as a writer.

Early Work

Eliot's introduction in 1914 to Ezra Pound, another expatriate* American writer, was perhaps the most important event of his artistic life. Pound's name is associated with anti-Semitism (a prejudice shared by Eliot, who, in a scandalous 1933 lecture, decried the presence of "free-thinking Jews," whom he found "undesirable" in large numbers) and an endorsement of fascism* during World War II. Nonetheless, he was a brilliant poet as well as a tireless advocate of promising young writers.

Through Pound's efforts, Eliot's first volume of poems, *Prufrock and Other Observations,* was published in 1917. The collection's best-known work, "The Love Song of J. Alfred Prufrock," is a monologue* wistfully narrated by a middle-aged man who feels that life has passed him by. The poem begins with an invitation:

> Let us go then, you and I,
> When the evening is spread out against the sky
> Like a patient etherised upon a table;

We quickly realize, however, that this invitation is misleading, for the traditional verse form established by the rhyming couplet as well as the seemingly upbeat tone of the speaker are both undercut by the third line, which jarringly breaks the rhyme scheme and introduces a bizarrely incongruous* image. Both in form and in content, Eliot signals that this poem is to be an assault on the reader's expectations. Even the title fools us, since the lines that follow it consist not of a love song, but rather a litany* of regrets for opportunities missed and an exhibition of the narrator's low self-esteem:

> No! I am not Prince Hamlet,* nor was meant to be;
> Am an attendant lord, one that will do

formal defense a session in which a candidate for an academic degree presents his or her thesis or dissertation and answers questions from a board of academic advisers; usually the last qualification needed before earning the degree

expatriate a person living outside of his or her native country

fascism a form of government that exalts a single ruler, greatly restricts personal freedom, and permits no opposition

monologue a text or speech given by a single person

incongruous inconsistent

litany a long list

Prince Hamlet the central figure of Shakespeare's tragedy *Hamlet*

To swell a progress, start a scene or two,
Advise the prince; no doubt, an easy tool,
Deferential, glad to be of use,
Politic, cautious, and meticulous;
Full of high sentence, but a bit obtuse;*
At times, indeed, almost ridiculous—
Almost, at times, the Fool.

obtuse inelegant or unclear in thought or expression

epigraph a quotation beginning a literary work that indicates the work's theme

The references to Shakespeare here, coupled with the poem's epigraph* from the medieval Italian poet Dante's *Inferno,* register Eliot's high estimation of these two writers. He viewed Dante in particular to have been history's greatest poet.

From 1915 to 1917 Eliot worked at a variety of jobs in England, including teaching, editing, and reviewing, until he landed a position at Lloyds Bank in London, where he was employed full time from 1917 to 1925. Although some of his artistic friends attempted to "rescue" him from his work at the bank by taking up a collection among potential patrons, the truth is that he prized daily routine and responsibilities; moreover, he was unable to write for more than three hours a day. As he put it, "I am too sceptical of my own abilities to be able to make a whole-time job of writing poetry, even if I had the means" (Behr, p. 40). Frugal, respectable, and with a good head for business, Eliot was the opposite of the impractical artist who lives only for art.

In 1920 Eliot published his first volume of criticism, *The Sacred Wood,* which contains many of his best-known early essays, such as "Tradition and the Individual Talent," in which he argued that "[p]oetry is not a turning loose of emotion, but an escape from emotion; it is not the expression of personality but an escape from personality" (*Selected Prose of T. S. Eliot,* p. 43). Despite the appearance in that same year of his *Ara Vos Prec* volume of poems, his reputation as a critic at this point surpassed his reputation as a poet. This changed in 1922 with the publication of a long poem he had been working on since 1919 and which a three-month leave of absence from the bank in 1921 (because of a bout of depression) gave him an opportunity to finish.

"The Waste Land"

A watershed year, 1922 saw the publication of both "The Waste Land" (in the inaugural edition of Eliot's important journal the

Preludes

I
The winter evening settles down
With smell of steaks in passageways.
Six o'clock.
The burnt-out ends of smoky days.
And now a gusty shower wraps
The grimy scraps
Of withered leaves about your feet
And newspapers from vacant lots;
The showers beat
On broken blinds and chimney-pots,
And at the corner of the street
A lonely cab-horse steams and stamps.

And then the lighting of the lamps.

II
The morning comes to consciousness
Of faint stale smells of beer
From the sawdust-trampled street
With all its muddy feet that press
To early coffee-stands.

With the other masquerades
That time resumes,
One thinks of all the hands
That are raising dingy shades
In a thousand furnished rooms.

Criterion, which he continued to edit until it ceased publication in 1939) and the Irish writer James Joyce's *Ulysses,* often taken, respectively, as the quintessential* poem and novel of modernist literature. In an essay published in the previous year entitled "The Metaphysical Poets," Eliot had contended that

> poets in our civilisation, as it exists at present, must be *difficult*. Our civilization comprehends great variety and complexity, and this variety and complexity, playing upon a refined sensibility, must produce various and complex results. The poet must become more and more comprehensive, more allusive,* more indirect, in order to force, to dislocate if necessary,

*__quintessential__ having the very essence of a quality in its purest form

*__allusive__ suggestive

language into his meaning. (*Selected Prose of T. S. Eliot,* p. 65)

This passage shows how Eliot used his literary criticism to create a readership that would appreciate his poetry on his own terms. "The Waste Land," in fact, is among the most difficult poems of the twentieth century; so perplexing did some early reviewers find it that they assumed it to be a hoax. Before the text of the poem begins, the reader is faced with an untranslated epigraph in Latin and ancient Greek as well as a dedication to Ezra Pound (who had heavily edited the work) in Italian; and the following English verse is strewn with passages in German, French, and Sanskrit as well as innumerable allusions to classical literature. Does this mean that the poem can be read only by someone fluent in seven languages and steeped in classical literature? Not at all. In fact, Eliot provided his readers with a good deal of help by later adding a series of explanatory notes that detail the sources for many of the poem's allusions.

"The Waste Land" consists of five sections: "The Burial of the Dead," "A Game of Chess," "The Fire Sermon," "Death by Water," and "What the Thunder Said." These titles signal Eliot's intention of bringing together a variety of cultures and religious traditions, as the first refers to Christianity, the second to Buddhism, and the last to Hinduism. And not only is the poem eclectic* in content, but it also uses the techniques of a variety of artistic media: its blending of voices is like a collage* in the visual arts, its five-part structure evokes traditional five-act plays, and its syncopated* rhythms mimic those of jazz.

The poem is filled with images of barrenness and desolation as well as tantalizing suggestions of potential fertility and regrowth, beginning with the opening lines:

> April is the cruellest month, breeding
> Lilacs out of the dead land, mixing
> Memory and desire, stirring
> Dull roots with spring rain.

Eliot drew on the death and rebirth patterns of a variety of ancient myths and legends, such as the quest for the Holy Grail, which concludes with the rejuvenation of the Fisher King. But it is an open question whether the poem allows for the possibility that the debased* modern world can be similarly revitalized. However the poem may be interpreted, the dominant

*eclectic** bringing together a number of differing elements

*collage** a work of art (or a method of composition) in which bits and pieces of different objects and media are glued together

*syncopated** marked by a temporary shift in the predominant musical or poetic rhythm

*debased** cheapened; of a lesser moral quality

mood it conveys is of a bleak pessimism, the mood of a world that had been ravaged by World War I. This quality is particularly evident in the picture it offers of contemporary London, whose language distinctly echoes Dante's account in the *Inferno* of the upper portion of Hell.

Conversion and Middle-Period Work

The success of "The Waste Land" secured Eliot's reputation as a poet, and in 1925 he left Lloyds Bank to join the publishing house of Faber and Gwyer (after 1929, Faber and Faber), where he worked for the rest of his life. Under Eliot's hand—first as editor and later as director—Faber and Faber became the foremost English publisher of twentieth-century Anglo-American poetry. Eliot's own poetry continued with the publication in 1925 of a sequence entitled "The Hollow Men," which stands out in his verse for its directness and accessibility. An apt sequel to "The Waste Land," it is dark and brooding:

> *This is the way the world ends*
> *This is the way the world ends*
> *This is the way the world ends*
> *Not with a bang but a whimper.*

After publishing "The Hollow Men," Eliot felt that he had no more poetry to write, but, in fact, he soon found a new poetic mission. In 1927 he became an Anglican* and then, several months later, was naturalized as a British subject. From this point forward, Eliot's poetry became explicitly Christian, beginning with the pieces collectively termed "The Ariel Poems," the first of which is "The Journey of the Magi," a work that reflects his transition of faith. In 1930 he published the most important of his conversion-era poems, the prayer-like "Ash-Wednesday." He also wrote a religious pageant-play* entitled *The Rock,* which enacts the development of the English church beginning with the Roman era. His increasing engagement with, and public endorsements of, Christianity led his friend the novelist and essayist Virginia Woolf to remark that he seemed to be turning into a priest. In a sense, he was.

Eliot returned to Harvard for the 1932–1933 academic year to deliver an important series of lectures. (His temporary

*Anglican a member of the Church of England

*pageant-play a drama consisting of a series of loosely unified scenes

*****pretext** a public justi-
fication

*****erratic** unpredictable

*****dogmatic** strictly in
accordance with an es-
tablished ideology or
text; "by the book"

*****secularized** focused
on the material, not
the spiritual

*****strident** harsh

*****denunciation** public
condemnation

*****paradoxically** relat-
ing to a statement that
seems to be a contra-
diction but may be
true

*****metaphysical** relat-
ing to such concepts as
being, substance,
essence, time, space,
and identity

return to America provided a pretext* for a final separation
from his wife, whose behavior had become increasingly erratic.*) He suggested in these lectures that theater is "the
ideal medium for poetry" (Behr, p. 43), a premise that would
guide him for much of the remainder of his career. His first
full-scale attempt to write for the stage was *Murder in the
Cathedral,* which is based on the life of the Christian martyr
Saint Thomas Becket. It was performed in 1935 in Canterbury
Theater (the site of Becket's murder) to great acclaim.

Late Work

As Eliot's renown grew, his pronouncements on a wide range of
issues, especially religion and politics, became increasingly dogmatic.* His chief theme was the necessity of reestablishing the
centrality of religion in an increasingly secularized* world. A series of lectures on this subject, delivered in 1939 at Cambridge
and subsequently published under the title *The Idea of a Christian Society,* are particularly strident.* They consist primarily of
a denunciation* of democracy and liberalism as insufficient de-
fenses against the double threat posed by fascism and commu-
nism. Christianity, he contended, is the sole dependable foundation upon which to construct civilization. Paradoxically,* 1939
also saw the publication of his entertaining collection of children's verse, *Old Possum's Book of Practical Cats,* which is
unique among his writings for its sheer playfulness.

In his last decades Eliot wrote mostly plays: *The Family
Reunion, The Cocktail Party, The Confidential Clerk,* and *The
Elder Statesman,* all of which were generally well received.
The summit of his later work, however, is the series of poems
that first appeared separately—"Burnt Norton," "East Coker,"
"The Dry Salvages," "Little Gidding"—and then were published together in 1943 as *Four Quartets.* Each of the four
parts of *Four Quartets* comprises five sections, indicating the
symmetry and structural rigor of the work as a whole. Thematically, the suite of poems, which Eliot characterized as having
been loosely based on the four seasons and the four elements,
is broadly inclusive, moving freely between the metaphysical,*
the political, and the personal. The opening poem, "Burnt
Norton," begins philosophically, with a series of mystical
propositions on the nature of time:

Time present and time past
Are both perhaps present in time future,
And time future contained in time past.
If all time is eternally present
All time is unredeemable.
What might have been is an abstraction
Remaining a perpetual possibility
Only in a world of speculation.
What might have been and what has been
Point to one end, which is always present.

Such abstract passages are offset by others, such as one in "East Coker" in which Eliot, reflecting on his efforts to perfect his craftsmanship as a poet, expresses his sense of the futility of such attempts: he has expended his energies

Trying to learn to use words, and every attempt
Is a wholly new start, and a different kind of failure
Because one has only learnt to get the better of words
For the thing one no longer has to say, or the way in
    which
One is no longer disposed to say it.

Elsewhere, *Four Quartets* celebrates English endurance during World War II under the most adverse circumstances. In the conclusion of the last of the four poems, "Little Gidding," however, all personal and political concerns are transcended in a passage that, appearing as a closing flourish to a poetic career, takes the form of an esoteric* prophecy:

All manner of thing shall be well
When the tongues of flame are in-folded
Into the crowned knot of fire
And the fire and the rose are one.

*esoteric known only
to a privileged few

Final Years

The crowning affirmation of Eliot's career came in 1948, when he was awarded the Nobel Prize in literature. His poetry writing by this point had all but ceased. "The Nobel is a ticket to one's funeral. No one has ever done anything after he got it,"

Eliot himself quipped after having learned that he had received this honor (Ackroyd, p. 290). In the next few years his health became increasingly precarious;* he had a heart attack in 1954 and suffered from chronic bronchial problems that would force him to spend winters away from England's damp and chilly climate. In 1956, at the age of sixty-eight, Eliot married Valerie Fletcher, his thirty-year-old secretary and a fan of his work from the age of fourteen. (His first wife had died a decade earlier, freeing him to remarry.) This relationship seems to have granted him a measure of the happiness and contentment he had previously been denied. Eliot died on 4 January 1965, and by his request his ashes were buried in East Coker, England, where his ancestor Andrew Eliot had lived before emigrating to America in the 1660s. On his tombstone are inscribed the first and last lines from the "East Coker" section of *Four Quartets:* "In my beginning is my end" and "In my end is my beginning."

Selected Bibliography

WORKS BY T. S. ELIOT
Poetry

Prufrock and Other Observations (1917).

Ara Vos Prec (1920).

The Waste Land (1922).

Poems, 1909–1925 (1925).

Collected Poems, 1909–1935 (1936).

Old Possum's Book of Practical Cats (1939).

Four Quartets (1943).

Plays

Sweeney Agonistes (1932).

The Rock (1934).

Murder in the Cathedral (1935).

The Family Reunion (1939).

The Cocktail Party (1950).

The Confidential Clerk (1954).

The Elder Statesman (1959).

Collected Plays (1962).

Prose

The Sacred Wood (1920).

Homage to John Dryden (1924).

For Lancelot Andrewes (1928).

Dante (1929).

Selected Essays, 1917–1932 (1932).

The Use of Poetry and the Use of Criticism (1933).

After Strange Gods (1934).

Elizabethan Essays (1934).

Essays Ancient and Modern (1936).

The Idea of a Christian Society (1939).

Notes Towards the Definition of Culture (1948).

On Poetry and Poets (1957).

George Herbert (1962).

Knowledge and Experience in the Philosophy of F. H. Bradley (1964). Eliot's doctoral dissertation, completed in 1916.

To Criticize the Critic, and Other Writings (1965).

Translation

Anabasis, a Poem by St. John Perse (1930).

Available Collections

The Complete Poems and Plays, 1909–1950. New York: Harcourt Brace, 1952. Rev. ed., New York: Harcourt Brace and World, 1971.

Inventions of the March Hare: Poems, 1909–1917. Edited by Christopher Ricks. New York: Harcourt Brace, 1996.

The Letters of T. S. Eliot, vol. 1. Edited by Valerie Eliot. San Diego: Harcourt Brace Jovanovich, 1988. The first volume of a projected multivolume edition.

Poems Written in Early Youth. London: Faber and Faber, 1967.

Selected Prose of T. S. Eliot. Edited by Frank Kermode. London: Faber and Faber, 1975.

The Waste Land: A Facsimile and Transcript of the Original Drafts Including the Annotations of Ezra Pound. Edited by Valerie Eliot. New York: Harcourt Brace Jovanovich, 1971.

WORKS ABOUT T. S. ELIOT

Ackroyd, Peter. *T. S. Eliot: A Life.* New York: Simon and Schuster, 1984.

Behr, Caroline. *T. S. Eliot: A Chronology of His Life and Works.* London: Macmillan, 1983.

Brooker, Jewel Spears, ed. *The Placing of T. S. Eliot.* Columbia: University of Missouri Press, 1991.

Bush, Ronald. *T. S. Eliot: A Study in Character and Style.* New York: Oxford University Press, 1984.

Cuddy, Lois A., and David H. Hirsch, eds. *Critical Essays on T. S. Eliot's* The Waste Land. Boston: G. K. Hall, 1991.

Gallup, Donald. *T. S. Eliot: A Bibliography,* rev. ed. New York: Harcourt Brace, 1969.

Gordon, Lyndall. *Eliot's Early Years.* Oxford, U.K.: Oxford University Press, 1977.

Gordon, Lyndall. *Eliot's New Life.* New York: Farrar, Straus, and Giroux, 1988.

Grant, Michael, ed. *T. S. Eliot: The Critical Heritage.* 2 vols. London: Routledge, 1982.

Headings, Philip R. *T. S. Eliot,* rev. ed. Boston: Twayne, 1982.

Kenner, Hugh. *The Invisible Poet: T. S. Eliot.* New York: Harcourt Brace Jovanovich, 1959.

Moody, A. David. *Thomas Stearns Eliot: Poet,* rev. ed. Cambridge, U.K.: Cambridge University Press, 1994.

Moody, A. David, ed. *The Cambridge Companion to T. S. Eliot.* Cambridge, U.K.: Cambridge University Press, 1994.

Southam, B. C. *A Student's Guide to the Selected Poems of T. S. Eliot,* rev. ed. New York: Harcourt Brace Jovanovich, 1996.

Tate, Allen, ed. *T. S. Eliot: The Man and His Work.* London: Chatto and Windus, 1967.

RALPH WALDO EMERSON

(1803–1882)

by Paul Kane

In his influential essay "The Poet," Ralph Waldo Emerson declares: "The poets are thus liberating gods. . . . They are free, and they make free"; the poet "unlocks our chains, and admits us to a new scene." Emerson's high regard for poetry comes from his sense that words and images can set a person's imagination on fire and open him or her to new ideas and new ways of seeing things. Poets make us free because they inspire us to look at the world afresh in our own way. For Emerson, the main point of reading poetry is not to find out what a particular poet says or means, but rather to be stimulated to become a kind of poet ourselves—a poet in the sense of someone whose imagination suddenly comes alive. When we are touched by poetry, says Emerson, "We are like persons who come out of a cave or cellar into the open air." His love of the liberating power of poetry came to Emerson early on, and as a poet and writer and thinker, he strove his whole life to help make others free.

Except where otherwise indicated, quotations from Emerson's work throughout are taken from Ports, Bloom, and Kane, eds., *Essays and Poems.*

Early Years

Emerson began writing poems at the age of nine. He was born into a family that valued books and ideas and encouraged him to pursue his interest in poetry. Emerson descended from a long line of ministers on both sides of his family, which meant that he grew up among well-educated people. His father, William Emerson, was a minister in Boston, where the poet was born on 25 May 1802, but when Emerson was seven years old, his father died, leaving the family in difficult financial circumstances. Emerson and his brothers were raised by his devoted mother, Ruth Haskins Emerson, and by a religiously stern but lively aunt, Mary Moody Emerson (who had her bed built in the shape of a coffin to remind her of her mortality). When he was fourteen Emerson enrolled at Harvard College (the youngest member of his class) and went on to graduate in 1821 as the "class poet." Emerson was not, however, a distinguished scholar at the time: out of a class of fifty-nine students, he was ranked thirtieth. Emerson went on to teach school for several years and then returned to Harvard to study at the new Divinity School. During this period he suffered from eye troubles and other health problems, but in 1829 he was finally ordained a Unitarian minister at the old Second Church in Boston. That same year he married Ellen Tucker, a beautiful woman he loved dearly (as we can tell from the many poems he wrote about her). By the age of twenty-six, Emerson seemed well on his way to a settled and successful career as a respectable minister in Boston.

Crisis

"People wish to be settled," says Emerson in his essay "Circles." "Only as far as they are unsettled is there any hope for them." "Life," he writes, "is a series of surprises." What might have looked like a secure life for Emerson was nothing of the sort. The next three years were full of turmoil and surprise. In the winter of 1831 Emerson's young wife died of tuberculosis. The terrible shock of this event is registered in the numerous elegies* he wrote for her at the time. In an untitled poem from his journal, dated 1831, Emerson writes:

> Dust unto dust! and shall no more be said
> Ellen for thee, and shall a common fate

*****elegy** a poem of sorrow or reflection, usually about one who is dead

Blend thy last hour with the last hours of all?
Of thee my wife, my undefiled, my dear?

Up to this point, Emerson had himself written quite conventional and "correct" verse, but now he became more experimental as a poet. In his time of crisis, he freed himself from the constraints of traditional forms, using what was later called "free verse."* He would go on to write in a variety of forms, some conventional and some unconventional. The important thing is that he felt free to choose.

In 1832, Emerson resigned his post as minister of the Second Church. He no longer believed in the church as an institution because it worshipped "the dead forms of our forefathers" and not the ongoing spiritual life of each individual. God, he declared, was to be found in each person. As he says in "Gnothi Seauton" (Greek for "Know Thyself," which was the inscription over the entrance to the Temple of Apollo at Delphi in ancient Greece):

Then take this fact unto thy soul—
God dwells in thee.—
It is no metaphor nor parable*
It is unknown to thousands & to thee
Yet there is God.

In December of that year Emerson sailed for Europe. When he returned nine months later he was ready to embark upon a new vocation* as a writer.

Poetic Maturity

With a renewed sense of purpose, Emerson set about to develop his skills as a writer, lecturer, and poet. In 1834–1835 he emerged into his full maturity as a poet with some of his best and most characteristic poems, including "The Rhodora," "Each and All," and "The Snow-Storm."

In "Each and All" we see Emerson's typical concern with what happens when you view things from different angles. The poem begins with three examples of how a person's actions might unknowingly influence others: a "clown," or rustic peasant, tending cows appears picturesque to an onlooker; a "sexton," or church maintenance man, rings a bell, which

*__free verse__ poetry that does not follow traditional forms, meters, or rhyme schemes

*__parable__ a short story that illustrates a moral or religious principle

*__vocation__ occupation

pleases the French emperor Napoleon, who is leading his army over the Alps; or you, the leader, might supply your neighbor with an example of how to conduct one's life. In each case, someone is part of a larger picture without knowing it. "All are needed by each one," says Emerson, "Nothing is fair or good alone." In other words, we are all connected to each other and to nature in ways we do not necessarily perceive, but this unity is crucial to our sense of what is beautiful or good.

The poem goes on to relate three personal incidents as further examples: the poet brings home a song sparrow because its singing delighted him, only to discover that taking the bird out of its natural setting takes away most of its charm. Or, again, the poet brings home lovely seashells, but without the context of "the sun and the sand and the wild uproar" he has "left their beauty on the shore." And, finally, he is entranced by a "graceful maid" singing in a choir, but when they marry and he takes her home, he finds out that she is not the "fairy" he had imagined: he had not taken into account the enchanting circumstances in which he had seen her. At this point the poet says he is fed up with pursuing beauty because it is no more than a "cheat," or child's toy; from now on he will seek truth only. At that moment a new perspective emerges:

> As I spoke, beneath my feet
> The ground-pine curled its pretty wreath,
> Running over the club-moss burrs;
> I inhaled the violet's breath;
> Around me stood the oaks and firs;
> Pine-cones and acorns lay on the ground,
> Over me soared the eternal sky,
> Full of light and of deity;
> Again I saw, again I heard,
> The rolling river, the morning bird;—
> Beauty through my senses stole;
> I yielded myself to the perfect whole.

Despite his decision to reject beauty in favor of truth, he is overcome by nature's presence and realizes that he is part of the perfect unity of nature. Instead of trying to grasp beauty and selfishly possess it as his own, he now yields himself to it. In arriving at this new perspective on beauty Emerson also arrives at a new truth about the world. Truth and beauty, like nature and humanity, are interconnected.

Emerson's Influence

Emerson made his living primarily from giving lectures at lyceums, or community education centers, around the country. He was a very popular lecturer and traveled throughout New England, the Midwest, and even as far as California (quite a long journey in those days). Emerson eventually worked his lectures into essays, which he collected and published in book form. Through his extensive lecturing and his publications, Emerson became one of America's most influential thinkers, and, in fact, his ideas have continued to shape how Americans see themselves. When people advise you to "hitch your wagon to a star" or refer to a "shot heard round the world" or suggest that "the reward of a thing well done, is to have done it," they are quoting Emerson. But Emerson's influence lies primarily in his capacity to challenge people to think for themselves, to encourage them to embrace what he calls "self-reliance." In his essay of that title, he writes: "Trust thyself: every heart vibrates to that iron string." Emerson has been particularly important to other poets. When Walt Whitman, for instance, was on the verge of becoming a poet, he was propelled forward by Emerson's essays. In his essay "On Emerson," Robert Frost ranked Emerson as one of "my four greatest Americans," the others being George Washington, Thomas Jefferson, and Abraham Lincoln (*Collected Poems, Prose, and Plays.* Edited by Richard Poirier and Mark Richardson. New York: Library of America, 1995).

Emerson, however, was not always admired and, in fact, has remained controversial. In his own time he was seen as a dangerous radical (an "infidel"), and in the twentieth century he was considered by some to be an anarchist. In 1981 the president of Yale University, A. Bartlett Giammatti, in *The University and the Public Interest* (New York: Atheneum, 1981), claimed that Emerson "is as sweet as barbed wire" (p. 174). Why do Emerson's ideas generate so much opposition? In the first place, he attacked social institutions like churches and reform societies and protested the enslavement of African Americans and the removal of Native Americans from their homelands. When Emerson delivered his "Divinity School Address"

Emerson "is as sweet as a barbed wire."

Maia

Illusion works impenetrable,
Weaving webs innumerable,
Her gay pictures never fail,
Crowds each on other, veil on veil,
Charmer who will be believed
By Man who thirsts to be deceived.

---

at Harvard in 1838, in which he advocated freedom of conscience over intellectual conformity, he was banned from the school for almost thirty years. As controversy swirled around him, he quietly withdrew to his home in Concord, Massachusetts, where he and his new wife, Lydia Jackson, waited out the storm. His poem "Uriel" is based on his banishment. In the poem, Uriel, an angel or demigod in heaven, announces a new doctrine of the relativity of evil:

> 'Line in nature is not found;
> Unit and universe are round;
> In vain produced, all rays return;
> Evil will bless, and ice will burn.'

*heresy dissenting opinions from official church doctrine

This heresy* wreaks general confusion and angers the "stern old war-gods"; the young god is disappointed by this hostile reception:

> A sad self-knowledge, withering, fell
> On the beauty of Uriel;
> In heaven once eminent, the god
> Withdrew, that hour, into his cloud;

*vindicate to justify or defend

But every once in a while, something would happen that would vindicate* Uriel's philosophy, and then,

> Came Uriel's voice of cherub scorn,
> And a blush tinged the upper sky,
> And the gods shook, they knew not why.

Emerson, too, has a way of shaking people up. His critique of society as a whole can be quite uncompromising. As he says in

"Self-Reliance," "Society everywhere is in conspiracy against the manhood of every one of its members." He goes on, "Whoso would be a man must be a nonconformist." To live by such doctrine requires great personal strength, for "It is easy in the world to live after the world's opinion; it is easy in solitude to live after our own; but the great man is he who in the midst of the crowd keeps with perfect sweetness the independence of solitude." As Emerson discovered, "For nonconformity the world whips you with its displeasure." But he persisted, and, in the end, the world took more pleasure than displeasure in what he had to say. Emerson went on to live a long and full life, and he became, in his own time, one of America's most beloved writers. He died 27 April 1882 of pneumonia.

Conclusion

In his poem "Days" Emerson writes about the possibilities open to us each day of our lives. Most of our time seems taken up with trivial events and repetitious duties, and we tend to forget that there is a tremendous spiritual potential within each of us. Emerson imagines our days as "Daughters of Time" and refers to them as "hypocritic," by which he means they play a role like actors or even set out deliberately to deceive people. In the poem, Emerson presents us with a representative day:

> Daughters of Time, the hypocritic Days,
> Muffled and dumb* like barefoot dervishes,*
> And marching single in an endless file,
> Bring diadems* and fagots* in their hands.
> To each they offer gifts after his will,
> Bread, kingdoms, stars, and sky that holds them all.
> I, in my pleached* garden, watched the pomp,
> Forgot my morning wishes, hastily
> Took a few herbs and apples, and the Day
> Turned and departed silent. I, too late,
> Under her solemn fillet* saw the scorn.

Sitting in his garden, Emerson watches the procession of possibilities that the Day presents. But in forgetting his wish for more than an ordinary humdrum existence, he takes only "a few herbs and apples" instead of something great and exciting. The Day turns and walks away silently, but Emerson notices her

*dumb mute; unable to speak

*dervish a member of a group of Islamic mystics (whirling dervishes) who do a turning meditation as part of their practices

*diadem crown

*fagot a bundle of sticks

*pleached interwoven, as vines or stems may become

*fillet headband

scornful expression. Too late, Emerson realizes he has made a poor choice: he has once again sold himself short. There is, of course, nothing wrong with taking a few herbs and apples from the Day—it even sounds pleasant—but when we compare that with Emerson's transcendent* experience described in the essay "Nature," when, enjoying a "perfect exhilaration," he becomes a "transparent eyeball" and the "currents of the Universal Being circulate" through him, then we can understand what is at stake each day. A day can be ordinary or extraordinary, depending upon how we approach it. For Emerson, poetry is one way to be reminded of what is beyond the ordinary; it can liberate us and show us how "Life is a series of surprises" ("Circles"). As he puts it in the poem "Merlin I," through poetry we can "mount to paradise / By the stairway of surprise."

Selected Bibliography

WORKS BY RALPH EMERSON
Poetry

> *Poems* (1847).

> *May-Day and Other Pieces* (1867).

> *Society and Solitude* (1870).

> *Selected Poems* (1876).

Prose

> *Nature* (1836).

> *Nature; Addresses, and Lectures* (1849).

> *Essays: First Series* (1841).

> *Essays: Second Series* (1844).

> *Representative Men* (1850).

> *English Traits* (1856).

> *The Conduct of Life* (1860).

> *Letters and Social Aims* (1875).

Available Collections

> *Essays and Poems*. Edited by Joel Porte, Harold Bloom, and Paul Kane. New York: Library of America, 1996.

WORKS ABOUT RALPH WALDO EMERSON

Baker, Carlos. *Emerson Among the Eccentrics: A Group Portrait*. New York: Viking, 1996.

Barish, Evelyn. *Emerson: The Roots of Prophecy*. Princeton, N.J.: Princeton University Press, 1989.

Bloom, Harold, ed. *Ralph Waldo Emerson*. New York: Chelsea House, 1985.

Burkholder, Robert E., and Joel Myerson, eds. *Critical Essays on Ralph Waldo Emerson*. Boston: G. K. Hall, 1983.

Carpenter, Frederic Ives. *Emerson Handbook*. New York: Hendricks House, 1953.

Gregg, Edith W., ed., *One First Love: The Letters of Ellen Louisa Tucker to Ralph Waldo Emerson*. Cambridge, Mass.: Belknap Press, 1962.

Konvitz, Milton R., and Stephen E. Whicher, eds. *Emerson: A Collection of Critical Essays*. Englewood Cliffs, N.J.: Prentice-Hall, 1962.

Matthiessen, F. O. *American Renaissance: Art and Expression in the Age of Emerson and Whitman*. New York: Oxford University Press, 1941.

Myerson, Joel, ed. *Emerson Centenary Essays*. Carbondale: Southern Illinois University Press, 1982.

Packer, Barbara L. *Emerson's Fall: A New Interpretation of the Major Essays*. New York: Continuum, 1982.

Paul, Sherman. *Emerson's Angle of Vision: Man and Nature in American Experience*. Cambridge, Mass.: Harvard University Press, 1952.

Poirer, Richard. *The Renewal of Literature: Emersonian Reflections*. New York: Random House, 1987.

Richardson, Robert D., Jr. *Emerson: The Mind on Fire*. Berkeley and Los Angeles: University of California Press, 1995.

Robinson, David. *Emerson and the Conduct of Life*. New York: Cambridge University Press, 1993.

Waggoner, Hyatt H. *Emerson as Poet*. Princeton, N.J.: Princeton University Press, 1974.

Whicher, Stephen. *Freedom and Fate*. 2d ed. Philadelphia: University of Pennsylvania Press, 1971.

Yoder, R. A. *Emerson and the Orphic Poet in America*. Berkeley: University of California Press, 1978.

✍️

More About Emerson

You can visit Emerson's house in Concord, Massachusetts, which is open mid-April through October.
For information, contact:
Ralph Waldo Emerson House
Box 33
28 Cambridge Turnpike
Concord, MA 01749
phone: (508) 369-2236

ROBERT FROST

(1874–1963)

by Geof Hewitt

Robert Frost is one of the most famous poets in U.S. history, but many people are surprised and disappointed to learn of his troubled childhood and the enormous contradictions in his adult life. For instance, having dropped in and out of school and never having completed a college degree, Frost maintained a lifelong disregard for formal education, once writing, "The chief reason for going to school is to get the impression fixed for life that there is a book side to everything" (Lathem, p. 412.) For many years throughout his life, Frost earned his living as a teacher, yet he once admitted, "I'm always skeptical about education. . . . I admire people who neglect their studies for dancing or sports. And especially those who neglect them to study, of course" (Vogel, p. 2).

Anyone who doubts that Robert Frost was human and full of human frailties should read his letters or spend some time with Lawrance Thompson's three-volume biography. Frost could be petty, menacing, and downright dangerous, yet his poems and his craggy* farmer-grandfather image have merged in the American psyche as the perfect image of a

Except where otherwise indicated, quotations of Robert Frost's work throughout are taken from Lathem and Thompson, eds., *Robert Frost Poetry and Prose*, and page numbers refer to that collection.

*craggy rugged

"poet." This was no gentle man who penned the poems that nearly every high-school student has heard, if not memorized, in one classroom or another. "Something there is that doesn't love a wall," "Whose woods these are I think I know," and "Two roads diverged in a yellow wood" (from "Mending Wall," "Stopping by Woods on a Snowy Evening," and "The Road Not Taken," respectively) are among his well-known lines of poetry.

Robert Lee Frost was born in San Francisco on 26 March 1874, the son of Isabelle Moodie Frost and William Prescott Frost, Jr., a Harvard educated newspaperman and politician. When Frost's father died in 1885, Isabelle Moodie Frost moved with her small family (Frost and his sister) from San Francisco to Lawrence, Massachusetts. Frost graduated from Lawrence High School in 1892, the class valedictorian along with Elinor Miriam White, whom he married in December 1895.

Following his high school graduation, Frost briefly attended Dartmouth (1893) and Harvard (1897–1899). Meanwhile, the Frosts had two children. In 1900 Frost and his family moved to West Derry, New Hampshire, where he tried his hand at farming and where four more children were born.

> *This was no gentle man who penned the poems that nearly every high-school student has heard. . . .*

From Chicken Farming to the Pulitzer Prize

From 1900 to 1906, all the while writing poems, Frost supported himself; his wife, Elinor; and their children as a chicken farmer and published at least ten short stories and sketches in two poultry magazines, *The Eastern Poultryman* and *Farm-Poultry.* The family lived on the edge of poverty, but Frost was determined to become a widely published poet.

Despite his ambition, Frost did not quickly find a wide audience for his poems. These very poems, which seem elegant now, may have been too radical in form and in focus for U.S. publishers in the early 1900s.

In 1912, having retired from chicken farming and a subsequent teaching stint, nearly forty years old and still seeking publication of his first book of poems, Frost moved to England with his family. Within a year, thanks to assistance from his fellow poet Ezra Pound, then living in London, Frost found a publisher. Two collections of poems, *A Boy's Will* and *North of Boston,* appeared in 1913 and 1914, respectively.

Returning to the United States in 1915, Frost discovered that success breeds success. His first two books were published in U.S. editions that year, and his third collection, *Mountain Interval,* appeared in 1916. Frost would never again have trouble publishing his poems. Indeed, during the next thirty years he won four Pulitzer Prizes for his books of poetry (*New Hampshire* in 1924, *Collected Poems* in 1931, *A Further Range* in 1937, and *A Witness Tree* in 1943), a record that stands at the beginning of the twenty-first century. In addition, he was honored throughout the rest of his adult life with virtually every poetry prize that existed. In 1961, at the age of eighty-six, he read his own poetry at the inauguration of President John F. Kennedy, and a year later, during a period of terrifying international tension between the U.S. and Soviet governments, he traveled to the USSR on a goodwill mission for the U.S. Department of State. When he died on 29 January 1963 of complications following surgery for prostate and bladder cancer, Frost could look back on a life that had at one time or another found him teaching school, supporting his family as a poultry farmer, scraping by as a freelance writer and poet, and visiting college campuses as a deeply honored, prize-winning, world-famous poet.

As his fame grew, Frost seemed to love to play the role of elderly Yankee philosopher, a kindly older man who had weathered a lifetime of encounters with nature and with human nature. At the same time that he played this role in public appearances across the country, he was credited behind the scenes with being a shrewd businessman. But Frost's public was more likely to see the image that he wanted to project, an image that included philosopher, wit, and practical thinker.

Having spent most of his life in California and then in England, Massachusetts, New Hampshire, and Michigan, Frost nevertheless was named poet laureate of Vermont in 1961. He remained that state's poet laureate* for nearly twenty-five years after his death in 1963, testimony to either Vermont's good taste or its lack of attention to the post.

How is it that a mean-spirited poet from California could become the poet laureate of Vermont? Perhaps it is because Frost's poems are almost always cast in a rural setting. Yet the rural themes are universal ones: the death of a hired man, a neighbor's need to maintain a fence, the temptation to wander off a well-trodden "path" for the sake of a little healthy exploration. Such themes are obviously of significance to readers in urban as well as rural environments.

*poet laureate in England, an outstanding poet once appointed for life as a paid member of the royal household and expected to write poems for certain national occasions. In other countries, the term refers to a poet honored and recognized for his or her achievements

Place and Person in the Poem

*transcend to rise above the limitations of

Evoking New England settings, Frost's poems transcend* place. In responding to circumstance, his primarily New England characters take on unique characteristics as they develop individuality, long considered the defining element in a Yankee farmer. "Oh, that's just the Yankee character," a reader in Virginia or Texas might say and thus paint all New Englanders with the same brush.

Although Frost was a reluctant student who never completed a college degree, he was an eager reader of Shakespeare's poems and plays. His readings of William Wordsworth and other eighteenth- and nineteenth-century British poets influenced his early poems and had a lifelong effect on his poetic style.

Compare Frost's first published poem (he wrote it as a high-school sophomore) to the first poem he published nationally, just four years later. The first is "La Noche Triste":

> Anon the cry comes down the line,
> The portals wide are swung,
> A long dark line moves out the gate,
> And now the flight's begun.
>
> What terror to each heart it bears,
> That sound of ill portent,*
> Each gunner to escape now looks,
> On safety all are bent.
> <div align="right">(<i>High School Bulletin,</i> April 1890, pp. 1–2)</div>

*portent an omen; something that fore-shadows events to come

The second is "My Butterfly":

> And didst thou think who tottered maundering* on
>   high
> Fate had not made thee for the pleasure of the wind,
>   With those great careless wings?
>   'Twas happier to die
>   And let the days blow by,—
>   These were the unlearned things.
> <div align="right">(<i>The Independent,</i> 8 November 1894, p. 1)</div>

*maundering meandering; wandering idly

Notice in "The Butterfly" that Frost maintains a "poetic" vocabulary ("who tottered maundering on high") at the same time that he appears to be experimenting with the length of lines and the regularity of rhyme. Reading the complete text of both poems, one sees a growing sense of independence in the young poet's approach. Continuing to respect the traditions of his predecessors, Frost was also discovering his own voice less and less relying on convoluted* phrases (like "Each gunner to escape now looks, / On safety all are bent") simply to fit into a prescribed rhythmic and rhyme scheme.

Yet in his later poems, Frost used such convolution to powerful effect, especially as a poem's opening line, as with "Something there is that doesn't love a wall. . . ." and "Whose woods these are I think I know. . . ." The difference is that he used this technique sparingly and for dramatic effect, not out of a necessity dictated by the poem's form.

This evolution of literary tradition is an important part of the development of any writer. Frost's poems continued to evolve as he learned to explore human interaction in specific, dramatic terms, saying more and saying it in greater detail than seemed possible in the predominantly form-bound verse that characterized much American poetry in the early 1900s. In his attention to the language and circumstances of his neighbors, Frost validated concrete human experience (in this case rural New England experience) as a building block for poetry.

*convoluted complicated or indirect

"Fire and Ice"

In addition to his keen portrayals of the New England landscape and Yankee character, one of the defining elements of Frost's poems is the mischief of his wit. In "Fire and Ice," he debates one of the greatest questions of all time, touching on religion, philosophy, and science—all at once.

> Some say the world will end in fire,
> Some say in ice.
> From what I've tasted of desire
> I hold with those who favor fire.
> But if it had to perish twice,
> I think I know enough of hate
> To say that for destruction ice
> Is also great
> And would suffice.
>
> "Fire and Ice"

Out, Out—

The buzz saw snarled and rattled in the yard
And made dust and dropped stove-length sticks of wood,
Sweet-scented stuff when the breeze drew across it.
And from there those that lifted eyes could count
Five mountain ranges one behind the other
Under the sunset far into Vermont.
And the saw snarled and rattled, snarled and rattled,
As it ran light, or had to bear a load.
And nothing happened: day was all but done.
Call it a day, I wish they might have said
To please the boy by giving him the half hour
That a boy counts so much when saved from work.
His sister stood beside them in her apron
To tell them "Supper." At the word, the saw,
As if to prove saws knew what supper meant,
Leaped out at the boy's hand, or seemed to leap—
He must have given the hand. However it was,
Neither refused the meeting. But the hand!
The boy's first outcry was a rueful* laugh,
As he swung toward them holding up the hand,
Half in appeal, but half as if to keep
The life from spilling. Then the boy saw all—
Since he was old enough to know, big boy
Doing a man's work, though a child at heart—
He saw all spoiled. "Don't let him cut my hand off—
The doctor, when he comes. Don't let him, sister!"
So. But the hand was gone already.
The doctor put him in the dark of ether.*
He lay and puffed his lips out with his breath.
And then—the watcher at his pulse took fright.
No one believed. They listened at his heart.
Little—less—nothing!—and that ended it.
No more to build on there. And they, since they
Were not the one dead, turned to their affairs.

*****rueful** pitiable;
mournful; regretful

*****ether** a type of anes-
thetic

In addition to mischief and wit, Frost brought the power of keen observation to his poems. In "Out, Out" he describes the death of a boy who has just lost his hand to a buzz saw, and the necessary, immediate resumption, by the boy's family and neighbors, of the very chores that have just cost a young life.

As Jay Parini acknowledges in *Robert Frost: A Life,* there is at once a heartless practicality and a Yankee nobility at work in the resumption of routine. Further, Frost may have been alluding to his own experience following the deaths of two of his six children. Is there an understandable, human need to "stay busy" as a way of dealing with grief?

Regardless of how one envisions Frost—whether as grandfatherly, gentle New England farmer-poet or as insecure, temperamental hustler of his poetry (or something between the two)—the word "genius" applies to his abilities as a poet. His poems range from the brief and aphoristic* delights of language and wit (as in "Fire and Ice") to a prolonged and playful meditation on "New Hampshire" to the full script of a play and even to bawdy subjects (see "Pride of Ancestry," which begins: "The Deacon's wife was a bit desirish / And liked her sex relations wild, / So she lay with one of the shanty Irish / And he begot the Deacon's child").

Varied as his poems may be, Frost's work is bound by one driving aesthetic, perhaps most aptly expressed in his preface to *A Way Out,* his one-act play originally published in *The Seven Arts* magazine in 1917, produced at Amherst College in 1919 and reprinted separately in 1929.

> **A dramatic necessity goes deep into the nature of the sentence. Sentences are not different enough to hold the attention unless they are dramatic. No ingenuity of varying structure will do. All that can save them is the speaking tone of voice somehow entangled in the words and fastened to the page for the ear of the imagination. That is all that can save poetry from sing-song, all that can save prose from itself (p. 272).**

Later, in a letter to the anthologist Louis Untermeyer, Frost talked about the poet's responsibility to use the language of his own locale and time:

> **There may be a few fools trying to anticipate their future selves and write poetry as of 4000 A.D. so as to be more American than the facts warrant. But most of us are willing to take our lives as given us. About all we can do is write about things that have happened to us in America in the language we have grown up to in America (p. 458).**

*__aphoristic__ characterized by aphorisms: brief, pithy statements of truth

The Fate of Good Poems

Phrases from Frost's poems are often used in conversation, sometimes so out of context that their meaning is reversed. For instance, "Good fences make good neighbors" often justifies the setting of boundaries, even though Frost's "Mending Wall," from which the phrase is quoted, suggests that building fences is antisocial! It is an ironic fate that great words risk, for any idea worth pondering can be misconstrued or intentionally misrepresented.

> He is all pine and I am apple orchard.
> My apple trees will never get across
> And eat the cones under his pines, I tell him.
> He only says, "Good fences make good neighbors."
> Spring is the mischief in me, and I wonder
> If I could put a notion in his head:
> "*Why* do they make good neighbors? Isn't it
> Where there are cows? But here there are no cows.
> Before I built a wall I'd ask to know
> What I was walling in or walling out,
> And to whom I was like to give offence.
> Something there is that doesn't love a wall,
> That wants it down."

Robert Frost, Poetry Guru

Frost expressed his notions with great force, almost as if they were the laws of nature, and his ideas have influenced most American poets after him, whether or not they agree with those ideas. The *Atlantic Monthly* (June 1951) published entries from Frost's notebooks, including this: "For my pleasure I had as soon write free verse as play tennis with the net down" (p. 31). Even in the world in which Frost was writing fifty or sixty years ago, such words were fighting words: Was Frost just an old crank, preaching in favor of his own special strength? Free verse observes neither a strict metrical* nor a rhyming pattern, and by mid-century was becoming widely acceptable. But, in addition to condemning free verse, Frost avoided it.

Meter makes Frost's poems memorable without calling undue attention to itself; in natural speaking patterns Frost

*****metrical** relating to the rhythmic pattern within each line of verse

recognized the heightened language of poetic tradition. By abbreviating a conversational statement here, adding an occasional syllable there, and sometimes starting a sentence in an unlikely place, he created poems where the content, not the style, was what mattered. He captured colloquial* speech patterns, demonstrating that iambic* pentameter* is the most common rhythm of speech in the United States. At the end of his life, he acknowledged having written only one free-verse poem in his entire career.

> A lady said to me one night, "You've said all sorts of things tonight, Mr. Frost. Which are you, a conservative or a radical?"
>
> And I looked at her very honestly and earnestly and sincerely, and I said:
>
> I never dared be radical when young
> For fear it would make me conservative when old.
> That's my only free verse poem (p. 458).

(It was published under the title "Precaution," in *A Further Range*.)

Frost's Legacy

To this day American poets are fond of analyzing the metrical patterns of conversation as well as of the prepared speeches delivered in important places. And although rhyme seems less and less a component of contemporary American poetry, Frost's attention to meter remains a driving force in the poems being written today.

In reading Frost's poems it is helpful to approach the work with a willingness to "read through" the rhymes and line breaks, to read for *content,* using the punctuation, not the line breaks, as a guide for pauses. This approach to reading poems, especially when reading them aloud (as Frost intended his poems to be appreciated), allows the rhyme and rhythm to work on a near-subconscious level, providing a sense of unity without obscuring* the poem's intent behind the singsong of regular rhythm and rhyme. Conversely, Frost's dependence on meter and rhyme can be demonstrated to the point of satire by singing the many poems that are in rhymed, iambic tetrameter to the tune of "Yellow Rose of Texas" or "Hernando's Hideaway."

colloquial characteristic of everyday conversation

iambic a rhythmic unit (or metrical foot) that consists of one unstressed syllable followed by one stressed syllable, as in "un-DO"

pentameter having five metrical feet

obscuring blocking from view

In Praise of the Slow Reader

"Poetry plays the rhythms of dramatic speech on the grid of meter," wrote Frost in one of his notebooks. "A good map carries its own scale of miles" (p. 415). Just as a musician needs a beat against which to play or to reinforce a melody, Frost recognized the importance of meter, the actual rhythm of speech. By insisting on "its own scale of miles," he emphasized the creative freedom that is still available to each poet on the grid of meter.

In the same notebook Frost defined the ideal reader in a way that reinforces his concern for the *sound* of the poem:

> **The best reader of all is one who will read, can read, no faster than he can hear the lines and sentences in his mind's ear as if aloud. Frequenting poetry has slowed him down by its metric or measured pace.**
>
> **The eye reader is a barbarian. So is the writer for the eye reader, who needn't care how badly he writes since he doesn't care how badly he is read (p. 415).**

In his praise of the slow reader, Frost opened the door to *all* readers. The seeming simplicity of his poems further broadens his invitation. Yet as so many critics and scholars have learned, the more one reads a poem by Robert Frost, the deeper it may become. And the more of Frost's poems one reads, the greater the resonance* one observes among the poems, with themes repeated and reexamined: the meaning of death, the nature of nature, the cost of pursuing one's own goals as opposed to those imagined by one's predecessors. As with Frost's very human personality, his poems, like a diamond, have many facets. The light that is brought to those facets will make a vast difference in how they are viewed.

*resonance richness of tone; applicability or relevance

Selected Bibliography

WORKS BY ROBERT FROST
Poetry

A Boy's Will (1913).

North of Boston (1914).

Mountain Interval (1916).

IF YOU LIKE the poetry of Frost, you might also like the poetry of Edwin Arlington Robinson, Carl Sandburg, or Richard Wilbur.

❦

New Hampshire: A Poem with Notes and Grace Notes (1923).

West-Running Brook (1928).

Collected Poems (1930).

A Further Range (1936).

A Witness Tree (1942).

A Masque of Reason (1945).

A Masque of Mercy (1947).

Steeple Bush (1947).

In the Clearing (1962).

Available Collections

The Letters of Robert Frost to Louis Untermeyer. Edited by Louis Untermeyer. New York: Holt, Rinehart, and Winston, 1963.

Robert Frost: Poetry and Prose. Edited by Edward Connery Lathem and Lawrance Thompson. New York: Holt, Rinehart, and Winston, 1972.

Selected Letters of Robert Frost. Edited by Lawrance Thompson. New York: Holt, Rinehart, and Winston, 1964.

WORKS ABOUT ROBERT FROST

Cady, Edwin H., and Louis J. Budd, eds. *On Frost.* Durham, N.C.: Duke University Press, 1991.

Cox, Sidney. *A Swinger of Birches: A Portrait of Robert Frost.* New York: New York University Press, 1957.

Francis, Robert. *Frost: A Time to Talk.* Amherst: University of Massachusetts Press, 1972.

Gerber, Philip. *Robert Frost,* rev. ed. Boston: Twayne, 1982.

Lathem, Edward Connery, ed. *Interviews with Robert Frost.* New York: Holt, Rinehart, and Winston, 1966.

Lathem, Edward Connery, and Lawrance Thompson, eds. *Robert Frost Poetry and Prose.* New York: Holt, Rinehart and Winston, 1972.

Parini, Jay. *Robert Frost: A Life.* New York: Henry Holt and Company, 1999.

More About Frost

You can visit/contact:
The Robert Frost Farm
P. O. Box 1975
Derry, NH 03038
phone: (603) 271-3556

The Robert Frost Trail in
 Ripton, Vermont, is also
 open to the public.

Pritchard, William H. *Frost: A Literary Life Reconsidered.* New York: Oxford University Press, 1984.

Thompson, Lawrance. *Robert Frost: The Early Years, 1874–1915.* New York: Holt, Rinehart, and Winston, 1966.

Thompson, Lawrance. *Robert Frost: The Years of Triumph, 1915–1938.* New York: Holt, Rinehart, and Winston, 1970.

Thompson, Lawrance, and R. H. Winnick. *Robert Frost: The Later Years, 1938–1963.* New York: Holt, Rinehart, and Winston, 1976.

Vogel, Nancy. *Robert Frost, Teacher.* Bloomington, Ind.: Phi Delta Kappa, 1974.

ALLEN GINSBERG

(1926–1997)

by Bob Rosenthal

In 1943 a skinny seventeen-year-old boy boarded a Hudson River ferry to cross from New Jersey to New York City to take his entrance exams for Columbia University. Allen Ginsberg made a vow to himself that if he passed his exams he would dedicate his life to helping the working class. To accomplish this end, he planned to become a labor lawyer.

Irwin Allen Ginsberg was born 3 June 1926 in Newark, New Jersey. He was the second son of Naomi and Louis Ginsberg, who were children of eastern European Jewish immigrants. Their lives were infused with hard work and political ideals. Louis's family were socialists, and Naomi's family were communists. Louis taught high school English and was a published poet. Naomi suffered from a disastrous case of paranoid schizophrenic psychosis.* She had her first major breakdown in the years before Allen's birth. During Allen's infancy, Naomi had many "good" years, but the breakdowns and hospitalizations occurred with increasing frequency.

At the age of eleven, Ginsberg started keeping a journal, which he continued all his life. In the earliest entries, he

Quotations from Ginsberg's poetry throughout are taken from *Collected Poems 1947–1980*.

***paranoid schizophrenic psychosis** a disorder characterized by loss of contact with the environment, difficulty functioning in everyday life, and hallucinations or delusions

381

mentions that his mother had had another hospitalization but that she had only a very slight chance of dying. Ginsberg devoted many pages to news of the war in Europe in the late 1930s. In the next few years, he took on much of the responsibility for the care of his mother, as his father grew exhausted by the continuing crisis. Still, Ginsberg felt that a distinctive future awaited him, as he reveals in his journal at age fourteen:

> If some future historian or biographer wants to know what the genius thought & did in his tender years, here it is. I'll be a genius of some kind or other, probably in literature. I really believe it. (Not naively, as whoever reads this is thinking). I have a fair degree of confidence in myself. Either I'm a genius, I'm egocentric, or I'm slightly schizophrenic. Probably the first two (unpublished journal, May 1941).

Beatnik* Fits and Starts

At Columbia University, Ginsberg became seriously interested in literature and studied with two famous professors, Lionel Trilling and Mark Van Doren. His teachers disparaged* the modern styles of poetry that Ginsberg loved, including the poetry of Walt Whitman and William Carlos Williams. Early in his college career, Ginsberg met people who became lifelong friends. First he met Lucien Carr, a journalist who challenged Ginsberg's hand-me-down ideals of helping the working class and forced him to develop his own ideas from his own experience. Carr also introduced Ginsberg to the older William Burroughs, an American novelist best known for settings of the universe of heroin users and for experimental writing techniques. It was Carr who also encouraged Ginsberg to introduce himself to the novelist and poet Jack Kerouac, a former Columbia student. Kerouac was enjoying an afternoon breakfast when the seventeen-year-old Allen Ginsberg walked into his kitchen. Ginsberg and Kerouac discovered that they shared the sensitivity of writers and soon became close friends. They visited Burroughs, and the three formed friendships that germinated the Beat Movement.

In March 1945 Ginsberg was suspended for one year from Columbia for letting Kerouac stay overnight in his dorm room and for writing lewd comments on the windows. He

*beatnik someone who chooses a lifestyle free of many social conventions and tends to have an affinity for jazz, poetry, intoxicants, and free love

*disparaged degraded; lowered in status

The Beat Generation of writers, including Allen Ginsberg, Jack Kerouac, and William Burroughs, began publishing their work in the United States during the 1950s. "Beat" is associated with the term "beatnik."

moved out of the dorms and worked at many minor jobs, even shipping out as a merchant marine. He also drew closer to the subterranean* world surrounding Burroughs and met Herbert Huncke, a con man and hustler working out of Times Square. Although Ginsberg was learning about life on the streets, his poetry was still rooted in the traditional. This can be seen in the following excerpt from the poem "A Lover's Garden":

> How vainly lovers marvel, all
> To make a body, mind, and soul,
> Who, winning one white night of grace,
> Will weep and rage a year of days,
> Or must forever on a kiss,
> If won by a more sad mistress—
> Are all these lovers, then, undone
> By him and me, who love alone?

He reentered Columbia in the spring of 1946 but lived off campus. Although he had several girlfriends, he had known from an early age that he was homosexual and was still uncomfortable with that notion.

Once, as Ginsberg was reading William Blake's poem, "Ah! Sunflower," he experienced an auditory hallucination of a mature voice reading the poem aloud. The voice was not coming out of his head. He felt that he was hearing the voice of William Blake himself. Ginsberg counted this as a spiritual experience and revelation. The sunlight took on an extraordinary clarity, and the blue sky deepened into infinity. Ginsberg recalled, "I suddenly realized that *this* existence was *it*! This was the moment I was born for. This initiation, this consciousness of being alive unto myself. The spirit of the universe was what I was born to realize" (Miles, p. 100). Ginsberg excitedly reported this experience to his friends, family, and teachers, who gave him little support; most of them wondered if he had inherited his mother's illness.

Ginsberg's circle of friends had broadened to include Neal Cassady, a hustler and sort of natural philosopher. Cassady was the first man to welcome Ginsberg into his bed, for which Ginsberg reciprocated with an enduring love. In February of 1949 Ginsberg took Huncke into his apartment during an illness and nursed him to health, but had a hard time supporting him and an even harder time getting rid of him.

Huncke and his criminal friends started to commit robberies and store the stolen loot in Ginsberg's house. Ginsberg finally persuaded the gang to move out and take their loot with them. He helped the thieves load the car and got in with them. Driving the wrong way down a one-way street, they were spotted by a police cruiser. The gang sped up, and during the chase their car struck the curb and turned over. Ginsberg, dazed but unhurt, walked home, but the police found his address and arrested him.

Ginsberg's father and his professors at Columbia plea-bargained so that instead of going to jail Ginsberg entered a mental hospital on 29 June 1949. In Columbia Presbyterian Psychiatric Institute, a young man peered at him and inquired, "Who are you?" "I'm Myshkin," Ginsberg replied, referring to the mystical saintly character in Fyoder Dostoyevsky's novel *The Idiot.* "I'm Kirilov," the man replied, referring to the demonic nihilist* in Dostoyevsky's novel *The Possessed* (Barry, p. 117). Ginsberg's new friend was Carl Solomon, a writer of short, witty polemics.* Ginsberg used the eight months in the hospital to steady his nerves and, under Solomon's tutelage, to broaden his reading to French writers such as Jean Genet, Henri Michaux, and Antonin Artaud.

After his release Ginsberg moved in with his father in Paterson, New Jersey. He wrote to William Carlos Williams, who was writing his long poem, *Paterson.* Williams was impressed by Ginsberg's letters and included one of them in his poem. Williams cautioned Ginsberg about traditional rhymed and metered verse, saying, "In this mode, perfection is basic" (interview of Ginsberg by Bob Rosenthal). Williams suggested a more direct approach to writing poetry in the American vernacular, or common speech, an approach he called objectivism.

Ginsberg moved back to New York City in 1950 and spent the next several years reading and writing. During this time he stayed with friends and supported himself with money from his father and by doing market research and various other jobs. From time to time he sent poems to Williams, who was not impressed. After many tries, Ginsberg sent a poem, "The Bricklayer's Lunch Hour," which Williams enthusiastically praised. Ginsberg then began to work more closely with Williams and put together his first book of poems, *Empty Mirror: Early Poems,* with an introduction by Williams. Ginsberg also spent much of his time trying to persuade publishers to publish the work of his friends Burroughs and Kerouac.

*nihilist someone who believes that traditional values are unfounded and that existence is useless

*polemics the practice of disputing the beliefs of someone else

For more on objectivism, see the essay on Twentieth-Century Modernist Poetry in volume 3.

San Francisco Renaissance

In this period Ginsberg took trips to Mexico and South America to visit friends and build new friendships. He also went to San Francisco in 1954 to visit Neal Cassady, but the reunion went poorly, since Cassady was married and living with his wife. Ginsberg rented an apartment and hung out with new friends whom he met in North Beach, an artists' and writers' neighborhood. A painter, Robert LaVigne, invited Ginsberg to his apartment. Ginsberg was admiring the nude portrait of a young man and falling in love with the person in the picture just as that young man walked in from the other room. This was Peter Orlovsky, a health care worker who became Ginsberg's lifelong lover and companion, and, under Ginsberg's tutelage, a poet. Soon Ginsberg and Orlovsky were inseparable. They took an eternal vow of poverty together, treating it as a wedding vow. In this period, Ginsberg also met the writers Gary Snyder, Philip Whalen, Philip Lamantia, Robert Duncan, Michael McClure, and Kenneth Rexroth.

In 1955, Ginsberg made the unusual decision to write a poem that he could not show to anyone. Its lines were long, like Walt Whitman's and filled with the objective details of the poetry of William Carlos Williams. Describing the lives and adventures of his friends, he also poured out his soul. He sent an early draft (called "Strophes") to Kerouac, who wrote back that he enjoyed Ginsberg's howl, which prompted Ginsberg to change the title to "Howl." On 13 October 1955 a historic poetry reading took place at the Six Gallery. Kenneth Rexroth introduced the readers: Lamantia, McClure, Whalen, Snyder, and Ginsberg. Ginsberg read "Howl" in a calm, even voice, but the power of the poem broke over the listeners like a tidal wave.

I

I saw the best minds of my generation destroyed by
    madness, starving hysterical naked, dragging them-
    selves through the negro streets at dawn looking for
    an angry fix, angelheaded hipsters burning for the
    ancient heavenly connection to the starry dynamo in
    the machinery of night,

who poverty and tatters and hollow-eyed and high
    sat up smoking in the supernatural darkness of

cold-water flats floating across the tops of cities contemplating jazz,
who bared their brains to Heaven under the El* and saw Mohammedan angels staggering on tenement roofs illuminated , . . .

Kerouac yelled, "Go!" at the end of each long line. The experience was unforgettable. That very night the poet and publisher Lawrence Ferlinghetti wrote to Ginsberg asking for a manuscript to include in his new City Lights books series. Ginsberg was now in full possession of his oratorical* voice and tremendous poetic, prophetic style. His "Footnote to Howl" culminates:

Holy New York Holy San Francisco Holy Peoria & Seattle
    Holy Paris Holy Tangiers Holy Moscow Holy
    Istanbul!
Holy time in eternity holy eternity in time holy the
    clocks in space holy the fourth dimension holy the
    fifth International holy the Angel in Moloch!*
Holy the sea holy the desert holy the railroad holy the
    locomotive holy the visions holy the hallucinations
    holy the miracles holy the eyeball holy the abyss!
Holy forgiveness! mercy! charity! faith! Holy! Ours! bodies! suffering! magnanimity!*
Holy the supernatural extra brilliant intelligent kindness
    of the soul!

Kaddish

When his mother, Naomi, died in 1955, Ginsberg was stunned and left so numb he did not know how to react. He did not travel east for the funeral, which was so small that there were not the required ten Jewish men present to recite the ancient prayer for the dead, Kaddish. Following several successful public readings of "Howl" and his other poems, "America," "Supermarket in California," and "Sunflower Sutra," Ginsberg and Orlovsky traveled in North Africa and Europe for a year and half. Meanwhile City Lights published *Howl* and was charged with obscenity. A trial followed, and the judge ruled that *Howl* did have the redeeming merit of being literature.

A Supermarket in California

What thoughts I have of you tonight, Walt Whitman, for I
walked down the sidestreets under the trees with a
headache self-conscious looking at the full moon.
In my hungry fatigue, and shopping for images, I went into
the neon fruit supermarket, dreaming of your enu-
merations!*
What peaches and what penumbras!* Whole families shopping at night! Aisles full of husbands! Wives in the avocados, babies in the tomatoes!—and you, García
Lorca,* what were you doing down by the watermelons?

I saw you, Walt Whitman, childless, lonely old grubber,
poking among the meats in the refrigerator and eye-
ing the grocery boys.
I heard you asking questions of each: Who killed the pork
chops? What price bananas? Are you my Angel?
I wandered in and out of the brilliant stacks of cans following you, and followed in my imagination by the store
detective.
We strode down the open corridors together in our solitary fancy tasting artichokes, possessing every frozen
delicacy, and never passing the cashier.

Where are we going, Walt Whitman? The doors close in an
hour. Which way does your beard point tonight?
(I touch your book and dream of our odyssey in the supermarket and feel absurd.)
Will we walk all night through solitary streets? The trees
add shade to shade, lights out in the houses, we'll
both be lonely.
Will we stroll dreaming of the lost America of love past
blue automobiles in driveways, home to our silent
cottage?
Ah, dear father, graybeard, lonely old courage-teacher,
what America did you have when Charon* quit poling
his ferry and you got out on a smoking bank and
stood watching the boat disappear on the black waters of Lethe?*

*enumeration inven-
tory; count

*penumbra space be-
tween complete
shadow and full light

*Lorca, Federico
García (1898–1936)
Spanish poet. See sep-
arate essay on Lorca in
these volumes.

*Charon in Greek
mythology, the ferry-
man of the dead, often
depicted as an old man

*Lethe in Greek
mythology, a river from
which the dead had to
drink in order to forget
about their past lives
on earth

*Aramaic** vernacular language of Israel, related to Hebrew. The Kaddish is recited in Aramaic.

Ginsberg and Orlovsky came back to New York City in 1958. Kerouac's novel *On the Road* had catapulted him to fame, but these were lean years for Ginsberg and Orlovsky, who remained true to their vow of poverty. In late 1958, Ginsberg was visiting a friend, Zev Putterman. They stayed up all night listening to the music of the rhythm-and-blues singer Ray Charles. Early in the morning, Zev pulled out his old prayer book and read Ginsberg the "Mourner's Kaddish" in its original Aramaic.* Ginsberg absorbed the blues and the ancient prayer, and went home at dawn. He sat down to start what became his greatest poem. It had been several years since Naomi died, and now he poured out her story and his onto pages of poetry. He wrote from 6 A.M. on Saturday until 10 P.M. Sunday, inspired finally to say Kaddish for his mother. The completed poem took Allen sixty-three minutes to read. "Kaddish" so emotionally drained him that he read it aloud only a handful of times in his life.

> No more to say, and nothing to weep for but the Beings
>   in the Dream, trapped in its disappearance,
> sighing, screaming with it, buying and selling pieces of
>   phantom, worshipping each other, worshipping the
>   God included in it all—longing or inevitability?—
>   while it lasts, a Vision—anything more?
> It leaps about me, as I go out and walk the street, look
>   back over my shoulder, Seventh Avenue, the battle-
>   ments of window office buildings shouldering each
>   other high, under a cloud, tall as the sky an in-
>   stant—and the sky above—an old blue place.
> (p. 209)

Cosmopolitan Greetings

Allen's fame and success were now secure. The press scornfully labeled him a "beatnik," but this made him even more famous. In the early 1960s, Ginsberg and Orlovsky traveled for several years in India. There, Ginsberg met many Hindu holy men and learned to sing the praises of God through chanting. When he returned to the United States, he included these chants in his public poetry readings.

Throughout the 1960s, Ginsberg's fame as a poet, speaker, and social activist spread. College campuses were fertile ground for his popularity. In 1965, he was deported from Cuba for protesting the treatment of homosexuals. He went to Prague, Czechoslovakia, where he was elected King of May by one hundred thousand students in an annual May 1 celebration. He was then summarily deported from Czechoslovakia.

Ginsberg worked closely with organizations to end the United States' war against Vietnam, and refused to pay taxes that would contribute to the war. The new youth social movement of the 1960s, known as the hippie movement, embraced him as a natural leader. He calmed the stormy protest crowds outside the Democratic National Convention of 1968 by chanting "om" through a megaphone till he had no voice. His poems about the war, collected under the title *The Fall of America: Poems of These States,* won the National Book Award in 1974.

In the early 1970s, Ginsberg met his most important religious teacher, the Tibetan Buddhist lama Chögyam Trungpa Rinpoche. Ginsberg embraced Tibetan Buddhism completely and practiced it the rest of his life. He collaborated with the folk rock musician Bob Dylan and made his own musical settings for the "Songs of Innocence" and "Songs of Experience" by William Blake. The mature Ginsberg realized that the mysterious voice chanting Blake, which he had heard as a young man, was his own future full voice.

In the final twenty years of his life, having become the most famous living American poet, Ginsberg took on a secretary in order to complete all the tasks he set before himself. He used his Buddhist training and extended his mindfulness teaching* to his many students. In 1974 Allen co-founded the Jack Kerouac School of Disembodied Poetics at the Naropa Institute in Boulder, Colorado, where he taught until his death. Allen Ginsberg had a seemingly endless capacity to undertake new projects and continue long-standing ones. In his final years he also became recognized as a photographer. He was widely interviewed as a living icon/prophet of each generation from the 1940s through the 1990s and was frequently asked to discuss the conclusion of the twentieth century and to make new millennial predictions. His telephone rang continually for talk and advice on every subject from presidential politics to baby namings. Ginsberg still lived modestly in a tenement apartment on New York City's Lower East Side. But in his seventieth year, using income from the sale of his manuscripts and papers, he bought and renovated a loft space. Several months after he moved into his new home, still in his old

*mindfulness teaching in Buddhism, teaching oneself to pay attention to all activities, even including everyday functions such as breathing and walking. This is seen as a way to bring the mind under control and to achieve a state of rest.

neighborhood, his health deteriorated rapidly. In March of 1997, doctors told him that he had incurable liver cancer. A week later, 5 April 1997, he died in his home surrounded by Peter Orlovsky, family, and friends. He had a Buddhist funeral, and his remains were buried next to his father's in B'nai Israel Cemetery in Newark, New Jersey.

IF YOU LIKE the poetry of Ginsberg, you might also like the poetry of Walt Whitman, Gregory Corso, or Gary Snyder.

Selected Bibliography

WORKS BY ALLEN GINSBERG
Poetry

Howl and Other Poems (1956).

Empty Mirror: Early Poems (1961).

Kaddish and Other Poems (1961).

Reality Sandwiches (1963).

Planet News (1968).

The Gates of Wrath: Rhymed Poems, 1948–1951 (1972).

The Fall of America: Poems of These States (1973).

Iron Horse (1973).

Mind Breaths: Poems, 1971–1976 (1978).

Plutonian Ode: Poems, 1977–1980 (1982).

White Shroud: Poems, 1980–1985 (1986).

Cosmopolitan Greetings: Poems, 1986–1992 (1994).

Howl (1995). Annotated by Ginsberg, with a facsimile manuscript.

Illuminated Poems (1996). Illustrated by Eric Drooker.

Death and Fame: The Last Poems, 1993–1997 (1999).

Prose

The Yage Letters (with William Burroughs) (1963).

Gay Sunshine Interview (with Allen Young) (1974).

Composed on the Tongue (1980). Literary conversations, 1967–1977.

Straight Hearts Delight: Love Poems and Selected Letters (with Peter Orlovsky) (1980).

Indian Journals (1970).

Luminous Dreams (1997).

Photography and Catalogs

Allen Ginsberg Photographs (1990).

Snapshot Poetics (1993).

Available Collections

Collected Poems, 1947–1980. New York: Harper Collins, 1984.

Deliberate Prose: Selected Essays, 1959–1995. Edited by Bill Morgan. New York: Harper Collins, 1999.

Journals: Early Fifties Early Sixties. Edited by Gordon Ball. New York: Grove Press, 1977.

Journals: Mid-Fifties. Edited by Gordon Ball. New York: Harper Collins, 1995.

Selected Poems, 1947–1995. New York: Harper Collins, 1996.

Spontaneous Mind: Selected Interviews. Edited by David Carter. New York: Harper Collins, 1999.

Works About Allen Ginsberg

Hyde, Lewis, ed. *On the Poetry of Allen Ginsberg.* Ann Arbor: University of Michigan Press, 1984.

Merrill, Thomas F. *Allen Ginsberg.* Boston: G. K. Hall, 1988.

Miles, Barry. *Ginsberg: A Biography.* New York: Simon and Schuster, 1989.

Watson, Steven. *The Birth of the Beat Generation.* New York: Pantheon, 1995.

THOMAS GRAY
(1716–1771)

by Gary Lenhart

In 1757, Thomas Gray was offered the poet laureateship* of England. At that time, he had published only eight poems. One of them, however, earned him acclaim immediately upon its publication. It would become one of the most popular poems in the language. Although Thomas Gray remains among the most famous of English poets, his poetic reputation continues to rest on that poem, "An Elegy Written in a Country Churchyard." It is so well known that it is commonly referred to only as the "Elegy," despite the many elegies* written by other great poets. Gray declined the honor of poet laureate, giving as his reason that he would be unable to compose easily the occasional verse required of the office.

Early Life and Career

Thomas Gray was born in London on 26 December 1716. His father, Philip Gray, was a London scrivener* and his mother, Dorothy (Antrobus) Gray, the co-owner with her sister of a

*poet laureateship in England, an honor given to an outstanding poet, who was appointed for life as a paid member of the royal household.

*elegy a poem of sorrow or reflection, usually about one who is dead

*scrivener a person who prepares contracts, lends money, solicits investors, and serves as a notary public

*milliner's shop hat store

milliner's shop.* Thomas was the fifth of twelve children, but was the only one to survive infancy. His mother lavished her sole surviving child with attention, but his father was a cruel, volatile man whose physical abuse of his wife was so frequent and extreme that his wife sought legal advice about obtaining a divorce. In eighteenth-century England, however, wife beating did not constitute sufficient legal ground for divorce. So Thomas's mother was forced to remain with her abusive husband, who also insisted that his wife use her earnings to pay all expenses for Thomas's support and education.

At age nine, Thomas was removed from this embattled household when his mother's two brothers, who were tutors at the famous English school Eton, obtained his admission. Gray was delighted by the change in environment and formed schoolboy friendships there that lasted the rest of his life. His first long poem, "Ode on a Distant Prospect of Eton College," praises the joy of student life from the melancholic perspective of an older, disillusioned eye.

> Alas, regardless of their doom,
> The little victims play!
> No sense have they of ills to come,
> Nor care beyond today:
> . . . .
> Thought would destroy their paradise.
> No more; where ignorance is bliss,
> 'Tis folly to be wise.

Quotations from Gray's poetry throughout are taken from Starr and Hendrickson, eds. *The Complete Poems of Thomas Gray: English, Latin, and Greek.*

Except for a brief period in his late middle age, Gray lived as a bachelor on school campuses for the rest of his life.

Gray's best friends at Eton included Richard West, a quiet and sickly boy who also became a poet, and Horace Walpole, son of the English prime minister. Walpole was a spirited, charming rich boy who would become famous for his energetic correspondence with a vast network of friends. After they left Eton, Gray and Walpole attended Cambridge University together. West, who went to Oxford University, remained in close touch with his friends through frequent letters. During his years at Cambridge and immediately following, Gray honed his poetic skills by translating passages of poetry from Latin and Italian.

Upon leaving Cambridge, Walpole invited Gray to join him on a grand tour* of the European continent. Gray could not afford to travel in Walpole's style, so Walpole agreed to sub-

*grand tour a long trip through Europe that was part of the education of British gentlemen in the eighteenth and nineteenth centuries

sidize the trip. For more than a year this unequal arrangement worked fine, as the friends traveled through France and northern Italy. Everywhere they went the studious Gray researched the local history, geography, and manners and towed the reluctant Walpole around to all the tourist sites. Walpole, however, preferred parties to ruins, enjoyed making the acquaintance of fashionable high society, and insisted that the retiring Gray attend a whirl of social events. Despite their genuine affection for each other, the differences in their finances and dispositions eventually led to a harsh falling-out. The offended Gray was forced to humble himself further and borrow money for his return to England from two other rich young Englishmen. Although Gray and Walpole eventually were reconciled and remained close friends for the rest of their lives, they did not speak to each other for the next two years. During these two years Gray began to direct his energy to poetry.

Gray returned to England and Cambridge. During the separation from Walpole, Richard West became Gray's closest friend. The friends shared poetic ambitions and relied increasingly on each other as readers and advisers. So it was with great anticipation that Gray mailed his "Ode on the Spring" to his friend in 1742. He was devastated to learn that West had died before receiving it, but the death of his closest friend seemed to spur him to composition.

During the period between West's death and Gray's reconciliation with Walpole in 1745, Gray wrote the Eton ode, "Hymn to Adversity," and composed the "Sonnet on the Death of Richard West" that was much admired during his lifetime, but later criticized by William Wordsworth in the preface to the *Lyrical Ballads* as an example of strained poetic diction, that is, language contorted for the sake of poetic effect. Yet Wordsworth exempted from that charge five lines:

> A different object do these eyes require.
> My lonely anguish melts no heart but mine;
> And in my breast the imperfect joys expire.
> . . . .
> I fruitless mourn to him, that cannot hear,
> And weep the more, because I weep in vain.

Despite his criticism of Gray's extravagances, Wordsworth used these lines to exemplify the direct language "no different than prose" that he was proposing as a new poetic standard.

*Phoebus** in Greek mythology, the god of the sun

*amorous** relating to love, especially sexual or romantic love

*wonted** usual; habitual

Sonnet on the Death of Mr. Richard West

In vain to me the smiling Mornings shine,
And redd'ning Phœbus* lifts his golden fire:
The birds in vain their amorous* descant join;
Or chearful fields resume their green attire:
These ears, alas! For other notes repine,
A different object do these eyes require.
My lonely anguish melts no heart but mine;
And in my breast the imperfect joys expire.
Yet Morning smiles the busy race to chear,
And new-born pleasure brings to happier men:
The fields to all their wonted* tribute bear:
To warm their little loves the birds complain:
I fruitless mourn to him, that cannot hear,
And weep the more, because I weep in vain.

Indeed, Wordsworth softened his criticism of Gray when he revised his preface in 1802.

By 1745, Gray had settled into the pattern that was to characterize the rest of his life. Walpole was again his closest friend; the two carried on a lively correspondence, and Gray visited Walpole once or more each year, first in London and Windsor and, after 1748, at Walpole's famous mansion at Strawberry Hill. Perhaps Gray's most charming poem was his "Ode on the Death of a Favourite Cat, Drowned in a Tub of Gold Fishes," occasioned by a fatal accident that befell Walpole's pet, Selima. Gray frequently went to London to visit friends and to see operas and plays. After his father's death, Gray spent pleasant summer vacations with his mother and aunts at their home in Stoke Poges. The rest of the time he lived a retiring scholar's life at Cambridge, where he became one of the most learned men in England. He read widely in history, geography, philosophy, and botany. His descriptions of English insects made him perhaps the greatest entomologist of his time. He read many languages, was particularly familiar with Greek and Latin literature, and translated from Norse and Welsh. He sang the music of Italian composer Giovanni Pergolesi and other contemporaries in his tenor voice and accompanied himself on the harpsichord. He was renowned for his fine taste in painting, prints, architecture, and gardening.

Whether distracted by his other interests or simply for lack of spirit, Gray did not write many poems. He suffered all his life from chronic depression and would endure great stretches during which he was incapable of writing. The few poems he did compose reflect his great erudition,* the acquisition of which was his sole enterprise. During more than thirty-five years at Cambridge, he never taught a class or gave a public lecture. He lived on a modest inheritance supplemented by a series of fellowships and professorships, including a well-paid position as Professor of Modern History—the only position that required that he deliver lectures. Nonetheless, Gray never fulfilled such duties. No effort was ever made to relieve him of his post. Over the years, he became a fussy old bachelor known for his solitary and delicate ways. At once, he was the pride of the college and favorite victim of its notorious pranksters. Many critics attribute the narrow emotional range of his verse to this academic seclusion. But readers of the great "Elegy" can attest that despite the limited range of Gray's experience, his imagination was ambitious and broad in its sympathies.

*erudition scholarly learning

The "Elegy"

Although subsequent shifts in English usage have caused Gray's elegy to be known as the "Elegy Written in a Country Churchyard," Gray's original title was "Elegy Wrote in a Country Churchyard." This change reminds us that we can never read a mid-eighteenth-century poem without being aware of changes in the language. The elegy is remarkable for its clarity, restraint, and concision.* There are three voice shifts in the poem. During the first part, the narrator wanders in early evening through the cemetery attached to a small rural church.

*concision brevity; lack of unnecessary detail

> The Curfew tolls the knell* of parting day,
> The lowing herd wind slowly o'er the lea,
> The plowman homeward plods his weary way,
> And leaves the world to darkness and to me.

*knell toll; the sound of a bell

As he watches the farmers return home from their fields, he laments the "rude forefathers" buried in the churchyard, peasants who lived and died anonymous to all the world except for their families and friends. He both pities and admires their circumscribed* lives, prevented as they were by lack of educa-

*circumscribed bounded; limited or restricted

tion, money, and opportunity from accomplishing anything that would have made them famous. He lists sentimentally the domestic pleasures of the rural hearth and then goes on to lament the unfulfilled potential of these uncelebrated dead.

> Let not Ambition mock their useful toil,
> Their homely joys, and destiny obscure;
> Nor Grandeur hear with a disdainful smile,
> The short and simple annals of the poor.
> . . . .
> Some village-Hampden, that with dauntless breast
> The little Tyrant of his fields withstood;
> Some mute inglorious Milton here may rest,
> Some Cromwell guiltless of his country's blood.

There is irony in the poet's invocation of Hampden, John Milton, and Oliver Cromwell. All were heroes of the English Revolution, a bloody civil war that preceded Gray's writing of the elegy by about one hundred years. A contemporary reader would have been well aware of the implication that if the anonymous farmers did not gain worldly fame, at least they caused no great civil strife and bloodshed.

> Far from the madding crowd's ignoble strife,
> Their sober wishes never learn'd to stray;
> Along the cool sequester'd vale of life
> They kept the noiseless tenor of their way.

Part of the elegy's vigor comes from the contradictions in the attitude of the narrator toward his subjects. He celebrates the quiet pleasures of the pastoral life while simultaneously lamenting the lack of opportunities available to the farmers. One source of this contradiction lies in the young man's own conflicted aspirations. He longs for peace from life's hardships and uncertainties but also for adventure and a chance to make a name for himself. He fears that he might die before he can achieve worldly success and, at the same time, deems worldly ambition less noble than the stoic* resolution of the poor. For himself, "who, mindful of the unhonoured dead / Dost in these lines their artless tale relate," he hopes only that a "kindred spirit" will someday be interested in his fate.

At this point the narrator jumps ahead to imagine what might happen after his own death. We are introduced to the

*stoic indifferent to pleasure and pain; unemotional

second voice in the poem, that of a "hoary-headed swain."* The swain does not know the young poet but often sees him wandering through the rural setting, not just at twilight but from "peep of dawn."

> Hard by yon wood, now smiling as in scorn,
> Mutt'ring his wayward fancies he wou'd rove,
> Now drooping, woeful wan, like one forlorn,
> Or craz'd with care, or cross'd in hopeless love.

Then, one morning, the swain misses the young poet. Two days later, the poet is buried among the "unhonour'd Dead" in the same churchyard that we have heard him describe.

The last lines of the poem, representing the third voice, are given to the epitaph inscribed on the young poet's tombstone. Critics of the poem have attacked the epitaph for shifting the focus of the poem from the anonymous laborers buried in the churchyard to the figure of the poet cut down in his youth. But it is the anxiety of the young poet, who imagines himself dying before he can write anything that might bring him fame, that renders him so sympathetic to the villagers who have died in anonymity. Like Gray's beloved friend Richard West, the young poet of the elegy, despite large talents and "soul sincere," dies "A Youth to Fortune and to Fame unknown."

Gray was noted for his taste and erudition, not his imagination. Because his critical instincts were so refined, he must have been aware of his own limits. His literary ambitions understandably refused them. In his effort to be as inventive and impassioned as the Norse and Welsh poetry he admired, he often pushed his poems into contortions and ornaments that strike us as ludicrously baroque.* The elegy shows none of these defects. In this poem Gray's skill is entirely at the service of his simple, but not-so-simple subject.

However personal its inspiration, Gray's poem had great relevance to his whole society. It came at a time when the laboring classes were entering the stage of history. The poet died just before the American and French revolutions, and his genuine sympathy for the rural poor is a new note in English poetry. Although the poems of Edmund Spenser and John Milton contained classical shepherds, Gray's elegy is the first great English poem in which the poor appear as themselves, working people who may be minor characters in grand historical terms but who have their own emotions and travails.* You

*hoary-headed swain a herdsman or shepherd whose hair is gray or white with age

*baroque highly ornate or decorated

*travails tasks; pains

*sea change a dramatic shift

*foreshadow to give clues that suggest events yet to come

*light verse verse that is written mainly to entertain and is usually humorous or witty. For examples and a more detailed explanation, see essay on Ogden Nash in these volumes.

*allusion a passing reference to fictional or historical characters, events, or places the writer assumes the reader will recognize

*contrived complicated or artificial

have only to compare Gray's country folk to Shakespeare's rural clowns or John Dryden's servants to appreciate the sea change* in attitude toward minor characters. In the elegy the poor no longer serve as merely backdrop to the actions of the nobility. Gray foreshadowed* the approach to common subjects that later seemed so revolutionary in Wordsworth and young Samuel Taylor Coleridge.

Other Writings

Among Gray's other poems, the best known are the "Ode on a Distant Prospect of Eton College" and the "Sonnet on the Death of Richard West." Of all Gray's poems, they are most in keeping with the style, diction, and mood of the elegy. Although like his contemporaries Gray composed light verse,* the wit ascribed to him by his friends does not translate well to our era. The social successes of "Ode on the Death of a Favourite Cat, Drowned in a Tub of Gold Fishes" and the poem "A Long Story" contributed to making Gray's poetic reputation.

But it was his two odes, "The Bard" and "The Progress of Poesy," that Gray deemed his greatest poems. The form suited the scholarly Gray; his odes were so rich in allusions* that even his closest friends begged him to footnote the poems so they might understand them. Gray refused, claiming that he wrote only for the few superior readers who might understand him without the assistance of scholarly notes, and the Odes languished in obscurity for ten years. Gray was so disappointed with their reception that he supplied plentiful notes when he included the odes in his collected *Poems* in 1768.

Even with Gray's notes, the odes appear contrived* and obscure to most readers. As their titles indicate, they are poems about poetry, entirely literary in inspiration and derivative in content. Originality was not as prized in the eighteenth century as it became during the Romantic era of the nineteenth century and remains today. Gray's odes did not fail because they lacked originality but because they failed to repay the demands they made on readers. The failure of the odes was a major disappointment to Gray, and after their publication he never again attempted to compose a major poem.

Gray devoted the last fifteen years of his life to writing a descriptive catalog of English insects and to researching Welsh and Norse poetry. When his health permitted, he took summer jaunts to what remained of the English wilderness and figured importantly in popularizing the Romantic taste for the picturesque. Although he wrote no more poems, his travel diaries—in their qualities of close attention, botanical curiosity, and precise description—anticipate the prose works of William Bartram, William Cobbett, and William and Dorothy Wordsworth. For many years Gray suffered from what may have been wrongly diagnosed as gout. In the summer of 1771, he experienced increasingly severe attacks of apparent kidney illness and died at Cambridge on 30 July.

Selected Bibliography

WORKS BY THOMAS GRAY
Original Publication

An Elegy Wrote in a Country Church Yard (1751).

Designs by Mr. R. Bentley, for Six Poems by Mr. T. Gray (1753).

Poems by Mr. Gray (1768).

Poems by Mr. Gray (1773).

The Works of Thomas Gray. 2 vols. Edited by Rev. John Mitford (1816).

Poems and Letters of Thomas Gray, with Memoirs of His Life and Writings by William Mason (1820).

Collected and Critical Editions

The Complete Poems of Thomas Gray: English, Latin, and Greek. Edited by H. W. Starr and J. R. Hendrickson. Oxford, U.K.: Clarendon Press, 1966.

The Correspondence of Gray, Walpole, West, and Ashton (1734–1771). 2 vols. Edited by Paget Toynbee. Oxford, U.K.: Clarendon Press, 1915.

Correspondence of Thomas Gray. Edited by Paget Toynbee and Leonard Whibley. Oxford, U.K.: Clarendon Press, 1935.

An Elegy Written in a Country Church Yard: The Text of the First Quarto with the Variants of the Mss. and of the Early Editions. Edited and with an introduction and appendixes by Francis Griffin Stokes. Oxford, U.K.: Clarendon Press, 1929.

The Letters of Thomas Gray, Including the Correspondence of Gray and Mason, 3 vols. Edited by Duncan Tovey. London: G. Bell, 1900–1912.

The Works of Thomas Gray in Prose and Verse, 4 vols. Edited by Edmund Gosse. New York: A. C. Armstrong, 1885.

WORKS ABOUT THOMAS GRAY

Arnold, Matthew. *Essays in Criticism: Second Series.* London: Macmillan, 1913.

Blake, William. *William Blake's Designs for Gray's Poems.* Introduction by H. J. C. Grierson. London: Oxford University Press, 1922.

Brooks, Cleanth. *The Well Wrought Urn: Studies in the Structure of Poetry.* New York: Harcourt, Brace, and World, 1947.

Hough, Graham. *The Romantic Poets.* London: Hutchinson's University Library, 1953.

Johnson, Samuel. *Lives of the English Poets.* London: Oxford University Press, 1964.

Ketton-Cremer, R. W. *Thomas Gray: A Biography.* Cambridge, U.K.: Cambridge University Press, 1955.

Weinfield, Henry. *The Poet Without a Name: Gray's* Elegy *and the Problem of History.* Carbondale: Southern Illinois University Press, 1991.

Wordsworth, William. *Lyrical Ballads by Wordsworth and Coleridge: The Text of the 1798 Edition with the Additional 1800 Poems and the Prefaces.* Edited by R. L. Brett and A. R. Jones. New York: Barnes and Noble, 1963.

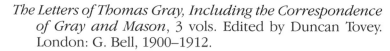

More About Gray:

You can find information about Thomas Gray on the Internet at: http://library.advanced.org /3247/poets/gray.thomas/

NICOLÁS GUILLÉN
(1902–1989)

by Alba Delia Hernández

I t is no surprise that the rebellious student who refused to continue attending Catholic school because his "great torture was to have to hear mass every day" went on to become one of Cuba's finest and most controversial poets (Augier, 1984, p. 17). Nicolás Guillén worked to create a Cuban-flavored poetry, one that was neither white nor black but that celebrated both Cuba's Spanish and its African heritage (until then ignored in poetry). Strongly believing in the need to break with tradition when the old ways no longer spoke to the present, Guillén sought to use his poetry to "express our time with things of our time" (Augier, 1984, p. 113). To this end, he shocked his critics and readers when he used the rhythms of popular Afro-Cuban dance music as a basis for his poetry.

Quotations from Augier's *Estudio biografico critico* throughout were translated by Alba Delia Hernández. Quotations from Guillén's *Prosa de prisa* throughout were translated by Alba Delia Hernández.

Childhood and Loss

Guillén came from a family committed to social change and to literature. His paternal grandfather had been a poet and

403

teacher. His father, a popular figure in the political affairs of his community, worked as a printer and was the director of the local newspaper. His mother was Argelia Batista y Arrieta. Guillén's entrance into this world was such a joyous occasion that news of his birth on 10 July 1902 was printed in his father's newspaper: "At two in the morning, the wife of our director, Sr. Nicolás Guillén, gave birth to a robust boy" (Augier, 1984, p. 11). Guillén was the oldest of six children. As a student, Guillén had difficulty conforming to the stuffy atmosphere of many of the schools he attended. It was in a Catholic school he briefly attended that Guillén first felt the pangs of racism and discrimination, being one of the very few black children there. His education, however, did not suffer; his father's teaching nurtured him more than any school could have.

Despite the obstacles present in a society that had only recently come out of slavery and oppression, Guillén's father rose to a position of influence and popularity in the provincial town of Camagüey, Cuba. A veteran of the Cuban War for Independence, he concerned himself with the struggles of the working class and spoke openly against colonialism. Guillén always thought of him as his greatest teacher and friend. While other children were asked to leave the company of older men, his father would occasionally allow young Nicolás to sit in on discussions of national politics. The smell of fresh ink was ever present as he helped his father with the production of his newspaper. This atmosphere undoubtedly fed what became Guillén's second great professional interest, journalism.

Books were readily available in the family library, and with the help of his father, Guillén read the Spanish classics. So intensely did his father encourage his love of journalism and literature that Guillén preferred the company of books to that of other children his age. By the age of fourteen, he had begun writing poetry. His first poems were about both nature and politics; he wrote poems to autumn leaves, but one poem in particular he dedicated to Robespierre, the French revolutionary. In that poem we find the subject enveloped in blood amid a pyramid of crushed skulls.

With such a committed and caring father, it is not hard to imagine the agony the fifteen-year-old Guillén felt when his father was murdered by members of conservative government troops. This tragedy left a lifelong wound in Guillén's soul. Thirty-five years after the murder, Guillén evokes the memory

The Cuban War for Independence was fought against Spain between 1895 and 1898. The war ended after the United States intervened.

of his father in "Elegía Camagüeyana" (Camagüeyan elegy), a poem from his book *Elegías* (Elegies):

> No puedo hablar, pero me gritan
> la noche, este misterio;
> No puedo hablar, pero me obligan
> el perfil de mi padre, su índice de recuerdo:
> no puedo hablar, pero me llaman
> su detenida voz y el sollozo del viento.
>
> (*Man-making Words*)

> I cannot speak, but they cry out to me
> the night, this mystery;
> I cannot speak, but they force me to
> the profile of my father, his index of memory;
> I cannot speak, but they call to me
> his arrested voice and the sobbing of the wind.
>
> (translated by Alba D. Hernandez)

For a poet to claim that he "cannot speak" reflects a moment of great anxiety. The job of the poet *is* to speak. The physical and aural* images of his father, however, prompt the poet to do what he claims that he cannot do—continue to write. Even after his tragic death, Guillén's father inspires him to go on writing.

*aural concerning the sense of hearing

Poet in Law School

After the death of his father, Guillén and his brother had to assume financial responsibility for the family. Guillén worked as a typesetter during the day, and during the evening he continued his studies. In the remarkably short time of two years, he finished his bachelor's degree. Within the community, he had already distinguished himself as a poet, publishing some of his verse in a local magazine.

In 1920 Guillén left Camagüey to study law in the capital, Havana. He remained there only one year, for he found the people of Havana too "excessive" and the city "a barbaric hubbub of the infernal metropolis" (*Prosa de prisa,* p. 290). The only fruit Guillén bore in law school was three sonnets he wrote expressing his repudiation of it. He soon returned to Camagüey and, in 1922, wrote his first small book of poems.

This poem is from Marzán, ed., *Luna, Luna: Creative Writing Ideas from Spanish, Latin American, and Latino Literature.*

Sensemayá

Mayombé—bombe—mayombé!
Mayombé—bombe—mayombé!
Mayombé—bombe—mayombé!

La culebra tiene los ojos de vidrio;
la culebra viene y se enreda en un palo;
con sus ojos de vidrio, en un palo
con sus ojos de vidrio.
La culebra camina sin patas;
la culebra se esconde en la yerba;
caminando se esconde en la yerba;
caminando sin patas.

Mayombé—bombe—mayombé!
Mayombé—bombe—mayombé!
Mayombé—bombe—mayombé!
Tú le das con el hacha, y se muere:
dale ya!
No le des con el pie, que te muerde,
no le des con el pie, que se va!

Sensemayá, la culebra,
sensemayá.
Sensemayá, con sus ojos,
sensemayá.
Sensemayá, con su lengua,
sensemayá.
Sensemayá, con su boca,
sensemayá . . .

La culebra muerta no puede comer;
la culebra muerta no puede silbar;
no puede caminar;
no puede correr.
La culebra muerta no puede mirar;
la culebra muerta no puede beber;
no puede respirar,
no puede morder!

Mayombé—bombe—mayombé!
Sensemayá, la culebra . . .
Mayombé—bombe—mayombé!
Sensemayá, no se mueve . . .
Mayombé—bombe—mayombé!
Sensemayá la culebra . . .
Mayombé—bombe—mayombé!
Sensemayá, se murió!

Sensemayá (Song to Kill a Snake)

Mayombé—bombe—mayombé!
Mayombé—bombe—mayombé!
Mayombé—bombe—mayombé!

The snake has eyes of glass;
the snake comes and wraps around a stick;
with its eyes of glass, on a stick,
with its eyes of glass.
The snake walks without feet;
the snake hides in the grass;
walking, it hides in the grass,
walking without feet.
Mayombé—bombe—mayombé!
Mayombé—bombe—mayombé!
Mayombé—bombe—mayombé!

You hit it with an ax and it dies:
Hit it now!
Don't hit it with your foot, or it'll bite you,
don't hit it with your foot, or it'll run!

Sensemayá, the snake, the snake,
sensemayá.
Sensemayá, with its eyes,
sensemayá.
Sensemayá, with its tongue,
sensemayá.
Sensemayá, with its mouth,
sensemayá . . .

The dead snake can't eat;
the dead snake can't hiss;
it cannot walk,
it cannot run.
The dead snake can't see;
the dead snake can't drink;
it cannot breathe,
it cannot bite!

Mayombé—bombe—mayombé!
Sensemayá, the snake, the snake . . .
Mayombé—bombe—mayombé!
Sensemayá doesn't move . . .
Mayombé—bombe—mayombé!
Sensemayá, the snake, the snake . . .
Mayombé—bombe—mayombé!
Sensemayá is dead!

These were never published, because Guillén found them of little artistic merit. Disappointed, Guillén immersed himself in editing and publishing a literary magazine he had founded and in writing for local newspapers. Despite his criticisms of the city, Guillén returned to Havana, where he published editorials in a local paper that gained him recognition as an intellectual opponent of the dictator of Cuba, Gerardo Machado. For five years Guillén wrote not one line of verse.

A Voice in the Dark

At the behest of a respected editor, Guillén published his old poems in a column of a Havana newspaper. His readers demanded more. "Who is this man?" one critic asked. "Bring him to light." But Guillén was in a bind. His poems were almost ten years old. In his own words: "The truth was that I had not even one more line" (*Prosa de prisa*, p. 293). This anxiety sparked a new voice. One night, while in a half-asleep, half-awake state, Guillén heard a voice clearly whisper into his ear, "Negro bembón." The voice, "accompanied by a special and new rhythm, continued for the rest of the night, each time more profound and imperious" (*Prosa de prisa*, p. 294). He could not sleep. Getting out of bed early, he set pen to paper and began writing. The lines came to him "as if remembering something he had once known" (*Prosa de prisa*, p. 294). At the end of a whole day, he had produced the eight poems that appeared in his first published book of poems, *Motivos de son* (*Son Motifs*).

The book was an immediate scandal and success. Based on the popular and rhythmic Afro-Cuban dance music, the *son*, the poems capture the mood and life of Havana. Both in form and content the poems were radically innovative. Never in Cuban history had anyone taken popular music, the authentic music of the black masses, and made it the basis for the rhythm in their poetry; never had any poet written about the black Cuban experience from an insider's perspective.

The poems are rhythmic and simple and use techniques of repetition, *jitanjáfora*,* and onomatopoeia* to evoke the beating of drums. At once a celebration of the beauty of the black community and a cry against the racial injustices blacks suffer, the poems capture the natural rhythms of the vernacu-

*jitanjáfora a word of no particular meaning invented by the artist

*onomatopoeia the use of words that mimic or suggest the sounds or physical qualities of the thing spoken about, as in "the door banged shut" or "out of the swamp in slimy, slippery shoes."

lar speech spoken by the Cuban poor. In "Negro bembón" (Big-lipped black man), Guillén takes a feature that was often a source of scorn, the big lips of the black man, and makes it a source of pride. In "Michiquita" ("My Little Woman"), a black man shows off his "little woman":

> Black as she is,
> I wouldn't trade
> the woman I got
> for no other woman.
>
> She wash, iron, sew,
> and man,
> can that woman cook!
>
> (*Man-making Words*)

Guillén received both praise and criticism for this collection. Some critics who had admired his early, more traditional poems argued that the new poems were "vulgar" and urged Guillén to abandon his new muse. Guillén countered his critics openly and vehemently. If a poet could write sonnets on imaginary "love queens," "gardens," "the moon, distant stars, lips like rubies," Guillén demanded, then why could a poet not write about black Cuban life (Augier, 1984, p. 116)? Black academics argued that the speech he captured was a voice they had never heard a black Cuban speak. To this criticism, Guillén responded, "They are the deaf who do not want to hear" (Augier, 1984, p. 111).

Drowning out the din of Guillén's critics was the ecstatic praise of his admirers. Guillén's poetry had won him the support of many people inside and outside Cuba. One prominent supporter and lifelong friend was the African American poet Langston Hughes, who was writing poetry in the United States based on the rhythms of blues and jazz, the music of the African-American people. Without question, Hughes's work inspired Guillén's poetry. Among other admirers was the young Spanish poet Federico García Lorca, who after visiting Cuba in March of 1930, wrote his own poem based on the rhythms of the *son,* "Iréa Santiago" ("I Will Go to Santiago"). There is no doubt that Guillén relished the stir he created. In a letter to Hughes, he mischievously wrote that he had created a great scandal.

True Color

Guillén's second book, *Sóngoro cosongo: Poemas mulatos,* reflects his lifelong attempt to create a truly Cuban poetry—a poetry that is neither white nor black but that embodies the influence of both the African and Spanish heritages that make up Cuba. This dynamic fusion is reflected not only in content but in form as well, where Guillén synthesizes the rhythms of the *son* with more traditional forms, like the romance,* and with meters* more typical of the classical Spanish literary tradition. Guillén explains in the prologue to his book:

> These are mulatto verses. They share the same elements that enter into the ethnic composition of Cuba. . . . And the two races that emerge on the surface on the island, though apparently distant, are linked subterraneously to each other, like those underwater bridges which secretly join two continents. Therefore the spirit of Cuba is mestizo.* And from the spirit through the skin our true color will emerge (*¡Patria o muerte!,* pp. 20–21).

Guillén's synthesis of both African and Spanish heritages is nowhere more evident than in his poem "Balada de los dos abuelos" ("Ballad of the Two Grandfathers"), published in *West Indies, Ltd.: Poems.* The poem draws on Guillén's own ancestry (he had a white great-grandfather and a black great-grandfather). In the poem he confronts them, one as the master and the other as the slave. The grandfathers speak alternating lines, his black grandfather repeating, "¡Me muero!" ("I'm dying!") and his white grandfather repeating, "¡Me canso!" ("I'm tired!"). In the last stanza Guillén unites them:

> los dos en la noche sueñan
> y andan, andan.
> Yo los junto.
>   —¡Federico!
> ¡Facundo! Los dos se abrazan.
> Los dos suspiran. Los dos
> las fuertes cabezas alzan;
> los dos del mismo tamaño,
> bajo las estrellas altas;
> los dos del mismo tamaño,
> ansia negra y ansia blanca,

romance a Spanish variation on the ballad—a short narrative folk song that focuses on the most dramatic part of a story

meter in poetry, the rhythmic pattern within each line

mestizo of mixed (normally European and American Indian) ancestry

los dos del mismo tamaño,
gritan, sueñan, lloran, cantan.
Sueñan, lloran, cantan.
Lloran, cantan.
¡Cantan!

(*Man-making Words*)

both dreaming in the night
and walking, walking.
I bring them together.
    "Federico!
Facundo!" They embrace. They sigh,
they raise their sturdy heads;
both of equal size,
beneath the high stars;
both of equal size,
a Black longing, a White longing,
both of equal size,
they scream, dream, weep, sing.
They dream, weep, sing.
They weep, sing.
Sing!

(*Man-making Words*)

The poem, a variation on the Spanish ballad,* employs repetitions of lines ("los dos del mismo tamaño") and of "o" and "a" sounds, to suggest the beating of drums, giving the poem a hypnotic, even primal feel. The repetitions in the last four lines, and their shortening length, rush the poem to its heightening end—the emphatic final drumbeat "¡Cantan!" that links the two grandfathers in song. There are no longer two distinct voices, but one of "equal size."

In *West Indies, Ltd.,* Guillén also published one of his most popular poems, "Sensemayá: Canto para matar una culebra" ("Sensemayá: Song to Kill a Snake"). The poem draws heavily on Guillén's signature use of *jitanjáfora.* The words "Mayombé-bombe-mayombé" and "Sensemayá," invented by Guillén, have no particular meaning but serve to suggest the beating of drums and the hissing of snakes; they give the poem a magical and primal aura. Through the chanting of these incantations,* the speaker of the poem finally kills the snake: "Sensemayá, se murió!" (Logan, pp. 146–148).

*ballad rhythmic poem that tells a story and is often meant to be sung

*incantation a spell or chant

Social Protest

Fulgencio Batista was a Cuban dictator (1933–1940) and president (1940–1944 and 1952–1958). He was overthrown by an armed revolt led by Fidel Castro in 1959.

The 1930s marked a period of political instability in Cuba. Several presidents were overthrown, and the military, headed by Fulgencio Batista (who later became president of Cuba), exercised most of the rule on the island. At the same time, the workers' movement steadily grew, criticizing, among many other things, the government's facilitation of the economic exploitation of Cuba by the United States.

In the midst of this social unrest, Guillén published *West Indies, Ltd., Cantos para soldados y sones para turistas,* (Songs for soldiers and poems for tourists), and *España: Poema en cuatro angustias y una esperanza* (Spain: a poem in four anguished voices and one of hope). These works firmly established Guillén as a poet of the people, one who sees poetry as a vehicle for social protest and as an expression of a national collective voice. His loyalties lie with the leftist workers' movement, decrying colonialism, imperialism, and the exploitation of not only the Cuban community but the whole of Latin America.

Guillén's drift toward the political left culminated in a visit to Spain during the Spanish Civil War (1936–1939), a visit he remembered as a defining moment in his life. Opposed to the fascist regime, he traveled to Spain in 1937 as one of the Cuban delegates to the antifascist Second International Congress of Writers for the Defense of Culture. In that same year, Guillén joined the Communist Party. Between 1942 and 1959, he traveled widely throughout Latin America, Europe, the USSR, and China, attending conferences and social events. During this period his poems take a militant tone that reflects his view of revolution as the only venue that will lead to Cuban and Latin American liberation.

After the triumph of the 1959 Cuban Revolution, Guillén returned to Cuba for good. His poetry of this period takes a less combative tone and reflects a sense of pride in and fellowship with the Cuban people. This pride is reflected in poems like "Tengo" ("I Have"; published in a 1964 collection of the same title), where he lists all the things that he, and by extension all the Cuban people, now have: "I have let's see: / I have the pleasure of walking my country, / the owner of all there is in it, / / / I have that having the land I have the sea." The poem ends with the proud declaration: "I have, let's see / I have what was coming to me" (*¡Patria o muerte!*).

Legacy of Compassion

Guillén's poetry reflects his intimate relationship with the people that surrounded him, particularly those whom Guillén saw as victims of oppression and discrimination. Even when addressing social concerns, his poetry is profoundly personal in tone and attempts to see humanity even in the face of tragedy and violence. In a poem he wrote during the Spanish Civil War, "No sé por qué piensas tú" (Why, soldier, does it seem to you; from his collection *Cantos para soldados y sones para turistas*), Guillén addresses an enemy soldier not as a cog in a military machine but as a palpable human being. He asks:

> No sé por qué piensas tú,
> soldado, que te odio yo,
> si somos la misma cosa
> yo,
> tú.
>
> Why, soldier, does it seem to you
> that I hate you,
> if we're exactly the same,
> me
> you.
>
>   (*¡Patria o muerte!*)

The poem continues the alternating line endings of "yo" and "tú"—"me" and "you"—to drive home what was most important to Guillén, equality and compassion. His life and poetry is testament to his mission of breaking down the walls of hatred, to see the humanity in all of us.

Selected Bibliography

WORKS BY NICOLÁS GUILLÉN
Poetry in Spanish

Motivos de son (1930).

Sóngoro cosongo: Poemas mulatos (1931).

West Indies, Ltd.: Poemas (1934).

IF YOU LIKE the poetry of Guillén, you might also like the poetry of Langston Hughes or Federico García Lorca.

Cantos para soldados y sones para turistas (1937).

España: Poemas en cuatro angustias y una esperanza (1937).

El son entero: Suma poética, 1929–1946 (1947).

La paloma de vuelo popular: Elegías (1958).

Tengo (1964).

El gran zoo (1967).

Nueva antologia (Compilation and prologue by Ángel Augier) (1979).

Prose

Prosa de prisa: 1929–1972, 3 vols. (Compilation, prologue, and notes by Ángel Augier) (1975).

Poetry in English Translation

The Daily Daily. Translation and with an introduction by Vera M. Kutzinski. Berkeley: University of California Press, 1989.

Man-making Words: Selected Poems of Nicolás Guillén. Translated, annotated, and with an introduction by Robert Márquez and David McMurray. Amherst, Mass.: University of Massachussetts Press, 1972.

¡Patria o muerte! The Great Zoo and Other Poems. Translated and edited by Robert Márquez. New York: Monthly Review Press, 1972.

WORKS ABOUT NICOLÁS GUILLÉN

Augier, Ángel. *Nicolás Guillén: Estudio biográfico-crítico.* Havana: Ediciones Union, 1984.

Logan, William Bryant. "Sound, Rhythm, Music: Using a Poem by Nicolás Guillén." In *Luna, Luna: Creative Writing Ideas from Spanish, Latin American, and Latino Literature.* Edited by Julio Marzán. New York: Teachers & Writers Collaborative, 1997.

Rampersad, Arnold. *I Too Sing America.* Vol. 1 of *The Life of Langston Hughes.* New York: Oxford University Press, 1986.

Smart, Ian Isidore. *Nicolás Guillén: Popular Poet of the Caribbean.* Columbia: University of Missouri Press, 1990.

ROBERT HAYDEN

(1913–1980)

by Odetta D. Norton

Born Asa Bundy Sheffey on 4 August 1913 to Ruth and Asa Sheffey of Detroit, Michigan, Robert Earl Hayden was raised by foster parents Sue Ellen Westerfield and William Hayden after his biological parents separated shortly after his birth. His birth mother soon moved to Buffalo, New York, drawn to the city's arts, culture, and urban life. Unlike his father, however, Ruth Sheffey maintained a relationship with her son and returned to Detroit to visit Hayden from time to time. It is likely that Sheffey was the only adult that encouraged and shared the young Hayden's interest in the arts.

Despite poor vision, Hayden taught himself to read before he entered school. Severely nearsighted by the age of eight, Hayden read books from the library and struggled to put his own words on paper while the other kids in his Detroit neighborhood played outside. When his violin teacher discovered that he was playing only by ear and not reading the music, she dismissed him. From then on, Hayden engaged his ear with language instead of music.

Quotations of Hayden's poetry throughout are taken from Glaysher, ed., *Collected Poems.*

*****paramours** passionate lovers

In her poem numbered 1129, Emily Dickinson prescribed, "Tell all Truth but tell it Slant / Success in Circuit lies / Too bright for our infirm Delight / The Truth's Superb Surprise / As Lightning to the Children eased / with explanation kind / The Truth must dazzle gradually / Or every man be blind."

*****baroque** excessively flamboyant or ornate

Years later, Hayden explained that the conflicts and tensions in his foster family were worse than the poverty the household endured. Divided affections upset the household. The poet's natural mother visited often; his foster mother's heartbreak over a man she loved and married before she met her second husband inspired "The Ballad of Sue Ellen Westerfield," published in Hayden's *Collected Poems.* Depicting a passionate love affair on a Mississippi riverboat just after the Civil War, the poem describes the paramours* as "fugitives whose dangerous only hidingplace / was love." Sue Ellen (later, Sue Ellen Hayden) cursed fate because of her doomed love affair and took out her anger against her foster son.

When, in his forties, Hayden applied for documents to leave the country for a visit to Bulgaria, he found out that he had never been legally adopted. This emotional discovery became the subject for his poem "Names." Hayden often wrote about subjects from his own life, although he told truth "slant," like his poetic forebear, the nineteenth-century American poet Emily Dickinson. In his *Collected Prose,* he explains, "Frequently I'm writing about myself but speaking through a mask, a persona" (p. 120). Hayden's personas include a diver, a tattooed man, and a witch doctor.

In Hayden's earliest world, joy was rare. He later vividly described the poverty-stricken neighborhood where he grew up. The ironic "Elegies for Paradise Valley," in his *American Journal,* the last of nine books he published in his lifetime, begins "My shared bedroom's window / opened on alley stench." Another poem that talks about his childhood is "Those Winter Sundays," in which Hayden explores the complexities of love and family. One of his most widely anthologized poems, it begins "Sundays too my father got up early / . . . with cracked hands that ached / from labor in the weekday weather made / banked fires blaze. No one ever thanked him." Hayden easily managed alliteration and assonance (the repetition of consonant and vowel sounds) in these and many lines in his poems.

Race and Narrative

Rich vocabulary also distinguishes such poems as "A Ballad of Remembrance," which Hayden described as "baroque"* and some critics considered an example of "hypererudition." Here are two typical lines from the poem: "What will you have? she inquired, the sallow vendeuse / of prepared tarnishes and jokes of nacre and ormolu. . . ." Because New Orleans is the setting for the poem, Hayden seems to have chosen words like "vendeuse,"* "nacre,"* and "ormolu"* to evoke the atmosphere of the French- and Spanish-influenced port city that prospered for centuries in the trade of African slaves. He also depicted personalities from Mardi Gras floats representing three popular political positions in the African American community. The "Zulu king" favors accommodation. The "saints and the angels and the mermaids" cry for love. The "gun metal priestess" demands hate, then "pinwheeled / away in coruscations* of laughter, scattering those others before her like foil stars." There is a subtle alliteration here, the repetition of two letters (*s* and *c*), which together make cutting sounds. In the complexity of the poem's vocabulary and its undertone of racial tension, Mark Van Doren, a white critic and friend of Hayden's, becomes a stabilizing character: "your presence was shore where I rested / released from the hoodoo of that dance, where I spoke / with my true voice again."

*vendeuse a saleswoman, particularly one who sells clothing (a feminine form of "vendor")

*nacre mother-of-pearl, a pearly substance from the inside of a mollusk shell

*ormolu bronze or brass that is gilded; typically used as furniture embellishment

*coruscations flashes of light; brilliant displays of wit

An Artist in Society

Throughout his life and writing career, Hayden struggled with the dilemmas of an artist in society. Inspired by the story "A Very Old Man with Enormous Wings," by Nobel Prize–winner Gabriel García Márquez, Hayden's "For a Young Artist" describes how society treats the artist: "Leftovers were set out for him; / he ate sunflowers / instead and the lice crawling his feathers." (Sunflowers recur in all his poetry as a symbol of life against all odds.)

Hayden revised his work endlessly, John Hatcher, in *From the Auroral Darkness: The Life and Poetry of Robert Hayden,* quotes Hayden: "If I have a missionary zeal about anything it is this. Technique is very important to me. I've not spent my life as a poet just to put words together in any old way" (p. 89).

"The Poet of Perfect Pitch"

For nearly two decades, beginning in the early 1950s, Hayden taught English at Fisk University in Nashville, Tennessee. A former student has said that few students or professors at Fisk knew that Hayden was a poet; even fewer cared. It was said that he had "the best underground reputation of any poet in America" (*Collected Prose,* p. 203). His work was seen in only a few magazines. He wrote for some thirty years before his poetry was taken on by a major book publisher.

Hayden had hoped his reputation would rise, and later in life, in some circles at least, it did. The poet and critic Michael S. Harper praised Hayden this way: "His gifts include a feel for the formality of pattern and a resolute purity of diction and tone which musicians would call *perfect pitch*" (Williams, pp. 34–35). More than one critic on more than one occasion has echoed Harper's words and hailed Hayden as the "poet of perfect pitch."

In Hayden's early years, the black American poet Langston Hughes was the first famous poet he ever met. Hughes was a Harlem Renaissance* poet. In his *Collected Poems,* Hayden recalls the mood of the Harlem Renaissance in " 'Summertime and the Living. . . ,' " which ends

> . . . then Elks parades and big splendiferous*
> Jack Johnson in his diamond limousine
> set the ghetto burgeoning* with fantasies
> of Ethiopia spreading her gorgeous wings.

The heavyweight champion boxer Jack Johnson is a symbol of glory in a neighborhood where the poet says no one plants roses, and no one offers them until someone dies.

Many famous people became subjects of Hayden's verse. In "Homage to the Empress of the Blues," a tribute to the blues singer Bessie Smith, the poet writes:

> Because there was a man somewhere in a candystripe
>   silk shirt,
> gracile* and dangerous as a jaguar and because a
>   woman moaned
> for him in sixty-watt gloom and mourned him Faithless
>   Love
> Twotiming Love Oh Love Oh Careless Aggravating
>   Love, . . .

The blues singer's ability to show grace despite life's hardships is the spirit embodied in the poem. In poems like "The Whipping," " 'As My Blood Was Drawn,' " and "Names," Hayden chronicled some of his own hardships.

*Harlem Renaissance** a period (1920s) of enormous creativity in literature, music, and art in the African American community of Harlem in New York City that was echoed in other major cities across the United States

*splendiferous** extravagantly showy

*burgeoning** rapidly expanding

*gracile** slender and graceful

Names

Once they were sticks and stones
I feared would break my bones:
Four Eyes. And worse.
Old Four Eyes fled
to safety in the danger zones
Tom Swift and Kubla Khan traversed.

When my fourth decade came,
I learned my name was not my name.
I felt deserted, mocked.
Why had the old ones lied?
No matter. They were dead.

And the name on the books was dead,
like the life my mother fled,
like the life I might have known.
You don't exist—at least
not legally, the lawyer said.
As ghost, double, alter ego then?

(Collected Poems)

Many of the poet's hard times had, in fact, ended well. As an eighteen-year-old, standing in a welfare line and reading *Copper Sun* and *Black Christ,* two books by Countee Cullen, another well-known poet of the Harlem Renaissance, Hayden caught a clerk's attention. He told her he intended to publish his own poetry some day. His determination impressed her so much so that she helped him get a scholarship to Detroit City College, now Wayne State University. Much later, Hayden himself met Countee Cullen. Hayden credited the poets Edna St. Vincent Millay, Carl Sandburg, William Butler Yeats, Paul Laurence Dunbar, and W. H. Auden as important influences on his poetry. He claimed to have found images and lines in Millay's poetry that inspired him to write. "And not only that," he said, "they made me look at trees, clouds, flowers, faces as I had never looked at them before" (*Collected Prose,* p. 131). Hayden went on to receive both his bachelor's and master's degrees at the University of Michigan, where he studied with the poet W. H. Auden. The professor from England taught Hayden something he never forgot. According to Hayden, Auden said that good poetry is like algebra; it requires "solving for x" (Hatcher, pp. 70, 250).

Riddles and Secrets

In response to the turmoil of the civil rights movement, the war in Vietnam, and the assassinations of the black leaders Malcolm X and Martin Luther King and President John F. Kennedy in the 1960s, Hayden wrote a book of poems, *Words in the Mourning Time.* The book opens with "Sphinx," in which he writes from the point of view of the Greek mythological figure who asked travelers, "What walks on four legs in the morning, two at noon, and three in the evening?" Those who did not know that the answer to the riddle was "human beings" were devoured. In the third stanza, the poem reads "It is your fate, she has often / said, to endure / my riddling." In his *Collected Prose,* the poet explained that "the poem revolves around the psychological, deals with some tic or block, some inner conflict you may have which gives you your particular inscape, makes you what you are" (p. 125). Pontheolla Williams, in her *Robert Hayden: A Critical Analysis of His Poetry,* relates "Sphinx" and other poems to Hayden's own struggle with sexual identity.

Another secret is explored when Hayden addresses his grandson in the poem "The Year of the Child." The poet wonders if the infant ponders a "subtle joke" but simply cannot tell it, because he has not yet learned to talk. Both "Sphinx" and "The Year of the Child" are poems in which Hayden contemplated cycles and secrets and drew upon Greek, Navaho, American, and Baha'i* beliefs and traditions.

*Baha'i an Eastern religion that believes in the universality of humankind

Hayden had been raised as a Baptist. The poet became a Baha'i after his wife, Erma, whom he married in 1940, introduced him to the religion. Although such poems as "The Year of the Child," "The Night-Blooming Cereus," and "Two Egyptian Portrait Masks" have a variety of religious overtones, the influence of Baha'i beliefs is most evident in poems like "Full Moon," "Bahá'ull'áh in the Garden of Ridwan," "The Broken Dark," and "Stars." "Stars" is more sparse than Hayden's earlier "baroque" poems. Some have called his later economical style "haiku-like," comparing it to the Japanese form in which words are simple and relate directly to things; nature should be involved in the content. Sounds or syllables are counted, usually restricting the poem to three short lines. "The Moose Wallow," "Gulls," and "Snow" are poems Hayden wrote in this style.

"Stars" ends

"And the Nine-Pointed Star,
sun star in the constellation

of the nuclear Will;
fixed star
whose radiance
filtering down to us lights mind and
spirit, signal future light."

Quietly, Hayden traces light as a symbol of knowledge. Stars guided Sojourner Truth, the famous escaped slave and early abolitionist who appears in an earlier part of the poem. In the Baha'i faith, the nine-pointed star is a symbol that represents the nine religions of the world and the successive revelation of their prophets.

As the poet explained, "I believe in the basic unity of all religions. I don't believe that races are important; I think that people are important. . . . These are all Bahá'í points of view, and my work grows out of this vision" (*Collected Prose,* p. 111).

Some critics questioned the religious influence on Hayden's poetry. Reprinted in *The Chelsea House Library of Literary Criticism* is a review from the July 1967 volume of *Poetry* in which David Galler writes ". . . witness his poems concerned with the Bahá'í Faith, a prominent nineteenth-century Persian sect whose leader was martyred. Might not the example of Jesus have sufficed? For the white man, probably" (p. 1738). Utterly dedicated to his poetry and religious beliefs, Hayden, nonetheless believed that "the work of the artist is considered a form of service to mankind and it has spiritual significance. If the work is done with great sincerity and devotion and . . . knowledge. . . , it is considered really a form of worship and a service to mankind" (*Collected Prose,* p. 111).

Criticism and Awards

At the same time that critics in the United States debated Hayden's political and social agenda, a committee in Dakar, Senegal, selected his book *A Ballad of Remembrance* for the "Grand Prix de la Poésie" at the 1966 First World Festival of Negro Arts. Langston Hughes; Leopold Sedar Senghor, the president of Senegal, and himself an accomplished poet; and Dr. Rosey E. Pool, who had nominated Hayden for the award, were important participants in the ceremony. Hayden had earlier received the University of Michigan's Hopwood Award for poetry and a Rosenwald fellowship to Mexico; his later honors included election as a Fellow of the American Academy of Poets in 1975, two National Book Award nominations, several honorary degrees, and a two-term appointment as poetry consultant to the Library of Congress.

Since his first volume of poetry, *Heart-Shape in the Dust,* Hayden had shown a passion for American history and for the African American personalities who shaped it. Inspired by the early-twentieth-century American poet Stephen Vincent Benét, author of *John Brown's Body,* Hayden dedicated himself to writing a volume of historical poems under the title "The Black Spear." Although the book was never completed, some of Hayden's most famous poems came from this project, including "Middle Passage," "Frederick Douglass," and "The Ballad of Nat Turner." Some critics were not pleased with the poet's spoofs of such black characters as "Witch Doctor" and "Aunt Jemima of the Ocean Waves," but many others were happy to honor Hayden with the unofficial title of "black poet laureate," a title that even Langston Hughes coveted in a friendly way.

In "Middle Passage," Hayden tried to expose some hard truths in American history by cataloging the names of the slave ships and the African ethnic groups who were forced on board. The poem was highly praised by critics like William Logan, who considered it the best poem ever written about the transatlantic slave trade. The poet writes in the voice of a crew member, "Which one of us / has killed an albatross? A plague among / our blacks—Ophthalmia: blindness—& we / have jettisoned the blind to no avail." He uses repetition and variation in another interesting way, stringing together words with the same consonants throughout the poem. "Jests," "jettisons," "justify," and "justice" are words uttered by people trying to make sense of the murderous proportions of the slave trade. The critic Arnold Rampersad, in his introduction to the revised edition of Hayden's *Collected Poems,* argues that "violence is everywhere" in Hayden's poetry but that "in the context of African-American history and the desire for freedom, violence is often seen as a necessary evil."

Shadow and Light

Hayden admitted in an interview in 1977 that it had always been a struggle to write: "I've always found it difficult to keep my teaching going and keep my other responsibilities going and write too" (*Collected Prose,* p. 101). To satisfy his responsibilities as husband, father, professor, and poet, Hayden waited patiently for his wife, Erma, and child, Maia, to fall asleep before composing his verse. In 1969, Hayden returned to the University of Michigan as a professor of English. He was also poetry editor of the Baha'i magazine, *World Order.* Called both a "romantic realist" and a "historical symbolist," Hayden was a deliberate writer who hoped for careful readers, readers who cared not just for poetry but also for people. His final poem unites his concern with the suffering of African Americans in history and his diligence in language.

Unfinished at the time of his death in 1980, "from THE SNOW LAMP," is a poem in three parts about Matthew Henson, an African American explorer and co-discoverer of the North Pole. The Inuit* welcome Henson as one of their own in the first part of the poem, a praise song, calling "Miypaluk." One of Hayden's favorite words, "chimera"* is featured in this poem ("Yeti's tract / chimera's land . . ."). It also appears in "The Tattooed Man" ("My jungle arms, / their prized chimeras") and "October" ("This chiming / and tolling / of lion / and phoenix / and chimera / colors"). Repetition like this shows that Hayden cherished words for their sound, sense, and emotional quality.

Written as a diary entry in the explorer's voice, "from THE SNOW LAMP" ends "We stink like Eskimos. / We fight our wish to die," recalling the line in "Elegies for Paradise Valley" about the "Gypsies" who "take on bad as Colored Folks, / . . . Die like us too." On 25 February 1980, Robert Hayden died of cancer at age sixty-seven, but his careful portraits live on in beautiful contours of shadow and light for his readers.

Selected Bibliography

WORKS BY ROBERT HAYDEN

Poetry

    Heart-Shape in the Dust (1940).

    The Lion and the Archer (1948).

    Figure of Time: Poems (1955).

    A Ballad of Remembrance (1962).

    Selected Poems (1966).

*Inuit native of the Arctic regions of North America and Greenland

*chimera a she-monster in Greek mythology with a lion's head, goat's body, and the tail of a snake; also an illusion of the mind, a vision, or a dream

IF YOU LIKE the poetry of Hayden, you might also like the poetry of W. H. Auden, Stephen Vincent Benét, Langston Hughes, Edna St. Vincent Millay, Rainer Maria Rilke, or William Butler Yeats.

Words in the Mourning Time (1970).

The Night-Blooming Cereus (1972).

Angle of Ascent (1975).

American Journal (1982).

Available Collections

Collected Poems. Edited by Frederick Glaysher. New York: Liveright, 1985; 1996, rev. ed.

Collected Prose. Edited by Frederick Glaysher. Ann Arbor: University of Michigan Press, 1984.

WORKS ABOUT ROBERT HAYDEN

Fetrow, Fred. *Robert Hayden.* Boston: Twayne, 1984.

Greenberg, Robert M. "Robert Hayden." In A. Walton Litz, ed., *American Writers,* Supp. II, part 1. New York: Charles Scribner's Sons, 1981. Pages 361–383.

Hatcher, John. *From the Auroral Darkness: The Life and Poetry of Robert Hayden.* Oxford, U.K.: George Ronald, 1984.

Williams, Pontheolla. *Robert Hayden: A Critical Analysis of His Poetry.* Urbana: University of Illinois Press, 1987.

Williams, Wilburn Jr. "Covenant of Timelessness and Time: Symbolism and History in Robert Hayden's *Angle of Ascent.*" In Michael S. Harper and Robert B. Stepto, eds., *Chant of Saints: A Gathering of Afro-American Literature, Art and Scholarship.* Urbana: University of Illinois Press, 1979. Pages 66–84.

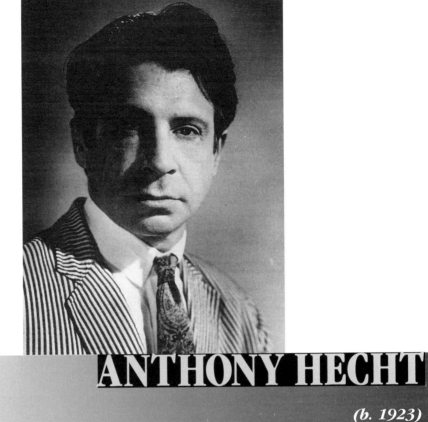

ANTHONY HECHT

(b. 1923)

by Brad Leithauser

Although he published no novels or short stories, Anthony Hecht is unusual in his strong links to writers of fiction. He is a natural storyteller. Many of his poems have a powerful narrative, and Hecht clearly relishes the little game of constantly adjusted speed by which a fiction writer maintains suspense—now leaning a little more on the accelerator, now tapping the brakes. He also has the born novelist's love of precise and elaborate scene-setting, whether of rich, crowded interiors (like the grocery store at the center of his longest poem, "The Venetian Vespers") or of sprawling, panoramic landscapes. In the loving attention Hecht lavishes on his landscapes ("The Short End," "The Gardens of the Villa D'Este," "See Naples and Die"), he is like Thomas Hardy, in whose novels the English countryside is portrayed with such grandeur and vividness that it almost becomes an additional character in his stories.

But Hecht's ties to fiction writers are perhaps most deeply felt in his efforts to see the world through another person's eyes. Ours is an era in which many poets have chosen to make themselves their primary subject matter. Many notable poems have resulted from this decision—but it is a decision that often proves disastrous for fiction writers, who generally require a populous world if their creations are to offer a gratifying three-dimensionality. Hecht shares the fiction writer's urge to paint a diversely peopled world, one whose inhabitants do not all look and think like him. It is typical of him that, although he was born Jewish, his poems often meditate on the meanings, riddles, beauties, and severities of Christian imagery and theology. He has aimed to understand how an immersion in Christian dogma and symbolism shapes the imagination. Likewise, he has frequently viewed the world from a feminine vantage. Some of his longest or most ambitious poems ("The Grapes," "The Short End," "The Transparent Man") either are about women's lives or are narrated by women.

One offshoot of Hecht's concern with other lives is that very little clear autobiography emerges from his work. And yet, working solely with the books themselves—the poems and the biographical material found on the dust jackets—the reader can piece together a capsule life history. Hecht was born in New York City in 1923. (His parents were Melvyn and Dorothea Hecht.) His first book of poems, *A Summoning of Stones,* appeared in 1954. Other volumes include *The Hard Hours, Millions of Strange Shadows, The Venetian Vespers, The Transparent Man,* and *Flight Among the Tombs.* He also published three books of essays and criticism. He married twice and had three sons. He served in the army during World War II and then spent most of his professional life teaching, chiefly at the University of Rochester and at Georgetown University. After retiring from Georgetown, he remained in Washington, D.C. He read widely, with a special, lifelong devotion to Shakespeare.

Civility and Grotesquerie

*diction choice of words

*allusion a passing reference to fictional or historical characters, events, literature, or places the writer assumes the reader will recognize

In the half-century or so of his writing career, Hecht was strikingly consistent. In two senses he took a formal approach: he embraced poetic forms—writing chiefly in rhyme and meter, composing sonnets, sestinas, villanelles, blank-verse narratives, and so forth—and he adopted elevated or "high" diction.* His work has extraordinary polish. He employs a broad vocabulary—he is likely to send even the most learned reader to the dictionary—and frequent literary allusions.* This formal polish helps create the characteristic surface of a Hecht poem. Readers can expect to meet up with a clear meter (strict or loose) and—particularly if the poem is short—a rhyme scheme. We look to Hecht for dexterity, wit, reserve, and an atmosphere of great scholarship and careful reflection. His poems are, in a phrase, refined and civilized.

But his subject matter is often the opposite of everything that is refined and civilized. Readers begin to appreciate Hecht's accomplishment only as they grasp the many ways in which subject matter plays off against style. Many of Hecht's poems are a beauty-and-the-beast sort of marriage, in which civility of form is wed to grotesquerie of content. His poems take up the horrors of warfare and torture ("Behold the Lilies of the Field"), Nazism and the death camps ("Rites and Ceremonies," "The Book of Yolek," " 'It Out-Herods Herod. Pray You, Avoid It.' "), madness and incarceration* ("The Venetian Vespers," "Coming Home"), plagues and mass death ("Tarantula"), executions ("More Light! More Light!"), and even a live entombment ("The Short End"). Hecht can be *extremely* dark. What may look like formal accomplishment for its own sake reveals itself in time as a strategy for achieving distance from a subject matter whose raw horror and enormity might otherwise look like mere sensationalism.

Hecht's poems often move cautiously, sometimes all but imperceptibly, toward their true subject. In many ways "A Hill," which opens *The Hard Hours,* is a perfect example of one of Hecht's short poems. It begins in a splash of sunshine and gaiety. The poem's narrator tells us we are in Italy. It is morning in a charming piazza, and he is walking with friends. Without warning, something peculiar happens: he has a sort of involuntary vision. His eyes go dark, and the bright palace standing before him disappears. In its place looms an icy hill, lifeless and mysterious. He hears the sound of distant gunfire. The vision is unnerving, but it does not last long. Soon the piazza returns—and the sunlight. The desolate hill eventually fades from the poet's mind—until, some ten years later, it reappears. Unexpectedly, he recognizes it. The hill belongs to his childhood, in Poughkeepsie, New York: "and as a boy / I stood before it for hours in wintertime." We suddenly understand that the hill never vanished, although it seemed to vanish for ten years. The hill has been standing there from the beginning—from childhood—and in its patient, timeless way it has pursued him on his travels throughout the world. For wherever the poet goes,

*incarceration
imprisonment

the hill will go with him, waiting for him with all the frozen finality of death and bereavement. Eventually, the distant rifle fire will bring down its target.

"The Deodand," from *The Venetian Vespers,* follows a similar arc, although at both ends the colors are more extreme: it begins with brighter brights and ends with darker darks. The poem's opening scene is taken from a painting called "Parisians Dressed in Algerian Costume" by Pierre-Auguste Renoir, the nineteenth-century French impressionist. The scene is delightfully luxurious: a number of beautiful, wealthy Frenchwomen are playing a little game of dress-up, in which they don exotic Arab finery. The "deodand" of the title is a legal term, referring to a payment offered in restitution or expiation of wrongdoing. In this case, the women's seemingly harmless, childish game—their teasing, toying manipulations of these symbols of colonialism and racial subjugation—demands a payment that will not be exacted for many years, not until the Algerian war of independence in the 1950s. What lies between Renoir's painting and that war is a steadily mounting series of resentments and hatreds. The gorgeous women call up for Hecht a particular atrocity in which Algerian rebels captured a boyish French legionnaire (a soldier) and "cut off all the fingers of both hands. / He had to eat from a fork held by his captors." The legionnaire was made to dress up as a girl and to sing for his supper. You must always be prepared, when reading Hecht, to come upon an image of horrific intensity, like the "meat-hooked ham, hung like a traitor's head / For the public's notice in a butcher shop" or a soldier hit by machine-gun fire: "They had sheared away / The top of his cranium like a soft-boiled egg" ("The Venetian Vespers"). In Hecht's work, golden daydreams have a way of sliding into the blood reds and blacks of nightmare.

> You must be prepared, when reading Hecht, to come upon an image of horrific intensity.

Darkness and Light

Poets often reveal a lot about themselves in their concept of true hell. For a poet like Theodore Roethke, hell is a zone of titanic raging. His poems are full of blackening skies and howling winds, of furious, gigantic father figures—some of them Zeus-like gods in the sky and others actual flesh-and-blood men. Either way, Roethke was haunted by notions of a male fury so potent and implacable that it could not be reasoned with.

Giant Tortoise

I am related to stones
The slow accretion of moss where dirt is wedged
Long waxy hair that can split boulders.
Events are not important.

I live in my bone
Recalling the hour of my death.
It takes more toughness than most have got.
Or a saintliness.

Strength of a certain kind, anyway.
Bald toothless clumsy perhaps
With all the indignity of old age
But age is not important.

There is nothing worth remembering
But the silver glint in the muck
The thickening of great trees
The hard crust getting harder.

(*The Hard Hours*)

What most haunts Hecht is the species of cruelty that is calm and collected. He returns again and again to images of barbarism derived from the seemingly rational mind—the torturer's inspired, fiendish ingenuities. For him, the image of the Nazi state—particularly the notion that engineers, professors, architects, and businessmen collaboratively, and with great, painstaking resourcefulness, contrived the death camps—has a natural resonance above and beyond questions of his religious background.

Yet for all the tragedy and ugliness in his books, reading Anthony Hecht can be surprisingly exhilarating. Independent of his content, there is a deep pleasure in his unfailing nimbleness—like watching professional tennis players cover the court as though they owned it. His poems brim with sharp, unexpected rhymes (like "ports" and "F. A. O. Schwarz") and humorous wordplay (as when Sigmund Freud's *Civilization and Its Discontents* becomes "civilization and its discotheques"). But what brightens his work more than anything else is his flair for visual imagery.

Again and again Hecht's poems celebrate the wonders of sight. Although he sings memorably in praise of all the senses (the smell of woods after a rainfall, the singing of choirs of insects, the feel of satin on the fingertips, and the taste of tea on the tongue), the experiences of the eye have a privileged place in his work. He loves the visual arts, especially painting, and in his poems he pays tribute to many painters besides Renoir: Giovanni Bellini, Rembrandt, Jan Vermeer, Pierre Bonnard, Henri Matisse.

His kinship with the impressionists is especially close, particularly in their love of variable, fleeting lighting effects. Some artists have come forward as champions of "art for art's sake"—art which advances no social message or agenda but which seeks to revel in the pure pleasure of artistic creation. Hecht's poems, like some impressionist paintings, celebrate light for light's sake. He loves the shifting light of sun through foliage, the dancing light of reflections within a water drop, the sliding light of dusk, the deepening light that often precedes a storm, as in "The Lull": "Some shadowless, unfocussed light / In which all things come into their own right" (*Millions of Strange Shadows*).

You might say that light balances dark in Hecht's poems: the literal light of the world (and all the worldly glories the light reveals—the flowers and stones and birds and shifting skies) balances the darkness of centuries of human mistrust and greed, selfishness, and savagery. More than anything else, it is this stubborn play of light—a scintillation at his heart's core—that keeps Hecht from seeming merely grim or gloomy. Both his joys and his sorrows are continually being infiltrated—darkened and brightened by movements of light and shadow. The reader comes away from the poems feeling that Hecht has never used others' grief for his own ends, but has used it only in true sympathy with the world's victims, and that his pleasures are never easy or idle but rather are hardwon satisfactions.

This dynamic interchange of pleasure and pain is on continual display in what may be Hecht's masterpiece, the long title poem to *The Venetian Vespers*. It is a work of what might be called an awkward size—neither long enough to step forth as a book-length poem nor short enough to appear in anthologies. Fiction writers often complain about the reception given to the novella*—a literary form slighted by publishers, who suspect that the book-buying public will be reluctant to

*novella a work of fiction that is, in length, between a short story and a novel

pay good money for something that looks insubstantial, and by critics, who often view it as an incomplete or lightweight novel. "The Venetian Vespers" may be the poet's equivalent of a novella.

And yet within its six sections and twenty-seven pages it tells a complicated, haunting story of an aging American expatriate* who has decided to live out his days in Venice, Italy. The poem can be read in one concentrated sitting, delivering more of a wallop—more feeling and beauty and lived life— than works many times its size. The expatriate has no name, but he is a fictional character—someone quite distinct from the poet himself. He eventually reveals that he grew up in Lawrence, Massachusetts, the son of Latvian immigrants. The poem vividly evokes his asthmatic childhood and the endless hours he spent in his family's store, inhaling the smells of fruit and coffee, playing and daydreaming on the floor behind the counter. His early years are glowingly evoked, blending the magical dreaminess of childhood with a vague, undefined, but palpable sense of foreboding. Childish dread gives way in time to concrete agonies—the death of his mother, the disappearance of his father, and a stint in the military that leaves him "mentally unsound." The darkness intensifies: it turns out that the protagonist's generous uncle, who has served as his patron and guardian, had a hand in the father's disappearance and may well have betrayed the family in other ways as well.

Living alone, convinced that his life is a "transparent failure," shaky of mind, subject to nightmares, the protagonist draws most of what strength he possesses from the pleasures of observation. He explicitly states a credo underlying so many of Hecht's poems when he describes rain falling in front of a cathedral:

> To give one's whole attention to such a sight
> Is a sort of blessedness. No room is left
> For antecedence,* inference,* nuance.*
> One escapes from all the anguish of this world
> Into the refuge of the present tense.

And near the poem's close: "I look and look, / As though I could be saved simply by looking." In its distinctive blend of tragic story and lyrical* imagery, "The Venetian Vespers" is one of the highlights of Hecht's career. The tale itself is heartbreaking. The craftsmanship is breathtaking. Light wrestles

*expatriate a person living outside of his or her native country

*antecedence priority

*inference conclusion; assumption; judgment

*nuance a subtle difference or characteristic

*lyrical having a musical quality

*opulent wealthy; rich

IF YOU LIKE the poetry of Hecht, you might also like the poetry of Richard Wilbur.

with darkness and praise with lamentation. The result is a complicated vision and opulent* music.

Selected Bibliography

WORKS BY ANTHONY HECHT

A Summoning of Stones (1954).

The Hard Hours (1967).

Millions of Strange Shadows (1977).

The Venetian Vespers (1979).

The Transparent Man (1990).

Flight Among the Tombs (1996).

WORKS ABOUT ANTHONY HECHT

Brown, Ashley. "Anthony Hecht." In *American Poets Since World War II.* Edited by Joseph Conte. Detroit, Mich.: Gale, 1996.

Lea, Sidney, ed. *The Burdens of Formality: Essays on the Poetry of Anthony Hecht.* Athens: University of Georgia Press, 1989.

GEORGE HERBERT

(1593–1633)

by Robert Cording

Izaak Walton's biography, *The Life of Mr. George Herbert,* published in 1670, created a lasting image of Herbert: the saintly country parson, known for the piety and sincerity of his life and for his one book of poems, *The Temple.* This image of the saintly poet won Herbert an enduring audience, but all too often at the expense of the poems, which have been valued for their religious sentiments.

Faith and Poetry

George Herbert was a religious poet, but his poetry is valuable even to those who do not share his religious beliefs. Like all good religious poetry, Herbert's *Temple* records the search for a life of the spirit. For those to whom religion means comfort and peace of mind, Herbert brings the agonizing appraisal* of the often conflicted workings of his own mind and heart. To those who would prefer an easy faith, Herbert reminds us that God must be experienced and that such an

Quotations from Herbert's work throughout are taken from Hutchinson, ed., *The Works of George Herbert.*

*appraisal** estimation of value

experience necessarily involves the difficulty of distinguishing between what one really feels and what one would like to feel, as the poet T. S. Eliot put it, singling out Herbert for his faithfulness to the truth.

Herbert's *Temple* poems are firm in their desire to plumb* the reality of their spiritual concerns. They continually question what Herbert feels and thinks, what is illusory* and what is not, and how Herbert should best live his life. The task of the poems is to express the experienced reality of the cosmos as a creation, an ordered, meaningful work of the Creator. For Herbert daily life is directed by these basic truths: that human beings live in a universe that they did not earn but received as a gift, and that the gift of our lives and the world in which we live should drive us toward thanks and praise and, most important, toward loving and the conviction that God acts spontaneously and lovingly to help humans satisfy their innermost needs.

To read George Herbert is to experience the common sense of another era, and many contemporary readers will not feel the urgency of Herbert's concerns. The world since his time has become more human-centered than God-centered; we depend more on science and the social sciences to provide us with an image of reality and standards to live by, as if the individual and what can benefit each one of us are of greatest importance.

The Temple

During his lifetime George Herbert published only a few Latin translations. His two books, *The Temple* and the prose work *The Country Parson,* were both published after his death. *The Temple* is the book on which Herbert's considerable reputation as a poet rests. It comprises poems that move between the spiritual conflicts of the speaker, a poet-priest, and the architecture, furnishings, and rituals of the church building in which his daily life is lived.

The Temple describes the poet's need to feel the reality and presence of God in all things as surely as the reader's hand feels the substance of the book itself. In many of the poems this presence makes itself felt more often than not as an absence. Yet, for Herbert, God does not so much go away as disappear, hidden by the very self that searches for God.

Imagine God as a mirror in which the entire world is reflected, except when the self appears and blocks the world from appearing. In "The Altar," Herbert brings the stone of his heart to the altar as a sacrifice, knowing that "if I chance to hold my peace, / These stones [of the altar] to praise thee may not cease." All that the speaker of "The Altar" possesses is the power to give his "I" to God. If God is all, we must give up all those habits of thought and perception that define our independence, that constitute our way of looking at the world, since the "I" that we think of as our identity is actually that which prevents us from seeing, and the stones from praising.

As if to remind himself and his reader that Christianity's paradoxes* are extreme and that all too often the professed believer protects himself against those paradoxes by turning them into platitudes,* Herbert insists throughout *The Temple* on the absoluteness of God. For Herbert,

> We say amisse,*
> This or that is;
> Thy word is all, if we could spell.
>
> "The Flower"

As Stanley Fish has pointed out, Herbert's poems often have two conflicting perspectives. On the one hand, there is the everyday world and the speaker who lives in it. On the other, there is the larger context of God that ultimately dissolves or consumes the speaker's perspective. Consider Herbert's little parable* "Redemption":

> Having been tenant long to a rich Lord,
>   Not thriving, I resolved to be bold,
>   And make a suit unto him, to afford
> A new small-rented lease, and cancell th' old.
> In heaven at his manour I him sought:
>   They told me there, that he was lately gone
>   About some land, which he had dearly bought
> Long since on earth, to take possession.
> I straight return'd, and knowing his great birth,
>   Sought him accordingly in great resorts;
>   In cities, theatres, gardens, parks, and courts:
> At length I heard a ragged noise and mirth*
>   Of thieves and murderers: there I him espied,
>   Who straight, *Your suit is granted,* said, & died.

paradox a statement that seems to be a contradiction but may be true

platitude a cliché or dull remark

amisse amiss; mistakenly or wrongly

parable a brief story that illustrates a moral or religious principle

mirth happiness

*__retrospective__ a look at what took place in the past

This little retrospective* poem is a cautionary tale about the misjudgment of the speaker, who, upset with the terms of his old lease with a wealthy landlord, goes in search of the landlord so that he may secure better terms for himself. Guided by his misperceptions of where such a wealthy man might reside, the speaker searches manors, great resorts, parks, and courts only to find his landlord among some "ragged" thieves and murderers. The landlord immediately grants his request and dies. The larger context is the story of Christ's redemptive death on the cross, a story that, as Herbert's poem reminds the reader, is too easily stored away in the back of the mind. Herbert's language does double duty, reminding the reader that "rich" can either mean possessing great wealth or abounding in desirable qualities. The Lord, seen from the speaker's original perspective is wealthy, of "great birth," and has the money to buy expensive property. He must be made to see the poor speaker's plight. But the larger context of the poem reveals that the Lord is good, of heavenly birth, and has purchased—at great cost and deep affection—our world with his life. In fact, the speaker who sets out to solve his problems is already having those problems solved by a Lord who knows what he needs before he knows it himself. For even before the speaker set out "to make his suit," Christ was giving his life so that this suit could be granted.

Poetry as Psychology

*__clerical collar__ a white collar worn by members of the clergy

*__rebuke__ to scold or reprimand

This kind of self-critical dialogue of the mind with itself underlies many of Herbert's poems, which often change directions, modifying or abandoning outright their original positions. Herbert's poems are psychological—they often investigate the many ways the self has of deceiving itself. In his famous poem "The Collar" (the title itself is a pun on choler, a fit of anger), Herbert strikes the Communion table, claiming that, despite entering the priesthood and putting on the clerical collar* of prayer and obedience, he has not received what he has asked for—a loving response from God. The poem imitates the disordered perceptions of the speaker: there is no apparent pattern to the rhyme, though no line is unrhymed, and the measure of the lines vary from two to five poetic feet. But after all the irregular lines and rhymes, the poem concludes with a patterned stanza that rebukes* this childish fit of rebellion.

But as I rav'd and grew more fierce and wilde
> At every word,
Me thoughts I heard one calling, *Child!*
> And I reply'd, *My Lord.*

The poem describes the unmaking of the speaker's overly self-centered perspective by the enlarging perspective of God, who both knows the speaker's childishness and loves him as his child.

But it is hard to write poems expressing the reality of God's infinite love using language that, bound by its own finite limitations, can only "say amisse / This or that is." This theme is examined in a number of poems about Herbert's art: "The Altar," "The Temper (1)," "The Temper (2)," "Jordan (1)," "The Quidditie," "Deniall," "Jordan (2)," "Dulnesse," "Mans Medley," "A True Hymne," "The Forerunners," "The Posie," and "A Wreath." Herbert knows his art—there is, seemingly, at least one example of every kind of short poem known in his time. More important, he loves his art. And loving his art as he does, even near the end of *The Temple* in "The Forerunners," Herbert cannot easily say farewell to his language so that God's word may speak—Herbert knows the temptation to show off his skills as a writer. Herein lies the very problematic nature of writing religious verse: the poet gets in the way of God. Over and over in these poems, Herbert is all too aware of how he "weave[s] [his] self into the sense" of the poems when he should only "copy out" what is "already penned" in the Bible. Herbert tries, but knows that substituting the Bible's words for his own words is often insufficient for a poem, even if sufficient for God.

Life and Poetry

Although early scholarship on Herbert saw him as a man of conscience who gave up all worldly ambition for the simple priestly life of a country parson, Herbert's actual life and the poems that make up *The Temple* are now seen as more complicated. Herbert lived in the world of civil affairs for much of his life. He was born 3 April 1593 to Richard Herbert, a sheriff and magistrate who served in Parliament, and Magdalene Newport. The family had high connections to King James and his court. Herbert attended Trinity College, Cambridge, from

*__dust__ the mortal frame of a human being; condition of humiliation

Love (3)

Love bade me welcome: yet my soul drew back,
    Guiltie of dust* and sinne.
But quick-ey'd Love, observing me grow slack
    From my first entrance in,
Drew nearer to me, sweetly questioning,
    If I lack'd any thing.
A guest, I answer'd, worthy to be here:
    Love said, You shall be he.
I the unkinde, ungratefull? Ah my deare,
    I cannot look on thee.
Love took my hand, and smiling did reply,
    Who made the eyes but I?

Truth Lord, but I have marr'd them: let my shame
    Go where it doth deserve.
And know you not, sayes Love, who bore the blame?
    My deare, then I will serve.
You must sit down, sayes Love, and taste my meat:
    So I did sit and eat.

*__disillusioned__ disenchanted; no longer viewing things idealistically

*__ordained__ officially given authority as a minister or priest

1609 to 1613. He did well, had influential friends, and from 1616 to 1620 received five prestigious appointments at Cambridge. But other such appointments did not follow. Herbert served as a member of Parliament from 1623 to 1624, but the experience seems to have disillusioned* him, and he applied to the Church of England to be ordained,* though he had postponed this step for years. In 1629 he married Jane Danvers. He died 1 March 1633 of consumption.

Though not much is known about his life, it is clear in such poems as the two "Employment" poems, "Affliction (1)" and "Submission" that Herbert's decision to leave public life for the priesthood and the small rectory at Bemerton, in southwest England, was not a simple one. His movement toward God both in life and in *The Temple* is more "bent" than "straight," to use two of his favorite words. Like all of us, Herbert found himself making the same mistakes over and over and learned that knowing the right thing to do is much easier than doing it. His poems chart the drama of all those veerings and reversals away from and toward God.

These are thy wonders, Lord of power,
Killing and quickning,* bringing down to hell
And up to heaven in an houre;

"The Flower"

quickning quickening; reviving or accelerating

Herbert wants to get beyond these seemingly endless emotional cycles of grief and joy. What he wants is a God that is predictable and intelligible. Instead Herbert learns that our lives are shifting and restless. We are not really like flowers that have roots; we are, instead, "flowers that glide." Our experience will always be one of many deaths and renewals, and to wish for more is a wish to be more than human. There is a strange, remarkable poem at the heart of *The Temple* called "The Bag," in which Herbert imagines the wound in Christ's side as a mailbag for conveying messages to heaven. The poem is a lesson about grief; Christ does not wish grief away, as Herbert has so often tried to do, but instead puts grief to use. The wound in his side gaping, Christ says, "That I shall minde, what you impart, / Look you may put it very neare my heart." What Herbert must learn is such openheartedness. Despair closes the heart. Herbert comes to see that he must not ask, Why me? Why did this happen to me? but instead open himself to the very gift of his life, to God's indiscriminate* love, which, as Herbert learns in the last poem, "The Church," has been serving always. When the speaker says in "Love (3)" that he cannot enter into Christ's paradise because of his sins, Christ responds, "And know you not . . . who bore the blame?" And when the speaker consents finally to come in, offering to serve Christ, Christ gently but firmly responds, "You must sit down . . . and taste my meat." Love serves in Herbert's conclusion, and has been serving from the beginning. This last poem is so ravishingly* direct that it seems as if Herbert has finally accomplished what all poems want to accomplish—to get beyond language to the experience itself, an experience that no words can accommodate.

indiscriminate not careful; random; haphazard

ravishingly very attractively; disarmingly

Selected Bibliography

WORKS BY GEORGE HERBERT
Available Collections

The Complete English Poems. Edited by John Tobin. London: Penguin, 1991. Includes *The Country Parson* and Izaak Walton's *The Life of Mr. George Herbert.*

IF YOU LIKE the poetry of Herbert, you might also like the poetry of John Donne.

ࣷ

The English Poems of George Herbert. Edited by C. A. Patrides. London: Dent, 1974.

The Works of George Herbert. Edited by F. E. Hutchinson. Oxford, U.K.: Clarendon Press, 1941; rev. ed., 1945. The standard text.

WORKS ABOUT GEORGE HERBERT

Biography

Charles, Amy M. *A Life of George Herbert.* Ithaca, N.Y.: Cornell University Press, 1977.

Critical Studies

Eliot, T. S. *George Herbert.* London: Longmans, 1962.

Fish, Stanley. *The Living Temple: George Herbert and Catechizing.* Berkeley: University of California Press, 1978.

Fish, Stanley. *Self-Consuming Artifacts.* Berkeley: University of California Press, 1972.

Gardner, Helen. *Religion and Literature.* New York: Oxford University Press, 1971.

Harman, Barbara Leah. *Costly Monuments.* Cambridge, Mass.: Harvard University Press, 1982.

Lewalski, Barbara Kiefer. *Protestant Poetics and the Seventeenth-Century Religious Lyric.* Princeton, N.J.: Princeton University Press, 1979.

Martz, Louis. *The Poetry of Meditation.* Rev. ed. New Haven, Conn.: Yale University Press, 1962.

Strier, Richard. *Love Known: Theology and Experience in George Herbert's Poetry.* Chicago: University of Chicago Press, 1983.

Tuve, Rosemond. *A Reading of George Herbert.* Chicago: University of Chicago Press, 1952.

Vendler, Helen. *The Poetry of George Herbert.* Cambridge, Mass.: Harvard University Press, 1975.

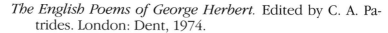

More About Herbert

You can find information about George Herbert on the Internet at:
http://www.luminarium.org/sevenlit/herbert/

ROBERT HERRICK

(1591–1674)

by Tom Clark

Robert Herrick has long been thought of as a "poet's poet"; his genius is appreciated by other poets, but little known otherwise. Herrick's astonishing lightness and delicacy in the realm of the senses give his poetry a unique tone* and touch. The lyric perfection of his poetry has few parallels in English, except for the songs in Shakespeare's plays. Only a handful of Herrick's 1,400 poems are available to the general reader today, but those few have established him as a great poet.

*tone the attitude of the writer toward the subject as shown in the writer's use of language

Early Life

Herrick was born in Cheapside, London, in August 1591. He came from an ancient family that went back to the days before the Norman Conquest,* and further back to Scandinavia. From this same family came the mother of Jonathan Swift, the author of *Gulliver's Travels,* who, like Herrick, was an out-of-the-ordinary clergyman.

*Norman Conquest the invasion of England by the French (Normans) in 1066

441

*a-Maying celebrating the pleasure of the incoming month of May

Corinna's Going A-Maying* (excerpt)

Come, let us go while we are in our prime;
And take the harmless folly of the time.
    We shall grow old apace, and die
    Before we know our liberty.
    Our life is short, and our days run
    As fast away as does the sun;
And, as a vapour or a drop of rain,
Once lost, can ne'er be found again,
    So when or you or I are made
    A fable, song, or fleeting shade,
    All love, all liking, all delight
    Lies drowned with us in endless night.
Then while time serves, and we are but decaying,
Come, my *Corinna,* come, let's go a-Maying.

(Selected Poems)

*apprenticed formally paired with a tradesman in order to learn the trade through hands-on experience, often working in exchange for a practical education (and sometimes room and board) rather than for pay

*luminous glowing; shining

*tangible real and concrete; capable of being touched; material

When Robert was an infant, his father, a prosperous London goldsmith and banker, died in a suspicious fall from an upper window of his house. Circumstances suggested suicide, which at that time was considered a felony and which, had it not been for certain friendly legal interventions on the family's behalf, would have resulted in the confiscation of the victim's estate. The mystery of his father's death long remained a shadow in Robert Herrick's imagination. As an adult poet with a bent for scholarship, he learned to include many of the beliefs of ancient Roman religion into his own view of things. Among these was the idea that a suicide could not be buried with formal religious rites but must remain a restless "shade," or ghost, until, over time, the proper purification rituals were performed. In Herrick's tender poem "To the Reverend Shade of His Religious Father," he begs forgiveness of his father's neglected ghost, then offers his poem as a tribute. The poet's deep sense of loss is expressed indirectly, through the symbolism of ancient Roman sacrifice rites.

Herrick's uncle took over the management of Robert's share of his father's estate, and in 1607 apprenticed* the sixteen-year-old boy to the goldsmith's trade. The six years Robert spent learning the secrets of the family craft leave their trace in the precise, luminous,* tangible* images of his poetry and in its quality of seeming to have been carefully carved from some hard, bright material.

The poet's understanding of the common speech of the streets probably dates from this period. Apprentices were among the fun-loving youth of London. With other young blades,* Herrick went often to the theater, seeing the latest productions of Shakespeare and of the team of dramatists Francis Beaumont and John Fletcher, and soaking up colorful poetic speech.

In 1613, Herrick's uncle ended the apprenticeship and sent Robert off to Cambridge University. Robert entered the university late, at age twenty-two; the poet Andrew Marvell, by contrast, would enter at fourteen. Young Herrick seems to have spent his time at Cambridge developing sophisticated tastes in studying the past as well as in pursuing the pleasures of the day; the principal theme of his correspondence with his uncle is requests for money to cover his continual overexpenditure at college.

Herrick and the "Tribe of Ben"

In 1617 Herrick received his bachelor's degree from Cambridge. The next thirteen years, a period in which he seems to have written most of his love poems, he spent in London, becoming one of the better-known members of the "Tribe of Ben"—a small circle of poets who gathered around Ben Jonson. Jonson, a professional man of letters, popular playwright, and self-taught classical* scholar, was a huge person, famous for eating and drinking. At the group's "lyric feasts" (*Selected Poems,* p. 24), as Herrick called them, Jonson was the master: we may imagine his confident presence at the center of things, authoritatively presiding, with Herrick as an eager disciple.

Over the years this informal poets' fellowship met at several different London taverns, including the Devil and St. Dunstan's, where for a while a special room was reserved for them. It was called the Apollo Chamber; above the door stood a statue of Apollo, the Greek god of poetry. In this sanctuary, Jonson, as a high priest of poetry, played the oracle* to his adopted "sons."

In Herrick's poems, the lyric feasts and the large figure of Jonson are evoked* with great warmth. A short "Ode for Him" recalls with nostalgic fondness their sessions "at the *Sun,* / The

blade a dashing, glamorous, pleasure-seeking young man

classical relating to Ancient Greece or Rome

oracle person through whom the will of the gods was revealed to humans

evoked re-created

Dog, the triple Tun"—three later sites of Ben's poetry club—and describes Jonson as the best poet in the house: "each verse of thine / Out-did the meat, out-did the frolic wine" (*Selected Poems,* p. 24).

Herrick took over verse forms and genres (categories) from Jonson the way an adopted son inherits parts of an estate. There are Jonson songs and lyrics that Herrick in effect rewrites, often improving on them. Jonson's interest in Greek and Roman poetry doubtless encouraged Herrick in his own project of imaginatively reconstructing the poetic worlds of ancient classic writers like Anacreon, Horace, Martial, Catullus, Tibullus, and Ovid. Herrick's playful yet reverent* and moving little "Prayer to Ben Jonson," offering its commemoration "For old *Religions* sake," reveals the central role of "Saint *Ben*" (*Poems of Robert Herrick,* p. 212) in Herrick's own nostalgia* for an imagined past.

A Living

In early seventeenth-century England, from one generation to the next, a son had to have twice as much income as his father in order to keep up a comparable standard of living. By his early thirties, Herrick, having spent his inheritance and abandoned his father's trade, lacked a means of supporting himself. At first he tried to win the favor of the royal court, writing lyrics he set to music; some of his songs were set by his friend the composer Henry Lawes and were performed by court singers and musicians before royalty. When King Charles I had a son in 1630, Herrick wrote a pastoral* for the occasion, set by the composer Nicholas Lanier for presentation to the king. Basing his pastoral on the event's timing—the child was born at noon, with Venus, thought to be the star of love and fortune, showing on the horizon—Herrick wrote of the starlike royal birth in such a way as to identify the infant prince with Christ.

It must have been apparent to Herrick that his best chance for obtaining a living was as a churchman, and it was in his religious career that he found himself best able to make use of his courtly and poetic connections. He was ordained a priest of the Church of England* in 1623. In 1628 a commission obtained through a friend at court, Endymion Porter, led to his setting off as chaplain* on a military expedition to the

*reverent worshipful or with great respect

*nostalgia a sentimental yearning to return to a past time

*pastoral a work dealing with rural life and tending to portray nature as sweet and beautiful

*Church of England the Anglican church, the state religion founded by king Henry VIII

*chaplain a clergyman who serves a branch of the military, an institution, a family, or a court

French coast. The expedition was a disaster—many of the English were slaughtered, and the survivors fled—and Herrick seems to have had a horrendous experience ministering to dying men aboard a threatened ship. At any rate, he never left dry land again, and his poetry contains numerous expressions of distaste for sea voyaging, such as "Trust to the shore" in the poem "Safely on the Shore" (*Poems of Robert Herrick,* p. 85).

Herrick's next post, however, was a little more to his liking: he was appointed to the vicarage* of Dean Prior, a rural parish located in far-off Devonshire. With its rustic meadows, orchards, cornfields, rocky moors, and limited cultural advantages, this remote country village in the west of England, to which Herrick retreated at age thirty-nine, provided the setting for most of the rest of his long life. Here the urban courtier traded his "lyric feasts" and "many fragrant mistresses" (*Selected Poems,* p. 37) for a different life, one that was pastoral in both senses—as a country parson and a poet of the countryside.

Country Pastor

Herrick occupied his West Country parish in 1630 and stayed on until 1647, when he was removed and deprived of his church privileges because he refused to submit to the conditions imposed by the victorious Puritan* side in the English Civil War.*

This time of widespread social, political and religious upheaval was very precarious* for Herrick. The "untuneable Times," he lamented, had "unstrung" his poetry, crippled his hand, and "palsy-struck"* his tongue (*Poems of Robert Herrick,* p. 84). Grief, he implied, had induced in him some kind of minor stroke. He was convinced—as he put it in another piece, titled "The Bad Season Makes the Poet Sad"—that England itself was "Sick to the heart" (*Selected Poems,* p. 37).

As one of those Englishmen who appeared to stand in the way of revolutionary change, Herrick was inevitably among those left most vulnerable to it—even though his conservatism was mainly literary. He felt nostalgia for a lost world of innocence, a "golden age" like that ideal past described by his beloved Roman poets, where sensory delights and morality could coexist without contradiction. "Corinna Goes A-Maying,"

*vicarage the house and grounds where an Anglican priest resides

*Puritan a Protestant Christian who opposed the Church of England. Most Puritans opposed elaborate ceremony and church hierarchy, believing that God's will was directly revealed to individuals.

*English Civil War (1640–1648) war between king Charles I and the Parliament, which was supported by the Puritans. The Puritans won, and Charles was beheaded in 1649. In 1660, however, the monarchy was restored.

*precarious uncertain or insecure

*palsy-struck afflicted with a paralytic condition

his lyric masterpiece, is a gentle lament for the passing of that golden age, placed in the context of a lively English springtime.

*exile forced absence from one's homeland

Herrick's feelings about his rural retreat in Devon had all along been mixed, but the sense of isolation and exile* was outweighed by its cozy security and modest comforts. For many years he had in fact found his parish a sanctuary, its unhurried seasonal rhythms paced to his own bookishness, and he had also found much material for poems in local folk ceremonies, pastimes, and customs. He cataloged the pleasures of country life in his delightful poem "His Grange, or Private Wealth," with its inventory of the little household company—a maid named Prew, a hen, a goose, a lamb, a cat, a spaniel named Tracy—"whereby / I please / The more my rural privacy" (*Selected Poems,* p. 25). It is said he also kept a pig that drank beer from a dish. When, in 1660, the English monarchy was restored, and along with it Herrick's former position at Dean Prior, he returned gratefully to "the dull confines of the drooping West" and spent his declining years there, hanging on among the country folk to the ripe old age of eighty-three. He died on 15 October 1674.

"Cleanly Wantonness" and "Times Trans-Shifting": Herrick's Poetry of Life and Death

*epigram a short poem dealing with a single, sharply observed thought or event; also, a brief witty statement of truth

*devotional religious

The only book Herrick ever published was a large volume of lyrics, epigrams,* and devotional* poems, which he saw through the presses in 1648 while living, down on his luck, in the city of London. But by then his kind of poetry was no longer being read or written in London. With their fun and ceremony, and in particular their erotic content, Herrick's poems could not have been more out of keeping with the triumphant Puritan attitude of the times. The collection went virtually unsold, and it was not until the nineteenth century that Herrick's poetry was read again.

The title Herrick gave his collection was *Hesperides,* after the mythical Fortunate Isles at the western extremity of Earth: golden apples were said to grow there, in the garden of the daughters of Hesperus. Herrick's poems were thus acknowledged by their author as fruits of his stay in the West Country, though how many of them he had actually written there remains a question to this day.

In the introductory poem of *Hesperides,* "The Argument of his Book," Herrick carefully listed all his work's major themes:

> I sing of brooks, of blossoms, birds and bowers:
> Of April, May, of June, and July-flowers.
> I sing of may-poles, hock-carts,* wassails,* wakes,
> Of bridegrooms, brides, and of their bridal-cakes.
> I write of youth, of love, and have access
> By these, to sing of cleanly wantonness.
> I sing of dews, of rains, and piece by piece
> Of balm, of oil, of spice, and ambergris.*
> I sing of times trans-shifting; and I write
> How roses first came red, and lilies white.
> I write of groves, of twilights, and I sing
> The Court of Mab,* and of the Fairy King.*
> I write of Hell; I sing (and ever shall)
> Of Heaven, and hope to have it after all.
>
> *(Selected Poems)*

Two themes are of particular interest: "cleanly wantonness,"* a term that represents the central contradiction of Herrick's poetry, its celebration of sensuality while leaving out the whole idea of sin; and "times trans-shifting" referring to the passing of time and the rites and ceremonies of renewal. Herrick was alerting his readers that life and death were his abiding concerns.

The poems of *Hesperides* embrace life and accept death in a way that is uniquely Herrick's. One of the religious poems, "A Thanksgiving to God, for His House," frames Herrick's concept of the good life not in spiritual terms but amid the warm lighting and pleasures of the hearth. For devotional poetry, this poem's realism is surprisingly worldly and specific: Herrick thanks God for his parlor, his hall, his kitchen, his pantry, his bread box, his kindling wood, his fire ("Close by whose living coal I sit, / And glow like it"); and also for his store of legumes* and grains, his vegetables ("my beloved Beet"), his bowl of spiced ale, his "teeming hen" (*Poems of Robert Herrick,* p. 350), his cows, his sheep. Out of gratitude to God for these blessings he offers a pagan sacrifice, stoking up incense like a proper ancient Roman.

Again, when Herrick writes of death, it is a matter not of agonized spiritual combat, as in the *Holy Sonnets* of John

*hock-carts wagons bringing in the last load of the harvest

*wassails drinking of healths on festive occasions

*ambergris waxy substance used in perfumes

*Mab and the Fairy King Oberon and Mabare—king and queen of the fairies

*wantonness lack of discipline; wildness

*legume a category of vegetables, including peas and beans

Donne, but of acceptance and resignation. A poem like Herrick's "To Daffodils" transforms the traditional Christian act of mourning into a cosmic appreciation of natural process. This poem presents the drooping of daffodils at nightfall as an attitude of prayer, thus charmingly and playfully humanizing the natural world. Though the brief life of the daffodils is quietly mourned, as in a Christian prayer service, the poem displays a pre-Christian affirmation of the natural process of death and, most importantly, offers no promise of an afterlife. He says to the daffodils:

> We have short time to stay, as you,
>   We have as short a spring;
> As quick a growth to meet decay,
>   As you, or anything.
>   We die,
>   As your hours do, and dry
>   Away,
>   Like to the summer's rain;
> Or as the pearls of morning's dew,
>   Ne'er to be found again.
>
> *(Selected Poems)*

IF YOU LIKE the poetry of Herrick, you might also like the poetry of John Donne, George Herbert, John Milton, or William Shakespeare.

Selected Bibliography

WORKS BY ROBERT HERRICK
Poetry

Hesperides (1648)

Available Collections

The Poetical Works of Robert Herrick. Edited by F. W. Moorman. Oxford, U.K.: Clarendon Press, 1915.

The Poems of Robert Herrick. 2d ed. Edited by L. C. Martin. New York: Oxford University Press, 1965.

Robert Herrick: Selected Poems. 2d ed. Edited by David Jesson-Dibley. Manchester, U.K.: Carcanet, 1989.

Anthologies

English Pastoral Poetry. Edited by Frank Kermode. New York: Norton, 1972.

Ben Jonson and the Cavalier Poets. Edited by Hugh MacLean. New York: Norton, 1974.

The Penguin Book of Renaissance Verse. Edited by H. R. Woudhuysen. London: Penguin, 1992.

WORKS ABOUT ROBERT HERRICK

Bush, Douglas. *English Literature in the Earlier Seventeenth Century, 1600–1660.* Oxford, U.K.: Clarendon, 1945.

Deming, Robert H. *Ceremony and Art: Robert Herrick's Poetry.* Paris: Mouton, 1974.

DeNeef, A. Leigh. *"This Poetick Liturgie": Robert Herrick's Ceremonial Mode.* Durham, N.C.: Duke University Press, 1974.

Macaulay, Rose. *The Shadow Flies.* New York: Harper, 1932.

Miner, Earl. *The Cavalier Mode from Jonson to Cotton.* Princeton, N.J.: Princeton University Press, 1971.

Patrick, Max, and Roger B. Rollin. *"Trust to Good Verses": Herrick Tercentenary Essays.* Pittsburgh, Pa.: University of Pittsburgh Press, 1978.

Riddell, Edwin. *Lives of the Stuart Age: 1603–1714.* New York: Barnes and Noble, 1976.

Rollin, Roger B. *Robert Herrick.* Rev. ed. New York: Twayne, 1982.

Sanders, Andrew. *The Short Oxford History of English Literature.* Oxford, U.K.: Clarendon, 1994.

Summers, Joseph H. *The Heirs of Donne and Jonson.* New York: Oxford University Press, 1970.

Tuve, Rosemond. *Elizabethan and Metaphysical Imagery.* Chicago: University of Chicago Press, 1947.

Williams, Raymond. *The Country and the City.* New York: Oxford University Press, 1973.

HOMER

(ca. eighth century B.C.)

by Lisa Hermine Makman

Imagine a world without books, without writing, without even an alphabet. The poet Homer lived in a world that was just emerging from such conditions. In Greece at the time of Homer, writing was just coming into use. It is probable that his first audiences could not read or write. Homer himself may have composed his works—the lengthy epics* the *Iliad* and the *Odyssey*—without writing them down.

Because Homer was the most admired poet of the ancient world, his works were preserved, whereas most literature of his period has been lost. Copies of Homer's epics, carefully handwritten by scribes on rolls of papyrus, were kept in the great libraries of antiquity—in Athens, Alexandria, and Pergamum. Influential classical philosophers and poets perpetuated the idea of Homer's greatness. To this day Homer is considered by many to be the father of Western literature.

*epic a long poem that tells the story of a hero's deeds

Who Was Homer?

Almost nothing certain is known about Homer's life. Some ancient writers claimed he was the child of a river nymph, and all believed he was blind. A few modern scholars maintain that Homer did not exist at all and that his works are the product of countless poets working in an oral tradition. However, most contemporary specialists agree that Homer did exist, that he was the master of an oral tradition that might have existed for centuries before him, and that he composed his works in the second half of the eighth century B.C., a period of great flux in Greek society. Many cultural and political developments accompanied the introduction of the alphabet. It was an age of exploration, colonization, and the growth of cities. Homer's work itself seems to be an exemplary product of this expansion.

Although Homer's birthplace is not documented, ancient writers consistently link the poet with cities in Ionia, particularly Chios and Smyrna, which are located across the Aegean Sea from mainland Greece. The language of Homer's poetry supports these claims, since it is predominantly Ionic dialect, a traditional poetic language that centuries of bards* developed for the purpose of performing their poetry.

Even if Homer was from Ionia, his works offer a conception of Greek nationality that goes beyond regional difference. The heroes of the *Iliad* and *Odyssey* are predominantly from central Greece, Thessaly, and the Pelopónnisos. In the *Iliad,* these Greeks unite to fight a foreign power from the east, the Trojans. This model of an allied national force became important after Homer, particularly during the wars between Greece and Persia at the beginning of the fifth century. His epics encouraged Greeks to define their civilization as distinct from what they saw as eastern "barbarism."

An Oral Tradition

Oral poetry is usually preserved and transmitted through special members of the community who memorize and perform it. In ancient Greece, professional reciters, called *rhapsodes* ("song-stitchers"), memorized and repeated traditional stories but also must have embellished and personalized them. *Rhapsodes* appeared frequently at public festivals.

According to twentieth-century scholars, the repetitions in Homer's poetry point to its origins in an oral tradition. Standard phrases ("formulas") are commonly repeated in the epics. Often these take the form of epithets.* For instance, Achilles, hero of the *Iliad,* is repeatedly called "brilliant Achilles" or "swift-footed

*__*bard__ a poet and singer*

Many of the characters' names in Homer are most familiar to us in their Latin forms (for example, Ajax and Hector), but you might find that some translators use spellings they consider closer to the original Greek (for example, Aias and Hektor). Both methods of translating the names into English are acceptable.

*__*epithet__ a descriptive phrase used along with or in place of a person's name*

Achilles." Furthermore, typical scenes, such as arming scenes, scenes of arrival and departure, and descriptions of sacrifices and fighting, are repeated. Such repetitions aid memorization. But the question remains: Was Homer an illiterate singer, or was he a literate poet using the techniques of an oral tradition?

There are three possible answers: first, that Homer composed with the help of writing; second, that the poet was himself illiterate, but the poetry was written down for him by scribes; and third, that the poetry was composed by an illiterate poet and then memorized by a collective of reciters for up to two hundred years before it was written down in the sixth or seventh century B.C. Those who believe that Homer must have been literate claim that his poems, because of their length, could not have been composed without the help of writing. The traditional songs that bards sang were probably between one hundred and five hundred lines long, whereas Homer's works are more than thirty times longer.

Homer's verse, called heroic or epic poetry, is written in the form of hexameters; that is, each line contains six metrical units.* Most of these metrical units are dactyls (a long syllable followed by two short syllables, as in the word "memory"—MEM-or-y), and there are between twelve and seventeen syllables per line. For the ancient Greeks, the rhythm was important, since the poems were originally sung by bards, accompanied by a stringed instrument called a lyre.

*metrical unit a group of syllables used to create poetic rhythm

The Stories

Both the *Iliad* and the *Odyssey* tell stories from a mythic, heroic past, a time when warriors were larger and stronger, when human beings spoke with gods face to face, and when some mortals were even related to the gods by blood. The epics recount the actions of heroes during and after the Greeks launched a massive military campaign against the city of Troy. The *Iliad,* which describes the war itself, probably was composed about 750 B.C., roughly twenty-five years before the *Odyssey.* The action of the *Odyssey* takes place after that of the *Iliad,* depicting the lengthy voyage home of the warrior Odysseus after Troy has been toppled.

But was there a Trojan war, and, if so, when did it occur? Historical evidence and the texts themselves suggest that the Achaeans, who destroy Troy in Homer's story, were, in fact, the Mycenaeans. The wealthy and powerful Mycenaean civilization, centered around the city of Mycenae in mainland Greece, controlled the area around the Aegean Sea during the Bronze Age, from about 1600 to 1150 B.C. Scholars believe that tales of the Trojan War may be age-old memories of a raid by Mycenaean rulers on Troy in the thirteenth century B.C. In the nineteenth century, when the archaeologist Heinrich Schliemann discovered the remains of Troy he found evidence of the city's violent destruction and Mycenaean artifacts, including weapons resembling those described in the *Iliad*.

Although both of Homer's works deal with the war against Troy, thematically the poems differ dramatically. The *Iliad* is a war poem, and the *Odyssey* is an adventure poem. Whereas the *Iliad* is a dramatic story and precursor to future works of tragedy, the *Odyssey* is a precursor to future works of comedy. These differences and others have led a few scholars to suggest that the works were composed by different poets. Most scholars, however, point to similarities in both the form and content to suggest that a single poet wrote both epics. Such common elements have led Homer's poems to become prototypes for what is now known as the epic.

Several conventions found in Homer's works define the epic form. First of all, the epic begins with an invocation of the muse, a female deity who provides artistic inspiration, and with an introduction of the poem's central theme. When the narrative begins, the poet immediately dives *in medias res,* that is, "into the middle of things," only later referring back to earlier events and projecting forward to what is to come.

Second, the main characters in these works have typical qualities; they are superhuman, protected by or related to the gods; they save or establish cities or nations; and they are concerned with their own glory or fame, called *kleos* in Greek. Third, the style of Homer's poetry has certain distinctive features, such as the repetition of stock phrases (epithets) and the inclusion of many extended similes,* which tend to be lengthy and detailed.

*extended simile
a long, detailed comparison

The *Iliad*

The *Iliad* opens with the poet's appeal to the muse to sing of the wrath of Achilles, the Greeks' mightiest warrior. The central theme and first word of the poem is *menin,* or "wrath," a

---

The *Iliad* (excerpt)

Like the swarms of clustering bees that issue forever in
fresh bursts from the hollow in the stone, and hang like
bunched grapes as they hover beneath the flowers in
springtime fluttering in swarms together this way and
that way, so the many nations of men from the ships and
the shelters along the front of the deep sea beach
marched in order by companies to the assembly . . .

(Book 2, lines 87–93)

---

term that denotes no ordinary anger, but rather a rage as potent as that of the gods. Achilles's fury is aroused by an argument with Agamemnon, the king who leads the tribes of
Greece in the campaign against Troy. The problems that fuel
this argument concern honor and power, central issues
throughout the *Iliad*. Because of the quarrel, Achilles refuses
to participate in the fighting. The epic traces the course of
Achilles's anger from the time he leaves the fighting through
his dramatic return to the battle, when he kills Hector, the
greatest Trojan warrior.

At the start of the narrative, Agamemnon has dishonored
the god Apollo and his priest Chryseis by stealing the priest's
daughter as war booty. The king must return the girl to her father to appease the god. Angered at being compelled to give
up his prize, Agamemnon claims another abducted girl, whom
he had given to Achilles as a "war prize." For Achilles, this is a
tremendous dishonor, and as a result, he withdraws himself
and his men from the fighting. Since Achilles is the most powerful fighter, the consequences of his withdrawal are cata-
strophic for the Greeks.

The struggle over the priest's daughter mirrors the feud
that initiated the Trojan War itself. The war began when the divinely beautiful Helen, wife of Agamemnon's brother, was seduced away from her home by Paris, son of Troy's king, Priam,
through the scheming of Aphrodite, the goddess of love. The
Greeks' aim in the war against Troy is to retrieve Helen and the
honor they lost owing to her seduction.

The *Iliad* covers only a short period of time, less than two
months during the Greeks' ten-year war against Troy. Although

the narrative projects forward into the future and looks back toward the beginning of the war, most of the poem (from book 2 to book 22) focuses on four days of fighting and two days of truce near the end of the war. During this period, Agamemnon, in desperation, sends word to Achilles (book 9), offering him the return of the controversial girl and, in addition, tremendous riches and multiple honors. Three great warriors convey Agamemnon's message: Odysseus, Ajax, and Phoenix, each of whom makes a powerful appeal. Achilles greets them as friends but refuses their offers.

The central action of the *Iliad* (books 11–18) takes place during a single day of fighting, just after Achilles has rejected Agamemnon's offer of reconciliation. At this point, the Trojans are clearly winning and almost all of the Greeks' best warriors are disabled. Achilles's closest friend, Patroclos, seeing the desperate situation, begs Achilles to lend him his armor and his army. Achilles assents, and Patroclos goes into battle.

Patroclos fares well until, striving for *kleos*, he takes on the Trojan's strongest fighter, Hector, who kills him and triumphantly strips his body of Achilles's armor. When Achilles discovers that Patroclos is dead, he redirects his fierce rage from Agamemnon to Hector. Thirsting to avenge his friend's death, Achilles enlists his mother to ask the god Hephaistos to craft magical armor for him. Protected by this armor and aided by the gods, Achilles slaughters Hector. Then, dragging Hector's dead body behind his chariot, he repeatedly circles the Greek camp in triumph. This behavior is perceived as irrational and barbaric by his fellow Greeks and also by the gods, who eventually compel him to stop.

The poem ends not only with Achilles's victory but with his humility. In the last book of the *Iliad*, Priam, Hector's father and the king of Troy, arrives at Achilles's tent alone in the night to beg for the return of his son's body. In this moving passage, Priam appeals to Achilles's pity. He says,

> . . . take pity upon me
> remembering your father, yet I am still more pitiful;
> I have gone through what no other mortal on earth has
>   gone through;
> I put my lips to the hands of the man who has killed my
>   children.
>
> (book 24)

Achilles and Priam then weep together, Achilles mourning for his father and Patroclos, and Priam lamenting the loss of Hector. The poem concludes with Hector's death and funeral, which presage* both the fall of Troy and the fall of Achilles, whose own death, according to prophesy, will follow shortly after Hector's.

> *presage* to warn or foreshadow

Although the subject of the *Iliad* is Achilles's anger, the epic's name points to another major theme; "Iliad" means "a poem about Ilium," and Homer's poem focuses almost as much on the tragic fall of the city as it does on the exploits of Achilles. Homer's portrait of life in Troy is vivid and compassionate; thus his depiction of the city's fall is tragic. Particularly moving are the poet's portraits of family relations in the city, such as the interactions between Hector and his faithful wife, Andromache. Homer contrasts Andromache with Helen just as he contrasts Hector with Achilles. Whereas Helen *abandons* her husband, child, parents, and city, Andromache *loses* her family and city to the war caused by Helen. Whereas Achilles fights to *acquire* war booty and *kleos,* Hector, a model citizen and family man, fights to *preserve* his city and to save his loved ones.

The *Odyssey*

At the start of the *Odyssey,* the poet asks the muse to sing of the "man of many ways," Odysseus. Over the course of this epic, Odysseus employs his "many ways," his trickiness and resourcefulness, in order to return from the Trojan War to Ithaca, his kingdom. As in the *Iliad,* in the *Odyssey* love of one's homeland is an important theme. While in the *Iliad* the destruction of a beloved city is delayed by the anger of Achilles, in the *Odyssey* the return home to a beloved city is delayed by the anger of the powerful sea god Poseidon. Odysseus has enraged Poseidon by blinding the god's son, the monstrous one-eyed giant Polyphemus. While Poseidon presents a direct danger to Odysseus, the peril of physical death, he also menaces the hero with a more subtle threat: the threat of being forgotten, of losing *kleos.*

Odysseus, whose name means "man of pain," experiences much suffering in his struggle to return to his city and to his faithful wife, Penelope. The poem broaches the question of human suffering in the first book, in which Zeus proclaims that although mortals blame the gods for their suffering, they cause it themselves through recklessness. Odysseus, however, suffers even though he is usually prudent. In fact, Odysseus exerts great self-control. Even in the face of undeserved suffering, he survives his journey and ultimately arrives home because of this restraint.

Just as the *Iliad* takes place in the tenth year of the war, the *Odyssey* takes place in the tenth year of Odysseus's voyage home after the war. So when the epic begins, Odysseus has been away from home for almost twenty years, during which time his wife, Penelope, has been staunchly faithful to him, and his son, Telemachos, has grown from infant to adult. The first section of the poem, known as the Telemachy, describes the boy's voyage in search of news of his father. After this, Homer presents Odysseus's homecoming voyage, called a *nostos* in Greek.

The Telemachy introduces the theme of guest-host relations, by presenting the terrible situation that has developed in Odysseus's kingdom. A band of suitors for Penelope's hand has taken over Odysseus's castle, behaving in a rowdy manner and abusing Penelope's hospitality. Also, the Telemachy introduces the theme of remembrance. Athena appears to Telemachos to incite him to travel in search of news of his father.

*paradisiacal like paradise

When we first encounter Odysseus, he is pining for home, held captive by the beautiful goddess Calypso on her paradisiacal* island. Calypso, whose name means "she who conceals," in effect conceals Odysseus from the world. She has sequestered him for many years and tempts him to remain with her forever, offering him immortality if he will forget his quest to go home. He selects home and *kleos* over eternal life and obscurity.

*edenic like Eden, or paradise

Liberated from Calypso's clutches by the goddess Athena, Odysseus finds himself on the shores of another edenic* isle, home to the Phaeacians, a peace-loving people who possess magical ships. He does not initially disclose his identity, but nevertheless the Phaeacian king and queen treat him generously and like him enough to express their hope that he will stay with them and wed their daughter. Odysseus remains determined to return home. He finally makes his identity known at a festival held in his honor just before he is to depart for Ithaca on a Phaeacian ship. During the revelry, the poet of the household sings of Odysseus's exploits in Troy, after which Odysseus, in tears, reveals himself to be the subject of song and goes on to tell the tale of his voyage from Troy.

The next four books (9–12) are Odysseus's narration of his own adventures. In this section of the epic, Odysseus displaces the anonymous narrator, becoming the purveyor* of his own *kleos.* Odysseus tells of the tremendous suffering he has undergone during his voyages. For instance, he had to descend into the underworld, a terrifying journey the Greeks called *katabasis.* In later epics the *katabasis* became an important element; heroes would undertake such journeys to test their will and strength.

There is a fairy tale quality to the stories Odysseus recounts. In many of them, powerful female characters play a key role as obstacles to Odysseus's homecoming—for instance, the witchlike goddess Circe, who transforms men into animals; the savage Scylla, who devours Odysseus's men with her many mouths; and the monstrous Sirens, who enchant sailors with their song, inspiring them to dive overboard and drown. In order to bypass such figures, Odysseus must use his wits. Sometimes, however, he is dependent on help from the gods, especially his patron goddess, Athena.

While Athena serves as an antidote to dangerously powerful female characters, Odysseus's queen, Penelope, does so as well. Penelope is both wily and wise. Also, in contrast to most of the creatures Odysseus encounters, Penelope behaves as a proper host to her husband when he finally appears, disguised as a beggar. Proper guest-host relations were extremely important to the Greeks, who believed that all guests should be treated with respect, fed and housed first, and only afterward asked to reveal their identity.

Homer devotes nine books to Odysseus's exploits after he returns to Ithaca. For most of this time the hero keeps his identity hidden. Athena disguises him as a beggar so that he can assess the situation in his kingdom and discern who has been faithful to him in his absence. In Ithaca, Odysseus's identity is disclosed to various characters through a series of poignant recognition scenes—Argos, his aged dog, joyfully recognizes him and promptly dies, and Eurycleia, his old nurse, recognizes a scar on his body.

Odysseus kills the suitors with the help of his faithful companions, including Telemachos and Athena. After Odysseus massacres them, he reveals his identity to Penelope. At first she refuses to believe that he is truly Odysseus. Her suspicion proves her to be an equal match for her wary husband. Odysseus and Achilles represent two distinct heroic types.

***purveyor** supplier

Odysseus succeeds through his cunning and intelligence. Achilles, on the other hand, succeeds through brute force.

Homer's Legacy

After the time of Homer, his works were recited in competitions at the great Greek festivals, such as the Panathenaic games, which first took place in 776 B.C. At these festivals—models for our Olympic Games—athletic as well as poetic competitions took place. The games began with a procession of women wailing for the death of Achilles, and the games themselves are like the funeral games in the *Iliad*.

By the end of the sixth century B.C., written manuscripts of Homer's works were available, but the tradition of learning the poems by heart had remained alive. Homer, memorized by students, continued to be an important part of education. Homer's works remained extremely popular throughout the Roman period. During this time, Virgil composed the *Aeneid,* an epic that imitates both the *Iliad* and the *Odyssey.* Since then Homer has been a model and inspiration for a remarkable variety of literary works. In 1667, the English poet John Milton published *Paradise Lost,* an epic account of the Judeo-Christian story of the fall of man. In 1922, the Irish writer James Joyce wrote the novel *Ulysses,* compressing Odysseus's wanderings into the tale of a representative modern man, Leopold Bloom, during a single day in Dublin, Ireland. More recently, in 1990, the West Indian poet and playwright Derek Walcott composed his epic poem *Omeros,* using the Homeric model to tell a story of contemporary Caribbean life.

Various significant poets and political thinkers have translated Homer's works into English, including Thomas Hobbes in the seventeenth century, Alexander Pope in the eighteenth century, and William Cullen Bryant in the nineteenth century. In the twentieth century there were many popular translations of Homer, notably by Robert Fitzgerald, Richmond Lattimore, and Robert Fagles.

IF YOU LIKE the poetry of Homer, you might also like the poetry of Virgil. ⮞

Selected Bibliography

WORKS BY HOMER

The Odyssey of Homer. Translated by Richmond Lattimore. New York: Harper, 1991. Reprint of 1967 edition.